DOGFIGHT

DOGFIGHT

THE GREATEST AIR DUELS OF WORLD WAR II

EDITOR
TONY HOLMES

OSPREY
PUBLISHING

“It’s just like being in a knife fight in a dirt-floor bar. If you want to fix a fella, the best way to do it is to get behind him and stick him in the back. It’s the same in an air fight. If you want to kill that guy, the best thing to do is get around behind him where he can’t see you… and shoot him.”

Captain William O’Brien, 357th Fighter Group, USAAF

First published in Great Britain in 2011 by Osprey Publishing.
This paperback edition first published in 2014.
PO Box 883, Oxford, OX1 9PL, UK
PO Box 3985, New York, NY 10185-3985, USA
Email: info@ospreypublishing.com

Osprey Publishing is part of the Osprey Group.

Material in this book has been previous published as:
Spitfire vs Bf 109: Battle of Britain by Tony Holmes
P-47 Thunderbolt vs Bf 109G/K: Europe 1943–45 by Martin Bowman
P-40 Warhawk vs Ki-43 Oscar: China 1944–45 by Carl Molesworth
P-51 Mustang vs Fw 190: Europe 1943–45 by Martin Bowman
Seafire vs A6M Zero: Pacific Theatre by Donald Nijboer

A CIP catalog record for this book is available from the British Library

ISBN: 978 1 47280 820 2

Page layout by Myriam Bell Design, France
Index by Alan Thatcher
Typeset in Adobe Caslon Pro
Maps by bounford.com
Originated by PPS Grasmere Ltd, Leeds, UK
Printed in China through Asia Pacific Offset Limited

14 15 16 17 18 10 9 8 7 6 5 4 3 2 1

Osprey Publishing is supporting the Woodland Trust, the UK's leading woodland conservation charity, by funding the dedication of trees.

www.ospreypublishing.com

Front cover artwork by Jim Laurier, © Osprey Publishing
Back cover image courtesy USAAF via Martin Bowman
Imprint page image IWM CH 20
Endpapers © Wiek Luijken (front) and Osprey Publishing (rear)

Imperial War Museum Collections

Many of the photos in this book come from the Imperial War Museum's huge collections which cover all aspects of conflict involving Britain and the Commonwealth since the start of the twentieth century. These rich resources are available online to search, browse and buy at www.iwmcollections.org.uk. In addition to Collections Online, you can visit the Visitor Rooms where you can explore over 8 million photographs, thousands of hours of moving images, the largest sound archive of its kind in the world, thousands of diaries and letters written by people in wartime, and a huge reference library. To make an appointment, call (020) 7416 5320, or e-mail: mail@iwm.org.uk.

Imperial War Museum www.iwm.org.uk

CONTENTS

INTRODUCTION

The term "dogfight" is an emotive one, conjuring up images of fighter aircraft dueling with each other for command of the skies. The earliest engagement between two airplanes that resulted in a machine being shot down (rather than being brought down by "aggressive maneuvering") took place on October 5, 1914 over Reims, in northern France. A German Aviatik reconnaissance biplane was shot down by French pilot Sergeant Joseph Franz, who was flying a Voisin. The latter aircraft was fitted with a free-mounted Hotchkiss gun.

The early clashes in the skies over Western Europe during World War I initially saw pilots and observers taking potshots at opposing airmen with rifles and pistols. It was not until the early spring of 1915, when Frenchman Roland Garros had a fixed forward-firing machine gun fitted to his Morane-Saulnier Type L parasol monoplane, that the era of true air combat, and dogfighting, commenced. Garros' machine had steel deflector wedges bolted to its propeller blades, and these deflected bullets that would have otherwise damaged his fighter. On April 1, 1915, Garros claimed an Aviatik destroyed with his Morane Type L, and by the time he was forced down behind enemy lines 18 days later he had achieved three victories.

The Frenchman's aircraft was closely examined by the Germans, who had already developed an interrupter gear that mechanically prevented the gun from firing whenever a propeller blade passed in front of the weapon's muzzle. This equipment was quickly incorporated into the Fokker E-type monoplane fighters that gained control of the skies in the summer of 1915. Allied observation aircraft proved extremely vulnerable to the German scouts with their forward-firing armament, so a new breed of British and French fighters was built to counter this threat. Thus the cycle began of Allied and German designers producing ever more effective aircraft in response to fighters fielded by their opposite numbers over the Western Front.

By the final months of World War I, the deadly practice of dogfighting had been honed to a fine art by such skilled exponents as Manfred von Richthofen, Mick Mannock and Georges Guynemer, all of whom had perished in combat. The great aces of Germany, France and Britain were revered both by their fellow pilots and the general public thanks to colorful stories of their exploits in the press. The aircraft these men flew looked very much like the machines flown by their forebears just four years earlier. However, improved engine performance and increased armament made the fighting scouts of 1918 far deadlier machines in aerial combat. For example, Roland Garros' Morane-Saulnier Type L of 1915 had a top speed of just 71mph and boasted a solitary 8mm Hotchkiss machine gun. By comparison, the 1918 SPAD XIII had a top speed of 135mph, could climb twice as fast as the Type L and was fitted with two 7.7mm Vickers machine guns.

With the cessation of hostilities on November 11, 1918, and the signing of the Treaty of Versailles early the following year, the requirement for more advanced fighters and bombers evaporated almost overnight. Air arms had to make do with the types already in service, or "warmed-over" aircraft that were only a modest improvement on what had come before.

In this environment of negative growth within the air forces of the major powers, many aircraft manufacturers focused on the fledgling air transport market in order to remain afloat. In an attempt to bestow upon these machines a useful range when carrying a payload of people and mail, rather than bombs, manufacturers turned to companies such as Bristol, Napier, Rolls-Royce and Curtiss to furnish them with more powerful, and reliable, engines. Although the transportation of people provided the impetus – and cash – for companies to produce more advanced aircraft that could in turn be easily adapted for use as bombers throughout the austere 1920s, no such carrot was dangled in the face of prospective fighter manufacturers. Therefore, no new fighter designs entered service until 1924, and even these machines relied strongly on wartime design traits. Small numbers of biplane fighters were periodically ordered by the major powers into the 1930s, thus ensuring a steady rise in the performance of these types.

Air racing proved popular during this period, and it gave both aircraft designers and engine manufacturers an outlet for performance aeronautics. Indeed, events such as the Schneider Trophy in Europe and the Thompson Trophy in the USA provided a crucial testing ground for new monoplane designs incorporating high-revving liquid-cooled inline or multi-cylinder radial engines and stressed-skin airframes. Rolls-Royce in particular learned much from air racing, and its V12 inline Kestrel engine – of nearly 500hp – powered the revolutionary Hawker Hart bomber of 1928. The first really advanced all-British design to enter service with the Royal Air Force since the end of World War I, the Hart was 10mph faster than Britain's principal fighter of the day, the Bristol Bulldog.

It was only a matter of time before the Hart sired a single-seat fighter derivative, and in 1931 the Fury was ordered into series production. It was the first production fighter in the world able to achieve 200mph in level flight.

The threat of conflict in Europe following the seizing of power in Germany by the National Socialist Party in 1933 ignited a rapid reequipment program across the globe. Money and manpower was poured into the development and production of better fighters and bombers, as well as the expansion of frontline units equipped with the new generation of predominantly monoplane machines now entering service. By the late 1930s, aircraft design and technology had developed rapidly from fabric, wire and wood to metal, glass and considerably more horsepower. By September 3, 1939, when Britain and France declared war on Germany following its invasion of Poland, the majority of the fighter aircraft in service with these countries featured all-metal monocoque construction, six to eight machine guns, hydraulically-operated flaps, retractable undercarriages and effective radio equipment. Enclosed cockpits were also very much the norm, while the majority of these machines were powered by reliable engines that produced upwards of 1,000hp. This in turn allowed the aircraft to operate at previously unheard-of altitudes in excess of 20,000ft.

Although the technology employed to create the fighters of 1939 had changed significantly since the world was last at war some 21 years earlier, the rules of aerial combat, or dogfighting, remained the same. Indeed, all the tactics evolved in World War I over the Western Front were brought to bear once again in the early actions of World War II. Height was the key to a successful engagement, as was achieving the element of surprise. The pilot who saw his enemy first and dived on him from out of the sun usually prevailed in just a matter of moments. During World War II the ultimate in winged perfection, the fighter, and its pilot, consistently grabbed the headlines, just as had been the case two decades earlier.

This volume analyzes the capabilities, history and exploits of some of the greatest fighters of this conflict – Britain's Spitfire and Seafire, Germany's Bf 109 and Fw 190, America's P-51 Mustang, P-40 Warhawk and P-47 Thunderbolt, and Japan's Ki-43 "Oscar" and Mitsubishi Zero. For six years, the pilots flying these legendary aircraft battled each other for aerial supremacy in the war-torn skies over Europe, the Pacific and Asia. From the desperate battles over southeast England during the Battle of Britain, through swirling dogfights around the Allied bombers that raided deep into Germany, to the last naval aviators' duels over defeated Japan, their stories make for compelling reading. Covering four air forces, three theaters, and ten iconic fighters, these pages tell the story of head-to-head aerial combat in World War II.

Tony Holmes

Part I

THE BATTLE OF BRITAIN: 1940

SPITFIRE vs Bf 109E

Fighter-versus-fighter combat has always held a particular fascination for historians and aviation enthusiasts alike, and perhaps the ultimate aerial joust of the 20th century took place over the skies of southern England during the long, hot summer of 1940. The fate of the free world effectively rested on the shoulders of several thousand aviators (supported by thousands more groundcrew, radar plotters, fighter controllers and observers) who flew with RAF Fighter Command in direct defense of the British Isles. Their opponents, the battle-hardened Luftwaffe, had been given the job of neutralizing Britain's aerial defenses so that a seaborne invasion could be launched across the Channel from occupied France. At the forefront of the action were 19 Spitfire squadrons, charged with defending their more numerous Hurricane brethren from attack by Bf 109s as the Hawker fighters attempted to repel the hordes of medium bombers dispatched by the Luftwaffe to knock out key industrial and military targets.

The similarities in terms of performance between the Bf 109E and the Spitfire I/II, the predominant models used by the rival air forces, are remarkable. Both were the product of several years' development during the 1930s as Britain and Germany rapidly rearmed, and they were the most advanced fighter types in frontline service in 1940. By examining the strengths and weaknesses of both aircraft, not only the technical nuances of each fighter can be revealed, but also the reality of using the fighters within a combat situation. But with both aircraft being so evenly matched, the outcome of a battle really came down to the skill of the pilots involved, and their employment of superior tactics, to ensure victory.

The Spitfire and Bf 109E had initially met over the evacuation beaches of Dunkirk in the final days of May 1940, and neither fighter managed to gain a clear advantage over the other. The German fighter pilots, near exhaustion and at the end of an overstretched supply chain following the rapid advances of the *Blitzkrieg* through the Low Countries of Western Europe, were flying their favored freelance sweeps into the areas patrolled by RAF Fighter Command.

Sensing that his 56th kill is just moments away, then ranking *Jagdwaffe* ace Major Helmut Wick turns in behind the already smoking Spitfire I of No. 609 Sqn's Plt Off Paul A. Baillon as the pair race over The Needles at the western end of the Isle of Wight, on the afternoon of November 28, 1940. Having power-dived into the Auxiliary squadron from a superior height, Wick quickly singled out his victim and hit the Spitfire hard with cannon and machine gun fire. Baillon bailed out about 20 miles off the coast, and his body was later washed up off Normandy. His conqueror had little time to celebrate, for Wick in turn fell victim to No. 609 Sqn's leading ace, Flt Lt John C. Dundas, less than five minutes later. (Artwork by Iain Wyllie, © Osprey Publishing)

The British units were also experiencing operational difficulties of their own as their "short-legged" fighters were operating at the extreme limits of their range.

Nevertheless, the Spitfire and Bf 109E pilots who survived the bloody clashes over the French coast gained a valuable insight into the strengths and weaknesses of their much-vaunted opponents. Fighter Command's tactics were quickly exposed as being terribly out of date, and therefore dangerous to those pilots ordered to adhere to them during the summer of 1940. The Spitfire more than held its own in combat with Europe's all-conquering fighter, however, and the majority of RAF pilots serving in the frontline felt confident that they could prevail over the Bf 109E when engaged by the Germans over home territory.

The *Jagdwaffe*, in turn, was anxious to exploit the apparent weakness in British fighter tactics, and the more senior pilots in the German Bf 109E ranks were also quietly confident that they could defeat even the most aggressively flown Spitfire. They were fully aware that the Messerschmitt fighter's endurance could pose problems, but they believed their preferred – and combat tested – slashing tactics, which meant that the *Jagdflieger* attacked with deadly accuracy from high altitude and then headed straight home, would alleviate any range issues.

Eager to fight each other for the mastery of the skies over southern England, Spitfire and Bf 109E pilots prepared themselves for possibly the most important aerial clash of World War II – the Battle of Britain.

THE MACHINES

SUPERMARINE SPITFIRE

Vickers Supermarine, the manufacturer of one of history's greatest aircraft, in fact had little experience of building fighter aircraft prior to placing the Spitfire into production. It had, however, been heavily involved in high-performance aviation through its family of flying-boat and floatplane racers of the 1920s and early 1930s. Based in Woolston, Southampton, the company and its chief designer, Reginald J. Mitchell, initially achieved prominence internationally when Supermarine's Sea Lion biplane won the Schneider Trophy in 1922. Over the next nine years the company would secure further racing successes, and set world speed records, with its S 4, S 5, S 6 and S 6B floatplanes. A fruitful relationship with Rolls-Royce's aero engine division was also cultivated during this period.

Vickers Aviation acquired a majority shareholding in Supermarine in 1928, and this helped the company survive the lean interwar period when few military orders were on offer. Indeed, the bulk of Supermarine's work during this time centered on the construction of 79 Southampton flying-boats for the RAF. In 1931 the Air Ministry issued Specification F7/30 for a new fighter for frontline service with the RAF that would boast a higher top speed than the 225mph Bristol Bulldog – little more than half the speed of the S 6B Schneider Trophy winner! The winning design would also have to be armed with four .303in machine guns, which was double the armament of the RAF's biplane fighters then in squadron service.

Because military orders were scarce for the British aviation industry at the time the F7/30 specification was issued, no fewer than eight manufacturers produced prototypes in response. Supermarine's 660hp Rolls-Royce Goshawk-powered Type 224 was one of three monoplane prototypes put forward. The Goshawk used the newly developed evaporative-cooling system rather than conventional external radiators, which meant that the aircraft could feature cleaner aerodynamics. The Type 224, with its distinctive low-mounted cranked wing and fixed "trousered" undercarriage, made its first flight in February 1934, and the combination of evaporative cooling and the low-wing monoplane design soon presented Supermarine with serious engine overheating problems. The aircraft's performance was also disappointing, with a top speed of just 238mph due to its overly thick wing and fixed undercarriage. It came as no surprise, therefore, that Gloster's SS 37 biplane, which was marginally faster and considerably more maneuverable, was chosen as the winner. Developed from the company's successful Gauntlet biplane, the new fighter would enter service with the RAF as the Gladiator – Britain's last biplane fighter.

Undaunted by this initial failure, Mitchell and his team started work on a far cleaner airframe that would feature a retractable undercarriage and a considerably more powerful engine. The latter had emerged from Rolls-Royce in late 1934 in the form of the PV 12 (later renamed the Merlin). The company rated the engine at 790hp when unveiled, but the manufacturer hoped to eventually get 1,000hp from it. By this time Mitchell was already seriously ill with cancer. In 1933 he had taken a holiday to Europe to convalesce after an operation, and had met with some German aviators. He became convinced that war was inevitable and he was determined to make his contribution by providing the design for a battle-winning fighter.

At the same time Vickers allocated funds for Mitchell and his team to proceed with their PV 12-powered fighter, which was designated the Supermarine Type 300. Although initially started as a private venture at Woolston, the Air Ministry quickly became interested in the aircraft. On December 1, 1934, it issued a contract worth £10,000 to Supermarine for construction of a prototype to Mitchell's "improved F7/30" design, the new fighter receiving the designation F37/34.

Rolls-Royce factory workers construct the various component parts required to create Merlin engines at the production plant in Derby. The company's V-shaped, inline 12-cylinder design, intended for the new generation of fighters, was originally designed and funded exclusively by Rolls-Royce. Air Ministry funding was granted from 1933 onward, and from this point on it was known as the Merlin engine. Like the Spitfire and Hurricane, the Merlin would go through various stages of refinements until eventually being replaced by the Griffon engine in 1942. (IWM D 12099)

The new Rolls-Royce engine was a third larger both in terms of its weight and size in comparison with the Goshawk, so in order to compensate for the forward shift in the center of gravity the sweepback of the leading edge of the fighter's wing was reduced. Soon, the wing had taken on an elliptical shape, as aerodynamicists at Supermarine calculated that it would create the lowest induced drag in flight. Such a flying surface also meant that the wing root would be thick enough to house the undercarriage when retracted. Beverley Shenstone, the aerodynamicist on the Type 300 team, told noted aviation historian Dr Alfred Price that:

> I remember once discussing the shape with R. J. Mitchell, and he said jokingly "I don't give a bugger whether it's elliptical or not, so long as it covers the guns!" The ellipse was simply the shape that allowed us the thinnest possible wing with sufficient room inside to carry the necessary structure and the things we wanted to cram in.

Mitchell's mentioning of the guns in this quote reflects the fact that in April 1935 Supermarine was asked by the Operational Requirements section of the Air Ministry to double the firepower being installed into the wings of its new fighter by fitting eight rather than four .303in Browning machine guns. Each gun would have its own 300-round ammunition box.

One of the final problems overcome with the prototype Type 300 prior to the aircraft being rolled out for the first time centered on the cooling for the PV 12 engine. Rolls-Royce had hoped to use the evaporative system once again, but this had performed so badly in the Type 224 that Mitchell was forced to go with an external radiator, and the drag it produced. However, a newly developed ducted radiator designed by Fred Meredith of the Royal Aircraft Establishment (RAE) promised to offset the drag through its ability to expel compressed, heated air at increased velocity through a divergent duct. Thus, when the prototype F37/34 was rolled out of the Woolston works on the banks of the Itchen River for the first time in February 1936, it boasted a Meredith-type ducted radiator beneath its starboard wing.

Following a series of ground runs, the fighter was dismantled and trucked to Supermarine's airfield at nearby Eastleigh. Once reassembled and passed fit to fly by the Aeronautical Inspection Directorate, the unpainted Type 300, wearing the serial K5054 and RAF roundels, took to the skies at 1630hrs. At the controls was Vickers' chief test pilot, Capt Joseph "Mutt" Summers, who was aloft for just eight minutes.

Spitfire IIA fuselages are mass-produced at the Nuffield Shadow Factory at Castle Bromwich, near Birmingham, in late 1940. The Shadow Factory plan was devised in the late 1930s to provide additional manufacturing capability in the event of war. Castle Bromwich's Spitfire IIs were virtually identical to the Spitfire Is built elsewhere.

By early April the initial test program had been completed, and on May 26 the prototype was delivered to the RAF trials establishment at Martlesham Heath. After a brief series of early flights that revealed the fighter's potential (including possessing a top speed of 349mph), the Air Ministry signed a contract with Vickers Supermarine for 310 fighters. There was some debate over what the new fighter should be called. According to the historian Robert Bungay, Vickers appeared to think of airplanes as "bad tempered women." They had previously come up with "Shrew" but Mitchell apparently objected to this denigration of his elegant design and was overheard to remark caustically that it was "just the sort of silly name they would give it." The eventual name actually came from Vickers' chairman, Sir Robert Maclean, who called his daughter "a little Spitfire," and it was approved by the Air Ministry.

As the sole prototype, K5054 was progressively modified into a more representative frontline fighter. For example, in August 1936 the aircraft returned to Eastleigh for the installation of eight .303in machine guns, a reflector gunsight and radio. Ever more powerful versions of the Merlin engine were also fitted during 1936 and 1937. On June 11, 1937, with K5054 still the only airworthy example of the Spitfire in existence, its creator, Reginald J. Mitchell, succumbed to cancer at the age of just 42, having dedicated his health and the final years of his life to creating the airplane. In the wake of his death, Supermarine's chief draftsman Joe Smith was promoted to chief designer, and he took charge of the Spitfire's development.

One of the more persistent problems facing Smith and his team was the freezing of the machine guns in the wings when the aircraft climbed up to 32,000ft. This issue first arose in March 1937, and it was not effectively cured until October of the following year – the ducting of hot air from the underwing radiator eventually cured the problem. By then the first production aircraft had at last reached Fighter Command, some 12 months later than scheduled.

The stressed-skin structure of the hand-finished prototype had proven difficult to replicate when it came to building production aircraft in jigs. The aircraft's elliptical wings could not be built using existing production techniques, and being all-metal, they were hard to make and hard to repair. Progress to this point had also been slowed by the redrafting of the prototype drawings so that they could be used as blueprints from which to build combat-capable Spitfires – this took a year to complete. Once it came time to cut, forge or cast metal, Supermarine encountered further problems employing sufficiently skilled workers to man its production line.

Mitchell had sacrificed everything for performance, and as a result, a Spitfire took two-and-a-half times as long to build as a Hurricane and twice as long as a

THE SPITFIRE IA THROUGH 360 DEGREES

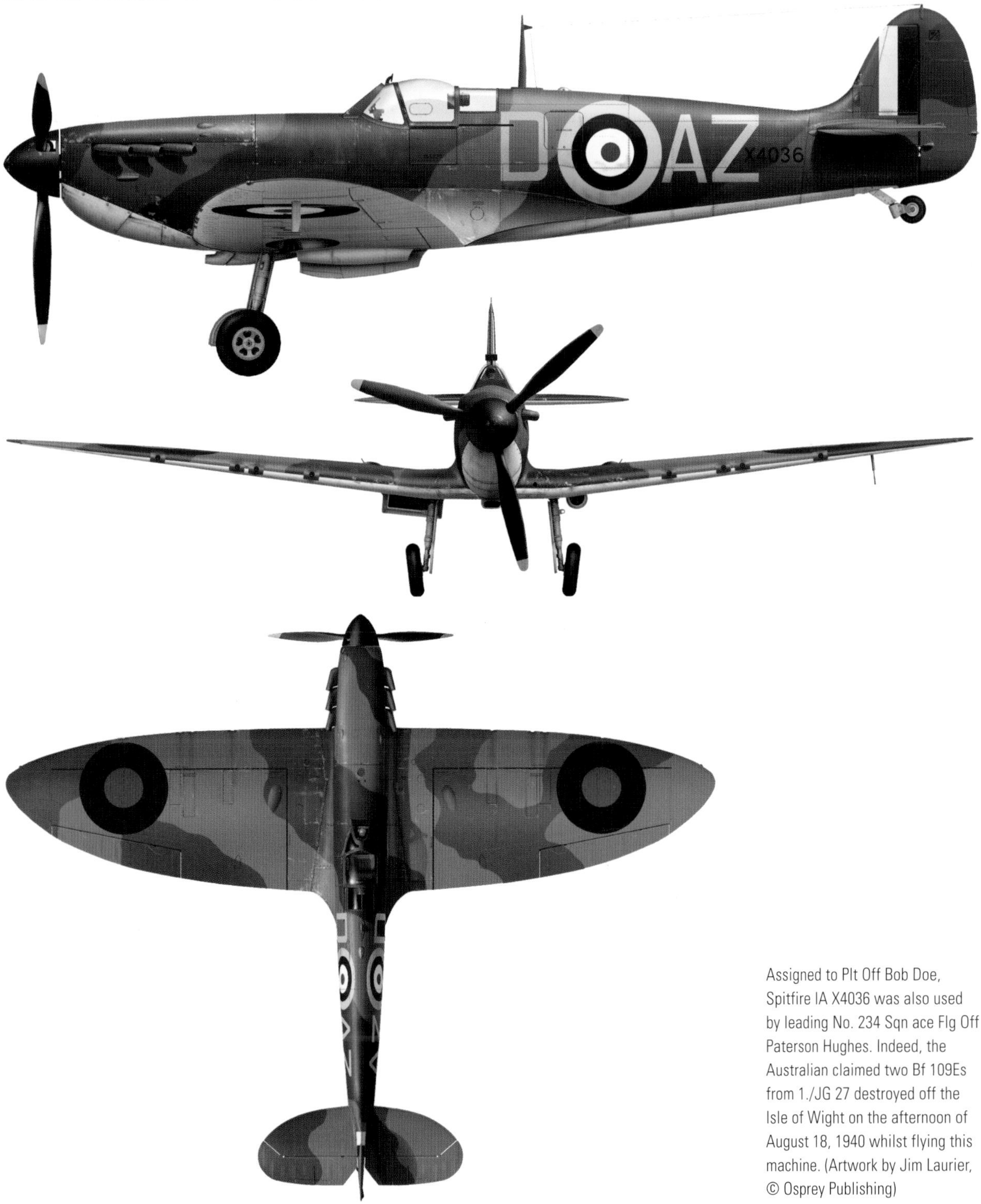

Assigned to Plt Off Bob Doe, Spitfire IA X4036 was also used by leading No. 234 Sqn ace Flg Off Paterson Hughes. Indeed, the Australian claimed two Bf 109Es from 1./JG 27 destroyed off the Isle of Wight on the afternoon of August 18, 1940 whilst flying this machine. (Artwork by Jim Laurier, © Osprey Publishing)

Bf 109E. With its 500-strong workforce fully occupied producing fuselages, Supermarine had to subcontract work on the wings out to General Aircraft and Pobjoy, wing ribs to Westland, leading edges to The Pressed Steel Company, ailerons and elevators to Aero Engines Ltd, tails to Folland, wingtips to General Electric and fuselage frames to J. Samuel White & Company. Final assembly and engine installation was completed at Eastleigh.

The Air Ministry was so dismayed by this convoluted process that in 1938 it contracted the Nuffield Organisation (which mass-produced cars) to build 1,000 Spitfire IIs in a new Shadow Factory at Castle Bromwich, and the first of these aircraft was delivered to the RAF in early July 1940. Again, these Spitfires were also delayed by various factors: changes to the production specification by the Air Ministry, the factory management's ignorance about aerospace technology and squabbles between the unions and management over pay. However, once war was declared Britain successfully converted to a war economy, with a huge drive resulting in Spitfire production eventually outstripping the German fighter production.

By then the production Spitfire I had matured into a frontline fighter to rival the best in the world. Amongst the numerous changes made to the aircraft was the replacement of the original two-bladed, fixed-pitch Watts wooden propeller with a three-bladed two-pitch or variable-pitch de Havilland or Rotol airscrew. The low, flat cockpit canopy had been replaced by a bulged canopy, thus giving more headroom for taller pilots, whilst steel armor had been fitted behind and beneath the pilot's seat. A thick slab of laminated glass was also fitted to the front of the windshield, and Identification Friend or Foe (IFF) transponders were built into the aircraft to identify the fighter as friendly to the all-new radar stations along the coast of Great Britain.

No. 19 Sqn became the first unit in Fighter Command to receive Spitfire Is in August 1938, and by September of the following year the RAF had ten squadrons equipped with the aircraft. It would now be just a matter of months before the world's best fighters of the period would meet in combat for the first time.

MESSERSCHMITT Bf 109

The Spitfire's great rival in the skies for much of World War II was the Bf 109. Design work on this airplane commenced in secret in March 1934 at the Bayerische Flugzeugwerke AG (BFW) facility in Augsburg-Haunstetten, in Bavaria. The company had a long history of aircraft construction, having taken over the Udet Flugzeugbau in July 1926. BFW had merged with fellow aircraft manufacturer Messerschmitt Flugzeugbau at this time, and company founder,

Diplomingenieur (Diploma Engineer) Willy Messerschmitt, assumed design control within the new enterprise.

German industry had been banned from producing military aircraft under the terms of the 1919 Treaty of Versailles, so manufacturers gained experience in the late 1920s and early 1930s building a series of ever more advanced mailplanes, airliners, touring and sports aircraft. Many advanced aviation design techniques such as low-set cantilever wings, stressed-skin semi-monocoque fuselage shells, retractable undercarriages and enclosed cockpits were incorporated into these machines made by manufacturers such as Heinkel, Arado, Dornier, Focke-Wulf and, of course, Messerschmitt.

Despite the restrictive Treaty of Versailles, senior officers in the Wehrmacht had secretly set up organizations in the 1920s to train future pilots for the air force. When, on March 1, 1933, Reich Chancellor Adolf Hitler announced the existence of the newly created Luftwaffe, it had sufficient pilots available to staff a number of units thanks to the various clandestine training schools run in the USSR.

The civil ministry created to oversee the running of the Luftwaffe was the *Reichsluftfahrtministerium* (RLM), headed by Hermann Göring. The department responsible for aviation design within the RLM was the *Technische Amt* (LC), and its requirements would exert considerable influence on the final configuration of the Bf 109. As the Luftwaffe's fighter force, the *Jagdwaffe* was initially equipped with Heinkel He 51 and Arado Ar 68 biplanes. These aircraft had braced and staggered wings, fixed and spatted undercarriages, and open cockpits, making them little removed from the fighters of World War I. Indeed, they were slower than civilian monoplane types such as the He 70, and only marginally faster than the He 111.

Clearly something had to be done to modernize the German fighter force, and on July 6, 1933 the RLM's LCII (Technical

Theo Osterkamp shown inspecting the Me 108 *Taifun* ("Typhoon") in 1938. Osterkamp was a fighter pilot during World War I, with 32 victories claimed. With the outbreak of World War II he commanded Jagdgeschwader 51 during the Battle of France and later commanded all fighter aircraft in Luftflotte 2. He was eventually dismissed from the Luftwaffe in 1944 following a series of disagreements with High Command. (Bundesarchiv Bild 183-H16409)

Office for Development) issued the Tactical Requirements for Fighter Aircraft (Land) document. This stated that the Luftwaffe needed a single-seat daytime fighter armed with two fixed machine guns (with 500 rounds per gun) or one fixed cannon (with 100rpg). It had to have a radio for air-to-air and air-to-ground communication, as well as a safety harness, oxygen system, parachute and heating for the pilot. The fighter had to be able to maintain a speed of 250mph for up to 20 minutes at 19,500ft, take no longer than 17 minutes to reach this height and possess at least an hour's flight duration. Its ultimate ceiling was to be 33,000ft.

From a handling perspective, the aircraft had to be capable of diving and turning without losing altitude, and be easily recoverable from a spin. The fighter also had to be operable from the average German airfield (which was 1,300ft x 1,300ft in size) by an average frontline pilot. It would also be required to fly in cloud and fog and to perform group (up to nine aircraft) take-offs and landings. Finally, the design had to be small enough to enable it to be transported by rail.

Having already built fighters for the Luftwaffe, Arado, Heinkel and Focke-Wulf were seen as frontrunners to win this lucrative contract, and Messerschmitt, which had no experience in designing fighters, was seen as the rank outsider. However, the latter company's series of fast sports aircraft from the late 1920s and early 1930s, boasting low-set, cantilever wings, gave LCII the confidence to instruct Messerschmitt to build a four-seater touring aircraft to compete in the 1934 European Flying Contest. The M 23 design by Willy Messerschmitt had won this prestigious international competition in 1929 and 1930, and the new aircraft produced by the company was eventually designated the Bf 108.

Many features embodied in this advanced machine would soon find their way into the Bf 109 prototype, including flush-riveted stressed-skin construction, cantilevered monoplane wings equipped with Handley Page "slots" along the leading edges (improving the aircraft's slow-speed handling), and a narrow track undercarriage that was attached to the fuselage and retracted outward into wells forward of the main spar. Although it did not win the 1934 contest, the Bf 108 was the fastest machine at the meet by some margin, and it would ultimately enjoy a long career with the Luftwaffe as a utility/training aircraft.

Buoyed by this success, Messerschmitt pressed on with the Bf 109, which incorporated all of the features previously mentioned. Aside from the wing "slots," the aircraft also had trailing-edge flaps, and these two features combined with the wing's small surface area (made possible by the growing power of aero engines) to ultimately give the Bf 109 unmatched maneuverability. The fuselage itself was made of light metal as a monocoque structure of roughly oval section, constructed in two halves and joined along the center line.

Right from the start, Messerschmitt had planned that the lightweight Bf 109 would be powered by one of the new-generation inverted-vee 12-cylinder engines under development by Junkers and Daimler-Benz. The former's 680hp Jumo 210 was ultimately selected because it was at a more advanced stage in its development than the 960hp DB 600Aa. As it transpired, delivery of the Junkers powerplant was delayed to the point where the first prototype Bf 109 V1 had to be fitted with a 695hp Rolls-Royce Kestrel VI engine.

Construction of the V1 was completed by early May 1935, and following a series of taxiing trials, on the 28th of that month Messerschmitt's senior test pilot, Hans-Dietrich "Bubi" Knoetzsch, made the fighter's first flight from Augsburg-Haunstetten airfield. Following initial factory trials, the aircraft was sent to the Rechlin-based *Erprobungsstelle* (testing center) for service trials. The latter soon proved that the Bf 109 was considerably faster and more maneuverable than its primary rival for the fighter contract, Heinkel's He 112 V1 (which was also Kestrel-powered).

The Messerschmitt Bf 109 V1 Wk-Nr 758 performed its first flight on May 28, 1935, from Augsburg-Haunstetten airfield, with Messerschmitt's senior test pilot, Hans-Dietrich "Bubi" Knoetzsch, at the controls. Like its He 112 V1 rival, this aircraft was powered by a 695hp Rolls-Royce Kestrel VI engine. This photograph was taken at Augsburg-Haunstetten during engine runs that preceded the first flight.

The Jumo 210A-powered Bf 109 V2 took to the skies in October 1935 and joined the trials program three months later. This aircraft also boasted two 7.92mm MG 17 machine guns in the fuselage upper decking. The V3, which had provision for an engine-mounted 20mm MG FF/M cannon firing through the propeller hub, flew for the first time in June 1936, and a short while later both Messerschmitt and Heinkel received contracts from the RLM to build ten preproduction aircraft.

In the autumn of that year the official trials culminated in a series of tests at Travemünde, where the Bf 109 proved its superiority in a memorable flight demonstration that included tailslides, flick rolls, 21-turn spins, tight turns and terminal dives. Being faster in level speed and in the climb than the He 112, and easily able to outdive the Heinkel, the Bf 109 could also perform much tighter turns thanks to its leading-edge slots. From rank outsider, Messerschmitt had become the obvious choice for the fighter contract, and the Bf 109 was duly announced the competition winner.

The first of ten preproduction Bf 109B-0s took to the air in November 1936, and the following month three aircraft were sent to war-torn Spain for an evaluation under operational conditions with the Condor Legion. The trials were beset with problems, but they did give both Messerschmitt and the Luftwaffe experience of what to expect when the production Bf 109B entered service in Germany in February 1937.

Early Bf 109Bs were built at Messerschmitt's Augsburg-Haunstetten plant, but it soon became obvious that a larger factory would be required. A new site at Regensburg was duly developed, and production of the Bf 109B (or "Bertha") was soon transferred there. However, the company's design offices remained at Augsburg.

The first production Bf 109Bs were issued to II./JG 132 "Richthofen" at Jüterbog-Damm as replacements for the *Geschwader*'s He 51 biplanes in February 1937. (*Geschwader* denotes a wing of aircraft; for more details on the structure of the Luftwaffe's fighter arm see the Unit Organization section on page 42) However, the dominance of the Republican forces' I-15 and I-16 *Ratas* in Spanish skies resulted in 16 Berthas being shipped to Spain just weeks after their delivery to the Luftwaffe. Accompanying them were II./JG 132 personnel, who formed 2./J 88. Operational by April, the unit ultimately did not see its first combat until the battle for Brunete in July, when it was discovered that the Bf 109B and the nimble Soviet-built Polikarpov fighters were evenly matched below 10,000ft. At higher altitudes, the Bertha was untouchable, and German pilots soon worked out that Republican aircraft could be easily picked off if attacked from above and behind using high-speed dives – this would be the Bf 109 pilots' stock tactic throughout World War II as well.

In Germany, meanwhile, development of the aircraft continued at a rapid pace, and in June 1937 the Bf 109 V10 flew for the first time with the promising 960hp Daimler-Benz DB 600Aa fitted. This new powerplant was much longer and heavier than the Jumo, and in order to offset the shift in the aircraft's center of gravity, Messerschmitt redesigned the fighter's cooling system. A shallow radiator bath was fitted under the nose and two radiators positioned beneath the wings. A three-bladed VDM propeller also replaced the two-blade VDM-Hamilton airscrew fitted to the Jumo-powered Bf 109B. Due to the fighter's higher all-up weight (when fully fueled and armed), its fuselage and undercarriage were also strengthened. This aircraft would effectively serve as the prototype for the Bf 109E.

The new fighter made its entrance on the international stage in late July 1937 when three Jumo- and two Daimler-Benz-powered Bf 109s were dispatched to the 4th International Flying Meeting at Zurich-Dübendorf, in Switzerland. Setting a series of speed records during the week-long event, the aircraft garnered Messerschmitt world recognition for its Bf 109. By year-end, production of the B model had commenced at the Gerhard Fieseler Werke at Kassel, and four *Gruppen* (groups) within the Luftwaffe and two *Staffeln* (squadrons) in Spain had reequipped with the aircraft.

In the early spring of 1938 deliveries of the Bf 109C, fitted with the 730hp fuel-injected Jumo 210Ga engine and wing-mounted machine guns, commenced, with the first aircraft being issued to I./JG 132. Only 58 were built prior to production switching to the four-gun Bf 109D, which was powered by the 680hp carburetored Jumo 210Da engine. Some 657 were built, with aircraft also being constructed by Erla Maschinenwerk in Leipzig and Focke-Wulf Flugzeugbau of Bremen.

Aside from service with the Luftwaffe, a handful of C and D models were also sent to Spain for service with the Condor Legion, where they continued to down Republican Polikarpov fighters with regularity. Amongst the leading aces from this campaign were Werner Mölders (14 kills), Wolfgang Schellmann (12 kills) and Harro Harder (11 kills), all of whom would enjoy more success with the Bf 109E in the first 18 months of World War II.

While the Luftwaffe's fighter pilots continued to gain valuable combat experience in Spain, at home, the *Jagdwaffe*'s enlargement continued apace. By September 19, 1938, a total of 583 Bf 109B/C/Ds were on strength, but limited availability of the Daimler-Benz engine had stymied plans for the rapid fielding

THE Bf 109E THROUGH 360 DEGREES

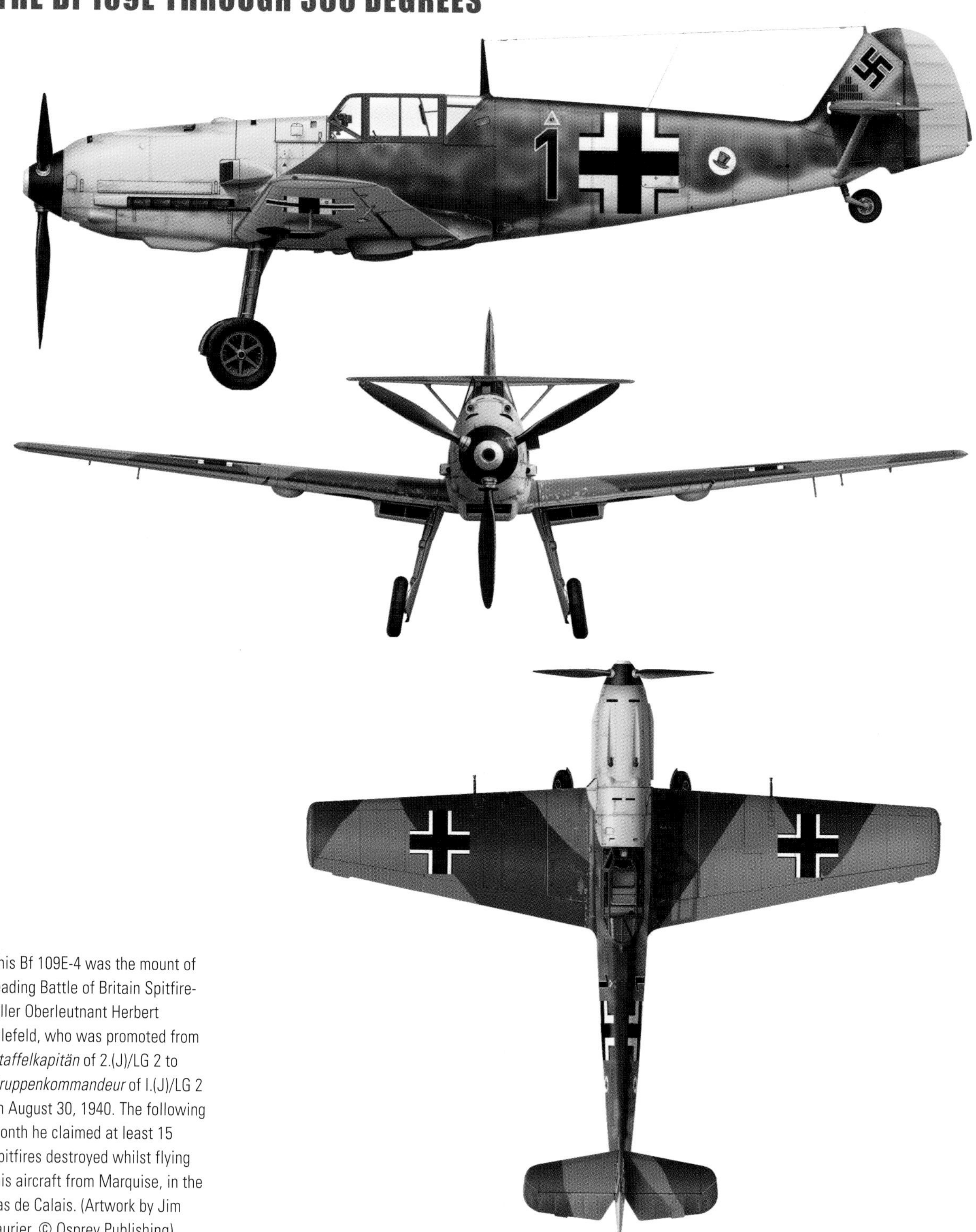

This Bf 109E-4 was the mount of leading Battle of Britain Spitfire-killer Oberleutnant Herbert Ihlefeld, who was promoted from *Staffelkapitän* of 2.(J)/LG 2 to *Gruppenkommandeur* of I.(J)/LG 2 on August 30, 1940. The following month he claimed at least 15 Spitfires destroyed whilst flying this aircraft from Marquise, in the Pas de Calais. (Artwork by Jim Laurier, © Osprey Publishing)

of the Bf 109E. This was because bomber production had priority over fighter procurement in the late 1930s, and most of the DB 600s produced were duly allocated to the He 111. Finally, in 1938 the focus shifted to fighter production, and by then the much delayed DB 601A was at last reaching maturity, so Daimler-Benz switched its efforts to perfecting this powerplant. This new engine was very similar to the DB 600, but crucially it featured fuel injection rather than a float carburetor. The engine meant that the Bf 109 could perform negative G flight, and also increased the fighter's range through improved fuel economy.

With its DB 601A engine rated at 1,175hp for takeoff, the Bf 109E-1, nicknamed the "Emil," finally entered series production in December 1938, the new aircraft boasting unmatched take-off and climb performance. The higher wing loading of the Emil increased the fighter's turning circle and stall speed, but it was still very much a pilot's aircraft. Like the D model before it, the E-1's armament consisted of two MG 17s in the upper fuselage decking and two more machine guns in the wings. The latter had 500rpg, and the fuselage guns had 1,000 rounds each. The aircraft was fitted with a Revi C/12C gunsight and FuG 7 radio, the latter having a range of about 40 miles.

In early 1939 the first Bf 109E-3s began rolling off the production line, these aircraft having their wing MG 17s replaced with MG FF 20mm cannon as initially trialled in the Bf 109C-3. Each weapon only had 60 rounds, but their destructive punch was unrivalled. Once in frontline service, the E-3 *Kanonenmaschine* (cannon machine) was rated as the best early generation Messerschmitt by those that flew it, with the aircraft enjoying a greater margin of superiority over its rivals than any other Bf 109 variant. Some 40 Bf 109E-1/3s were sent to Spain for service with the Condor Legion, although it appears that these aircraft did not get the chance to prove themselves in aerial combat prior to the Republicans surrendering in March 1939.

A total of 200 German pilots had flown with *Jagdgruppe* (Fighter Group) 88 in Spain, and these men would be in the vanguard of the *Jagdwaffe*'s fighting force during the first 18 months of World War II. They would primarily be flying Bf 109Es during this period, and between January 1 and September 1, 1939, 1,091 Emils were delivered. Four engine plants had been established to allow production of the DB 601 to keep pace with airframe construction, with Bf 109s being built by Messerschmitt at Regensburg, and by Erla and Fieseler, as well as by the Wiener-Neüstadt Flugzeugbau in Austria. By the time the Wehrmacht advanced east into Poland on September 1, 1939, no fewer than 28 *Gruppen* were operating Bf 109B/C/D/Es. The Messerschmitt fighter was now well placed to dominate the skies over Europe.

TYPE HISTORY

THE SPITFIRE

PROTOTYPE SPITFIRE K5054

Remarkably, just one prototype Spitfire was built by Vickers Supermarine, in the form of K5054. This aircraft conducted all the preproduction development work associated with the aircraft between March 5, 1936 and the first flight of the first production Spitfire I (K9787) on May 14, 1938. Thoroughly tested by both the manufacturer and the RAF, the handbuilt K5054 was progressively altered during this period to more closely represent the 310 Spitfire Is ordered by the Air Ministry in mid-1936. Guns were installed and fired in flight, a modified propeller fitted to improve its top speed and the external skin finishing changed to help reduce the time and cost involved in building production Spitfires. Improved versions of the Rolls-Royce engine were also progressively installed, including the Merlin "C" (later designated the Merlin II) of 990hp, the Merlin "F" of 1,035hp and finally the Merlin III of 1,030hp. Gun heating trials were also undertaken with this aircraft. Badly damaged twice in its brief lifetime during landing accidents, K5054 soldiered on in its testing role until late October 1938, by which time some of the 20 production Spitfire Is that had flown by then were conducting trials work. Sent to Farnborough to serve as a "high-speed hack," the aircraft was finally written off on September 4, 1939, in a fatal landing accident.

SPITFIRE I

The jig-built Spitfire I differed significantly from the handbuilt K5054 in a number of key areas, primarily internally. The fighter's distinctive elliptical wing had been considerably strengthened so as to raise its never-to-be-exceeded maximum speed from 380mph to 470mph. Flap travel was also increased from 57° to 90°, and fuel tankage boosted from 75 to 84gal. Other equipment and minor changes were also introduced, which resulted in the first production Spitfire I weighing in at 5,819lb fully loaded – 460lb heavier than K5054. The first 64 airframes were fitted with the Merlin II engine, whilst the remaining Spitfire I/IAs were powered by the 1,030hp Merlin III. From the 78th airframe onwards, the Rolls-Royce engine would be driving a three-bladed de Havilland or Rotol two-pitch or constant speed propeller, rather than the Watts two-bladed fixed-pitch wooden airscrew. The new propeller shortened the take-off run from 420 yards to 225 yards (with the constant-speed airscrew), increased the rate of climb,

The very first production Spitfire I built, K9787 made its maiden flight on May 5, 1938 – a full 26 months after the prototype K5054 had taken to the skies for the first time. Used extensively by Supermarine as a trials and testbed aircraft, K9787 was eventually stripped of its armament and converted into a photo-reconnaissance platform in the spring of 1941, but was lost later that year.

boosted the top speed from 361mph to 365mph and made the Spitfire much easier to handle in combat. The first Spitfire Is reached No. 19 Sqn in August 1938, and further modifications were brought in following early months of service flying. Engine start problems were cured with a more powerful starter motor, an engine-driven hydraulic system to raise and lower the undercarriage replaced the hand pump that was originally fitted, and a bulged canopy was introduced to provide the extra headroom that was needed to allow taller pilots to fly the aircraft in comfort.

Early in World War II, once it became clear that pilots of modern fighters needed armor protection, the previously unarmored Spitfire I had a thick slab of laminated glass fitted to the front of its windshield. A .12in-thick light alloy cover was also fitted over the upper fuel tank in the fuselage, and 75lb of steel armor was installed behind and beneath the pilot's seat. In the spring of 1940, the RAF also introduced 100-octane fuel in place of the 87-octane that it had previously used. The Spitfire I's Merlin engine had to be modified to use this gasoline, and the higher octane rating allowed pilots to select double the supercharger boost for a maximum of five minutes (raising the top speed by up to 34mph) without the risk of damaging the Merlin III. IFF transponder equipment was also introduced soon after the outbreak of war, thus allowing radar operators on the ground to identify the aircraft they were tracking on their plots. Finally, just prior to the Battle of Britain commencing, all frontline Spitfires were fitted with "two-step" rudder pedals, with the upper step six inches higher than the lower step. Just prior to combat, the pilot lifted his feet on to the upper steps, thus giving his body a more horizontal posture, which in turn raised his blackout threshold by about 1G, allowing him to sustain tighter turns in action. Production of the Spitfire I ran from April 1938 through to March 1941, by which time 1,567 examples had been built.

SPITFIRE IA

In the summer of 1940, non-Castle-Bromwich-built aircraft that were still equipped with eight Browning .303in machine guns were redesignated Spitfire IAs so as to differentiate them from the recently introduced cannon-armed Spitfire IBs.

SPITFIRE IB

Soon after the Spitfire I entered service, the RAF stated that it required the fighter to pack a heavier punch in order to down bombers that boasted armor and self-sealing tanks. Having evaluated a series of heavier-caliber cannon, it selected

Armorer Fred Roberts rearms Sgt Bernard Jennings' Spitfire IA at RAF Fowlmere, September 1940. The eight rifle-caliber .303in Brownings of the IA were felt to lack punch, and on the Spitfire IB four of the machine guns were replaced by two 20mm cannon. (IWM CH 1458)

the French 20mm Hispano-Suiza Type 404 as the best weapon of its size then in production. The cannon boasted a high muzzle velocity and the ability to fire armor-piercing shells, and a deal was quickly struck with the manufacturer to build the gun under license in the UK. In June 1939, Spitfire I L1007 was fitted with two cannon in place of all eight machine guns, and the following month it commenced flight testing at Martlesham Heath. Small blisters were added to the upper surfaces of the fighter's wing so that the cannon's drum magazines could be housed within the slender structure. The cannon barrels also extended from the leading edges of the wings. The Hispano-Suiza guns had to be mounted on their sides in order for them to fit in the thin wings, and if they were fired when the fighter was pulling G, used cartridge cases tended to bounce back into the cannon and cause stoppages. If only one gun jammed, the recoil forces from the remaining weapon made it virtually impossible for the pilot to accurately sight his target.

RAF engineers worked hard to solve these problems, and by the spring of 1940 the armament was deemed reliable enough to enter series production. The first examples were delivered to No. 19 Sqn at Duxford in June 1940, but when the unit went into action two months later its aircraft were plagued with chronic cannon jams, and the Spitfire IBs were hastily replaced with all-machine gun Spitfire IIAs within days. During the fall further work was done to rectify the jamming problem, and to address the issue of the weapon's modest 60-round magazine per cannon – enough ammunition for just five seconds' worth of firing – it was decided to retain four .303in Brownings in the outer troughs, and the first of these revised Spitfire IBs was issued to No. 92 Sqn in November 1940.

SPITFIRE IB GUNS

The Spitfire IB was fitted with a single French-designed 20mm Hispano-Suiza Type 404 cannon in each wing. Small blisters were added to the upper surfaces of the fighter's wing so that the cannon's drum magazines could be housed within the slender structure. Early Spitfire IBs were plagued by chronic shell jams.

SPITFIRE IIA/B

Following a series of delays, the massive Shadow Factory established by the Nuffield Organisation in Castle Bromwich at last began to produce Spitfires in June 1940. These aircraft were virtually identical to late-production Spitfire Is built elsewhere in the UK, but they were fitted with the slightly more powerful

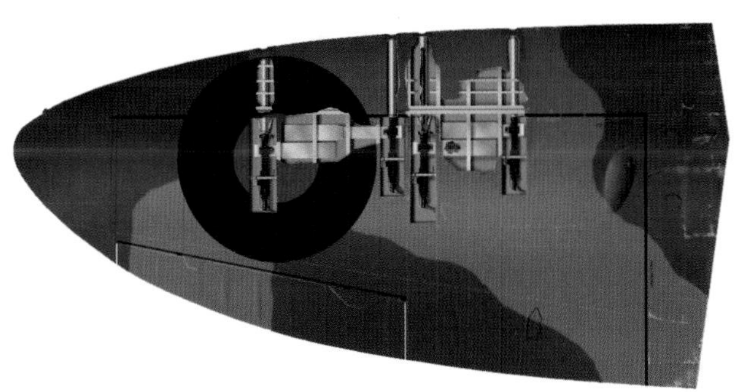

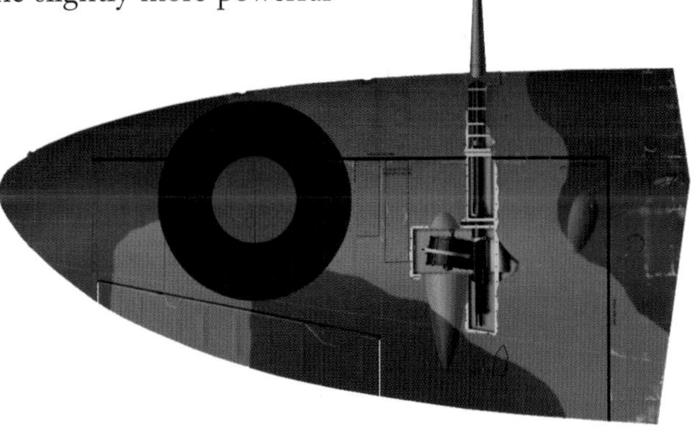

Merlin XII engine which produced 110hp more than the Merlin III. Designated the Spitfire IIA, the first examples were delivered to No. 611 Sqn in July 1940, followed by Nos 19, 74 and 266 Sqns. Towards the end of the aircraft's production run at Nuffield, 170 cannon-armed Spitfire IIBs were built at the factory, these aircraft also boasting four .303in machine guns. By the time production of the Spitfire IIA ended in July 1941, 751 examples had been built.

SPITFIRE IIA LONG RANGE

Operations over Dunkirk in May–June 1940 had revealed the Spitfire's limited radius of action, so Supermarine looked to extend its fighter's range through the provision of an external tank. Spitfire I P9565 flew with a 30gal tank fitted beneath its port wing in the summer of 1940, but the advent of the Battle of Britain stymied development until Fighter Command commenced offensive operations into Europe in early 1941. Eventually, 60 Spitfire IIA Long Range (LR) fighters were built with a 40gal fixed tank fitted under the port wing, these lopsided aircraft initially seeing service in the spring of 1941. Although less maneuverable and 26mph slower than a standard Spitfire IIA, the tank-equipped fighter carried nearly half as much fuel again, thus making it ideally suited to bomber escort missions.

THE Bf 109E

The Bf 109E was the dominant model of the Messerschmitt to serve during the Battle of Britain. All major derivatives of this model are described in detail below.

Bf 109 V10

This preproduction Bf 109 started life fitted with a 730hp Junkers Jumo 210Ga direct fuel-injection engine. In June 1937 this powerplant was replaced by a 960hp Daimler-Benz DB 600Aa. The Bf 109 V11, V12, V13 and V14 (the latter two participating in the 4th International Flying Meeting in Switzerland, in July 1937) were also subsequently flown with the DB 600Aa. All four aircraft featured a redesigned engine cooling system that saw a shallow oil radiator bath replace the huge coolant radiator beneath the nose of the Jumo-powered Bf 109, and rectangular coolant radiators under each wing replace the small oil radiator beneath the port wing. The upper cowling was also revised, with the supercharger air intake on the upper starboard side being replaced by an intake midway down the port side. Finally, a three-bladed VDM propeller was fitted in place of the two-blade VDM-Hamilton airscrew employed by the Jumo-powered Bf 109B. This trio of aircraft served as the prototypes for the Bf 109E which would follow in late 1938.

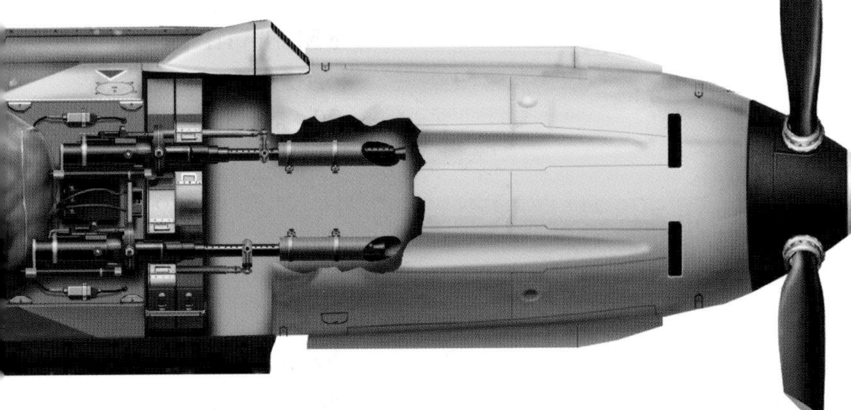

Bf 109E-4 COWLING GUNS

Like previous versions of the Emil, the Bf 109E-4 was fitted with a pair of rifle-caliber Rheinmetall MG 17s immediately above its DB 601 engine. Each 7.92mm weapon had a magazine holding 1,000 rounds per gun. Note how the guns are staggered, with the port MG 17 being set slightly forward the width of the ammunition feed chute.

Bf 109E-4 WING GUNS

The Oerlikon MG FF "M" cannon made its frontline debut in the Bf 109E-4. This version of the 20mm weapon fired *M-Geschosse* (Mine) shells, which inflicted more damage than a standard round. Boasting a low cyclic rate of fire, pronounced recoil and oversized Trommel T60 drum magazine, the weapon was replaced by the superb MG 151 from late 1940. (Artwork by Jim Laurier, © Osprey Publishing)

Bf 109 V14-16

These three V-series aircraft were fitted with the early-development DB 601A engines of 1,050hp in the summer of 1938, although the reliability of the powerplant was so poor that the introduction of the Bf 109E-1 to frontline service was delayed until year-end. Previously powered by a DB 600Aa, the V14 was fitted with two MG FF 20mm cannon in the wings and a pair of 7.92mm MG 17 machine guns in the fuselage. The V15 had only the latter weapons installed.

Bf 109E-0

A preproduction series of ten Bf 109E-0s was built for service evaluation and engine and armament development in the autumn of 1938. These aircraft were very similar to the V14, but they were all armed with two fuselage- and two wing-mounted MG 17s.

Bf 109E-1

With final clearance of the DB 601A for service use in late 1938, production of the Bf 109E-1 had commenced in earnest by year-end. Indeed, a substantial number of

This propaganda photograph shows an early Bf 109B, fitted with a provisional wooden Schwarz propeller, being used to provide cover for Wehrmacht infantrymen during maneuvers held in mid-1937. The first Messerschmitt fighters had reached the Luftwaffe in February of that year.

engineless airframes had been stored from the autumn of 1938 at Augsburg-Haunstetten pending the availability of powerplants. The E-1 was exclusively equipped with MG 17s, two in the fuselage and one in each wing. Some 1,540 E-1s were built at four manufacturing plants in Germany and Austria in 1939 alone. In 1940, a number of E-1s were factory-modified into E-1/B fighter-bombers with the fitment of ETC 500/IXb or ETC 50/VIIId bomb racks on the fuselage center line. A number of E-1/Ns were also built following the replacement of the standard DB 601A engine with the 1,270hp DB 601N that had flattened instead of concave piston heads for improved compression, and used 96-octane C3 fuel. The E-1/B *Jagdbomber* concept was tested in combat by Erprobungsgruppe (Operational Test Group) 210 during anti-shipping operations in the Channel in July 1940. Used principally as a dive-bomber, dropping bombs ranging in size from 110 to 551lb, the aircraft enjoyed great success. Indeed, every *Jagdgeschwader* was ordered to create a *Jabo Staffel* during the summer of 1940, and numerous E-1s, E-3s and E-4s were modified into *Jagdbombers*.

Bf 109E-3

In the early summer of 1939 a preproduction E-0 had been equipped with the improved 1,175hp DB 601Aa engine intended for the E-3 and flown as the Bf 109 V17. This version of the Daimler-Benz engine could mount an MG FF 20mm cannon on its crankcase, the weapon in turn firing through the airscrew hub. However, the problems of vibration, seizing and overheating that had beset the engine-mounted MG FF in the Bf 109D-1 persisted, and the weapon was rarely used in frontline service. The two wing-mounted MG FFs that replaced the MG 17s in the E-3 were retained, with each weapon being fed by a 60-round magazine. Production E-3s began to replace the E-1 on the assembly lines in late 1939 – the armament was the only thing that differentiated an E-1 from an E-3, and the latter proved to be the most-produced E-series fighter. E-3s were also retrofitted with a series of revisions following lessons learned during the French campaign in May–June 1940, including 8mm armor for the pilot: seat armor and a curved armor plate over the pilot's head that was attached to the hinged canopy. Heavier framing and flatter, squarer Plexiglas panels in the folding part of the canopy hood also began to appear in the early summer of 1940, these being more economical to produce than the original transparencies. Like the E-1, E-3/B and E-3/N variants were constructed in 1940, and many more were rebuilt as E-4s and E-7s.

An early Bf 109E-3. The problematic engine-mounted cannon was deleted on later Emils, but the concept was later reintroduced on the Bf 109F. (© Museum of Flight/Corbis)

Bf 109E-4

Nearly identical to the E-3, the E-4, which entered production in mid-1940, had the engine-mounted MG FF finally discarded. The aircraft featured two new MG FF/M cannon in the wings, these weapons boasting an improved rate of fire over the 20mm cannon installed in the E-3. Armor plating was fitted to protect the fuselage fuel tank and head armor was installed in the canopy. Many E-4s were not new production aircraft, instead being factory-modified E-1s and E-3s. Again, E-4/B and E-4/N variants were produced too. In early 1941 Bf 109E-4s of I./JG 27 that were destined for operations in the Mediterranean and North Africa were tropicalized through the fitment of a dust filter over the supercharger air intake and the installation of a emergency desert survival equipment. These aircraft were redesignated E-4/N Trops.

SPITFIRE I/II: IN THE COCKPIT

1. Seat
2. Control column
3. Rudder pedal adjusting wheel
4. Rudder pedal
5. Radiator flap control lever
6. Map case
7. Oil dilution push button
8. Rudder trim wheel
9. Pressure head heater switch
10. Elevator trim wheel
11. Crowbar
12. Door catch
13. Camera indication supply plug
14. Mixture lever
15. Throttle lever
16. Propeller control lever
17. Boost control cut-out
18. Radio controller
19. Ignition switch
20. Brake triple pressure gauge
21. Elevator tabs position indicator
22. Oxygen regulator
23. Navigation lights switch
24. Flaps control
25. Airspeed indicator
26. Altimeter
27. Gun button
28. Cockpit light switches
29. Direction indicator setting knob
30. Artificial horizon
31. GM 2 reflector gunsight
32. Rearview mirror
33. Ventilator control
34. Rate of climb indicator
35. Turn and slip indicator
36. Booster coil pushbutton
37. Engine starting pushbutton
38. Oil pressure gauge
39. Oil temperature gauge
40. Fuel gauge and pushbutton
41. Radiator temperature gauge
42. Boost pressure gauge
43. Fuel pressure warning lamp
44. Engine rpms
45. Stowage for reflector sight lamp
46. Cockpit light
47. Signaling switchbox
48. Remote contactor and switch
49. Fuel tank pressurizing cock control
50. Slow running cut-out control
51. Priming pump
52. Fuel cock
53. Compass
54. Undercarriage control lever
55. Harness release
56. Oxygen hose
57. IFF controls
58. CO_2 cylinder for undercarriage emergency lowering
59. Oxygen supply cock
60. Windshield de-icing pump
61. Windshield de-icing needle valve
62. Undercarriage emergency lowering control
63. Windshield de-icing cock

Bf 109E-4: IN THE COCKPIT

1. Machine gun firing button
2. Control column
3. Rudder pedal
4. Fuel cock
5. FuG VII radio control switch
6. Fuel contents gauge
7. Cockpit light control
8. Pitot head heating warning lamp
9. Circuit breaker
10. Airspeed indicator
11. Engine starter switch
12. Turn and bank indicator
13. Altimeter
14. Compass
15. Instructions for flap settings, landing speed, etc
16. Clock
17. Revi C/12D gunsight
18. Boost gauge
19. Compass deviation table
20. Tachometer
21. Propeller pitch indicator
22. Undercarriage position indicator
23. Fuel and oil pressure gauge
24. Undercarriage control lever
25. Undercarriage emergency control lever
26. Mechanical undercarriage position indicator
27. Filter pump control lever
28. Coolant temperature gauge
29. Oil temperature gauge
30. Low fuel warning lamp
31. Elevator control wheel
32. Landing flap control
33. Oil cooler flap control
34. Throttle control
35. Main instrument light
36. Engine instant-stop lever
37. Engine ignition lever
38. Starter coupling lever
39. Canopy release lever
40. Seat height adjustment lever
41. Tailplane incidence indicator
42. Circuit breaker panel
43. Oxygen hose
44. Main instrument light
45. Radiator flap control
46. Fuel pump auto switch
47. Map holder
48. Pilot's seat
49. Seat harness adjustment lever
50. Fuel injection pump
51. Remote control ventilator
52. Oxygen apparatus

(Artwork by Jim Laurier, © Osprey Publishing)

Bf 109E-5/6

Built in small numbers alongside the E-4, the E-5 variant had its wing cannon removed and a single vertical Zeiss Rb 21/18 camera mounted in the rear fuselage immediately behind the cockpit. The E-6 retained its full armament, but featured a smaller Rb 12.5/7 x 9 camera, again aft of the cockpit. A small number of tropicalized E-5/Trops were also operated by I./JG 27 in early 1941.

Bf 109E-7

Evolved directly from the E-4/N, the E-7 differed primarily in its ability to carry either a 66gal auxiliary drop tank or bombs of differing weights (E-7/B). The E-model's relatively modest range had proven an embarrassment for the *Jagdstaffeln* during the final phases of the invasion of France, and a rack and jettisonable drop tank made of moulded plywood were duly produced. The tank leaked badly, and pilots suspected that it would easily ignite in combat, so it saw no operational service through to the end of 1940. Factory-installed internal drop tank connections, a bomb-release mechanism and associated wiring were fitted into the E-7 as standard equipment, and this allowed units in the field quickly to convert fighter-bomber-configured aircraft into extended-range fighters, and vice versa – the E-7 and near-identical E-8 were the only E-model aircraft capable of carrying the drop tank. Operational experience with the E-1/B, E-3/B and E-4/B

Bf 109E-3 vs SPITFIRE IA COMPARISON SPECIFICATIONS		
	Bf 109E-3	Spitfire IA
Powerplant	1,175hp DB 601Aa	1,030hp Merlin III
Dimensions		
Span	32ft 4.5in	36ft 10in
Length	28ft 4.5in	29ft 11in
Height	8ft 2.333in	12ft 7.75in
Wing area	174.05 sq ft	242 sq ft
Weights		
Empty	4,685lb	4,517lb
Loaded	5,875lb	5,844lb
Performance		
Max speed	348mph at 15,000ft	346mph at 15,000ft
Range	410 miles	415 miles
Climb	to 20,000ft in 7.75min to 20,000ft in	7.42min
Service ceiling	34,450ft	30,500ft
Armament	2x 20mm MG FF 2x 7.92mm MG 17	8x .303in Brownings

had shown that the aircraft's engine was forced to work harder to overcome the drag associated with external stores, so Messerschmitt fitted an extra 2gal oil tank to help improve lubrication of the DB 601 when operating at higher power settings. The first E-7s reached frontline units in France in August 1940, and again many of these aircraft were not new production machines, but factory-modified E-1s, E-3s and E-4s. A Bf 109E-7 Trop variant was also produced in 1941, and later that same year the Bf 109E-7/Z introduced a nitrous oxide power-boosting system (GM 1) to the DB 601N, thus turning those aircraft fitted with this equipment into high-altitude fighters.

Werner Mölders, shown here in November 1940, displaying his Knight's Cross with Oak Leaves. A veteran of the Spanish Civil War, where he had developed his "finger four" flying tactic, Mölders was shot down on July 29, 1940, shortly after assuming command of JG 51. He survived and returned to combat a month later. He was eventually killed in an air accident when he was a passenger in a Heinkel 111 en route to the funeral of Ernst Udet. (Bundesarchiv Bild 146-1971-116-29)

Bf 109E-8 AND -9

The E-8 and -9 were the final versions of the E-series produced by Messerschmitt. All were rebuilt E-1s, E-3s and E-4s, and appeared in the autumn of 1940. The principal innovation of these aircraft was the introduction of the DB 601E, which was capable of generating 1,350hp thanks to increased revolutions and improved supercharging. Additional back armor was also added, and as with the E-7, the E-8 could carry a drop tank. The E-8/N was fitted with the DB 601N engine rather than the E-series powerplant, and the E-8/B boasted bomb-rack modifications. A Bf 109E-8 Trop variant was also produced in 1941. Finally, the Bf 109E-9 was the reconnaissance version of the E-8, with an Rb 50/30 camera located in the rear fuselage. The last E-series Bf 109 was finally completed in early 1942, by which time more than 4,000 had been built.

THE STRATEGIC SITUATION

The vulnerability of southern England to aerial attacks had been graphically shown during the Zeppelin and Gotha bomber offensives of World War I. British biplane scouts had struggled to defend London and other cities in the region, and following the fall of France to the German forces in June 1940, southeast England steeled itself once again for an assault from the skies. In the vanguard of this defense would be 19 Spitfire squadrons assigned to RAF Fighter Command. Their principal opponent in the skies during 1940 would be the much-vaunted, and combat-proven, Bf 109E, which had initially seen action in the Luftwaffe's highly successful aerial campaign that had been waged as part of the revolutionary *Blitzkrieg* (lit. "lightning war") offensive, firstly in Poland and then in western Europe. *Blitzkrieg* had seen the Wehrmacht's mechanized infantry, supported by Panzers and waves of fighters and bombers, capture huge swathes of territory in just a matter of days.

Yet despite the German success in Poland, the Bf 109 had played only a peripheral part in the 18-day air war. This was primarily because it was feared that French and British bombers would attack German cities upon their countries' declaration of war in support of Poland on September 3. Those units that were involved in the Polish campaign duly found aerial targets hard to come by, and most of the 67 Bf 109s lost during the campaign fell victim to ground fire as pilots searched for well-hidden Polish aircraft.

In between the invasion of Poland and the launching of the *Blitzkrieg* in the west on May 10, 1940, Bf 109 units, like the rest of the Luftwaffe, endured the *Sitzkrieg* (lit. "Sitting-down War"), or the "Phoney War," as it was dubbed by the Allies. Aircraft from both sides would periodically venture across their respective defensive borders (the Maginot Line in France and the Westwall or Siegfried Line in Germany) on tentative reconnaissance flights. Most action during this period took place over the *Dreiländereck* ("three-nations corner") on the northernmost corner of the Franco–German border, as this was the shortest route for Allied reconnaissance aircraft heading for the Ruhr.

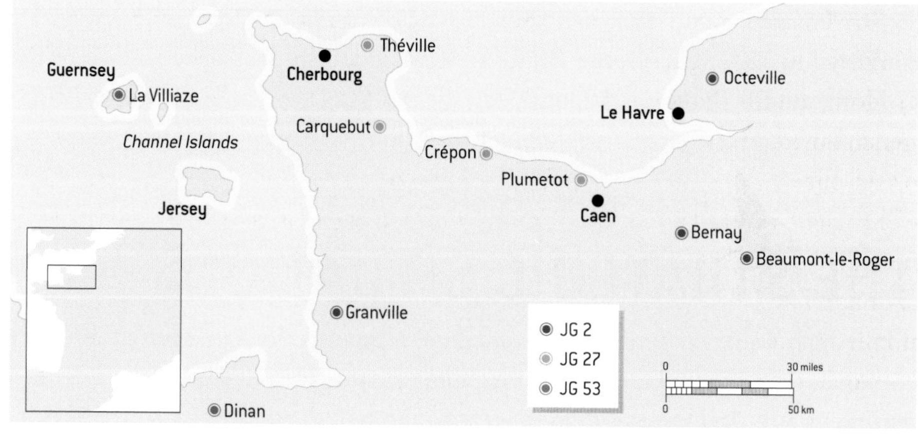

Luftwaffe single-seat fighter disposition in Normandy, Brittany and the Channel Islands during the Battle of Britain. Each *Jagdgruppe* had 35–40 pilots and more than 300 groundcrew, and was led by a *Gruppenkommandeur* who was usually a Hauptmann or Major.

Many of the leading Bf 109E aces claimed their first victories during this period, including Oberleutnant Werner Mölders, Oberleutnant Rolf Pingel and Oberleutnant Hans von Hahn. Aside from engaging French fighters, the *Jagdflieger* also took on RAF Hurricanes that were based in France in support of the British Expeditionary Force (BEF), as well as Blenheim and Wellington bombers sent to attack German ports along the North Sea coast. The only Spitfires encountered were unarmed Photographic Development Unit (PDU) aircraft, two of which were brought down in March and April 1940. By the time the "Phoney War" ended, the *Jagdgruppen* had claimed no fewer than 160 victories, and numerous Bf 109 pilots had received their first taste of aerial combat.

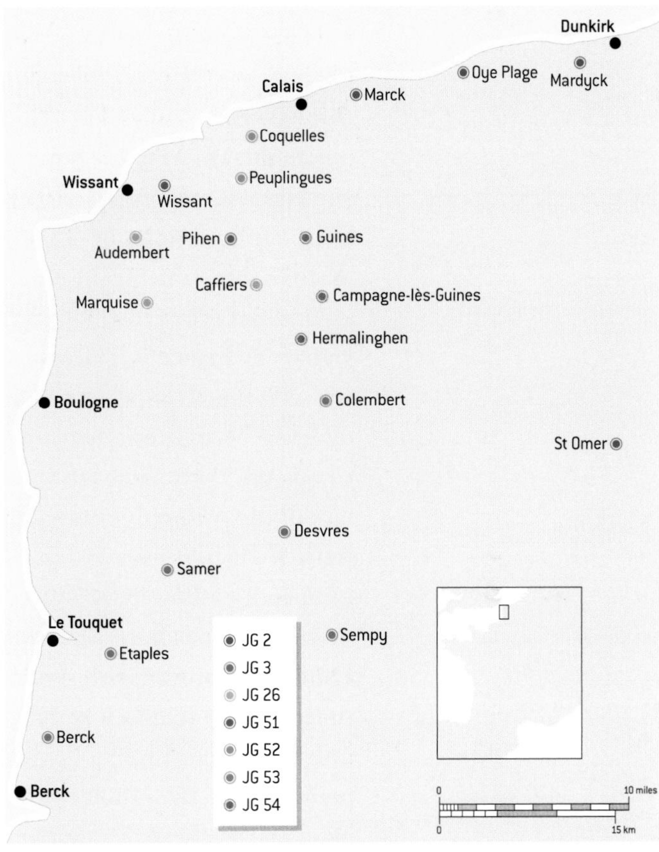

Luftwaffe single-seat fighter disposition in the Pas de Calais. A total of eight *Jagdgruppen* were equipped with Bf 109Es during the Battle of Britain.

In a forerunner of what was to come in the Battle of Britain, practically the whole of the Lufwaffe's single-engined fighter strength was brought together for the invasion of France and the Low Countries. In all, 27 *Jagdgruppen* were brought forward to airfields scattered along the Westwall, these units being split between Luftflotten (Air Fleets) 2 and 3. More than 1,016 Bf 109Es and over 1,000 pilots prepared themselves to wrest control of the skies over western Europe.

The German campaign itself was divided into two parts, codenamed *Gelb* (Yellow) and *Rot* (Red). Operation *Gelb* would commence with an all-out attack on Holland and Belgium, which, it was calculated, would cause the BEF and French northern armies to rush to the aid of the Low Countries. With the Allies forced out of their prepared defensive positions along the Maginot Line, the Wehrmacht would launch its primary offensive against the vulnerable rear of the Allied forces, with Panzers sweeping around behind them and racing for the Channel. The Low Countries and Anglo-French divisions would be cut off from supplies and reinforcements in the process, and thus quickly defeated. Operation *Rot* would then swing into action, with German troops advancing west across the Somme into central France.

The *Jagdgruppen* assigned to Luftflotte 2 would be in the vanguard of Operation *Gelb*, and the pilots of JG 2, JG 26, JG 27 and JG 51 cut swathes through the obsolescent Allied fighters that attempted to blunt the German onslaught. On May 12, with the launching of the armored thrust at the rear of the stretched Allied forces, Luftflotte 3's units at last joined in the action too. Two days later, during a series of actions over Sedan that saw Allied bombers attempt to destroy the strategically crucial Meuse River bridge crossings, Bf 109 units downed no fewer than 89 aircraft in an action that effectively sealed the German victory in France. Yet despite successes such as this, the campaign in the West was very much a calculated risk for the *Jagdwaffe*, as it possessed insufficient reserves of fighters, fuel and ammunition in order to support a sustained campaign. Fortunately, the rapidity with which Allied forces capitulated in the face of the *Blitzkrieg* meant that resources never reached breaking point. Indeed, just 147 Bf 109s were lost in May (including aircraft destroyed in the Norwegian campaign), followed by 88 in June.

Supply lines became stretched as the fighting in northern France reached Dunkirk, however, with serviceability amongst the *Jagdgruppen* reaching an all-time low due to a lack of fuel, poor parts supply, austere operating bases (often little more than farmers' fields) and sheer pilot exhaustion. Ironically, it was at this point that Bf 109 units began at last to encounter Spitfire squadrons flying from bases in southern England in support of the sea evacuation of troops from Dunkirk. RAF Fighter Command succeeded in preventing German bombers from sinking many of the vessels that transported troops back to England primarily because the *Jagdstaffeln*, lacking serviceable aircraft and suitable bases, could not adequately protect the vulnerable *Kampfgeschwader* (bomber wings) and *Stukageschwader* (Stuka wings) – a portent of things to come later that summer.

Although the evacuation of Dunkirk had ended on the morning of June 3, fighting in France continued as part of Operation *Rot* until a ceasefire was agreed some 22 days later. By then, most of the Bf 109 units that had played such a key part in the success in the West had returned to Germany to rest, recuperate and refit in preparation for an all-out attack on the United Kingdom.

UNIT ORGANIZATION

As with the *Blitzkrieg* in the West, Luftflottenkommando 2 and 3 would again be at the forefront of the fighting during the Battle of Britain, controlling all Bf 109 units assigned to the offensive through the offices of Jagdfliegerführer (Fighter Aircraft Command) 2 and 3.

Unlike British fighter squadrons at the time, which only officially formed into wings as the RAF went on the offensive in 1941, German fighter units had been grouped together prewar. The *Jagdwaffe* equivalent of a typical 12-aircraft squadron in Fighter Command in 1940 was the *Staffel*, which consisted of nine aircraft (rising to as many as 16 as the war progressed). It was led by a *Staffelkapitän* of Oberleutnant or Hauptmann rank, who controlled a further ten pilots and around 80 groundcrew. *Staffeln* were usually numbered 1, 2, 3 etc.

In 1940, typically, three *Staffeln* and *Stab* (headquarters flight) would be assigned to a single *Gruppe*, which was the Luftwaffe's basic flying unit for operational and administrative purposes. Normally, one complete *Gruppe* occupied a single airfield, and this was typically the case during the Battle of Britain, with linked *Staffeln* being spread amongst austere sites in the Pas de Calais, Normandy, Brittany and the Channel Islands. The *Gruppenkommandeur* was usually a Hauptmann or Major, and he led somewhere between 35 and 40 pilots and more than 300 groundcrew. *Gruppen* were usually numbered I., II., III. etc.

The *Geschwader* was the largest Luftwaffe flying unit to have a fixed strength of aircraft. Eight *Jagdgeschwader* flew Bf 109Es during the Battle of Britain, with five (JGs 3, 26, 51, 52 and 54) assigned to Luftflottenkommando 2 in the Pas de Calais and three to Luflottenkommando 3 (JGs 2, 27 and 53) in Normandy, Brittany and the Channel Islands. Additionally, Bf 109E fighter-bombers were flown by Erprobungsgruppe 210's 1 Staffel and II.(Schl.)/LG 2. Assigned some 90–95 aircraft, the *Geschwader* was usually led by a *Kommodore* of Major, Oberleutnant or Oberst rank.

The *Jagdgeschwader* were in turn locally controlled by *Jagdfliegerführer* (those involved in the Battle of Britain were numbered 2 and 3), which issued operational directives to the frontline flying units. The *Jagdfliegerführer* were in turn part of the larger, locally based *Fliegerkorps* (air corps), which were ultimately subordinated to the *Luftflotten* (of which the Luftwaffe had four in 1940). These were self-contained organizations, each with its own fighter, bomber, reconnaissance, ground-attack and transport units. The *Jagdwaffe* slowly began to return to the Channel coast in strength during July and early August 1940, some 809 Bf 109Es being in France by July 20, and this number increased to 934 by August 10.

Opposing the growing ranks of German fighters were 29 squadrons of Hurricanes (462 aircraft) and 19 squadrons of Spitfires (292 aircraft). As previously mentioned, these aircraft were not organized into air fleets or groups as per the Luftwaffe model. Instead, all RAF fighters in the UK were centrally controlled by Fighter Command, headed by Air Chief Marshal Sir Hugh Dowding. The latter had calculated prewar that he needed a minimum of 46 squadrons (typically

Fighter Command's plotting table at Bentley Priory – the nerve center of Britain's defenders. From here information would be sent to Group Headquarters and then to sector stations. (RAF Hendon PC71/19/124)

numbering 12 aircraft) and 736 fighters to defend all possible targets in the UK ranging from Portsmouth to the River Clyde. During the Battle of France and the evacuation of Dunkirk, Fighter Command had lost around 300 aircraft, but these had been replaced by July. Therefore, Dowding felt reasonably confident that he had sufficient resources to hand to defend the UK from attacks by the Luftwaffe.

Fighter Command had been formed in 1936 as one of four commands into which the flying strength of the RAF was broken up by the Air Ministry, primarily in response to the growing rearmament of Germany. With its HQ at Bentley Priory, Fighter Command initially controlled three groups created by Dowding to defend the UK. No. 11 Group was charged with protecting the southeast, No. 12 Group the Midlands and No. 13 Group the North and Scotland. On July 8, 1940, following the fall of France, No. 10 Group was established to cover potential targets in the southwest.

Each Group was split up into Sectors, which were given letters for identification purposes, although they were ultimately known by the name of their Sector Station, which was the airfield controlling them. Defending London and the southeast, No. 11 Group would be the vital organization in the UK's defense in 1940. Its HQ was in Uxbridge, not far from Bentley Priory, and its

Sectors (centered on London) were lettered A, B, C, D, E, F and Z, controlled from Tangmere, Kenley, Biggin Hill, Hornchurch, North Weald, Debden and Northolt respectively.

The fighters based at these stations, and nearby smaller "satellite" airfields, were the teeth of Fighter Command in 1940, but the pilots flying these aircraft relied on other assets within the command to effectively take the fight to the Luftwaffe. Undoubtedly the most important of these was the chain of radar stations built during the late 1930s along the south and east coasts of England and Scotland. Codenamed Chain Home (CH), the stations (there were 18 between Portsmouth on the south coast of England and Aberdeen in northeast Scotland) were able to detect and track enemy aircraft approaching from medium or high level at distances of more than 100 miles. This equipment proved unable to track aircraft flying at altitudes below 5,000ft, however, so in late 1939 the RAF introduced Chain Home Low (CHL) stations that could detect aircraft flying at

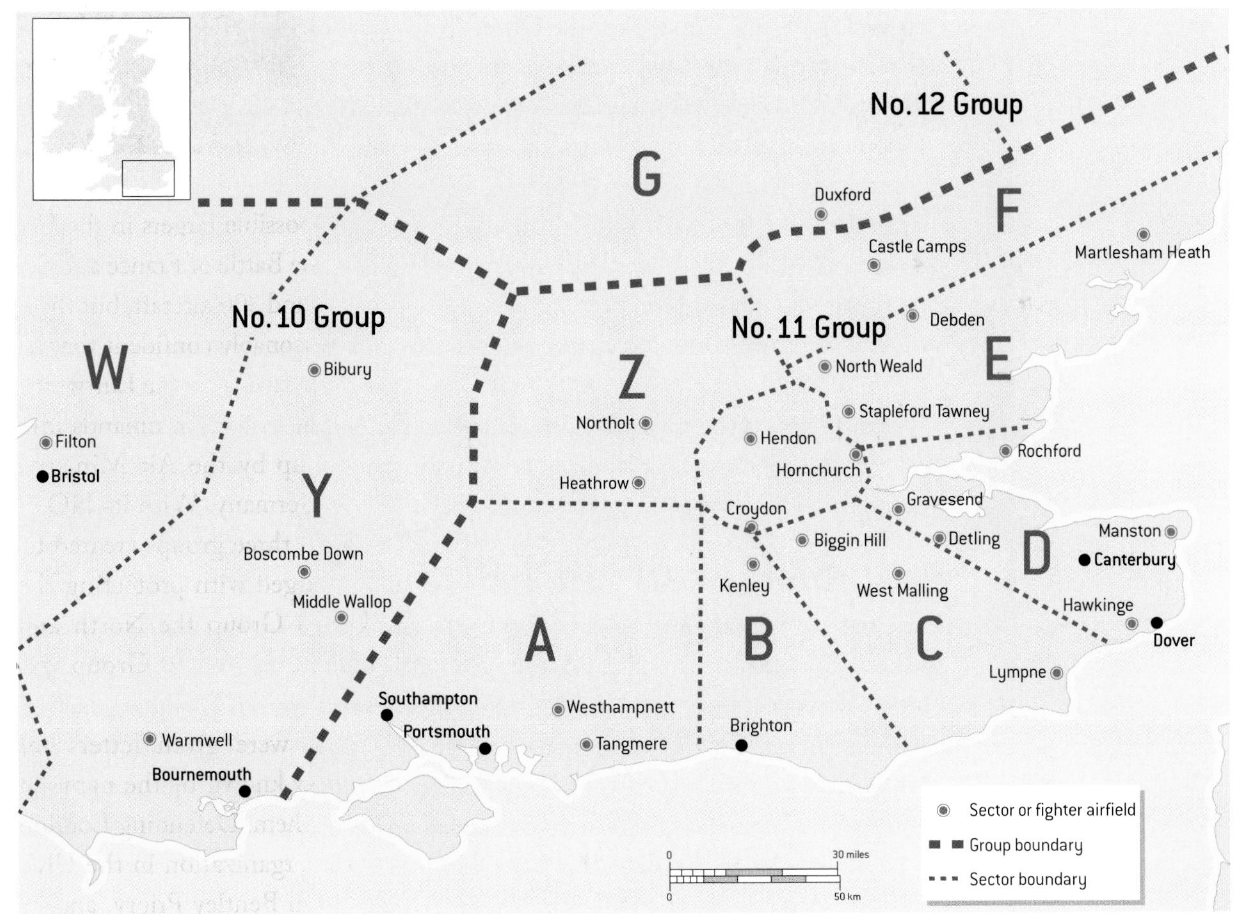

RAF Fighter Command Sector and fighter airfields in southeast England during the Battle of Britain.

2,000ft some 35 miles from the British coastline. CHL sites were interspersed between the CH towers.

A complex network of landlines, linking these various sites with Fighter Command HQ and Group and Sector operations rooms, was another asset that proved vital during the Battle of Britain. When enemy aircraft were detected by radar, their grid position, altitude and estimated strength were passed via a landline to the Filter Centre at Fighter Command HQ. Once the plot had been classified as "hostile," it was passed to the Operations Room and noted as a marker on the situation map. This information was also relayed to relevant Groups and Sector operations rooms, where it also appeared on their situation maps. The fighter controller at the Group HQ tasked with defending the area that appeared to be threatened by the "hostile" plot then ordered his units to "scramble." It was crucial that this order was given early enough to allow the fighters to get up to the raiders' altitude.

Radar of this period could not track aircraft overland, so once German aircraft crossed the English coastline, the Observer Corps took over the responsibility of tracking formations. They would pass plot information via a landline to their own Group HQ, which in turn relayed details to the Fighter Command Filter Centre for onward transmission. Once airborne, a fighter unit remained under the radio control of one of the Sector operations rooms, the fighter controller guiding the squadron until it visually sighted the enemy. At this point the formation leader would call "Tally Ho!" over the radio, signaling to the controller that he needed no further help from him.

Fighter Command squadrons were thoroughly familiar with ground-based fighter control come the summer of 1940, having regularly exercised with this system prewar. According to noted Battle of Britain historian Dr Alfred Price, "in the forthcoming air actions over Britain, the ground control system would be Fighter Command's ace of trumps."

THE BATTLE OF BRITAIN

For the second and last time in the Luftwaffe's history, the Battle of Britain would see virtually the entire frontline strength of Bf 109Es concentrated in one area – this time, the Channel coast. Once again, these aircraft would be charged with achieving aerial supremacy as the German *Kampfgeschwader* and *Stukageschwader* strived to knock out Fighter Command in preparation for the seaborne invasion of southern England, codenamed Operation *Sealöwe* (Sea Lion).

The Battle of Britain has been split into four phases by historians, commencing in early July with *Kanalkampf* (Channel Battle). During this period,

German aircraft probed British defenses primarily through attacks on coastal convoys, as well as port facilities on the south coast. Only JG 26 and JG 53 were initially assigned to this phase of the campaign, as most other *Jagdgeschwader* were still making good their losses suffered during the occupation of France. *Kanalkampf* would last until August 12, and although Fighter Command succeeded in matching the Luftwaffe in trying circumstances, it had suffered significant losses – including 27 Spitfires destroyed and 51 damaged. Many of these had been claimed by Bf 109E pilots conducting *Freie Jagd* (Free Hunt) sweeps independently of the bombers, seeking out RAF fighters.

The date August 13 was dubbed *Adlertag* (Eagle Day) by the Luftwaffe, and it signaled the start of the sustained campaign against RAF airfields, radar stations and other key military targets such as aircraft and aero engine factories. The bombers sent to strike at these targets were well escorted by Bf 109Es from eight *Jagdgeschwader*, as the single-seat fighter force reached its peak strength. During 11 days of sustained attacks, which saw both sides suffer heavy losses, the Luftwaffe hoped to assert its dominance through sheer weight of numbers. Certainly the Luftwaffe enjoyed some success on Eagle Day and immediately afterwards, when a number of the more inexperienced RAF pilots were lost.

The view from a German He 111 bomber on a mission against England on either 25 or 26 August 1940. (akg images/ullstein bild)

However, all three of the major raids that day were picked up by radar and then intercepted. Although runways were damaged, they were quickly made operational again as the craters were filled in and key radar stations were always back up-and-running in a matter of hours. Eagle Day was designed to be the beginning of the end of Fighter Command. In this respect, the Luftwaffe did not even come close to success.

Between August 24 and September 6, the Germans continued to target Fighter Command airfields and aircraft factories, with growing success. The RAF would later call this "the critical period" of the Battle of Britain, as it found losses ever harder to replace, stretching the pilots and their aircraft to the limits of their endurance. Yet despite suffering serious casualties (136 Spitfires were lost in August alone), Fighter Command was in turn inflicting heavier losses on German forces. Indeed, Bf 110 *Zerstörer* (Destroyer) and Ju 87 Stuka *Gruppen* had been so badly affected that they would play little part in the rest of the campaign. Critically, Reichsmarschall Hermann Göring questioned the tactics of continuing to attack radar stations when the British had so many, and he was also explicit in his order that airfields which "had been successfully attacked one day should not be attacked the following day," presumably because he regarded it as a waste of effort. With this Göring virtually guaranteed the continued operational capabilities of the frontline Spitfire and Hurricane squadrons. German Bf 109 pilots' chances of winning the battle were therefore scuppered by the amateurish interference of Göring.

In contrast, British Spitfire pilots fell under the command of Air Chief Marshal Hugh Dowding. He had been responsible for introducing the "Dowding system" whereby radar, raid plotting and radio control of aircraft were integrated. In the hands of this dedicated professional, ably assisted by Air Vice-Marshal Keith Park, commander of No. 11 Fighter Group, the British enjoyed a distinct advantage despite the scores of German bombers and fighters increasingly darkening the skies over southeast England.

On September 7, believing that Fighter Command was finished, Reichsmarschall Göring ordered his forces to target London instead in an effort to bring more RAF fighters into the air. Eventually, the capital would be attacked both by day and night, culminating in two massive daylight raids (involving more than 250 bombers and 300-plus Bf 109Es) on September 15 – immortalized thereafter by the British as Battle of Britain Day.

By now the *Jagdflieger* were forbidden to fly their favored *Freie Jagd* sorties, ranging far and wide in front of the bombers. Instead, Reichsmarschall Göring ordered them to provide close formation escort for the bombers, which had suffered growing losses to the seemingly indestructible RAF. As if to prove that Fighter Command did indeed still have plenty of fight left in it, both waves of bombers were met by close to 300 Hurricanes and Spitfires. In what would prove to be one of the final large-scale raids made by the Luftwaffe during the campaign, 19 Bf 109Es were shot down. These aircraft were the last of nearly 400 Emils that had been lost or badly damaged in the four weeks from August 13. Fighter Command lost seven Spitfires and 20 Hurricanes on September 15.

On September 30, the last massed daylight raids on London and the southwest were flown. Some 300 bombers attacked the capital in two waves, and the escorting 200 Bf 109Es suffered their worst losses of the Battle of Britain – 28 Emils were shot down, whilst the RAF lost 13 Hurricanes and four Spitfires.

His bombs gone, Unteroffizier Josef Heinzeller of 2./JG 3 races back across the Channel towards the Pas de Calais at low altitude in his distinctively marked Bf 109E-3/B. Protecting him on this *Jabo* mission, flown in late September, are two less elaborately marked Emils from the same *Staffel*. Heinzeller, who claimed five victories in 1940, named all of his aircraft after his pet dog, "Schnauzl."

Clearly Fighter Command was far from beaten, and Operation *Sealöwe* was shelved on October 12. By then Göring had ordered that a third of all his Channel-based *Jagdgeschwader* strength had to be converted into fighter-bombers for "tip and-run" *Jabo* sorties due to the vulnerability of the medium bomber force in daylight raids. These missions were flown at high altitudes of between 26,000ft and 33,000ft, and Spitfire units struggled to intercept the Bf 109E *Jabos*. Conversely, little damage was done by the attacks, which were flown for nuisance value as much as anything else.

The Battle of Britain officially ended on October 31, by which time 610 Bf 109Es had been lost in combat – a little more than one-third of the Luftwaffe's total losses of 1,792 aircraft. During the same period, Fighter Command had seen 361 of its Spitfires destroyed. Both the Spitfire I/II and the Bf 109E would continue to clash in the skies over England and, increasingly, occupied Europe through to the end of 1941, but the battle to prevent the fall of Britain, like the fall of France several months earlier, was over.

THE MEN

The majority of the single-seat fighter pilots that faced each other in 1940–41 were amongst the best-trained aviators to see combat in World War II. This was particularly true for the *Jagdflieger*, many of whom had been flying with the Luftwaffe since its formation in the early 1930s. A significant number of Bf 109E pilots had also been blooded in Spain during the civil war, which had run from 1936 to 1939. Fighter tactics trialed and perfected in action against Republican aircraft influenced the way the *Jagdwaffe* trained and fought during the early years of World War II.

The pilots of RAF Fighter Command had no such combat experience, but they were very well trained nonetheless thanks to constant drilling and exercises. As detailed previously, the ground control system in place in the UK was unmatched anywhere in the world, and fighter pilots were familiar with its operation. As with the *Jagdwaffe*, Fighter Command only really began to feel the pinch in respect to the quality of the pilots reaching the frontline during the latter stages of the Battle of Britain, when heavy losses forced Training Command to cut corners in order to keep units operational. By late 1940 the pilot crisis was over within the RAF, and training schemes both in the UK and overseas in southern Africa, Australia, the United States and Canada ensured that Fighter Command would never again suffer from a lack of personnel.

The same could not be said for the *Jagdwaffe*, however, which struggled to replace pilots lost as the war progressed. Although losses in 1940 were swiftly made good, poor organization of its training units eventually resulted in serious pilot shortages from 1943 onward.

BRITISH PILOT TRAINING

The RAF was blighted by a lack of funding from 1919 until 1936, when the overt rearming of Germany prompted the government of the day to at last provide funding that would allow the air force to carry out its duties effectively in a modern war. Central to this reequipment was the purchase of new single-seat monoplane fighters in the shape of the Hurricane and Spitfire. A large number of pilots would be needed to fly these aircraft in the frontline, and it was obvious that the existing Flying Training Schools (for short-service commission officers and airmen pilots) and RAF College training (for permanent officers) output of around 400 pilots a year was grossly inadequate.

As part of the shake up of the RAF instigated by the Air Ministry in 1936, which saw four specialist commands created in place of the Area Commands that had previously existed, Training Command was established. Three years prior to this change, the RAF had already taken steps to improve the volume of its pilot training by establishing a handful of civilian-manned Elementary and Reserve Flying Training Schools (E&RFTSs), equipped with Gipsy Moths, Tiger Moths and Blackburn B 2s. It had also established a standardized training program for future officer pilots at the RAF College at Cranwell, Lincolnshire, that same year.

Coinciding with the formation of Training Command, the Air Ministry had created the RAF Volunteer Reserve (RAFVR) to train 800 pilots a year. Open to all comers, no matter what their financial or social status, this scheme proved so popular that by 1940 a third of Fighter Command's pilots had joined as RAFVRs – a considerable number were posted to frontline units as sergeant pilots. Prior to this, all recruits entered either as permanent or short-commission officers and NCOs, or via the Auxiliary Air Force (AAF). The latter, created in 1925, mirrored the Territorial Army in that units consisted of groups of men from particular areas who trained together at weekends. These squadrons were quickly manned by wealthy gentlemen, who set the tone for the auxiliaries into the early stages of World War II. By late 1938, close to 30 E&RFTSs had been established, setting student pilots on the path to obtaining their wings through training on Tiger Moths, Magisters and B 2s. An element of advanced training had also been introduced at these schools through the provision of Harts, Battles and Ansons.

Amongst the pilots to experience the RAF's revised pilot training was future Spitfire ace Al Deere, who was one of 12 New Zealanders selected to travel to the UK in September 1937 – many young men from across the Empire took up short-service commissions in the air force during this period. Deere was initially sent to the de Havilland Civil School of Flying at White Waltham, where he underwent an *ab initio* flying course for the next three months prior to being accepted into the RAF. Towards the end of this initial training phase, pilots were asked to make a choice as to whether they wanted to fly bombers or fighters – Deere, of course, chose the latter.

Following graduation from the E&RFTS, pilots destined to be commissioned then spent two weeks undergoing officer training at RAF Uxbridge, where they were fitted with uniforms, prior to heading to a Flying Training School (FTS). Deere went to No. 6 FTS at Netheravon, in Wiltshire, where he flew Hart biplanes in his junior term. Upon completion of this phase of his training, he was awarded his pilot's wings, after which he flew Fury biplane fighters (then still very much in service with Fighter Command) during his senior term. Completing his nine months of flying training in August 1938, Deere was duly posted to Hornchurch, in No. 11 Group, to fly Gladiators with No. 54 Sqn.

Like most prewar fighter pilots already serving with frontline or auxiliary units, Al Deere made the transition from biplane to monoplane at squadron level, as there were insufficient Spitfires and Hurricanes available to supply them to Training Command. Most pilots had plenty of flying experience under their belts by the time the switch was made, and the change in types posed few problems, as Deere noted in his autobiography, *Nine Lives*:

> On 6 March 1939, I flew my first Spitfire. The transition from slow biplanes to the faster monoplanes was effected without fuss, and in a matter of weeks we were nearly as competent on Spitfires as we had been on Gladiators. Training on Spitfires followed the same pattern as on Gladiators, except that we did a little more cine-gun work to get practice on the new reflector gunsight with which the aircraft was fitted.

Fighter Command did, however, try to fill the obvious performance gap between an obsolescent biplane fighter or Harvard advanced trainer flown by a brand-new pilot in an FTS and the monoplane fighter that awaited him in the frontline. It established several Group Pools in 1939 and equipped them with a handful of Hurricanes and Spitfires. New pilots would now be able to get a precious few flying hours in their logbooks on-type before joining Fighter Command proper.

With the declaration of war, all E&RFTSs were brought within the RAF Training Command structure as Elementary Flying Training Schools (EFTSs). Once finished here, pupils would then progress to Service Flying Training Schools (SFTSs), boosted in number from six to 11 by early 1940. The types operated at both stages in the training process remained much the same during the first 18 months of the war, although the interwar biplane fighters used at the SFTSs slowly began to be replaced by more Harvards and the all-new Miles Master.

The Group Pool system, from which operational squadrons were able to draw replacement pilots, and thus relinquish their own training responsibilities so as to concentrate on performing combat missions, soon showed signs of failure in wartime. Indeed, literally thousands of trainee pilots (many with considerable flying hours) were transferred into other trades in late 1939 and early 1940 because of a chronic shortage of monoplane fighter types within the Group Pools. Spitfires and Hurricanes were urgently needed in the frontline, leaving none for training purposes. In the spring of 1940, all Group Pools were redesignated Operational Training Units (OTUs) within Training Command, and the Air Ministry instructed Fighter Command to make sure that sufficient aircraft were

SPITFIRE PILOT: BRIAN JOHN GEORGE CARBURY

The RAF's leading Spitfire ace during the Battle of Britain, and also the only pilot in Fighter Command to down five Bf 109Es in a single day during 1940, Brian Carbury was born in Wellington, New Zealand, on February 27, 1918. A giant of a man at 6ft 4in, he was also a fine sportsman and an excellent marksman. Following brief employment as a shoe salesman in Auckland, he traveled to England in June 1937 and secured a short-service commission in the RAF after being turned down by the Royal Navy for being too old. Undertaking his flying training at No. 10 E&RFTS, Carbury was eventually posted to No. 41 Sqn at Catterick in June 1938, where he flew Fury II biplanes.

His unit converted to Spitfire Is in January 1939, and in October of that same year he was temporarily reassigned to No. 603 "City of Edinburgh" Sqn at RAF Turnhouse to help with its transition from Gladiator biplanes to Spitfires. He was permanently assigned to the auxiliary squadron upon the outbreak of war and saw his first action in December 1939 when he damaged an He 111 near Arbroath. Carbury followed this up with a share in the destruction of a second Heinkel bomber off Aberdeen on March 7, 1940 and a Ju 88 near Montrose on July 3.

On August 28, No. 603 Sqn was sent south from Scotland to RAF Hornchurch, in Essex, to relieve battle-weary Spitfire unit No. 65 Sqn. In the coming weeks the squadron would claim 67 German aircraft destroyed for the loss of 30 Spitfires. Four of its pilots would also claim five or more Bf 109Es destroyed. Carbury emerged as the unit's "ace of aces," downing eight Emils during the first week of No. 603 Sqn's operations with No. 11 Group. Five of these victories came during the course of three sorties on August 31, thus making him one of only two Fighter Command pilots to make "ace in a day" during the Battle of Britain (the other was No. 610 Sqn's Sgt Ronnie Hamlyn, who claimed four Bf 109Es and a Ju 88 on August 24).

Carbury was awarded a DFC and Bar in September and October 1940, and by year-end his tally stood at 15 and two shared destroyed, two probables and five damaged. Like many prewar fighter pilots to survive the Battle of Britain, he was posted as an instructor to Training Command in December 1940, joining No. 58 OTU. Carbury remained an instructor until dismissed from the service in 1944 following a court martial for bouncing checks that had been written to cover his wife's opulent lifestyle. He had his British pilot's license suspended in 1948 for ferrying aircraft to Israel (which was not allowed at the time), and eventually found work as a salesman for a heating firm. Carbury was diagnosed with terminal acute monocytic leukaemia and died on July 31, 1961.

made available to these units so that a steady flow of replacement pilots could be sent through them. The OTUs eventually succeeded where the Group Pools had failed, thanks to an influx of combat-weary fighters and equally battle-seasoned staff to instruct would-be frontline pilots.

When losses began to mount in August 1940, OTU courses for new pilots were drastically cut in length from several months to just four weeks, leaving squadrons to apply the finishing touches. As a result of this, Fighter Command began receiving replacement pilots who had not yet mastered the Spitfire or Hurricane, and who had received little more than basic training in blind or night flying, navigation or gunnery – indeed, a number of pilots had never fired their guns at all prior to engaging the enemy for the first time.

Despite the corners that were cut in pilot training, ever-more pilots were needed as replacements as the Luftwaffe continued to exact a heavy toll on the RAF. With no time to train them from scratch, Fighter Command sought out pilots from other commands within the RAF, as well as from the Fleet Air Arm – the best pilots from Army Cooperation, Coastal and Bomber Commands were posted in, as were 75 partly trained naval pilots. Combat-seasoned fighter pilots also came from Poland, Czechoslovakia, Belgium and France, having fled to Britain following the German occupation of their respective countries. These were the men that manned the 19 Spitfire squadrons that helped defend Britain in the summer of 1940.

GERMAN PILOT TRAINING

Prior to the official creation of the Luftwaffe, all air activity in Germany had been geared towards training because of the ban on military flying under the terms of the 1919 Treaty of Versailles. Those quasi-military aviation organizations that were formed in Germany during the late 1920s and early 1930s functioned under the cover of civilian activities. Although the restrictions stalled the development of both combat aircraft and tactics, the focus on flying training provided the newly formed Luftwaffe with plenty of military-trained aircrew. Men came from Lufthansa, gliding clubs and, until 1936, the army. However, the latter was expanding rapidly too, and senior officers forbade the Luftwaffe from recruiting from within the Wehrmacht. Conscripts and volunteers would make up the numbers from 1936 on.

In Germany, pilot recruitment and training was strongly influenced by Prussian military tradition. Initially, all future officers and NCOs could expect to undertake six months of labor service, organized in a paramilitary fashion, with the *Reichsarbeitdienst* (Reich Labor Service). Those that were particularly air-minded chose service with the Party-controlled *Nationalsozialistisches Fliegerkorps* (National Socialist Flyers' Corp) instead, flying gliders. However, with the Luftwaffe desperately short of personnel, labor service was reduced to just three months.

Induction into the Luftwaffe then followed, after which all recruits spent between six and 12 months undertaking basic infantry training at a *Flieger-Ersatzabteilung* (flying replacement unit). Once deemed to be effective infantrymen, all recruits were reviewed for possible advancement as pilots. Likely candidates were sent to a *Flug-Anwärterkompanie* (aircrew candidate company) for evaluation in a series of tests in basic aviation theory.

Most *Jagdflieger* flying Bf 109Es in 1939–40 would have gone through the full Luftwaffe training course. However, from late 1940 onwards, with the growing demand for pilots following the commencement of World War II, training and recruiting staff rationalized and compressed the initial stages of aircrew selection to enable trainees to embark upon the most appropriate training regime more expeditiously. The *Flieger-Ersatzabteilung* was now replaced by a series of *Flieger-Ausbildungsregiments* (flyer training regiments), where recruits would receive basic military training and preliminary aviation instruction. Potential pilots were then sent to undergo the standard selection process within a *Flug-Anwärterkompanie*, where the rest of their basic training, conducted over a period of three to four months, was completed alongside the aircrew evaluation tests.

Upon assignment to a *Flug-Anwärterkompanie*, the *Flugzeugführer-Anwärter* (pilot candidate) would receive instruction in basic flight theory and rudimentary aeronautics in aircraft such as the Bü 131, Ar 66C, He 72 Kaddett, Go 145 and Fw 44 Stieglitz biplane trainers. Assessed for advancement throughout this phase, those candidates displaying the required aptitude were then sent to *Flugzeugführerschule A/B* (Pilot School A/B) as soon as a space became available – typically two months after arriving at the *Flug-Anwärterkompanie*. Here, flight training proper would be undertaken.

At such schools, students underwent four principal levels of instruction, each requiring qualification for its own license, before advancing to the next stage. These licenses, earned over a period of six to nine months, gave the schools their name. The A1-Schien introduced students to basic practical flying in dual-controlled training aircraft, the instructors teaching recruits how to take off and land, recover from stalls and attain their solo flight rating. Prewar and through to early 1941, instructors would have been assigned four trainees each – this number rose as the conflict progressed. At the A2-Schien, cadets were required to learn the theory of flight, including aerodynamics, meteorology, flying procedures and aviation law, as well as the practical application of aeronautical engineering, elementary navigation, wireless procedure and Morse code. In the air, they gained more flying experience on larger single-engine two-seat aircraft.

The next level of training, known as the B1-Schien, saw pilots progress on to high-performance single- and twin-engined machines typically fitted with a retractable undercarriage – if destined to fly fighters, older types of combat aircraft such as early Bf 109s would be flown for the first time. Precision landings, night flying and cross-country flying were all tested in this phase of the course. The student pilot would also have to complete at least 50 flights in a B1-category aircraft. Upon graduation from the B1-Schien, students would then undertake training aimed at acquiring the final B2-Schien, having accumulated 100 to 150 hours of flight time over the previous 14 to 17 months.

In late 1940 the *Flugzeugführerschule A/B* was streamlined to take into account wartime demand for pilots, with a far greater emphasis now being placed on practical flying skills from the outset. The A2 license was dropped, with that phase being amalgamated into the remaining grades. The A license generally took three months to complete, with the B phase seeing pilots flying more advanced types. An elementary *K1 Kunstflug* (stunt-flying) aerobatics course was also included in the latter phase to provide all pilots with a good understanding of rudimentary evasive maneuvers (barrel rolls, loops and formation splits). This phase also allowed instructors to identify any potential fighter pilots among their students, who thereafter received more flying time than their fellow students.

Upon completion of the B2 phase, the cadet would finally be granted his *Luftwaffeflugzeugführerschein* (air force pilot's license), accompanied by the highly prized *Flugzeugführerabzeichen* (pilot's badge) – his "wings." After an average of ten to 13 months at *Flugzeugführerschule A/B*, he was now a fully qualified pilot.

It was at this point that new pilots were categorized for service on single- or multi-engined aircraft, with each being assigned to a specialist flying school. Here each pilot would undergo intensive training for his allotted aircraft type, with potential fighter pilots being sent directly to *Jagdfliegervorschulen* (fighter school) or *Waffenschule* (military school) for three to four months, where they carried out 50 hours of flying on semi-obsolescent types. For Bf 109E pilots this usually meant Ar 68 and He 51 biplanes, Bf 109B/C/Ds and Ar 96s. By the time he was eventually posted to a frontline unit, a pilot could expect to have 200 hours of flying time under his belt. Officer candidates would have also attended *Luftkriegschule* (air war school) to learn tactics, air force law and military discipline, prior to their assignment to a *Jagdfliegervorschulen*.

The realities of war led the Luftwaffe to further modify the final stages of its training syllabus in 1940, with the creation of *Erganzungsgruppen* (operational

MESSERSCHMITT PILOT: HERBERT IHLEFELD

Although credited with more Spitfire I/IIs destroyed than any other Bf 109E pilot, Herbert Ihlefeld, uniquely, claimed all of these victories flying with a mixed-formation *Lehrgeschwader* (training wing) tasked with the development of new tactics, rather than an out-and-out fighter *Jagdgeschwader*. Born in Pinnow, Pomerania, on June 1, 1914, Ihlefeld was an original member of the *Jadgwaffe* upon its formation in 1933. Following service with JG 132 "Richthofen," where he flew He 51s and the all-new Bf 109B-1, Ihlefeld volunteered for duty with the Condor Legion in late 1937.

Assigned to 2./J 88 upon his arrival in Spain, Feldwebel Ihlefeld's previous flying experience with the Messerschmitt fighter stood him in good stead, and he was issued with one of the first Bf 109B-1s to arrive in-theater. His unit saw much action during the Aragón offensive in the spring and summer of 1938, and Ihlefeld finished his tour with nine victories to his credit. Returning to Germany in 1939 with the rank of Leutnant, he was posted to the newly formed Lehrgeschwader 2 at Garz, whose I Gruppe was equipped with Bf 109Ds. This *Geschwader* was the second Operational Instruction and Evaluation Group to be formed by the Luftwaffe, and I.(J)/LG 2 was its fighter component, equipped with 45 Bf 109Es by fall 1939. Leutnant Ihlefeld was attached to the *Stab* of this unit, and saw action in Poland and during the *Blitzkrieg* in the West.

He claimed his first success – a French Morane-Saulnier MS.406 fighter – on May 29, 1940, and followed this up with an RAF Blenheim and a Spitfire on June 30 after I.(J)/LG 2's move to Marquise, in the Pas de Calais. The latter aircraft would be the first of no fewer than 33 Spitfire I/IIs victories credited to Ihlefeld between the end of June 1940 and March 23, 1941. Made *Gruppenkommandeur* of I.(J)/LG 2 on August 30, 1940, Hauptmann Ihlefeld downed no fewer than 15 Spitfires in September alone, being awarded the Knight's Cross that same month.

His success against the RAF's best fighters ended in April 1941 when he led his unit to the Balkans to participate in the invasion of Yugoslavia. Ironically, Ihlefeld's Bf 109E-7 was shot down by groundfire on the opening day of Operation *Marita* and he spent several days as a PoW. The I.(J)/LG 2 duly participated in Operation *Barbarossa* as I Gruppe of JG 77 from the very start of the offensive, and Ihlefeld, who eventually joined the *Stab* of I./JG 77 in late 1941, scored heavily in the first ten months of the campaign and duly became only the fifth pilot in the Jagdwaffe to reach the 100-kill mark, attained on April 22, 1942. By then *Gruppenkommandeur* of I./JG 77, he then became *Geschwaderkommodore* of JG 52, again in the east, on June 22, 1942.

Ihlefeld, eventually promoted to the rank of Oberst, would subsequently lead JGs 103 (a fighter training unit), 25, 11 and 1, scoring his final 13 victories during Defense of the Reich operations in 1944. He was also awarded the Oak Leaves and Swords to his Knight's Cross. Ihlefeld survived the war as the last *Geschwaderkommodore* of JG 1, having completed more than 1,000 combat missions and having scored 123 aerial victories in World War II.

training schools) for the teaching of tactics and further familiarization with frontline types. In the *Jagdwaffe*, these units were directly linked to and controlled by operational *Geschwader*. Designated IV Gruppe, these units were intended to allow new pilots to gain precious operational experience before being hurled into combat.

Surviving Bf 109Es soldiered on with *Erganzungsgruppen*, and the three Fighter Pools that replaced them in the summer of 1942, well into 1943.

INTO COMBAT

The first documented action between an armed Spitfire I and a Bf 109E took place just south of Calais late in the morning of May 23, 1940. With the campaign going badly for the Allies, Prime Minister Winston Churchill had ordered that more Fighter Command squadrons be moved to France. Air Chief Marshal Dowding strongly resisted this order, instead ordering six No. 11 Group units to be moved to forward airfields along the south coast.

A number of squadrons previously not involved in the Battle of France would commence operations along the French coast from May 16, including Spitfire-equipped Nos 54 and 74 Sqns which were now ordered to provide fighter cover and support for Allied forces withdrawing to the Dunkirk region from the Low Countries.

On the morning of May 23, Spitfires from No. 74 Sqn had engaged a Henschel Hs 126 observation aircraft and shot it down. However, defensive fire from the aircraft had hit the radiator of one of the fighters and forced its pilot, Sqn Ldr F. L. White, to land at nearby Calais-Marck airfield. The latter was under threat by advancing German troops, so it was decided that a rescue mission needed to be sent, involving a two-seat Master and two escorting Spitfires from No. 54 Sqn. Flying the latter were future aces Plt Offs Johnny Allen (who would later be killed in action by Hauptmann Adolf Galland on July 24, 1940 – the first Spitfire downed by the German ace) and Al Deere.

Once over the French airfield, they were engaged by a number of Bf 109Es from I./JG 27. With the Master safely on the ground, the two Spitfire pilots engaged the German fighters and claimed three destroyed. Al Deere later recalled:

> This was my first real combat, and the first recorded combat of a Spitfire with a Bf 109. My abiding memory was the thrill of the action – there was no sense of danger at that early stage in the war. So much so that I stayed behind the second

> of the two Bf 109s that I encountered after I had run out of ammunition just to see if I could do so. I only broke off when petrol became a factor. My prolonged fight with this Bf 109 allowed me to assess the relative performance of the two aircraft.
>
> In early engagements between the Hurricane and Bf 109 in France, the speed and climb of the latter had become legendary, and were claimed by many to be far superior to that of the Spitfire. I was able to refute this, and indeed was confident that, except in a dive, the Spitfire was superior in most other fields, and was vastly more manoeuvrable. My superior rate of climb was, however, due mostly to the type of Spitfire with which my squadron was equipped. We had the first Rotol constant-speed airscrews on which we had been doing trials when the fighting started. Other Spitfires were, at that stage, using a two-speed airscrew (either fully fine pitch or fully coarse), which meant they lost performance in a climb. The constant-speed unit changed its pitch as the engine revs went up.
>
> There was a great deal of scepticism about my claim that the Spitfire was the superior fighter, but the big thing for me was that we shouldn't have any fear of the Bf 109 in combat.

Although this was the first recorded clash in combat between the Spitfire and Bf 109, it was not the first time that these machines had come up against one another in the air. On November 22, 1939, Bf 109E-3 Wk-Nr 1304 of 1./JG 76 was landed intact at Strasbourg-Woerth airfield in France by Feldwebel Karl Hier after he had become disorientated in thick fog. His Emil was thoroughly tested by the *Armée de l'Air*, after which it was flown to the UK in May 1940 for trials at the RAE at Farnborough.

In a series of mock combats fought between the German fighter and a Spitfire I fitted with a two-speed airscrew (most constant-speed units were being allocated to bombers at the time, although this would change during the early summer of 1940), the Bf 109E was found to be superior in all aspects bar its maneuverability and turning circle. The margins reduced rapidly when the Spitfire was fitted with a constant-speed airscrew, however, as Al Deere proved over France later that month.

In level flight, the Spitfire had little trouble staying behind the Bf 109E, nor did a dive present the pursuer with many problems. However, when the Messerschmitt was pulled out of the dive and into a steep climb at slow speeds, the Spitfire pilot had difficulty in following the German fighter. When the Spitfire was being pursued in a turning fight at medium altitude, the trials proved that the RAF fighter was the superior aircraft. Thanks to its outstanding rate of roll, the Spitfire pilot could shake off the Bf 109E by performing a flick half-roll

Spitfires of No. 234 Sqn duel with Messerschmitts over southern England, July 1940. (Artwork by Wiek Luijken, © Wiek Luijken)

and quickly pulling out of the subsequent dive. The Messerschmitt pilot found it difficult to counter this defensive maneuver because his elevators became too heavy to effect a quick pull-out, due to the fighter's rapid buildup of speed in the dive. An experienced German pilot could, however, remain on the Spitfire's tail throughout this maneuver if the latter was flown by a novice who failed to tighten his turn for fear of stalling his fighter.

During the course of the trial it was discovered that a Bf 109E pilot could also push his aircraft into a sudden dive in an effort to elude a pursuing Spitfire, and the German fighter's DB 601 engine would continue to deliver full power thanks to its direct fuel injection. However, if a Spitfire tried to follow, its Merlin engine would splutter and stop because its normal float-type carburetor ceased to deliver fuel. RAF pilots quickly learned to half-roll and pull down in pursuit of a bunting Bf 109E, thus negating the fuel flow problems.

The Bf 109E drew praise from the RAF trials team for its excellent handling and low- and medium-speed response, good low-speed climb angle, gentle stall, lack of any tendency to spin and short take-off run. It was criticized for its control-heaviness at the upper end of its speed range, but the Spitfire was just as difficult to fly at around 400mph, losing any clear advantage in maneuverability that it enjoyed over the Bf 109E. Indeed, German pilots soon discovered in combat that if they kept their speed up, and flew evasively, the Spitfire pilot would struggle to bring his guns to bear. The absence of a rudder trimmer in the Bf 109E was also noted by the RAF trials pilots, who grew weary of constantly having to apply the rudder in order to fly straight at high speeds. They also commented unfavorably on the Bf 109E's uncomfortably cramped cockpit.

Dr Alfred Price, when commenting on the results of this trial in his volume *Spitfire At War*, noted:

> Overall, the Spitfire I and Bf 109E matched each other fairly evenly. If they fought, victory would almost invariably go to the side which was the more alert, which held the initiative, which understood the strengths and weaknesses of its opponent's aircraft, which showed better teamwork and which, in the last resort, could shoot the more accurately.

The fall of France in June 1940 also presented the Luftwaffe with the opportunity to test-fly a Spitfire after three examples were captured on the ground. Amongst the pilots to evaluate the captured Spitfire at the Luftwaffe's Rechlin test center was then-ranking German ace (with 39 kills, including 14 in Spain) Hauptmann Werner Mölders, who flew both the Spitfire and the Hurricane. Writing to his comrades in III./JG 53 about his Rechlin experiences, Mölders noted:

Originally captioned "So sties ich auf die Engländer herunter" ("So that is how I discovered the English hunter"), the German ace Hauptmann Helmut Wick describes to his colleagues how he succeeded in yet another duel with English pilots, in September 1940. The German tactic of operating in pairs ensured success against many RAF pilots who were too inexperienced to know better than to stick to the rigid Flying Attack formations. (Bundesarchiv Bild 146-1986-013-04, Bild 146-1968-015-19)

Spitfires of No. 610 Sqn on July 24, 1940. Throughout the course of the Battle of Britain, Fighter Command squadrons continued to practice such outmoded tactics, with dire consequences. After having borne the brunt of many German attacks throughout July and August No. 610 Sqn had to be posted away from the frontline for rest and recuperation. (IWM CH 740)

> In our terms, both British fighters are easy to fly... Take-off and landing in both types is child's play... The Spitfire is one class better [than the Hurricane], being very nice to the touch, light, excellent in the turn and almost equal to the Bf 109E in performance, but a rotten dogfighter, as any sudden dive and the engine cuts out for seconds at a time, and because the propeller's only two-pitch (take-off and cruise), it means that in any vertical dogfight at constantly changing heights it's either continually overrevving or never develops full power at all.

Fellow ace Oberleutnant Erwin Leykauf (who survived the war with 33 kills to his credit) of 7./JG 54 was also quite candid about the capabilities of the Spitfires he encountered during the summer of 1940, recalling in Armand van Ishoven's *Messerschmitt Bf 109 At War* volume:

> The essential difference between the Bf 109E and the Spitfire I was that the latter was less maneuverable in the rolling plane. With its shorter, square-tipped wings, the Bf 109E was more maneuverable and slightly faster. It also had leading edge slots. When the Bf 109 was flown, advertently or inadvertently, too slow, the slots would shoot out forward of the wing... Many fresh young pilots thought that they were pulling very tight turns even when the slots were closed against the wing. For us more experienced pilots, real maneuvering only started when the slots were out. For this reason, it is possible to find pilots from 1940 who will tell you that the

> Spitfire turned better than the Bf 109… I myself had many dogfights with Spitfires and could always outturn them.

In light of the combat experiences over Dunkirk and in the early stages of the Battle of Britain, the RAF rapidly fitted Rotol variable-pitch propellers to all of its Spitfires in frontline units, thus allowing the fighter to match the performance of the Bf 109E.

RAF TACTICS

As good as the Spitfire was, its employment in the first 18 months of the war was adversely affected by the rigid implementation of unwieldy tactics. In the 1930s the greatest perceived threat was from the bomber. Given the range of fighters, and the fact that France was an ally, it was assumed that the bombers would be unescorted. However, RAF fighters were armed exclusively with rifle-caliber .303in machine guns at this time, and their weight of fire was deemed to be insufficient to bring down bombers flying in tight, massed formations when attacking independently of one another. The RAF's Air Fighting Development Establishment (AFDE) therefore decided that the only way to solve this problem was to mass fighters in close formation so as to bring a large number of guns to bear. Pilots in frontline fighter units were well drilled in formation flying, so a series of six basic patterns known as Fighting Area Attacks were duly formulated and published in the RAF *Manual of Air Tactics* of 1938. These were at the heart of standard squadron air drills, as Al Deere recalled:

Spitfire Is of No. 19 Sqn head away from Fowlmere in 1940 in tight battle formation. The RAF's rigid adherence to the "vic" formation and outmoded tactics saw Spitfire and Hurricane units sustain heavy losses to marauding Bf 109Es during the Battle of Britain.

SPITFIRE: THROUGH THE GUNSIGHT

In 1940, most fighters had enough ammunition for 12 to 15 seconds' worth of fighting, so the pilot had to be selective about what he chose to fire at, and when, with a careful judgement of distance and angle. Most decisive fighter encounters ended within a few seconds of the attack commencing. One aircraft dived on another from behind or out of the sun ("Beware the Hun in the Sun" was a common adage in the RAF), opened fire for two or three seconds and then broke away – a classic aerial ambush known as the "bounce." However, if neither side had an initial advantage, then the fighters would "dogfight" – the aim being to get on the opponent's tail – hence the name. Speed and maneuverability were crucial in such an instance, with the tighter the turn, the greater the ability to get behind an opponent.

Robert Bungay in his book *The Most Dangerous Enemy* identified four key factors. The first factor was the pilot's ability to exploit his aircraft's performance to the maximum. Secondly, excellent eyesight was necessary, a skill some pilots sought to improve upon. "Sailor" Malan used to fix on a dot on a wall, look away and then turn his head and see how quickly he could focus on it again. Bob Doe used to search the sky systematically, dividing his view into four separate quarters with an emphasis on peripheral vision. One also had to be a good shot. Early experience with shotguns often characterized the famous aces. Malan grew up on a farm in South Africa and began shooting when he was a boy. The great German ace Adolf Galland had been taken on his first hunting trip when he was just five. And of course they all needed a certain mental ability – the courage to know how to overcome fear and attack aggressively. For those that succeeded in aerial combat, it was a life-changing experience.

This illustration shows the Barr and Stroud GM 2 reflector unit which replaced the ring and bead sight in the Spitfire I from 1939 onwards. With the reflector gunsight in position and switched on, the pilot would see a white dot surrounded by a ring reflected onto his windscreen. Small rearview mirrors, similar to those in cars, were fixed above the windshield to improve the view behind. (Artwork by Jim Laurier, © Osprey Publishing)

> The majority of our training in a prewar fighter squadron was directed at achieving perfection in formation, with a view to ensuring the success of the flight and the squadron attacks we so assiduously practiced. The order to attack was always preceded by the flight commander designating the number of the attack, such as "Fighting Area Attack No. 5 – Go." These attacks provided wonderful training for formation drill, but were worthless when related to effective shooting. There was never sufficient time to get one's sights on the target, the business of keeping station being the prime requirement.

The standard RAF fighter formation at the time was the V-shaped "vic" of three aircraft. A squadron of 12 aircraft would be split into two flights, A and B, and these were in turn made up of two sections of three fighters. When in full-strength Battle Formation, all 12 aircraft would be tightly grouped together in four sections of three fighters. Leading the "vic" would be the squadron CO or senior flight commander, with succeeding "Vs" following in close line astern. Once bombers had been spotted, the commander would position his formation in behind them and then lead the attack in section after section. Such attacks would have worked well against German bombers had it not been for the presence of agile escort fighters sweeping the skies ahead of them. As RAF Fighter Command would soon find out to its cost, Fighting Area Attacks (FAAs) were useless against small, nimble formations of high-performance fighters such as the Bf 109E. Indeed, upon seeing British fighters flying into combat in tight, neat rows of three, German pilots, who invariably enjoyed a height advantage, quickly dubbed the vics "*Idiotenreihen*" (lit. "rows of idiots").

Those pilots that survived their initial encounters with the enemy soon came to realize that a successful combat formation had to be able to maneuver whilst maintaining cohesion. Pilots also had to be able to cover each other's blind areas so as to prevent surprise attacks on the formation. Finally, individual members of the formation had to be able to support each other should they come under attack.

The Luftwaffe's four-strong *Schwarm* (based on the loose pair, or *Rotte*, which was at the heart of all *Jagdwaffe* formations) met all these criteria, but Fighter Command's tight vics did not. The *Schwarm* could turn as tightly as any individual aircraft within the formation, whereas a vic's rate of turn was limited by the need for it to pivot on the aircraft on the inside of the turn.

When looking for the enemy, all the members of the looser *Schwarm* enjoyed the freedom to search the skies (and cover blind areas astern of the formation) without the fear of running into a wingman. In the vic, only the leader searched for the enemy, as his two wingmen had to concentrate on remaining in tight

A *Schwarm* of Bf 109Es heads for England in the late summer of 1940. The aircraft have closed up for the benefit of the camera in this shot, as normally they would have been well spaced in "finger four" formation. The *Schwarm* would then fly as two *Rotten*, or loose pairs, with 200m of separation between each aircraft. This formation was far better suited to the fighter-versus-fighter combat that predominated from May to December 1940.

formation. This left them highly susceptible to attack from behind and below, and this blind spot was repeatedly exploited by the *Jagdwaffe* in 1940.

Finally, if a *Rotte* or *Schwarm* was attacked from behind, a quick turn by the formation would see the attacker immediately come under threat himself. If the rear section of an RAF formation was bounced, the aircraft under attack had usually been shot down well before another pilot could attempt to fend off the enemy fighters.

In the vic, only the leader searched for the enemy, as his two wingmen had to concentrate on remaining in tight formation. This left them highly susceptible to attack from behind and below, and this blind spot was repeatedly exploited by the *Jagdwaffe* in the opening days and months of the battle.

The futility of these formations, and the FAA, were brought home to the Spitfire squadrons in their first engagements over Dunkirk. Al Deere was lucky to escape with his life when No. 54 Sqn tried to carry out such an attack on He 111s over the French coast on May 24, 1940:

> The squadron had not been on patrol very long before Flt Lt Max Pearson's voice screeched over the R/T, "Tally ho, Tally ho, enemy aircraft above and ahead." About 3,000ft above us, and clearly silhouetted against a blue sky, a large formation of German bombers ploughed westwards towards Dunkirk unmolested and apparently unprotected. "Sitting ducks," I thought.
>
> "Hornet squadron, full throttle, climbing to attack," came the order from Flt Lt "Prof" Leathart, who was leading the squadron. "Hornet squadron, No. 5 attack, No. 5 attack, GO."
>
> Simultaneously, the sections fanned out into the various echelons necessary for this type of attack, and as they did so individual pilots selected a particular bomber

> target. But we had reckoned without interference from fighter escort – after all, no consideration had been given to it in designing this type of attack, and our peacetime training had not envisaged interference from escort fighters. Experience is dearly bought.
>
> "Christ, Messerschmitts – BREAK, BREAK."
>
> There was no need for a second warning. At the word "Break," and with one accord, the squadron split in all directions, all thoughts of blazing enemy bombers ousted by the desire to survive.

Somehow, No. 54 Sqn suffered no losses to the attacking Bf 109Es, its pilots instead claiming nine German fighters destroyed – a testament to the skill of the pilots if not the original tactics. Such tactics were questioned by the pilots once back at their Hornchurch base. Plt Off Colin Gray, who like Al Deere was a Kiwi, and would also become a leading Spitfire ace, having had his aircraft turned upside down by an exploding cannon shell commented:

> From behind me, I felt them. In future, I've no intention of offering myself as a target to Hun fighters while the rest of the squadron disappears in all directions other than that in which some unfortunate like me is getting hell beaten out of him.

Although No. 54 Sqn vowed there and then to abandon FAAs, however, vic formations would continue well into 1941 until falling out of practice. Indeed, officially, pilots were forbidden from implementing new tactics at unit level. In reality there was no actual time available for Fighter Command to rectify this problem through the issuing of new tactics on the eve of the Battle of Britain. Future ace Plt Off Bobby Oxspring, who was flying Spitfires with No. 66 Sqn at the time, explained the predicament facing frontline pilots at the time:

> We knew that there was a lot wrong with our tactics during the Battle of Britain, but it was one hell of a time to alter everything we had practiced. We had not time

Overleaf: The Battle of Britain
At 1630hrs on August 30, 1940, No. 603 Sqn's Flg Off Brian Carbury was leading a section in B Flight when, near Canterbury, Kent, he sighted three Bf 109s north of him. "I attacked the rear aircraft, and the leading two aircraft turned for my tail. I got a good burst in and the propeller of the rear enemy aircraft stopped, started and finally stopped, with white vapour coming out behind. The enemy aircraft went into a glide for the east coast. I veered off as other aircraft were closing in on me." The Bf 109E-1 of 3./JG 27's Feldwebel Ernst Arnold had been badly shot up, but its pilot managed to perform a controlled belly landing in a field near Faversham, Kent. (Artwork by Mark Postlethwaite, © Osprey Publishing)

> to experiment when we were in combat three or four times a day. Moreover, we were getting fresh pilots straight out of flying schools who were trained, barely, to use the old type of close formation – they simply could not have coped with something radically different.

In an effort to improve the operability of the vic, Fighter Command permitted squadrons to widen out the formations, thus allowing pilots to search the skies for the enemy more freely, rather than concentrating on close formation keeping with the lead fighter. A section or pair of aircraft would also now fly as "weavers" some 1,000ft above and behind the main formation in an effort to prevent surprise attacks from the rear – without anyone to protect their tails, countless "weavers" were duly shot down during the Battle of Britain. These modifications certainly improved the search and mutual support capabilities of Fighter Command's formations, but did nothing to improve their ability to perform tight turns without losing cohesion.

A number of squadrons that had seen action over Dunkirk began to modify their tactics. Amongst these was No. 74 Sqn, which included the great tactician Flt Lt "Sailor" Malan within its ranks. During the closing stages of the battle, Malan divided his aircraft into three sections of four. If the formation broke up, Spitfires would then become fighting pairs. Clearly, combat experience and some amount of "bending of the rules" ensured survival. He, along with Al Deere and Bob Stanford Tuck, also began to question the gun harmonization distances of their Spitfires. The official thinking prewar had been to fill the air with .303in bullets at a distance of 400 yards ahead of the line of flight. However, following combat experience, Malan was adamant that the distance should be reduced to 250 yards, thus forcing pilots to get in close to their targets so that one could not miss. This change was finally officially sanctioned in the summer of 1940.

At about the same time as this change was made, Spitfires also began to be armed with a new kind of incendiary round known to pilots as De Wilde ammunition. Unlike the standard incendiary ammunition in use at the start of the war, De Wilde had no flame or smoke trace. However, it did produce a small flash on impact with the target, thus for the first time providing pilots with the confirmation that their aim was good.

Despite their initially inferior tactics, it was the sheer ability of Fighter Command's pilots, combined with the superb command-and-control network and the combat performance of the Spitfire and, to a lesser degree, the Hurricane in combat, that allowed the RAF to retain air supremacy over the UK.

LUFTWAFFE TACTICS

The German fighter force that engaged the RAF during 1940 was by far the most experienced and tactically advanced anywhere in the world at that time. Although less than a third of its pilots had seen action in Spain, the lessons learned there had been introduced throughout the *Jadgwaffe*. Werner Mölders was the most influential of all Condor Legion veterans, and what he had learned fighting Spanish Republican aircraft was officially institutionalized in training in the lead up to World War II.

His philosophy for success in combat saw the emphasis placed more on fighting than flying. Experience had taught Mölders that the best way to achieve this was to abandon the three-aircraft vic and go with the two-aircraft *Rotte*, which in turn formed the basic fighting unit for all *Jagdwaffe* formations. Within the pair, the *Rottenführer* (pair leader) was responsible for making the kills and his wingman (the *Katschmarek*) protected the leader's tail. The wingman did not worry about where he was flying, or what to do next – he simply had to follow his leader. He usually held position some 200 yards away from the *Rottenführer*, flying almost in line abreast formation. Each pilot concentrated his search of the sky inwards, so as to cover his partner's blind spot.

Two *Rotten* made up a *Schwarm* (flight), flying some 300 yards apart – roughly the turning radius of a Bf 109E at combat speed. The leading *Rotte* typically flew to one side and slightly ahead of the other, and a *Staffel* formation comprised three *Schwarme* either stepped up in line astern or in line abreast. The *Jadgwaffe* also devised the "cross-over turn" to avoid aircraft on the outside of a *Schwarm* becoming stragglers when the formation turned at high cruising speed in an area where contact with the enemy was likely. Each pilot held his speed going into the turn and the *Rotte* simply changed position in the formation during the maneuver.

During the early stages of World War II, the Bf 109E enjoyed a superior altitude performance to all the fighters it came up against, so the favored tactic of the *Jagdwaffe* was to get above their opponents and attempt to bounce them, if possible using the sun to mask their approach. After a single firing pass, the *Jagdflieger* would use the speed gained in their diving attack to climb back up into a position from which to perform any repeat attacks. With enemy fighters usually being slower and more maneuverable, German pilots tried to avoid turning dogfights wherever possible.

If bounced, the *Rotte* or *Schwarm* would typically turn individually to meet the attack, and if there was no time for this, they would take advantage of the direct injection system fitted to their Bf 109Es by bunting over into a dive. The *Abschwung* (or "split-ess") was also used as an alternative escape route, the pilot performing a half-roll pulled through into a steep dive at full throttle – this maneuver could only be done with plenty of altitude in hand, as up to 15,000ft in height would be lost.

These formations and tactics served the *Jagdwaffe* well over Dunkirk and for much of the Battle of Britain, with *Rottenführer* having just one job to do – find and destroy the enemy. When they were found, the formation leader was the one who went in for the kill, leaving his wingmen to cover his tail. By sticking to the *Freie Jagd* tactic, pilots of the caliber of Mölders, Galland, Ihlefeld, Oesau and Wick all racked up impressive scores. Lesser-known pilots were also well served by these tactics, including 3./JG 52's Oberleutnant Ulrich Steinhilper on September 26, 1940:

> We were approaching Dover when we saw a whole squadron of Spitfires spread out in line astern below us, with a weaver on either side at the back. They were so well defined against the blue-green of the sea that we couldn't have missed them. My *Staffelführer*, Oberleutnant Helmut Kühle, instructed me to take one of the weavers and he said that he'd take care of the other. When the rest of the squadron saw that this had been accomplished, they could then pick their own targets. These were good tactics, as the weavers were there to protect the rear of the flight, and if

Having been made *Gruppenkommandeur* of I./JG 52 on August 28, 1940, future 77-victory *experte* Hauptmann Wolfgang Ewald celebrated his promotion five days later when he was one of three pilots from the *Gruppe* each to claim a Spitfire destroyed. The latter were almost certainly from Croydon-based No. 72 Sqn, which was attacked whilst patrolling over Lympne, in Kent. (Artwork by Jim Laurier, © Osprey Publishing)

> they could be taken out without raising the alarm, there would be a good chance of the rest of the squadron bagging the majority of the enemy aircraft. This was what was so foolish about flying this kind of formation.
>
> We peeled away and I began to position my fighter. The red ring of the Revi gunsight was projected onto the windscreen, and I'd already flipped over the trigger for both the nose guns and the wing cannon, ready for the attack. Gradually, the Spitfire filled the ring of the sight and I increased the pressure on the triggers. Four lines of tracer hosed out towards the target and I saw strikes, the aircraft spinning away. Instead of chasing it down, I altered course slightly and went for the next Spitfire in line. Again I saw hits before I broke away to safety.

As the Battle of Britain progressed, however, the tactical advantage enjoyed by the *Jagdwaffe* was steadily eroded by the unbreakable spirit of Fighter Command, its radar coverage of the Channel and its efficient fighter control system. The Bf 109E's short range also became more of a problem as the *Kampfgeschwader* started to go after targets farther inland from the south coast. Oberstleutnant Adolf Galland, *Geschwaderkommodore* of JG 26 by the end of the Battle of Britain, wrote at length about this problem in his autobiography *The First and the Last*, stating that the Messerschmitt fighter's lack of range was critical to the outcome of the Battle of Britain:

> It used to take us roughly half an hour from take-off to crossing the English coast at the narrowest point of the Channel. Having a tactical flying time of about 80 minutes in the Bf 109E, we therefore had about 20 minutes to complete our task. This fact limited the distance of penetration, German fighter squadrons based on the Pas de Calais and on the Contentin peninsula barely being able to cover the southeastern part of England. Circles drawn from these two bases at an operational range of 125 miles overlapped approximately in the London area. Everything beyond was practically out of our reach. An operating radius of 125 miles was sufficient for local defense, but not enough for such tasks as bomber escort, which were now being demanded of us.
>
> It was assumed that the appearance of German fighter squadrons over England would draw the British fighters into the area within our range, where they would be destroyed, beaten, or at least decimated in large-scale air battles. Things turned out differently. Our fighter formations took off. The first air battles took place as expected and according to plan. Due to the German superiority, these attacks, had they been continued, would certainly have achieved the attempted goal, but the RAF fighters were recalled from this area long before this goal was achieved.

> The weakened squadrons left their bases near the coast and used them only for emergency landings or to refuel and rearm. They were concentrated in a belt around London in readiness for our bomber attacks. Thus they evaded the attack in the air in order to encounter more effectively the attack from the air, which would logically follow. The German fighters found themselves in a similar predicament to a dog on a chain who wants to attack the foe but cannot harm him because of the limitations of the chain.

As losses to both German fighters and bombers mounted, and Fighter Command's resolve seemingly remained intact, senior officers in the Luftwaffe sought to lay the blame at the feet of the *Jagdgeschwader*, as Galland recalled:

> We had the impression that, whatever we did, we were bound to be wrong. Fighter protection for bombers created many problems which had to be solved in action. Bomber pilots preferred close screening in which their formation was surrounded by pairs of fighters pursuing a zigzag course. Obviously, the visible presence of the protective fighters gave the bomber pilots a greater sense of security. However, this was a faulty conclusion, because a fighter can only carry out this purely defensive task by taking the initiative in the offensive. He must never wait until attacked because he then loses the chance of acting.
>
> We fighter pilots certainly preferred the "free chase during the approach and over the target area." This in fact gives the greatest relief and the best protection for the bomber force, although not perhaps a sense of security for the latter.

Reichsmarschall Göring, however, did not side with *Jagdflieger* when it came to allowing them to continue to wage the Battle of Britain on their terms. Indeed, in late August he ordered that all *Jagdgeschwader* were to remain close to the bombers that they were escorting, and on no account were they to engage enemy fighters unless they or their bombers came under a direct threat of attack. With the bombers cruising at a much slower speed than the fighters, the *Jagdflieger* had to weave in order to maintain station, and yet still retain a high cruising speed in the combat area. By ordering the *Jagdwaffe* to fly close-formation missions, Göring totally nullified the effectiveness of the previously superior German fighter tactics, thus surrendering the initiative in the skies over southern England to the RAF.

Losses amongst the Bf 109E *Geschwader* rose steeply once they were "chained" to the bomber formations, and one of those men shot down was six-victory ace Feldwebel Heinrich Hoehnisch of 1./JG 53.

February 1941 and the pilots and non-operational officers of No. 92 Squadron pose proudly at RAF Manston with the squadron scoreboard, reflecting their 130th enemy aircraft destroyed. Squadron Leader Johnny Kent, formerly of No. 303 Sqn, is shown propping up the board. (IWM CH 2538)

On my last mission, on September 9, 1940, our task was to give direct fighter cover to the rear of an He 111 bomber formation. One *Kette* [three aircraft in a "vic" formation] of bombers got separated, so our *Staffel* looked after them. We had only seven Bf 109s, and I was tail-end Charlie with Oberfeldwebel Mueller. Approaching London Docks, there was no contact with the enemy, but I was sure that we could expect attacks out of the sun as soon as we turned 180 degrees for our return flight. To my surprise, I saw, when I was looking towards the rest of my *Staffel*, six Spitfires on a reciprocal course in line astern about 50 metres above me. To avoid the inevitable attack, I tried to come up with my *Staffel* flying in front and below me. When I was level with my *Staffelkapitän*, I thought I had made it.

However, there was a rattle like an explosion in my aeroplane and, with the pressure of a blowtorch, flames hit my face. With the greatest difficulty, I got out of my aeroplane. I landed with severe burns to my face and bullet wounds to my right calf. I stayed in the hospital in Woolwich for two months.[1]

Hoehnisch had been shot down by No. 19 Sqn Spitfire ace Flt Lt Wilf Clouston in an engagement that had lasted just a matter of seconds, a typical example of the Spitfire-versus-Bf 109E clashes that occurred throughout the Battle of Britain.

[1] Goss, *The Luftwaffe Fighters' Battle of Britain*

ANALYSIS

Bf 109Es and Spitfires fought each other from May 23, 1940, when No. 54 Sqn engaged aircraft from I./JG 27 near Dunkirk, to December 21, 1940, when No. 92 Sqn downed a Bf 109E-4 of 7.(F)/LG 2 over Dungeness, Kent. The two types continued to engage in mortal combat well into 1941 too.

Fighter Command (and No. 11 Group in particular) had done its best throughout 1940 to send its 19 Spitfire squadrons up against the *Jagdwaffe*'s eight *Jagdgeschwader*, leaving units equipped with slower, less capable Hurricanes to engage the bombers. Of course both RAF types would end up "mixing it" with Bf 109Es on a daily basis, and Spitfire pilots also downed their fair share of bombers. Nevertheless, a large proportion of the aircraft claimed destroyed by Spitfire pilots, and aces in particular, were Bf 109Es, and the same applied to the *Jagdwaffe*.

Fighter Command suffered significant Spitfire losses in 1940, with 72 (nearly one-third of its frontline strength of these aircraft at this time) being lost during operations to cover the evacuation of Dunkirk. August 1940 would prove to be the worst month for Spitfire losses, with 136 fighters destroyed. Overall, during the four months of the Battle of Britain, 361 Spitfires were lost and a further 352 damaged. Fortunately for Fighter Command, and the free world, production of the aircraft far outstripped attrition, with 747 Spitfire I/IIs being delivered in the summer and autumn of 1940.

During this same period, the *Jagdwaffe* lost 610 Bf 109Es, which compares favorably to Fighter Command's 1,023 Spitfires and Hurricanes. Of course, the only targets presented to the *Jagdflieger* during this period were fighters, and it appears that they claimed around 770 of the aircraft lost by Fighter Command. This gave the Bf 109E pilots a favorable kill ratio of 1.2:1, but this was nowhere near the 5:1 target that Oberst Theo Osterkamp (Jagdfliegerführer 2) had set his pilots in July in order to achieve the desired air superiority required for *Sea Lion*.

As the campaign ground on, the *Jagdwaffe*, like Fighter Command, also began to see its pilot numbers decrease, although production of Bf 109Es kept ahead of losses with an average of 155 being delivered per month. Some 906 Emil pilots were deemed to be operational in July, and this number had fallen to 735 by September.

Both sides certainly enjoyed significant aerial successes during the course of the Battle of Britain, but the overclaiming of victories was rife in both the *Jagdwaffe* and Fighter Command. For example, the 19 Spitfire units claimed 1,064.5 victories between July 1 and October 31, but exhaustive research by historian John Alcorn (published in the September 1996 issue of *Aeroplane Monthly* magazine) has shown that only 521.49 of these claims can be substantiated – an average of

27 kills per squadron – a result no doubt, of the confusion of aerial combat. The accuracy of these figures is borne out by the fact that the Luftwaffe lost 1,218 aircraft in total to fighter attacks during this period.

Of the ten top-scoring units by substantiated claims, six flew Spitfires, and two of these squadrons proved to be Bf 109E killers to boot as per the No. 11 Group strategy. No. 603 Sqn topped the list with 57.8 kills (from 67 originally claimed), with 47 of these being Bf 109Es, and No. 41 Sqn, which was third on the list, was credited with 45.3 kills (from 89.5 claimed), of which 33.5 were Emils. Unsurprisingly, the two leading Spitfire aces of 1940, Flg Off Brian Carbury and Plt Off Eric Lock, both of whom were credited with 15 Bf 109E victories apiece, served with these units in 1940.

German kill claims were, if anything, even more wildly optimistic than those of Fighter Command, leading senior Luftwaffe officers to believe that the RAF was literally on its knees – this, of course, was not the case. The postwar comparison of German kill claims with RAF losses shows that very few match up! This was partly the result of the inherent confusion associated with air combat – a number of pilots often claimed the same victim. Overclaiming was also to be expected when the Luftwaffe's system of medals, promotion and profile was closely linked to a pilot's score. It was also virtually impossible to confirm a kill by the examination of wreckage, as most Spitfires and Hurricanes fell either on British soil or in the Channel.

Plt Off Bob Doe of No. 234 Sqn, flying his Spitfire IA X4036, keeps a watchful eye on a second Bf 109E shortly after claiming his 11th victory of the Battle of Britain, and the fifth Bf 109E he had destroyed in three days. Bob Doe routinely hunted German aircraft along the Kent coast near Dover following bombing raids on London, as he recalled in his autobiography *Fighter Pilot*. "I assumed that enemy aircraft would be crossing the coast at about 10,000–12,000ft in a gentle dive, heading for home – and trade should be brisk, as they would be thinking of home, more than Spitfires." (Artwork by Jim Laurier, © Osprey Publishing)

The German tactical system was geared up for a chosen few to claim the bulk of the kills, with the rest supporting – and protecting – them, often with their lives. The victory and attrition figures for JG 51 prove just that, its statistics being typical for most of the *Jagdgeschwader* in 1940. The unit lost ten pilots in July of that year, half of which had failed to score a single kill prior to their demise. The remaining five had claimed just 11 between them. This ratio was to remain remarkably constant through to June 1941, when the unit headed east for the invasion of the USSR.

Just over half of the 100 pilots lost by JG 51 during this time had not claimed a single victory, and of the rest, 35 had fewer than five kills. Aerial combat in 1940–41 was "natural selection" at its harshest, and if a new pilot survived his first few missions, his chances of survival were significantly improved, at least in the short to medium term.

At the other end of the scale, 16 *experten* who claimed at least five Spitfire I/IIs destroyed scored some or all of their victories flying with JG 51 during this period. Leading the pack was Hauptmann Walter Oesau, who claimed 26 Spitfire I/IIs whilst flying with III./JG 51. Oberleutnant Hermann-Friedrich Joppien (13 kills), Major Werner Mölders (ten kills) and Hauptmann Ernst Wiggers (ten kills) were the other pilots to achieve Spitfire victories in double figures in 1940–41, although the latter was killed in action by a Hurricane pilot on September 11, 1940.

At the end of the day the Battle of Britain provided the Allies with their first victory in World War II. Although the Bf 109E *Jagdgeschwader* more than held their own, despite operating at the very limit of their range, the seemingly invincible Luftwaffe had been comprehensively beaten. However, Fighter Command had emerged from the 123-day campaign stronger than it had gone into it, despite losing 1,023 fighters and having 515 pilots killed. It would then eventually move onto the offensive as the threat of invasion ebbed away.

LEADING SPITFIRE Mk I/II Bf 109E KILLERS 1940–41			
	Bf 109E kills	Final score	Unit
Flg Off Brian Carbury	15	15 (+2sh)	No. 603 Sqn
Plt Off Eric Lock	15	26	No. 41 Sqn
Plt Off Colin Gray	12	27 (+2sh)	No. 54 Sqn
Flg Off Pat Hughes	12	14 (+3sh)	No. 234 Sqn
Sgt William Franklin	11	13 (+3sh)	No. 65 Sqn
Flg Off Des McMullen	10.5	17 (+5sh)	Nos 54 and 222 Sqns
Flg Off John Webster	9.5	11 (+2sh)	No. 41 Sqn
Sqn Ldr John Ellis	9	13 (+1sh)	No. 610 Sqn
Sqn Ldr Adolf Malan	9	27 (+7sh)	No. 74 Sqn
Flt Sgt George Unwin	8.5	13 (+2sh)	No. 19 Sqn

LEADING Bf 109E SPITFIRE I/II KILLERS 1940–41			
	Kills	Final score	Unit
Hptm Herbert Ihlefeld	33	132	Stab I.(J)/LG 2, 2.(J)/LG 2 and 2.(J)/LG 2
Hptm Walter Oesau	26	127	7./JG 51 and Stab III./JG 51
Maj Adolf Galland	25	104	Stab JG 27, Stab III./JG 26 and Stab JG 26
Maj Helmut Wick	24	56	3./JG 2, Stab I./JG 2 and Stab JG 2
Ltn Erich Schmidt	15	47	9./JG 53
Oblt Hermann-Friedrich Joppien	13	70	1./JG 51
Oblt Werner Machold	13	32	9./JG 2 & 9./JG 2
Maj Werner Mölders	13	115	III./JG 53 and Stab JG 51
Oblt Josef Priller	13	101	6./JG 51 and 1./JG 26
Hptm Gerhard Schöpfel	13	45	9./JG 26 and III./JG 26
Ltn Horst Ulenberg	13	16	2./JG 26
Ltn Friedrich Geisshardt	12	102	1.(J)/LG 2 and 2.(J)/LG 2
Oblt Hans Hahn	12	108	4./JG 2
Oblt Gustav Rödel	12	98	4./JG 27
Oblt Hans-Ekkhard Bob	10	60	9./JG 54, 7./JG 54 and Stab III./JG 54
Hptm Ernst Wiggers	10	13	2./JG 51

AFTERMATH

Officially, the Battle of Britain ended for the RAF on October 31, 1940. However, both Fighter Command and the *Jagdwaffe* continued to lock horns regularly until the end of the year. Indeed, on November 1 four Biggin Hill-based Spitfires were shot down by Bf 109Es from JG 26 that were escorting Ju 87s sent to attack a convoy off Dover – the kind of attack that had signaled the start of the Battle of Britain four months earlier! This particular raid was unusual for the period, as the Luftwaffe had by then reassigned the majority of its dedicated bomber units to night raids, using high-flying Bf 109E *Jabos* to attack targets in the southeast during daylight hours.

These raids were carried out at altitudes of between 26,000ft and 33,000ft, and at high speeds, presenting Fighter Command with little chance to intercept them. Fortunately, the bombloads carried by the *Jabos* was small, and accuracy of the weapons released from 18,000ft was generally poor. Nevertheless, *Jabo* attacks by Emils would continue well into 1941.

By then the Bf 109E's days as the premier German fighter on the Channel front were well and truly numbered. As early as October 9, 1940, Major Werner Mölders, *Geschwaderkommodore* of JG 51, had flown his first combat sortie over southern England in the Emil's successor, the Bf 109F. Over coming months, the improved "Friedrich" would be issued to JG 53, JG 3, JG 2 and JG 26, in that order. The last frontline Emils on the Channel front, flown by the latter unit's II Gruppe, were still "mixing it" with the RAF's Spitfires and Hurricanes over France as late as September 7, 1941, after which they were replaced by the all-new Fw 190A-1.

The RAF, meanwhile, had gone from being on the defensive in 1940 to taking the fight to the Germans in 1941. In the vanguard of this campaign was Fighter Command, whose new commander-in-chief, Chief Marshal Sir Sholto Douglas, wanted his squadrons "leaning forward into France." The first such mission had actually been performed by two pilots from Spitfire-equipped No. 66 Sqn on December 20, 1940, when they strafed Le Touquet. This was the first time Spitfires had sortied over France since the fall of Dunkirk. Large-scale operations aimed at enticing the *Jagdwaffe* into combat over France and the Low Countries commenced in earnest in January 1941, with the first "Circus" mission taking place on the 10th of that month. Spitfire units from Nos 10 and 11 Groups were heavily involved in this long-running offensive from the very start, escorting medium bombers sent to attack various military targets in occupied Europe.

More and more Hurricane units now switched to Spitfires – often battle-tired Mk Is, but also newer Mk IIs and the significantly improved Mk V. And with operations progressing ever deeper into occupied Europe, the short-ranged Spitfire was finding it difficult to offer the vulnerable medium bombers the protection they required. In a desperate effort to stretch the endurance of the Supermarine fighter, 60 Spitfire IIs were built with a fixed 40gal tank fitted under the port wing. Designated the Spitfire II Long Range, these aircraft saw considerable service from the spring of 1941 onwards. Despite being built in only modest numbers, the Spitfire II (LR)s flew with no fewer than eight units, as aircraft were passed between squadrons rotating in and out of No. 11 Group.

By then the tactics being employed by Spitfire squadrons in the frontline had also altered dramatically from those in place for much of the Battle of Britain. Several units had taken it upon themselves to modify the formations they flew when going into combat, and at the forefront of these changes was Spitfire-equipped No. 74 Sqn. Its CO, Sqn Ldr "Sailor" Malan, was effectively the Werner Mölders of Fighter Command, being one of the best tacticians in the RAF. He had also claimed nine Bf 109Es destroyed during 1940, so his theories on fighter formations had been formulated through bitter combat experiences.

During the final stages of the Battle of Britain, Malan began dividing his 12-aircraft formations into three sections of four, rather than the traditional four sections of three in an unwieldy vic. Now, if a formation of Spitfires broke up after being bounced, its four-aircraft sections would split into two fighting pairs, which operated similarly to the German *Rotte*. With the three section leaders flying in a widely-spaced "V," and the rest of their sections in line astern behind them, Malan's formation now possessed mutual support, coverage of blind spots to the rear and cohesion if forced to turn in combat. The loose line-astern formation was also

Having just claimed his 21st kill (a Hurricane), Oberfeldwebel Werner Machold of 1./JG 2 smiles for the camera as he looks at the new victory bar applied to the rudder of his Bf 109E on September 4, 1940. Machold would claim 13 Spitfire I/IIs destroyed between May 26, 1940 and May 19, 1941. Hit by antiaircraft fire whilst attacking a convoy off Portland on June 9, 1941, Machold force-landed his Bf 109E-7/Z near Swanage, in Dorset, and was captured. His score stood at 32 victories at the time of his imprisonment.

much easier to fly than tight "Battle Formation," thus freeing pilots to devote most of their time looking out for the enemy, rather than watching what their section leader was up to. Malan's new formation was soon officially implemented throughout Fighter Command, as was the German "finger four" *Schwarm*.

Virtually all Spitfire I/IIs had either been relegated to Training Command or rebuilt as Mk VBs by December 1941, and, fittingly, veteran Battle of Britain unit No. 152 Sqn had the honour of flying the final sweeps over enemy territory in these early mark fighters the following month. Later marks of Spitfire would, of course, continue to take the fight to the *Jagdwaffe*, dueling with improved versions of the Bf 109 to help the Allies ultimately claim final victory in Europe in World War II.

The importance of the victory of the Battle of Britain, and the success that the Spitfire pilots achieved, cannot be overstated. It was the first victory secured by the Allies against the Third Reich and it was a necessary victory to ensure later successes. Without victory here the Battle of the Atlantic could not have been fought, it is doubtful whether America would have been convinced to enter the European conflict, and Britain could not have fulfilled her final destiny as a staging ground for the D-Day invasion force of June 1944. Like Stalingrad, the Battle of Britain was one of the true turning points of the war, but one that was achieved without costing millions of lives. Indeed, as Churchill so famously concluded, "Never was so much owed by so many to so few."

B
L
L DX
B
F
F DX

Part II

THE BATTLE FOR THE BOMBERS: EUROPE 1943–45

P-47 THUNDERBOLT vs Bf 109G/K

By 1943, the fiercest battles in the skies of Europe had long swung away from the English Channel and Britain's southern counties, and toward the heart of Germany. With America's entry into the war, the growing force of USAAF B-17 and B-24 bombers joined the RAF's strategic bombing campaign against Germany. Targeting industrial facilities and major population centers, the massed bombers would devastate Germany's ability to wage war.

For much of 1942, the defense of the German Reich had been entrusted predominantly to Luftwaffe units equipped with the Messerschmitt Bf 109. Pilots of this iconic fighter, along with their brethren flying the equally deadly Focke-Wulf Fw 190, were inflicting increasing losses on the heavy bomber groups of the fledgling Eighth Air Force as the United States Army Air Force (USAAF) attempted to make its presence felt in the European Theater of Operations (ETO). On average, some 13.6 percent of the attacking force sent out to hit targets in western Europe would fall victim to the *Jagdwaffe*. Such losses could not be allowed to continue, but at the time neither the RAF or the USAAF had a fighter in-theater with sufficient range to protect the vulnerable B-17 Flying Fortresses and B-24 Liberators as they ventured ever deeper into enemy territory.

In late 1942, as a first step in providing the "heavies" with much-needed strategic escorts, 200 Republic P-47C Thunderbolts were shipped to the UK. Although some believed the Lockheed P-38 Lightning to be the better strategic fighter thanks to its twin engines and longer range, demand for it in other theaters meant that the Thunderbolt was the only modern fighter available in sufficient quantity to serve as the principal interceptor for the Eighth Air Force in the short term.

Three groups in VIII Fighter Command were initially equipped with the P-47, and they were declared operational in April 1943. These groups subsequently endured some hard knocks at the hands of battle-seasoned German fighter units, and despite their best efforts, Thunderbolt pilots were initially handicapped by poor tactics and combat inexperience.

Eastern Front *experte* (with 202 kills) Major Hermann Graf was appointed to the command of JG(r) 50 in August 1943. This specialist Defense of the Reich unit was tasked with combating US heavy bombers, as well as high-flying RAF reconnaissance aircraft. For this dual role, the *Geschwader* equipped its Bf 109G-6s either with underwing rockets (as depicted here) or additional cannon gondolas. Graf's Bf 109G-6 "Red 1" is seen just seconds after performing a head-on attack on a formation of B-17Fs from the 92nd BG, which has left one Flying Fortress streaming smoke from its outer port engine. The 92nd lost seven bombers on this day, at least one of which almost certainly fell to Major Graf. (Artwork by Iain Wyllie, © Osprey Publishing)

One of the P-47's primary tormentors in 1943 was the Bf 109; now developed into the G model, it was to be the Messerschmitt fighter's most-produced version. Having seen four years of combat in European skies, the German interceptor had been continually modified in order for it to remain a viable fighter in the face of growing Allied aerial opposition. The *Jagdwaffe* pilots equipped with Bf 109Gs were, in the main, as "salty" as the aircraft they flew. Their experience was brought to bear throughout 1943 and into early 1944, as the P-47 groups struggled to protect the longer-ranging heavy bombers that were still being brought down in growing numbers by German fighters.

Both the Thunderbolt and the Bf 109G represented astounding advances in fighter engine and armament design, but they could not have been more different. The sleek, aesthetically pleasing Messerschmitt was half the weight of the heavyweight, barrel-shaped American fighter. Indeed, the Thunderbolt was the largest and heaviest single-engined single-seat propeller-driven fighter ever built. It climbed like a homesick angel and dived for the deck like a rock. This was due to the mighty power of its air-cooled, turbosupercharged Pratt & Whitney R-2800 Double Wasp engine. Pilots disparagingly dubbed it the "seven-ton milk bottle." Other sobriquets included "the Repulsive Scatterbolt," "Thunderjug" and "Thundermug."

But sheer size was not to prove detrimental to the Thunderbolt's operational career. Indeed, P-47s flew 546,000 combat sorties from March 1943 to August 1945, and only 0.7 percent of them were lost in combat. Yet although the "Jug" could outdive any other fighter at low and medium altitudes, it could not match the rate of climb or maneuverability of the Bf 109G and later Bf 109K variant. Another shortcoming was insufficient range to permit deep penetration into Germany, and this was only rectified with the introduction of progressively larger wing drop tanks.

P-47 pilots came to typify the might of the Eighth Air Force's fighter strength from the summer of 1943 through to mid-1944, when the P-51 assumed the crown of king of USAAF fighters in the ETO. Nonetheless, while the Mustang became the finest long-range fighter of the war, more Thunderbolts were built than any other US fighter.

Like the P-47, the Bf 109 was eventually usurped as the best piston-engined fighter in Luftwaffe service, with the improved Fw 190 (radial and inline-engined versions) being seen as the better aircraft as the war progressed. However, through sheer weight of numbers, and hasty upgrades, the Bf 109G/K remained a deadly opponent in the hands of combat veterans. Unfortunately for the *Jagdwaffe*, the latter were in very short supply by the summer of 1944, as so many of its *experten* had fallen trying to repel the overwhelming Allied aerial onslaught – at the heart of which was the Thunderbolt.

THE MACHINES

REPUBLIC P-47 THUNDERBOLT

In June 1940, the United States Army Air Corps (USAAC) issued a requirement for new lightweight fighter designs, and among those manufacturers to respond was the Republic Aviation Corporation of Farmingdale, New York. Although a relatively new company, Republic had inherited vast experience in fighter design from its predecessor, the Seversky Aircraft Corporation. Republic's chief engineer, Alexander Kartveli, who, like his former chief, Maj Alexander P. Seversky, was of Russian extraction, had previously designed the P-35 to meet a 1935 USAAC fighter requirement. Republic had also received contracts in September 1939 for limited production of the P-43 Lancer. This aircraft had good high-altitude performance, but it was deemed to be inferior overall to European fighter types such as the Spitfire and Bf 109E.

Kartveli, meanwhile, had a new fighter project on the drawing board called the AP-10, which was a relatively lightweight machine designed around a 1,150hp Allison V-1710-39 liquid-cooled V12 inline engine and armed with two .50in machine guns in the nose. The Allison was more powerful and less expensive than the air-cooled Pratt & Whitney R-1830 radial that had powered the Seversky pursuits, and in 1939 the Curtiss XP-40, with its mechanically supercharged Allison V-1710-19 inline engine, had relegated the Seversky fighters to also-rans.

However, the estimated performance of the AP-10, designated the XP-47 (armed with two .50in nose guns and four .30in machine guns in the wings) and lightweight XP-47A (two nose guns only) by the USAAC, did not meet with official approval. Kartveli therefore abandoned his inline-engined designs so that he could concentrate all of Republic's resources on the development of a radically different fighter aircraft.

The most powerful engine then available was the huge 2,000hp Pratt & Whitney R-2800-21 Double Wasp 18-cylinder two-row radial. Adapting this massive engine to power a fighter aircraft required a great feat of engineering, but Kartveli and his team knew that without it, their design could not possibly meet the performance and load-carrying demands required of the new fighter by the USAAC. A four-bladed 12ft-diameter propeller had to be used to harness the power created by the R-2800, and Kartveli produced an efficient supercharging duct system that offered the least interrupted airflow, using the unorthodox method of designing this feature first and then building up the fuselage around it.

The engine's huge turbosupercharger was stowed internally in the rear fuselage, with the large intake for the air duct mounted beneath the powerplant, together with the oil coolers. Exhaust gases were piped back separately from the engine to the turbosupercharger and expelled through a waste gate in the bottom of the fuselage, with ducted air fed to the centrifugal impeller and returned under pressure via an intercooler to the engine.

Kartveli designed a telescopic landing gear that was nine inches shorter when retracted than when extended so as to make room for the wing installation of no fewer than eight .50in machine guns and their ammunition, which when fired imposed immense loads and stresses on the aircraft that had to be taken into consideration. Last, but not least, the great quantities of fuel necessary to power the 12,086lb beast required internal tanks to hold 307 US gallons of fuel.

The XP-47B Thunderbolt prototype was larger than all previous fighters by a substantial margin. Indeed, it was more than twice the weight of most of its contemporaries, yet the powerful radial engine enabled it to reach a maximum speed of 412mph shortly after making its maiden flight on May 6, 1941.

Across the Atlantic, the appearance of another radial-engined fighter in the shape of the BMW 801-powered Focke-Wulf Fw 190 over France just weeks earlier had caused alarm within the ranks of the RAF. In European terms, the P-47 and the Fw 190 were unusual in concept, as the majority of fighter types in frontline service were powered by liquid-cooled inline engines. However, the Fw 190 in particular outperformed all existing types by a wide margin, with its compact radial engine rendering the Focke-Wulf especially effective at low altitude – a trait that the P-47 would also exhibit once it reached the ETO later in the war.

While the Fw 190 cemented its reputation in combat both on the Channel Front and in the east against the Soviet air force in the early months of 1942, production difficulties and numerous technical problems hindered the development of the Thunderbolt. The first of 171 P-47Bs left the Republic plant in March of that year, but it was not until June that the 56th Fighter Group (FG) was issued with the first examples to reach a frontline unit.

From September 1942 production switched to the P-47C, some 602 examples eventually being built. This variant differed from the B-model in having a slightly lengthened (by 10.5in) forward fuselage, a new engine mounting, changes to the rudder and elevator balance system to improve its flight characteristics and the ability to carry a 200gal ventral drop-tank. The latter permitted units equipped with the aircraft in England (the 56th and 78th FGs had arrived from the US in January 1943, joining the 4th FG, which would swap its Spitfire VBs for P-47Cs) to fly deep penetrations into occupied Europe from July 1943.

THE P-47 THROUGH 360 DEGREES

Assigned to leading P-47 ace LtCol Francis "Gabby" Gabreski, P-47D-25 42-26418 was one of the first "bubbletop" Thunderbolts issued to the 56th FG in the ETO. The leading P-47 Bf 109-killer, Gabreski downed at least four "Gustavs" with this aircraft in June–July 1944, taking his final wartime tally of aerial victories to 28 (11 of which were Bf 109s). Gabreski hit the ground in 42-26418 whilst strafing He 111s at Bassenheim airfield on July 20, 1944, forcing him to crash-land. He spent the rest of the war as a PoW. (Artwork by Chris Davey, © Osprey Publishing)

The P-47C-1 had fixed deflection plates fitted between the oil cooler shutters and the exhaust waste gates, improvements made to its electrical system, undercarriage and brakes, and the addition of a hydraulic flap equalizer. The P-47C-2 differed from the C-1 only by being fitted with a metal-covered rudder and elevators. All early-build P-47s left the factory equipped with the Mk VIII reflector gunsight, as well as a simple ring and post sight, as standard. The K-14 gyroscopic gunsight was eventually factory-installed in Thunderbolts from late 1944, although many P-47s in the ETO had had the sight fitted through base- or depot-level modification.

The factory-installed rear view mirror above the windscreen framing was generally considered inadequate for a pilot to see behind him in combat, so P-47 units tried various mirror arrangements. It was not uncommon for some of the fighters to have three mirrors, with additional ones fitted to the sides of the windscreen framing. Others sported two large Spitfire-type mirrors fixed to the top of the windscreen framing. Plexiglas "bubble" panels originally supplied for better observation on bombers were also fitted in place of the side Plexiglas of the P-47's canopy. Such modifications were rendered superfluous with the development of the "bubbletop" P-47D in the spring of 1944, however.

The P-47D-1, of which 114 were built from December 1942, was the first Thunderbolt model produced at the company's new Evansville, Indiana, plant. It differed little from previous models except for the standardization of water

P-47D-28 44-19790 has its R-2800 Double Wasp radial fettled in the autumn sunshine outside the No. 2 hangar at Boxted on October 11, 1944. This aircraft was assigned to Capt Michael Jackson of the 56th FG's 62nd FS, the eight-kill ace scoring five of his victories (including two Bf 109s) in 44-19790.

injection into the intake manifold to produce more prolonged combat power of 2,300hp at 27,000ft. Other changes included additional armor protection for the pilot, fuel and oxygen system upgrades, and the exhaust ducting was again modified for improved reliability and performance. The 114 P-47D-RAs from Evansville were identical to Farmingdale-built P-47C-2-REs. P-47D-1-REs differed from earlier versions in having an additional pair of flaps on the engine cowl to vastly improve cooling of the R-2800-21 engine, which suffered from cylinder head overheating.

Paddle-bladed airscrews of increased diameter were fitted to the D-models as standard, and these helped absorb the full war emergency power of the R-2800-59 engine. One of the first pilots to fly a P-47D fitted with broader chord propellers in the ETO – in early 1944 – was 1Lt Robert S. Johnson of the 56th FG's 61st FS, who would eventually claim 27 kills (nine of which were Bf 109s) in the Thunderbolt. He provided details of his first flight in a modified P-47 in his postwar autobiography, *THUNDERBOLT!*:

> New Year's Day, and what a present we received. We flew to a maintenance depot at Wattisham to have the Thunderbolts modified. Our engineering officers were making a terrific fuss over a new propeller designed especially for the Thunderbolt. They insisted that the fat paddle blades of the new propellers would bring a tremendous boost in performance, as the increased blade area would permit the props to make the greatest use of the Thunderbolt's 2,000 horsepower. We listened to their enthusiastic ramblings with more than a grain of salt – and never were we more mistaken. What a difference the blades made when I took my modified fighter up for the first time. It quivered and began to shake badly as if partially stalled. The next thing I knew I was in dive and wow! I hauled back on the stick, afraid that the engine would tear right out of the mounts. What I didn't realize was that the new propeller was making all the difference. At 8,000ft I pulled the Thunderbolt into a steep climb. Normally, she'd zoom quickly and then slow down, rapidly approaching a stall. But now the Jug soared up like she'd gone crazy. Another Thunderbolt was in the air, and I pulled alongside, signaling for a climb. I left that other fighter behind as if he were standing still. The Jug stood on her tail and howled her way into the sky. Never again did an Fw 190 or Me 109 outclimb me in the Thunderbolt. The new propeller was worth 1,000hp, and then some.

According to Johnson's CO, the legendary 17.75-kill ace Col Hubert "Hub" Zemke, the "wide blade propeller took a much bigger bite of air and improved the fighter's rate of climb at low altitudes." The props, when combined with the newly introduced water injection equipment which boosted the engine's performance for short intervals, gave the P-47D a dramatic improvement in its rate of climb by around 600ft per minute. "We could now top 30,000ft in about 13 minutes, instead of 20," Zemke recalled. The P-47D's top speed of 433mph at 30,000ft and its formidable performance in the dive made it ideal for flying top cover for high-flying B-17 and B-24 heavy bomber formations that eventually reached as far as Berlin from bases in eastern England.

For the fighter-bomber role, the aircraft's "universal" wing and underbelly mountings permitted various combinations of up to 2,500lb of bombs, two 150gal tanks and one 75gal tank and, later, rocket projectiles in a tube cluster. A full bombload meant that ammunition for each of the six or eight .50in machine guns was reduced from 425 to 267 rounds, but the Thunderbolt's firepower remained undiminished.

P-47 ace Bob Johnson poses for an official USAAF photo with his crew chief and armorer. With his score at 27, beating that of America's legendary World War I ace Eddie Rickenbacker, USAAF chiefs sent him home to a publicity tour, factory visits and War Bond fundraising. (USAAF)

During strafing attacks, the weight of the bombload and drop-tanks added to that of the aircraft resulted in a terrific increase in speed when the fighter went into a dive. It could cause a surge or vapor lock in the fuel lines, as the fuel pump was unable to meet the G-loads imposed, and a number of P-47s suffered engine failure over enemy territory as a result of this problem. The P-47D-15 was the first Thunderbolt built with underwing pylons and fuel system plumbing within the wings to allow the aircraft to fly with expendable fuel tanks. Internal fuel capacity was also boosted to 375gal and the overall bombload increased to 2,500lb. Finally, the canopy was made completely jettisonable too. The "razorback" P-47D was built in numerous sub-variants, ranging from the D-1 up to the D-24, and these differed from one another in respect to their engine specification and wing weapon/plumbing fit.

The first major structural change to the Thunderbolt came with production of the P-47D-25 in late 1943. In July of that year, the last D-5 built was given a cut-down rear fuselage and a clear-view bubble canopy sourced from a British Hawker Typhoon. Designated the XP-47K, the aircraft proved to be so popular with test pilots that the new "blown" Perspex canopy was immediately introduced to the Thunderbolt production line starting with the P-47D-25-RE at Farmingdale and the P-47D-26-RA at Evansville.

Prior to the phasing out of production of the "razorback" Thunderbolt, some 3,962 D-models had been built at Farmingdale and 1,461 at Evansville. From the "Dash 25" onwards, the two plants produced 2,547 and 4,632 D-models. By the time the first of these aircraft – unofficially dubbed "Superbolts" by frontline pilots – reached the ETO, aircraft were being delivered to the USAAF unpainted. The 56th FG received its first P-47D-25s in May 1944, and Col "Hub" Zemke was an early recipient as he recalled in his autobiography *The HUB – Fighter Leader*:

> The one-piece clear cockpit canopy provided the pilot with excellent all round visibility, and helped cut down the fatigue from neck twisting. The only drawback was that the rear fuselage cockpit fairing had been removed, affecting the directional stability of the aircraft. The other welcome change with the Superbolt was an enlarged internal fuel tank providing an extra 65 gallons. This allowed us to take the maximum advantage of our external tanks, for we could push much farther into Germany and still be able to return on internally held fuel.

P-47D-25 WING GUNS ▲

All versions of the P-47 Thunderbolt were armed with either six or eight Browning M2 .50in machine guns, split three or four per wing. The wing magazines contained 425 rounds per gun, although this number had to be reduced to 267 rounds per gun from the P-47D-15 onwards if the fighter was carrying a bombload of 1,000lb or additional fuel tanks affixed to its newly introduced underwing pylons (one per wing). (Artwork by Chris Davey, © Osprey Publishing)

By the time production of the P-47D ended with the D-40-RA, which featured a dorsal fin (first installed as a retrofit in the field on the D-27) to cure instability problems that had always afflicted the "bubbletop" Thunderbolt, some 12,602 D-models had been built – the largest production quantity of one sub-type of any US fighter ever produced.

The next P-47 variant to attain series production was the high-speed M-model, hastily built to combat the V1 flying bomb threat in the summer of 1944. The aircraft was essentially a late-build P-47D fitted with a more powerful R-2800-57(C) engine that boasted an uprated CH-5 turbosupercharger, the latter having been trialed in the XP-47J – this machine attained 504mph during flight tests in 1944. The P-47M was also fitted with airbrakes in the wings to help the pilot slow the big fighter down when trying to achieve a firing position behind a slower enemy aircraft.

Just 130 "sprint" P-47Ms were built, and these were used exclusively by the 56th FG from the late summer of 1944. Abnormally low cylinder head temperatures, breakdown of the ignition systems at high altitude and other engine problems dogged P-47M operations, and the group enjoyed only moderate success with the aircraft.

The final variant to attain production was the P-47N, which was significantly different to the ubiquitous D-model. The aircraft was fitted with a new long-span wing tailored to cope with the much-increased weight of the Thunderbolt – it also contained fuel cells for the very first time. The wing, which was 18in greater in span and boasted 22 sq ft of extra area, incorporated larger ailerons and square-cut tips that significantly increased the roll rate. The fighter's undercarriage was also strengthened to meet the rise in weight by 750lb to 21,200lb. Large orders were placed for the aircraft, but Farmingdale had completed just 1,667 airframes and Evansville 149 when contracts were canceled in December 1945 in the wake of VE- and VJ-Days.

It was intended that the P-47N would equip the 56th FG, but the war ended before the "Wolf Pack" could get them into combat, and the type was used exclusively in the Pacific theater, where its extended range made the aircraft an excellent strategic bomber escort. P-47D/Ns remained in USAF service for a number of years after the war, passing to Air National Guard units before being phased out of service in 1955. By then all surviving Thunderbolts had been redesignated F-47D/Ns. Altogether, 15,683 examples of the Thunderbolt were built. Although not as high a number as for the Bf 109, Spitfire or Yak series of fighters, this figure makes the P-47 the most-produced American fighter of all time.

MESSERSCHMITT Bf 109 F/G/K

In the autumn of 1940, Messerschmitt's E-model replacement in the form of the Bf 109F-1 began rolling off production lines in Germany. This aircraft differed from its Battle of Britain-era predecessor primarily in its weaponry. The F-model saw the wing guns deleted in favor of a single engine-mounted cannon firing through the propeller hub, in addition to two upper cowling-mounted machine guns. Various hydraulic and cooling system improvements were also incorporated, as was additional pilot and fuel tank armor. Externally, the fighter was also more streamlined around the nose, and lengthened overall. The tail section was tidied up aerodynamically, with the deletion of the horizontal stabilizer bracing. Finally, the F-model's wing was completely redesigned, with the wingtips extended and rounded.

Production of the Bf 109F numbered 3,300-plus airframes built over four sub-variants (F-1 to F-4), and ran from September 1940 through to May 1942. Like the Emil, the "Friedrich" performed both fighter and fighter-bomber missions in eastern and western Europe, the Mediterranean and in North Africa.

The F-model was replaced on the production line in June 1942 by the Bf 109G, which combined the Friedrich's refined airframe with the larger, heavier and considerably more powerful 1,475hp DB 605 engine. Cockpit pressurization was also introduced for the first time with the G-1, although most later sub-variants lacked this feature. Produced in staggering numbers from mid-1942 through to war's end, some 24,000-plus Bf 109Gs were constructed in total – including an overwhelming 14,212 in 1944 alone.

Numerous modifications to the basic G-1 were introduced either in the factory (as *Umrüst-Bausätze* factory conversion sets) or in the field (*Rüstsätze* kits), and these included the provision for extra armament, additional radios, introduction of a wooden tailplane, the fitting of a lengthened tailwheel and the installation of the MW-50 water/methanol-boosted DB 605D engine. In an attempt to standardize the equipment of the frontline force, Messerschmitt began production of the Bf 109G-6 in February 1943, and this model included many of these previously ad hoc additions. The G-6 would ultimately prove to be the most important variant of Messerschmitt's famous fighter, with 12,000-plus examples being built – more than a third of the overall production run for the Bf 109.

Unfortunately, the continual addition of weighty items like underwing cannon gondolas, rocket tubes and larger engines to the once slight airframe of the Bf 109 eliminated much of the fighter's once legendary maneuverability, and instead served to emphasize the aircraft's poor slow-speed performance, tricky lateral control and ground handling. Yet in the late-war Bf 109G-10 model, fitted

Bf 109G-5/6 UPPER COWLING GUNS

Like previous versions of the Bf 109, the Gustav was fitted with a pair of upper cowling guns. These had initially taken the form of Rheinmetall MG 17 7.92mm weapons, but from the G-5/6 onwards, the weapons installed were MG 131 13mm machine guns produced by the same company. Each weapon had a magazine holding 300 rounds.

Bf 109G UNDERWING GUN

The Gustav could supplement its engine and cowling guns with two 20mm Mauser MG 151/20 cannon in underwing gondolas (a MK 108-equipped gondola was also developed). These were fitted to the aircraft as part of a field-installed Rüstsätze R kit. Each weapon drew its ammunition from a 120-round magazine. The widely used G-6 was the version most associated with underwing cannon, with this fitment rarely being seen on subsequent Gustav variants.

Bf 109G ENGINE-MOUNTED GUN

As with some earlier versions of the Bf 109, the Gustav also boasted an engine-mounted cannon – either a 20mm Mauser MG 151/20 or 30mm Rheinmetall MK 108 weapon. The MG 151/20 had a 200-round magazine and the MK 108 60 rounds of ammunition. The latter weapon, although highly destructive, was unreliable and prone to jamming. (Artwork by Chris Davey, © Osprey Publishing)

with the Erla Haube bulged canopy, tall wooden tailplane and DB 605D engine, Messerschmitt had a fighter capable of achieving speeds up to 429mph at 24,280ft. Confusingly, although the G-10 appeared numerically after the lightened G-14 in the sub-variant list for the Bf 109G, it was in fact the last production G-model to see service!

The last main operational version of the Bf 109 was the K-series, which was developed directly from the Gustav. The K-4 was the only sub-variant to see frontline service, and this aircraft boasted a DB 605DM engine, wooden tail construction and single cannon and twin machine gun armament. All major Bf 109G/K variants that fought with the P-47 in 1943–45 are described in detail in the next section.

TYPE HISTORY

P-47 THUNDERBOLT

P-47B

The P-47B was the initial production version of the Thunderbolt, which differed from the prototype only in having a sliding hood in place of the hinged canopy, an SCR-774 radio (with a redesigned forward-slanted aerial), metal-skinned control surfaces, production 2,000hp R-2800-21 engine and General Electric A-13 turbosupercharger. The addition of internal operational equipment increased the aircraft's gross weight by 1,270lb to 13,356lb, although maximum level speed was increased to 429mph. The first five B-models built became preproduction test and evaluation aircraft. A total of 171 P-47Bs were completed in total, all at Farmingdale.

P-47C

Similar to the P-47B, the P-47C-1-RE (RE was factory designation for Farmingdale) was fitted with a 2,300hp R-2800-59 that featured an A-17 turbosupercharger regulator. Aircraft also had a slightly longer forward fuselage, which had been extended 8in at the firewall (increasing overall length from 35ft to 36ft 1in) to create a better center of gravity and make the engine accessories compartment roomier and easier to work in. This variant also had the provision for a belly-mounted bomb or drop tank. The C-2-RE featured metal-covered rudder and elevators, as well as a revised oxygen system. The follow-on C-5-RE had an upright radio mast in place of the forward-sloped example previously fitted. The first P-47C was completed on September 14, 1942, and a total of 602 were eventually built.

P-47D-1 THROUGH TO D-10

The D-1-RA (114 built) was the first P-47 model to emerge from the new Evansville, Indiana, plant from December 1942 – RA was the Evansville factory designation. It was essentially similar to the C-5. The D-1-RE had additional cowling flaps, improved pilot armor and a new radio mast – all 105 were built at Farmingdale. The D-2-RA (200 built) was similar to the D-1-RE, as was the D-2-RE (445 built), which also featured minor upgrades to the fuel system. Some 100 D-3-RAs were then constructed, and these were similar to the D-2-RE. The D-5-RE (300 built) was based on the D-1-RE, but with modifications to the aircraft's fuel and hydraulic systems. The D-4-RA (200 built) was similar to the D-5-RE. The D-6-RE (350 built) was effectively a D-1-RE with two-point shackles for a bomb or a drop tank under the fuselage. The D-10-RE (250 built) was also based on the D-1-RE, but with further improvements to the hydraulic system and the fitment of a General Electric C-23 turbosupercharger.

P-47D-11 THROUGH TO D-23

The D-11-RE (400 built) was fitted with a 2,300hp R-2800-63 engine that featured water injection, as was the identical Evansville D-11-RA (250 built). The D-15-RE (496 built) introduced single stations for a bomb or drop tank beneath each wing panel and an increased payload that meant it could carry two 1,000lb or three 500lb bombs. The D-15-RA (157 built) was identical in specification. The D-16-RE (254 built) was based on the D-11-RE, but it could run on 100/150-octane fuel – just 29 D-16-RAs of a similar specification were built. The D-20-RE (250 built) was powered by a 2,300hp R-2800-59, and it also had a raised tailwheel strut, General Electric ignition harness and other minor airframe modifications – Evansville built 187 D-20-RAs to an identical specification. Delivered in natural metal finish, the D-21-RE (216 built) had manual water injection control for the engine, but was otherwise similar to the D-11-RE. The D-21-RA (224 built) was essentially the same as the D-21-RE. The D-22-RE (850 built) featured the 13ft Hamilton Standard paddle-blade propeller and an A-23 turbosupercharger regulator. Featuring the same engine modification, the D-23-RA (889 built) was fitted with a Curtiss Electric 13ft paddle-blade propeller.

P-47D-25 THROUGH TO D-40

The D-25-RE (385 built) was the first P-47 fitted with a teardrop canopy and cut-down rear fuselage. The aircraft also had an increased supply of oxygen and some of its fuselage-located systems repositioned to allow its fuel capacity to be increased to 270 US gallons. The D-26-RA (250 built) was similar to the D-25-RE, as was the D-27-RE (615 built) bar minor fuel system modifications. The D-28-RA (1,028 built) was based on the D-26-RA. The D-28-RE (750 built) was similar to the D-25-RE, although it was fitted with a Curtiss Electric 13ft paddle-blade propeller. The D-30-RE (800 built) was also based on the D-25-RE, but it had five stubs beneath each wing for High-Velocity Aerial Rockets – the D-30-RA (1,800 built) was built to the same specification. The final D-model sub-variants to be built were the D-35-RA and D-40-RA, of which 665 were constructed in 1944–45. These versions featured a dorsal fin for increased stability.

Tracer and a night gunnery exercise demonstrate the configuration and power of the P-47's eight .50cal machine guns. (USAAF)

P-47G

Basically similar to the C-1-RE, 20 P-47G-CUs were the first Thunderbolts built on the new Curtiss-Wright line at Buffalo, New York, in late 1942. These were fitted with R-2800-21 engines and Curtiss Electric 12ft 2in propellers. Subsequent production covered the G-1-CU (40 built), similar to the C-5-RE, G-5-CU (60 built), similar to the D-1-RE, G-10-CU (80 built), similar to the D-6-RE, and G-15-CU (154 built), similar to the D-11-RE. Most were assigned to training units in the USA, where they were fitted with the mounting points for a blind-flying hood inside the canopy. They were designated as TP-47Gs when used by training units.

P-47M-1

Farmingdale hastily constructed the M-1-RE (130 built), featuring a 2,800hp R-2800-57 with an uprated CH-5 turbosupercharger. The aircraft was also fitted with airbrakes in the wings, but was otherwise identical to the D-30-RE. All were sent to the 56th FG in the autumn of 1944, where dorsal fins were fitted in the field.

P-47N

The final production variant, the N-1-RE (550 built) saw the P-47D-27-RE fuselage, fitted with an R-2800-57 engine and CH-5 turbosupercharger driving a Curtiss Electric 13ft paddle-blade propeller, combined with a new long-span wing

P-47D-25: IN THE COCKPIT

1. Rudder trim tab control
2. Aileron trim tab control
3. Elevator trim tab control crank
4. Cockpit spotlight
5. Wing flap control handle
6. Landing gear control handle
7. Gun safety switch
8. Fuel selector valves
9. Supercharger control
10. Throttle
11. Microphone push-to-talk button
12. Propeller control
13. Mixture control
14. Hydraulic hand pump
15. Main switch box
16. Circuit breakers
17. Dive flap controls
18. Canopy open/close switch
19. Control switch box for constant speed propeller
20. Ammeter
21. Master battery switch
22. Ignition switch
23. Air speed indicator
24. Clock
25. Rear radar warning lamp
26. K-14A gunsight
27. Rearview mirror
28. Landing gear warning lights
29. Directional gyro turn indicator
30. Artificial horizon
31. Carburetor air temperature gauge
32. Turbo rpm gauge
33. Fuel pressure warning lights
34. Oil and fuel pressure temperature gauge
35. Defroster control lever
36. Engine primer
37. Oil temperature gauge
38. Cowl flap control lever
39. Control column
40. Rudder pedals
41. Altimeter
42. Turn and bank indicator
43. Accelerometer
44. Rate of climb indicator
45. Suction gauge
46. Engine hours gauge
47. Compass
48. Fuel warning light
49. Fuel contents gauge
50. Gun firing button
51. Manifold pressure gauge
52. Hydraulic and oxygen pressure gauges
53. Engine starter switches
54. Tachometer
55. Recognition light switches
56. Oxygen regulator
57. Flare pistol port cover
58. Crystal filter selector switch
59. Cockpit vent control
60. Tailwheel lock
61. VHF radio control box
62. Command transmitter control box
63. Identification light switches
64. IFF radio destroyer buttons
65. Command receiver control box
66. Pilot's seat

Bf 109G-6: IN THE COCKPIT

1. Revi C/12D reflector gunsight (later series used Revi 16B)
2. Gunsight padding
3. Ammunition counters
4. Armament switch
5. Repeater compass
6. Artificial horizon/turn and bank indicator
7. Manifold pressure gauge
8. AFN2 homing indicator (for FuG16ZY only)
9. Tumbler switch
10. Canopy jettison lever
11. Main light switch
12. Instrument panel light
13. Ignition switch
14. Start plug cleansing switch
15. Altimeter
16. Airspeed indicator
17. Tachometer
18. Propeller pitch position indicator
19. Fuel warning lamp
20. Combined coolant exit and oil intake temperature indicator
21. Starter switch
22. Fuel contents gauge
23. Undercarriage position indicator
24. Undercarriage control switch
25. Undercarriage switch
26. Undercarriage emergency release lever
27. Dual oil and fuel content gauge
28. Throttle
29. Throttle-mounted propeller pitch control thumbswitch
30. Dust filter handgrip
31. Bomb release button
32. Firing trigger
33. Control column
34. Auxiliary fuel contents indicator
35. Rudder pedal
36. Radiator cut-off handle
37. Ventilation control lever
38. Oil cooler flap control
39. Fuel cock lever
40. 20mm MG151/20 cannon breech cover
41. Radiator shutter control lever
42. FuG16ZY radio control panel
43. Drop tank fuel pipe
44. Oxygen supply indicator
45. Oxygen pressure gauge
46. Radio control panel
47. Oxygen supply
48. Fuel injection primer pump
49. Tailplane incidence indicator
50. Undercarriage emergency lowering handwheel
51. Tailplane trim adjustment wheel
52. Seat
53. Radio tuner panel

(Artwork by Jim Laurier, © Osprey Publishing)

18in greater in span and 22 sq ft larger in area. The latter also incorporated larger ailerons and square-cut tips. Numerous detail design changes were also incorporated, and extra fuel in the wings gave a total of 186 US gallons – single 300 US gallon drop tanks could be carried beneath each wing. A further 550 N-5-REs followed, and these were similar to the N-1-REs bar the addition of rocket launchers, AN/APS-13 tail warning radar and provision for a General Electric C-1 autopilot. The N-15-RE (200 built) was similar to the N-1-RE except for the addition of an S-1 bomb rack and K-14A/B gunsight. The N-20-RE (200 built) was also similar to the N-1-RE, bar a new radio, as was the N-20-RA (149 built) except for minor cockpit changes. The N-25-RE (167 built) was the final production version, and this too was similar to the N-1-RE except for the addition of autopilot, a new cockpit floor and strengthened ailerons to deflect rocket blast.

MESSERSCHMITT Bf 109G/K

Bf 109G-1 AND -2

Although looking very similar to the Bf 109F, the G-series was built to take advantage of the increased power output of the DB 605 engine, and the ability of the latter to be power-boosted to increase its performance in speed and altitude. Pressurized versions were also built in an effort to counter increased high-altitude raids being made by USAAF heavy bombers. Additional armor was also a feature of G-series aircraft, as was their improved armament, whereby rifle-caliber machine guns were replaced by hard-hitting 13mm, 20mm and 30mm cannon. This also meant the return of wing armament. Both the G-1 and -2 entered service in June 1942, with the former being pressurized for high-altitude combat and the latter unpressurized. Both were to be powered by the DB 605A, B or C, with each version being essentially the same bar different gear ratios – early G-1s also featured GM 1 nitrous oxide power boosting. Armament initially consisted of two nose-mounted 7.92mm MG 17 machine guns and a hub-firing MG 151 20mm cannon. A G-2 Trop version was used in tropical and rough theaters such as North Africa, this variant having additional engine filtering. Like all G-series aircraft, many

A III./JG 2 *Gruppe Spiess* (senior NCO), with his hand on the exhaust shroud, supervises the return of a Bf 109F-2 into its small wooden hangar at St Pol in the summer of 1941.

G-1/2s were modified in the field to meet specific operational requirements. These *Rüstsätze* alterations allowed the aircraft to be carry a centerline bomb rack (R1 and R2), drop tank (R3) or antipersonnel bombs (R4), underwing MG 151 pods (R6), or fuselage-mounted cameras (R2, and R3 from 1943). Some 164 G-1s and 1,614 G-2s were built.

Bf 109G-3 AND -4

The unpressurized Bf 109G-4 actually appeared in the frontline before the pressurized G-3, making its combat debut in November 1942. A total of 1,100 G-4s were produced between September 1942 and May 1943 (with additional aircraft built in Hungary between July and September 1943). Just 50 G-3s were constructed in January–February 1943. The G-3/4 differed from the G-1/2 by having a FuG 16Z radio installed in place of the FuG 7a – the aerial wire arrangement was changed also. The *Rüstsätze* sets made available were identical in content and designation to those fitted to the G-1/2, and Messerschmitt also produced an *Umrüst-Bauzätze U* modification for the G-3 too. Designated the U2, it referred to an uprated type of GM 1 power-boosting, combined with the fitment of a propeller from an Me 210.

Bf 109G-5 AND -6

The unpressurized Bf 109G-6 and pressurized G-5 were issued to frontline units from February and September 1943, respectively. In their initial form, they only differed from the G-3/4 in having cowling-mounted 13mm MG 131 machine guns rather than 7.92mm MG 17 weapons. The large breechblocks associated with the MG 131 could only be housed by modifying the upper fuselage engine cowlings to incorporate distinctive *beulen* (boils) that in turn came to symbolize all late war Bf 109Gs. Powered by a DB 605A with GM 1 or a DB 605AS incorporating the larger supercharger of the DB 603 (designated the G-5/AS, and with no *beulen*), fewer than 500 G-5s were built. These were the last pressurized Bf 109s constructed for frontline use, as cockpit pressurization was found to be of dubious operational value. Once again, with the G-5 the *Rüstsätze* sets made available were identical in content and designation to those fitted to previous G-series aircraft, with the addition of the R2 (reconnaissance), R5 (underwing cannon pods) and R7 (extra navigation aids). *Umrüst-Bauzätze U* modifications, often combined with *Rüstsätze* sets, were also produced, with the U2 being GM 1 power-boosted and featuring a wooden tailplane of increased height (and revised fin-and-rudder assembly), and the U4 having a MK 108 30mm cannon replacing the hub-firing MG 151. Finally, the Bf 109G-5/AS was

THE Bf 109G THROUGH 360 DEGREES

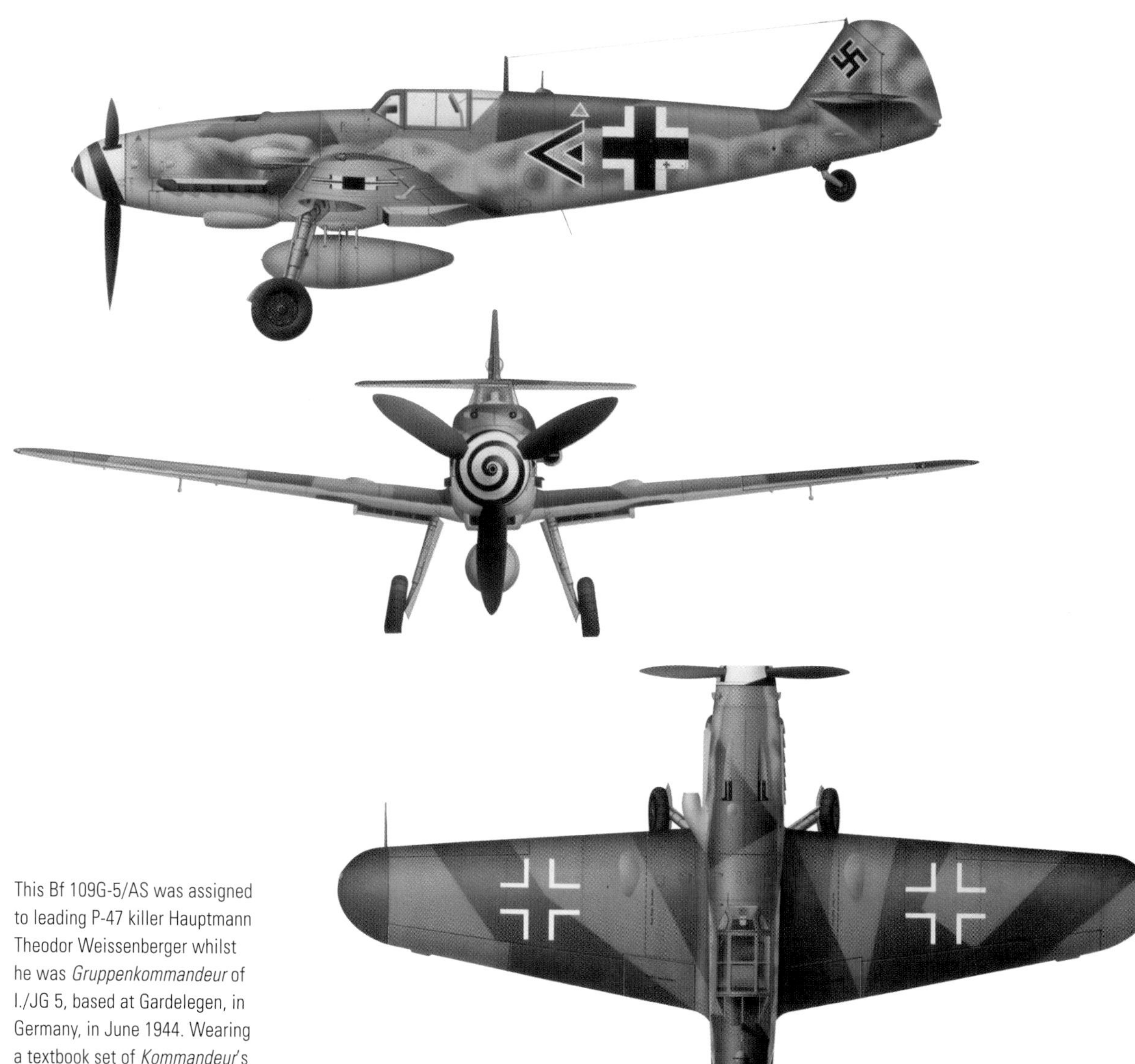

This Bf 109G-5/AS was assigned to leading P-47 killer Hauptmann Theodor Weissenberger whilst he was *Gruppenkommandeur* of I./JG 5, based at Gardelegen, in Germany, in June 1944. Wearing a textbook set of *Kommandeur*'s markings in the form of "double black chevrons" on either side of its fuselage, this was reportedly the aircraft that newly appointed Weissenberger flew to the Normandy front shortly after the Allied invasion of June 6, 1944. He used this Gustav to down the majority of the 13 P-47s he claimed destroyed in June–July 1944. (Artwork by Chris Davey, © Osprey Publishing)

powered by the DB 605AS engine, and its supercharger was housed within a bulged fairing on the port side of the forward fuselage – this variant had no *beulen* as a result. Unlike the G-5, the Bf 109G-6 was built in staggering numbers, with more than 12,000 examples rolling off production lines between the late autumn of 1942 and June 1944.

Built as the first "standard" model Gustav that was intended from the outset to accept any of the ever-increasing number of *Rüstsätze* sets emanating from Messerschmitt, the G-6 was also capable of being powered by several versions of the DB 605A – the uprated DB 605D was also made available from January 1944. The G-6 was also the first Gustav variant capable of carrying the engine-mounted MK 108 cannon. However, production of this awesome 30mm weapon was delayed to the extent that a considerable number of G-6s were built with the MG 151 fitted instead. As with the G-5, the Rüstsätze sets available for the G-6 followed the R designation pattern put in place with the G-1/2. The only real changes unique to this variant centered on the late (1944) R2 set, which covered the fitment of a single WGr 21 mortar launcher beneath each wing. Numerous *Umrüst-Bauzätze* modifications were to feature, however, starting with the U2 that saw the fighter fitted with a GM 1-boosted engine and a wooden tailplane similar to that used by the G-5/U2. The U4 saw the MK 108 replace the MG 151, while the U5 had underwing MK 108s instead of the 20mm cannon. The U6 was similarly armed, but also had the engine-mounted MG 151 replaced with an MK 108. Various G-6s had clear vision Erla Haube hoods fitted in the field in place of the conventional framed canopy. Finally, the Bf 109G-6/AS was powered by the DB 605AS engine, and like the G-5/AS, it had a supercharger bulge rather than MG 131 *beulen*.

Bf 109G-8

Produced in small numbers, the G-8 was a specialized tactical photo-reconnaissance version of the G-6 that was built to support ground forces. This variant appeared in August 1943, and featured a vertically-mounted camera (either an RB 12.5/7 or RB 32/7) in the center fuselage. Again, the *Rüstsätze* sets available for the G-8 followed the R designation pattern put in place with the G-1/2, with the only unique one to this variant being the R5 set which saw the aircraft fitted with a FuG 16 ZS radio – the latter operated on Army frequencies. Two *Umrüst-Bauzätze* kits were also made available, with the U2 seeing the aircraft fitted with the GM 1-boosted engine modification and the U3 featuring a DB 605D with MW 50 methanol-water injection. All G-8s had their MG 131 fuselage guns deleted, the aircraft relying on the hub-firing MK 108 or MG 151 for self-defense.

Bf 109G-12

Produced ahead of the Bf 109G-14 and G-10, the G-12 was a dedicated two-seat trainer version of the Gustav created through the conversion of existing G-2/4/6 airframes. A total of 494 G-12s were modified by Blohm & Voss between September 1943 and December 1944. To make room for the second seat, the aircraft's fuel capacity was reduced from 400 to 235 liters. The instructor sat in the rear seat and spoke with the student pilot via an intercom. The sole *Rüstsätze* kit available for the G-12 was the R3, which allowed the aircraft to carry a 300-liter drop tank.

Bf 109G-14

Very similar in specification and appearance to late-build G-6s, the DB 605AM-powered Bf 109G-14 began appearing in the frontline in July 1944 after Messerschmitt decided to incorporate the MW 50 power-boost as standard equipment on all piston-engined fighters then in production – this was previously available as the U3 modification on the G-6. The G-14 also had the FuG 16ZY radio fitted as standard too, this equipment being retrofitted to late-build G-6s. The *Rüstsätze* kits available for the aircraft covered fighter-bomber conversion with a bomb rack (R1), extended range with a 300-liter drop tank (R3), heavy fighter with two underwing MG 151s (R5) and an all-weather fighter with autopilot and FuG 125 radio (R6). The sole *Umrüst-Bauzätze* kit was the U4, which saw the G-14 replace its hub-firing MG 151 with a MK 108, and a wooden tail assembly fitted instead of one in metal. The Bf 109G-14/AS was powered by the DB 605AS engine, and like the G-5/AS, it had a supercharger bulge rather than MG 131 *beulen*. The Erla Haube hood was widely fitted to this variant, but it did not totally replace the original framed G-model canopy. The aircraft had an underwing Morane mast as well as a Zielfluganlage D/F loop and a FuG 25a IFF antenna below the fuselage.

Bf 109G-10

Appearing after the Bf 109K series, and thus earning the distinction of being the last sub-type built before war's end, the Bf 109G-10 first appeared in the autumn of 1944. Officially defined as a "bastard type" by the Luftwaffe, the aircraft combined the 1,850hp methanol-water injected DB 605DM engine of the Bf 109K-4 with the G-14/AS airframe. However, a chronic shortage of these engines saw DB 605ASs routinely fitted in their place, and as with all AS-powered Bf 109G/Ks, these particular aircraft had a supercharger bulge rather than MG 131 *beulen*. As with the G-12, the Erla Haube hood was widely fitted to this variant also, but once again it did not totally replace the original framed

Firmly chocked, a Bf 109G-14 of 9./JG 26 has its DB 605AM engine run up at Lille-Nord just a few weeks prior to the D-Day landings. The distinctive *beulen* synonymous with late-build Gustavs are clearly visible in this close-up view. Note also the original-style canopy and 300-liter centerline drop tank.

G-model canopy. The *Rüstsätze* kits available were identical to those for the G-14, with the addition of the R2 reconnaissance fit that included RB 50/30 or RB 75/30 cameras, the R7 underwing WGr 21 launcher kit and the R8, which featured a BSK 16 gun camera. And like the G-14, the only *Umrüst-Bauzätze* kit for the G-10 was the U4, which replaced the hub-firing MG 151 with a MK 108, and saw a wooden tail assembly fitted instead of a metal one.

Bf 109K-4

Continuing delays with the mass production of new German jet fighters forced the RLM to keep building Bf 109s until war's end. Realizing that production of various *Umrüst-Bauzätze* and *Rüstsätze* kits was slowing overall production, the RLM decided to rationalize things by ordering Messerschmitt to incorporate the best of the G-model upgrades into a single airframe, which was in turn designated the Bf 109K-4. Like the G-10 (which actually appeared after the K-4), the new aircraft would be powered by the DB 605DM with MW 50 boost. The K-model would also incorporate as much non-strategic material (such as wood and steel sheeting) within its structure as was possible. The armament was upgraded to two 13mm MG 131 machine guns in the cowling and a hub-firing MK 108 30mm cannon. As with several other late-build variants of the Bf 109G, the aircraft's tail assembly was made entirely of wood, and a longer, retractable, tailwheel was also fitted to some, but not all, K-4s. Yet another late-build G-model modification to be found in the K-4 was the employment of broad chord propeller blades.

P-47D THUNDERBOLT vs Bf 109G COMPARISON SPECIFICATIONS		
	P-47D-25	Bf 109G-6
Powerplant	2,300hp R-2800-59	1,800hp DB 605AM
Dimensions		
Span	40ft 9.25in	32ft 6.5in
Length	36ft 1.75in	29ft 7in
Height	14ft 2in	8ft 2.5in
Wing area	300 sq ft	174.37 sq ft
Weights		
Empty	10,000lb	5,893lb
Loaded	19,400lb	7,491lb
Performance		
Max speed	429mph at 27,800ft	385mph at 22,640ft
Range	475 miles (without tanks)	447 miles (without tanks)
Climb	to 20,000ft in 11 min	to 18,700ft in 6 min
Service ceiling	42,000ft	37,890ft
Armament	8x .50in Brownings	2x 13mm MG 131 1x 20mm MG 151

The fighter also lacked an antenna mast. The first K-4s entered service in October 1944, and they were the only sub-type of the final Bf 109 series to see combat – some 1,500-plus had been built by VE-Day. Again, *Rüstsätze* kits were available, covering the fitment of a bomb rack (R1), RB 50/30 or RB 75/30 cameras and FuG 16ZS radio (R2), extended range 300-liter drop tank (R3), two underwing MG 151s (R4) and the installation of a BSK 16 gun camera (R6) in the left wing. Many K-4s had no MG 131 *beulen*, and most were fitted with the Erla Haube hood. Finally, the aircraft had an underwing Morane mast as well as a Zielfluganlage D/F loop and a FuG 25a IFF antenna beneath the fuselage. There were no *Umrüst-Bauzätze* kits produced by Messerschmitt for the K-4.

THE STRATEGIC SITUATION

Following the invasion of the Soviet Union in June 1941, the *Jagdwaffe* fighter force in the west consisted of JG 1 in northwest Germany, JG 26 in the Pas de Calais and the Low Countries and JG 2 defending the Atlantic coast ports of France. JG 2 and JG 26 had nine *Staffeln* each (a *Staffel* having a strength of 12 aircraft), grouped into three *Gruppen* apiece. A total of around 200 Bf 109E/Fs therefore defended the Channel Front at any given time in 1941–42.

At intervals, *Gruppen* or *Staffeln* from JG 2 and JG 26 would be sent to other fronts, and their place taken by units from *Jagdgeschwaderen* posted in from the

Mediterranean or the Eastern Front. Such rotation allowed the Luftwaffe to maintain its fighter strength at approximately 200 aircraft.

With Allied air power in the west steadily increasing throughout 1942, and the USAAF's Eighth Air Force arriving in the UK in the late summer of that year, this force of 200 Bf 109Fs and Fw 190As found it increasingly hard to repel daylight bombing raids on industrial and strategic targets. In the spring of 1943, when the P-47 groups of VIII Fighter Command commenced operations in defense of USAAF heavy bombers, the *Jagdwaffe* in the west was forced to call on reinforcements from *Gruppen* in the east. By late July, a further five *Jagdgruppen* had been withdrawn from the southern USSR and Italy and sent to Germany to strengthen the day fighter arm defending the Third Reich.

One of the first units pulled back was Bf 109G-equipped III./JG 54, which arrived from the east in February 1943. I./JG 27 followed from North Africa shortly afterwards, and the last of the trio of Gustav-equipped *Gruppen* posted in was I./JG 3, transferred west from Stalingrad. A further increase in the ranks of the *Jagdwaffe* in the west was achieved in April when two of JG 1's four *Gruppen* were redesignated as units of the newly-formed JG 11, which continued to fly Bf 109Gs. Thus,

VIII Fighter Command's fighter groups were based in East Anglia so that they could be as close to targets in occupied Europe as possible. Most of these airfields were built from scratch especially for the USAAF, in a massive construction program launched in 1942.

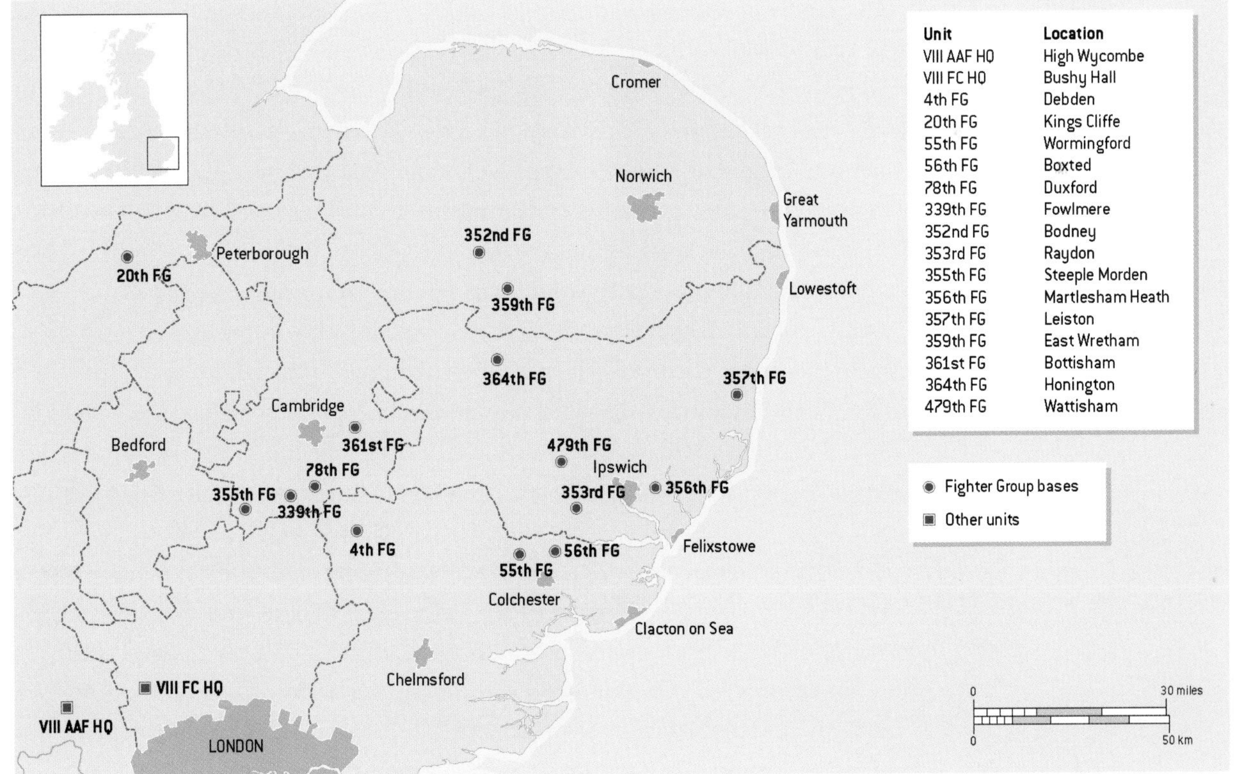

by mid-1943, the Bf 109 strength in the west consisted of eight main *Gruppen*, five of which were deployed along the Channel and North Sea coastlines from Biscay to the German Bight – the main routes used by the Eighth Air Force.

From west to east, the five *Gruppen* were II./JG 2, III./JG 26, III./JG 54 and II. and III./JG 11. The first two units formed part of Luftflotte 3, which was the frontline "air fleet" guarding outermost ramparts of occupied northwestern Europe. Bf 109G-equipped I./JG 27 was also part of Luftflotte 3, as was III./JG 54 for a short while. The three Bf 109 *Gruppen* of JGs 1 and 11, together with I./JG 3, were subordinated to Luftwaffenbefehlshaber Mitte (the forerunner of Luftflotte Reich), although purely for defense of the homeland. Sitting astride the "heavies'" main routes of approach into northwestern Germany, JGs 1 and 11 bore the brunt of much of the action in 1943.

The early official pedantry issued by Luftwaffe HQ that the Bf 109 units were to engage only fighter escorts that were in attendance, leaving the Fw 190As to concentrate on the bomber boxes, soon became an irrelevance in the heat of battle. Now, entire *Gruppen* and, on occasion, *Geschwader* of defending fighters would be sent up to do battle in the latter half of 1943 where previously single *Schwärme* or *Staffeln* had sufficed.

Buoyed by its successes against the USAAF heavy bombers in the summer, the *Jagdwaffe* introduced a second wave of reinforcements to the Reich's Defense organization in the autumn of 1943. II. and III./JG 3 were duly pulled out of Russia and sent to join I./JG 3 in western Germany. In line with persisting doctrine, which stipulated that home defense *Geschwader* should consist of two anti-bomber *Gruppen* and one *Gruppe* of covering fighters, II./JG 3 received a batch of new Bf 109G-5 high-altitude fighters to add to its G-6s. In reality, the "light" fighter *Gruppe* would down as many bombers as fighters in coming months.

II./JG 27 and II./JG 51 were also transferred in for homeland defense from Italy at this time, both units again being equipped with Bf 109Gs. These new *Gruppen* combined with those already in-theater to inflict such severe losses on USAAF bomber formations during raids on Schweinfurt and Regensburg in August, September and October that the Americans halted long-range penetration missions until suitable fighter cover could be provided.

The Bf 109G was in the vanguard of these missions, and the defense of Germany in the late summer and early autumn of 1943 marked the pinnacle of the *Jagdwaffe*'s performance in the west. From then on, as the Eighth Air Force's fortunes improved with the fielding of genuine escort fighters in the form of drop-tank-equipped Thunderbolts and the arrival of the superb Merlin-engined Mustang, the German fighter force would find itself in an ever-steepening spiral of decline.

P-47C/Ds from the 62nd FS/ 56th FG form up in echelon-down formation for the benefit of the press, who were huddled in a B-24 during a photo flight over Suffolk on May 25, 1943.

Despite the bloody reversals over Schweinfurt and Regensburg, USAAF senior planners were generally of the opinion that precision bombing attacks by B-17 Flying Fortresses and B-24 Liberators could be flown in daylight against targets in Europe without escort and without suffering heavy losses. Nothing the RAF or anyone else said was going to sway this dogmatic resolve, and some Eighth Air Force generals even believed that escort fighters were unnecessary. However, just as the Luftwaffe had discovered in 1940 during the Battle of Britain, VIII Bomber Command eventually realized that bomber losses could be reduced in proportion to the distance escorting fighters could escort the "heavies."

The Luftwaffe had been powerless to implement an effective daylight bombing strategy because a lack of organization in the production of fighters restricted the numbers of Bf 109s available to it in the summer and autumn of 1940. Those that did operate over Britain were severely restricted in radius of action by limited fuel reserves. The Luftwaffe was eventually forced to switch to night bombing, as was RAF Bomber Command when horrendous daylight losses left it with little choice but to undertake nocturnal raids on German targets in 1941.

But even when American bomber losses reached epidemic proportions in the autumn of 1943, the Eighth Air Force never abandoned its daylight precision bombing concept. That the USAAF daylight offensive did not go the same way as that of the Luftwaffe and RAF Bomber Command is due entirely to the advent of the long-range escort fighter.

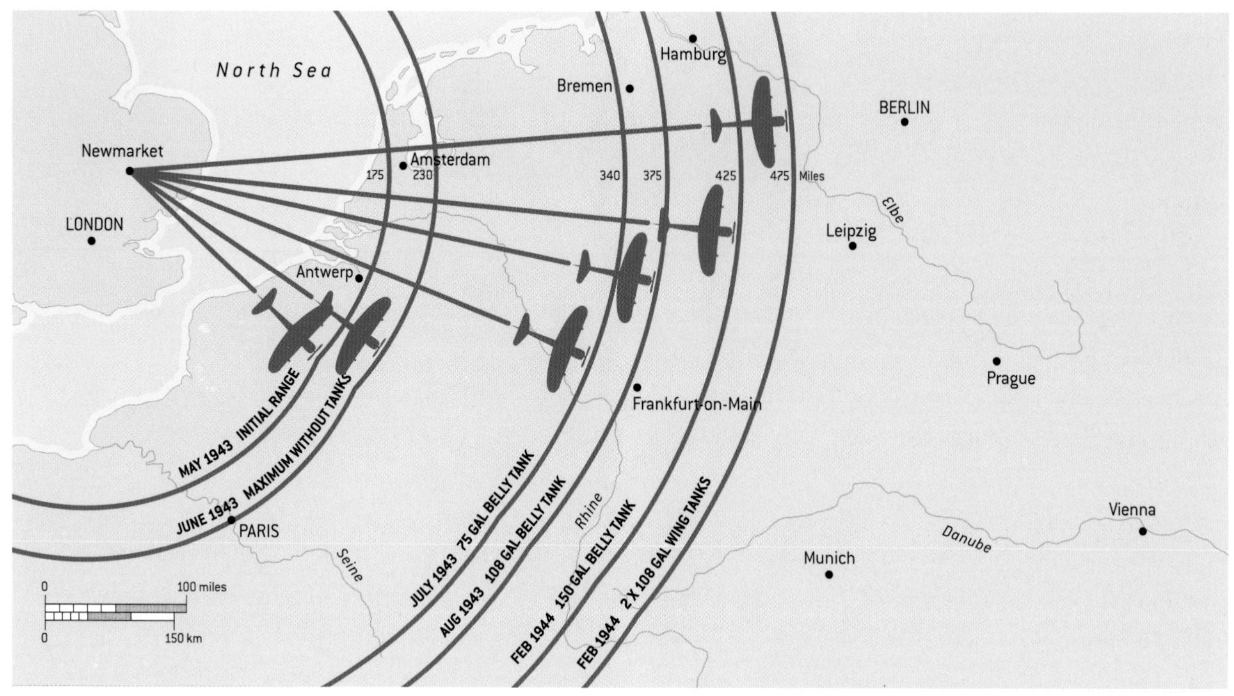

This map reveals how the range of the P-47 was progressively extended through the introduction of ever-larger external fuel tanks. Yet even when fitted with two underwing 108gal tanks, the P-47D still only possessed half the endurance of a similarly equipped P-51D. Indeed, the latter could escort bombers to targets east of Vienna.

In the autumn of 1942, all but one of VIII Fighter Command's fighter groups (the 4th FG) had been transferred to North Africa in support of the Operation *Torch* landings. The rebuilding of the Eighth Air Force's fighter arm commenced in December of that year when the P-38-equipped 78th FG arrived in England from the US. A decision was then made to reequip both groups with P-47C/D Thunderbolts, and VIII Fighter Command also welcomed the 56th FG in January 1943 – both the 4th and 78th reequipped with Thunderbolts later that same month. All three units were declared operational with the P-47C in April, and by year-end there were ten Thunderbolt groups in England.

The Eighth Air Force planned to use the P-47 force to support its daylight bomber operations, but pilots new to the theater were first to gain operational experience under the watchful eye of RAF Fighter Command. Spitfires had been employed in offensive cross-Channel operations since early 1941, mostly on "Rodeos," whereby several squadrons carried out a high-speed sweep over France or the Low Countries to lure Bf 109s into combat. However, the Luftwaffe often refused to take the bait, so a "Circus" consisting of a small number of bombers with strong fighter support was despatched. A fighter escort for a dedicated bomber operation was known as a "Ramrod."

When planning P-47 operations, the prime consideration in 1943 was range. Early Thunderbolt missions without belly tanks lasted between 1hr 45min and

2hrs 5min. With 75gal pressurized tanks, missions could last up to 2hrs 50min. The 165gal tanks gave another 45–50 minutes' range, and with aircraft utilizing two 108gal wing tanks, P-47 groups could fly sorties that lasted up to 5hrs 30min – made of metal, the 108gal tanks were initially in very short supply. The far more common treated pressed-paper wing tanks gave further range, but they also caused some problems.

The paper tanks were sometimes difficult to drop in combat because they occasionally froze at high altitude. One of the tricks used to jettison a recalcitrant tank was to have a wingman slip his wingtip between the tank and the wing and knock it off the pylon! By late 1943, P-47 groups were using up to 480 tanks a month, and they tried to keep a six- to eight-mission back stock on hand. Fighter units were assigned their escort relay points by the size of the tanks they carried on the mission, which of course dictated their range. Although the drop tanks gave the escort fighters a much-needed boost in their range, they had a detrimental impact on the handling of the Thunderbolt, as Col "Hub" Zemke recalled:

> Flying a P-47 with a loaded tank was not a pleasant experience because the tank affected the aircraft's aerodynamics. I figured out that if the Luftwaffe caught us while hugging these things, we would be in trouble. Extra range, however, was a priority for our fighters due to the growing losses our B-17s were sustaining.

In late 1943, when returning home from escort missions, Thunderbolt pilots began strafing targets of opportunity on the ground. The aircraft proved so

Natural metal finish and olive drab P-47Ds and P-38s crowd the disperal at Base Air Depot 1 (better known as RAF Burtonwood) in April 1944. Behind P-47D-22 42-25862 in the foreground is P-47D-6 42-74647 LM-V of the 71st FS/56th FG. Note the various bombers parked in the distance.

successful in this role that the P-47D was subsequently adapted to carry wing-mounted bombs to add to the destructive power of its six or eight machine guns.

With more USAAF fighters now appearing over Germany, the *Jagdwaffe* quickly transferred in additional Bf 109G-equipped units in the shape of IV./JG 3 and II./JG 53 from Italy. Despite their arrival, and the bolstering of other Reich Defense units in Germany, the early months of 1944 were to prove costly for the Bf 109G *Gruppen*, as the rate of attrition amongst its experienced and irreplaceable leaders rose dramatically due to the extended range of the USAAF fighters. The latter were now spending much longer with the bombers, and their numbers were increasing all the time.

Four more Bf 109G-equipped *Gruppen* were added to the homeland defensive line-up in the first half of 1944, as the *Jagdwaffe* struggled to make good rising losses. I./JG 5 arrived from Bulgaria in February, with II./JG 5 following two months later from the Arctic Front. Finally, III. and IV./JG 27 moved north from Italy to Austria in March to protect southern Germany from strategic raids by the Fifteenth Air Force.

February–March 1944 proved to be the Thunderbolt's heyday when it came to air fighting with VIII Fighter Command. Thereafter, the *Jagdwaffe* would be more difficult to encounter, and the P-51 Mustang's advantage of greater endurance over the P-47 saw groups equipped with the North American fighter regularly running up substantial scores, as they saw widespread use escorting long-penetration raids deep into Germany. The Mustang had the lowest fuel consumption rate of the three main USAAF fighters in the ETO, with the P-51B using 65 gallons per hour compared with the P-47D, which consumed as much as 200 gallons per hour, depending on power settings.

The P-51 equipped all but one of the Eighth Air Force's fighter groups by the late autumn of 1944, with most Thunderbolts in the ETO being used as fighter-bombers by units assigned to the tactical Ninth Air Force. These groups (some 13 in total) of IX and XIX Tactical Air Commands had departed bases in southern England for France shortly after the June 6, 1944 invasion of Normandy. D-Day had seen Allied air forces boasting no fewer than 4,100 fighters, of which 2,300 were USAAF P-38s, P-47s and P-51s. In response, the *Jagdwaffe* could muster just 425 Bf 109Gs and Fw 190As in Normandy, of which only 250–280 were serviceable on any given day.

In the lead up to D-Day, Channel-based JGs 2 and 26 had been bearing the full brunt of growing Allied air power. Unlike the *Jagdgruppen* stationed deep within Germany's borders, theirs was a campaign constantly being fought on two levels. For not only did they have to contend with high-flying US "heavies" attacking strategic targets within their own areas of responsibility (from U-boat pens in the west to airfields and industrial sites in the east) and beyond; they also had to oppose the swelling tide of tactical missions being mounted by the RAF and the Ninth Air Force as the coastal regions of northwest Europe were "softened up" ahead of the invasion.

Prior to the actual storming of the beaches of Normandy, despite lengthening casualty lists, the *Jagdwaffe* had managed to hold its own in the west. But in the wake of the invasion, the long retreat to final surrender had commenced. The Luftwaffe had reacted quickly to the D-Day landings, and within hours of the first troops coming ashore, the whole Defense of the Reich organization that had been so painstakingly put together over past months was torn apart. By the evening of June 9, no fewer than 15 *Jagdgruppen* – all but four of then flying Bf 109Gs – had left Germany for the threatened Western Front. Although carefully assigned areas to operate in, such was the Allies' overwhelming superiority (approaching 20:1 in fighter strength alone) that the *Jagdgruppen* soon abandoned their bases and began flying from widely dispersed, and heavily camouflaged, landing strips. Even here they were not safe from marauding fighter-bombers (including numerous P-47Ds from the Eighth and Ninth Air Forces), and by the end of June more than 350 German aircraft had been destroyed or damaged on the ground.

For many pilots who had only just begun to get to grips with the high-altitude anti-bomber air war over the Reich, the additional low-level dimension dictated by their opponents during the Normandy fighting proved too much. During the last three weeks of June more than 170 German fighter pilots were killed in action. Within a fortnight of their arrival in France, many *Jagdgruppen* had been reduced to single figure strength. Although the losses in men and machinery were constantly being made good, the inexperienced replacement pilots fared even worse. Nevertheless, the Bf 109G *Gruppen* still managed to claim a large number of Allied aircraft shot down, with the Ninth Air Force's P-47 fighter-bomber units suffering particularly badly.

And with more and more P-51s now being present in-theater, the Thunderbolts of the Eighth Air Force (now flown by just the 56th, 78th, 353rd and 356th FGs, as the remaining groups had switched to Mustangs) subsequently missed out on the renewed fighting over the German homeland in the late summer of 1944, primarily because the P-47 lacked the Mustang's endurance.

The aircraft being encountered by VIII Fighter Command in August were the surviving remnants of those *Gruppen* (together with JGs 2 and 26) that had been thrown into France three months earlier. They had now been ordered back to Germany, as the *Jagdwaffe* in the west was in irreversible decline. The units now

The wing magazines of a P-47, which could hold up to 425rpg. A three-second burst from the Thunderbolt's eight Browning machine guns would expend 200 rounds of ammunition.

fought alongside *Gruppen* that had been spared the carnage of Normandy, but had nevertheless been fighting a war of attrition with Eighth Air Force "heavies," and their escorts. In July alone, Defense of the Reich units claimed 329 aircraft destroyed for the loss of 341 of their own. But whereas the former constituted just a fraction of the USAAF's strength (and could be rapidly replaced), the latter represented the equivalent of almost the entire single-seater homeland defense force.

The return of the shattered remnants of the Normandy *Gruppen* brought no immediate relief to the embattled Defense of the Reich units either, for it would take several weeks before many of them could be deemed ready for frontline service again. Consequently, one final round of reinforcements was added to homeland defense in the late summer and early autumn of 1944. Elements of JGs 4 and 77 were withdrawn from the southern and southeastern perimeters of Hitler's rapidly shrinking "Fortress Europe," and two "new" Bf 109G *Gruppen* in I. and III./JG 76 – ex-*Zerstörer* units I./ZG 76 and II./ZG 1, respectively – were converted to Gustavs. The latter soon became IV./JG 300 and IV./JG 53.

These new units, and the increased production of aircraft that saw no fewer than 3,013 single-seat fighters delivered to the *Jagdwaffe* in September 1944 alone, did little to improve the situation, however, as the Luftwaffe no longer had the infrastructure to support their effective employment, the fuel to power their aircraft or the trained pilots to fly them. Even the introduction of the Bf 109K-4 in October 1944 had virtually no impact on the aerial battles taking place over Germany, despite some 20 *Jagdgruppen* operating them alongside late-model Gustavs until war's end.

Both I. and II. Jagdkorps, which controlled fighter units in the west and in Defense of the Reich, continued to take the fight to the Allies as best they could.

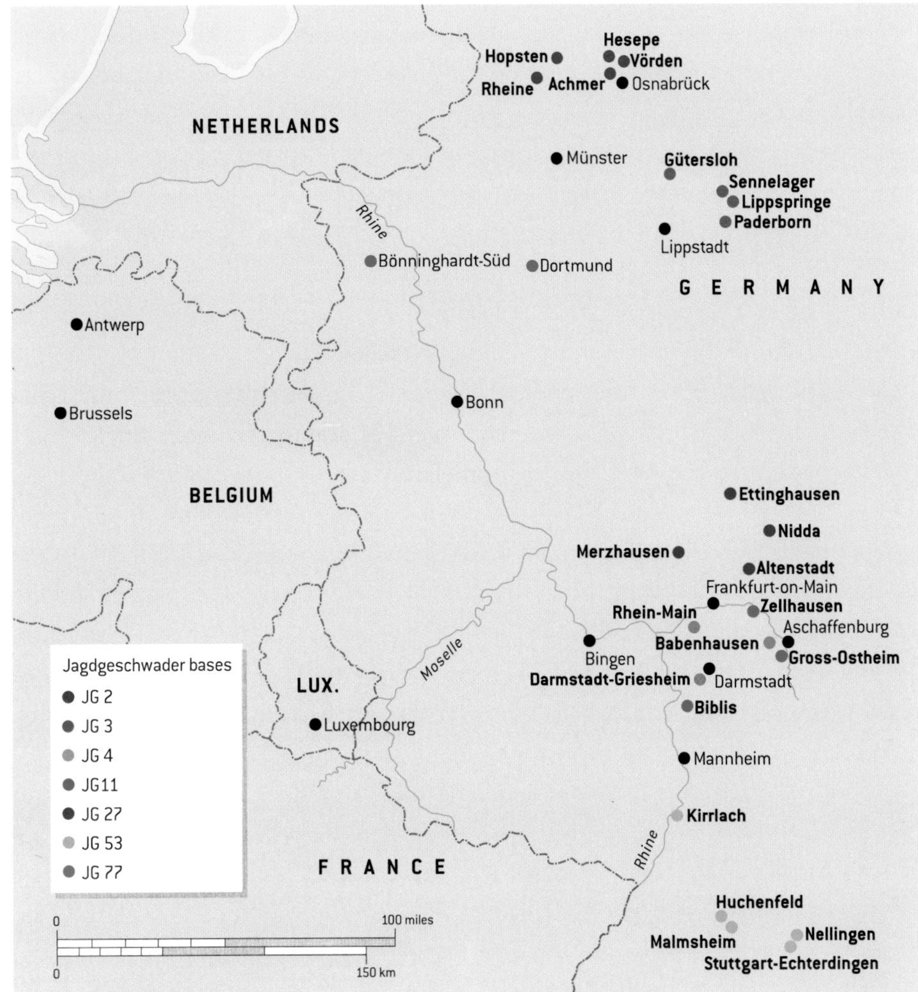

The principal *Jagdwaffe* Bf 109G/K bases from which Operation *Bodenplatte*, the *Jagdwaffe*'s last major air offensive in the west was launched. Carried out at dawn on January 1, 1945, *Bodenplatte* was intended to support the Wehrmacht's Battle of the Bulge counteroffensive by striking at Allied forward tactical bases, many of which operated P-47s, now chiefly relegated to the fighter-bomber role.

And in an effort to replicate the successes of Schweinfurt a year earlier, General der Jagdflieger Adolf Galland, who headed up the fighter arm, began hoarding fuel and aircraft for "the big blow" – the commitment of every available fighter in the west (some 2,000 aircraft in total) against USAAF "heavies" on a single day. He hoped to shoot down 400–500 bombers for the loss of 400 fighters and, possibly, 100–150 pilots. Galland thought that such a blow would force the USAAF to halt its bombing offensive.

However, Galland's carefully husbanded force, trained in high-altitude anti-bomber tactics, was ordered by Hitler instead to support the Wehrmacht's new land offensive in the west, dubbed the "Battle of the Bulge." The campaign was launched on December 16, 1944, and the *Jagdwaffe* took advantage of bad weather to offer close support to the ground troops. With the skies clearing, however, losses mounted as the counteroffensive was targeted by overwhelming Allied air power. In an effort to blunt the latter, the *Jagdwaffe* was ordered to conduct one massive attack against the Allies' forward tactical airfields in the Low Countries and France – many occupied by Ninth Air Force P-47 groups.

Codenamed Operation *Bodenplatte*, 33 *Jagdgruppen* (19 of them equipped with Bf 109G/Ks) attacked bases soon after dawn on New Year's Day 1945. Close to 1,000 German fighters participated in the mission, which inflicted only minimal damage and cost the lives of 214 Luftwaffe pilots. *Bodenplatte* sounded the death knell for German fighter operations in the west.

With Soviet forces getting perilously close to Berlin, Hitler transferred much of what was left of his once-mighty *Jagdwaffe* eastward. The only Bf 109 *Geschwader* left in the west in the final weeks of the war in Europe was JG 53, which claimed its last P-47 victory on April 19, 1945.

As previously mentioned, most of the P-47s encountered by Bf 109 pilots following *Bodenplatte* were flown by Ninth Air Force fighter-bomber groups supporting the advance of Allied forces on the ground. Controlled by IX and XIX Tactical Air Commands, the 14 P-47-equipped groups that were in the vanguard of Ninth Air Force operations post-D-Day saw intensive action through to war's end. These units suffered heavily at the hands of German flak batteries, and they also endured occasional reversals when engaged by *Jagdwaffe* fighters. The latter, however, primarily focused their efforts against the strategic bombers of the Eighth Air Force, and in so doing they allowed the 56th FG (the sole P-47 outfit in the Eighth Air Force after November 1944) to continue to claim Bf 109 kills through to April 7, 1945.

Although neither the P-47 or the Bf 109 were the best piston-engined fighters available to the USAAF or the Luftwaffe in the final months of the war in Europe, they still played an important part in aerial combat through to VE-Day.

THE MEN

AMERICAN PILOT TRAINING

In the late 1930s, while the future cream of the *Jagdwaffe*'s fighter force was receiving a blooding in the skies over Spain, across the Atlantic in the USA the USAAC had finally recognized that it would face monumental problems in developing a tremendously expanded air arm, should the war that now seemed inevitable in Europe escalate into a worldwide conflict. In early 1939, USAAC chief of staff Gen "Hap" Arnold realized that US military forces had to plan for the possibility of involvement in the European war. He and other senior officers in the USAAC duly devised a scheme that would facilitate the training of 1,200 pilots by the end of 1939, increasing to 7,000 in 1940 and 30,000 in 1941. The USAAC could not accomplish this task alone, however, so Arnold's scheme called for the establishment of civilian-operated training schools.

The latter would be responsible for the primary training phase of flight instruction, with civilian schools providing all services and facilities, bar the aircraft, but with USAAC control of the methods and manner of the instruction. In the spring of 1939, eight successful civilian pilot training school owner-operators agreed to become contractors to the USAAC to provide primary pilot training for 12,000 pilots per month. The program that Arnold recommended was to take up to 36 weeks to complete, with 12 weeks each for primary, basic and advanced pilot training (ultimately, these training sessions would be conducted in ten-week periods to save time).

By July 1939, nine civilian schools were giving primary phase flying training to USAAC Aviation Cadets. Within 12 months nine more schools were in operation, and by the end of 1940, Arnold's ambitious expansion program would be training more than 30,000 pilots a year. One such school was Darr Aero Tech, located some four miles southwest of Albany, New York, which by September 14, 1940, had its first class of 50 cadets conducting training flights with its 15 USAAC-supplied Stearmans.

By early 1942, the bulk of the US training program was being carried out by the Technical Training Command and Flying Training Command (renamed USAAF Training Command in 1943). By 1944, the standard USAAC program for the minimum number of flying hours required to produce a qualified pilot was 65 hours in Primary training, 70 in Basic training and 75 in Advanced training. Primary training consisted of 225 hours of ground school instruction and 65 hours of flight training to produce cadets who could fly single-engined, elementary aircraft. Most recruits had never even driven a car before, let alone flown an aircraft, but they were expected to fly solo after just six hours of tuition.

Potential pilots who reached the Primary stage arrived via Classification and Pre-Flight Training. College Training Detachments were established by the USAAF in early 1943, and everyone entering the Aviation Cadet Program from then until war's end was assigned to one of these detachments for a period of between one and five months, depending on the scores the recruits achieved on a battery of tests administered at both Basic training and at the College Training Detachment.

The distinctively marked engine cowling panels of a 84th FS/78th FG P-47D-22 "razorback" are carefully positioned in front of the fighter at Duxford in the early spring of 1944. This aircraft was one of the first natural metal Thunderbolts to arrive in the ETO from America. It was assigned to Capt Quince Brown, who claimed 12.333 aerial kills, including seven Bf 109s, prior to being shot down by flak on September 6, 1944 and executed by an SS officer.

By 1942 the USAAF had four Classification and Pre-Flight Centers in Nashville (Tennessee), Maxwell Field (Alabama), San Antonio (Texas) and Santa Ana (California). Classification consisted of general education tests, 50 questions per test, multiple-choice, physiomotor tests (to measure coordination) and a 64-point physical examination. Those who did not "wash out" awaited cadet classification for pilot preflight training. The latter normally lasted seven to ten weeks, during which time cadets attended academic classes, marched in formation, took part in PT and drill, pistol shooting and aquatic training, where they learned ditching procedures. Cadet pilots studied armaments and gunnery, with 30 hours spent on sea and air recognition, 48 hours on codes, 24 hours on physics, 20 hours on mathematics and 18 hours on maps and charts. All who were successful moved on to the next stage of flight training. Potential pilots were now given the chance to learn to fly.

An average of 600 potential pilots attended each Primary training school, students spending 94 hours on academic work in ground school, 54 hours on military training and 60 hours in 125–225hp PT-13/17 or PT-21/22 open-cockpit biplanes or PT-19/23/26 low-wing monoplanes. The standard Primary school flight training was divided into four phases. The first was the pre-solo phase, which saw students taught the general operation of a light aircraft, proficiency in landing techniques and recovery from stalls and spins. The second phase covered a pre-solo work review and development of precision control by flying patterns such as elementary figure 8s, lazy 8s, pylon 8s and chandelles. In the third phase, students developed a high proficiency in landing approaches and landing. Finally, the fourth phase focused exclusively on aerobatics.

THUNDERBOLT PILOT: FRANCIS S. GABRESKI

Born to Polish parents in Oil City, Pennsylvania, on January 28, 1919, Francis Stanley "Gabby" Gabreski was studying medicine at the University of Notre Dame when he decided to join the Army Reserve in July 1940. Enrolling in the USAAC, he graduated from flying training at Maxwell Field, Alabama, on March 14, 1941. Initially assigned to the 15th Pursuit Group's 45th Pursuit Squadron at Wheeler Field, Hawaii, Gabreski witnessed the Pearl Harbor raid on December 7, 1941. Having seen no combat flying P-40s in defense of the Hawaiian islands, he volunteered to be sent to the UK to gain combat experience with a Polish squadron – he was a fluent Polish speaker. After spending two months in the ETO ferrying USAAF aircraft to various bases in the UK, a chance meeting with Polish Spitfire pilots in London's Embassy Club saw Gabreski temporarily assigned to No. 315 Sqn. He fitted in well at RAF Northolt and flew 11 combat and two rescue missions in Spitfire IXCs in January–February 1943.

With combat experience under his belt, Gabreski was transferred to the Thunderbolt-equipped 61st FS/56th FG at Boxted in late February. Made CO of the latter unit on June 9, 1943, "Gabby" claimed his first kill (an Fw 190) on August 24. Further claims were made in the autumn, and on November 26 he downed two Bf 110s over Germany to attain ace status. The first of an eventual 11 Bf 109s destroyed by Gabreski followed three days later.

Promoted to lieutenant colonel in January 1944, "Gabby" continued to add to his score until by mid-July he was the ETO's leading ace with 28 victories. Volunteering to lead his unit on one final mission on July 20, prior to heading home tour-expired, he was in the process of strafing a number of He 111 bombers at an airfield at Bassenheim when he flew too low in his Thunderbolt and struck the ground with its propeller. Managing to clear the airfield, Gabreski bellied the aircraft into a nearby field. He spent the rest of the war in Stalag Luft I.

Leaving the USAAF postwar, "Gabby" returned to active duty in April 1947. In June 1951 he was sent to Korea to fly F-86s with the 4th Fighter Interceptor Group, and he shot down three MiG-15s while with this unit. He then became CO of the 51st Fighter Interceptor Wing (FIW) and destroyed 3.5 more MiG-15s, taking his final tally of aerial victories in two wars to 34.5. Following a series of command appointments, Col Gabreski retired from the USAF as CO of the 52nd FIW in November 1967, whereupon he joined the Grumman Aerospace Corporation. Subsequently becoming president of the Long Island Railroad in 1978, Gabreski lived in retirement on Long Island until he passed away on January 31, 2002.

During this training, at least half of the flights were made with an instructor and the remainder would see the pilot flying solo. Each cadet had to make at least 175 landings. Those who soloed went on to Basic flying training school, where they undertook a ten-week course. Here, a further 70 hours was flown in a 450hp BT-13/15 basic trainer (later replaced by the AT-6, because the BT was considered to be too easy to fly), 94 hours spent in ground school and 47 hours conducting military training.

In ground school, five major topics were covered; aircraft and equipment (understanding the aircraft and how everything worked, including engines and mechanical theory); navigation (preparation for cross-country flights); aircraft recognition (both "friendly" and "hostile"); principles of flight; and, finally, radio codes and radio communication for pilots. A link trainer was also available for use by rated pilots, and this introduced cadets to the art of instrument flying.

By the end of Basic school, trainees would have learned to fly an aircraft competently. Further training taught them to pilot a warplane the USAAF way. Before the end of Basic training, trainees were classified – on the basis of choice and instructors' reports – for single-engine training (fighter pilots) or twin-engine training (bomber, transport or twin-engined fighter pilots). There were two final stages in the training phase prior to a pilot reaching the front line – Advanced flying training and Transition flying training. Advanced flying training was a ten-week course (single-engine and twin engine), involving 70 hours flying, 60 hours ground school and 19 hours military training. Single-engine trainees flew 600hp AT-6s during this period, and also used the aircraft to undertake a course in fixed gunnery.

At the end of Advanced training, the graduate was awarded the silver pilot's wings of the USAAF and given the rank of flight officer, or commissioned as a second lieutenant. Transition flying training followed, pilots learning to fly the type of aircraft they would take into combat. Fighter pilots received a five-week Transition course, with single-engine pilots flying ten hours in aircraft like the P-39, P-40, P-47 or P-51. Gunnery was part of fighter Transition training.

For early Thunderbolt pilot Robert Johnson, he did not get to fly his future frontline mount until he joined the 56th FG in late July 1942. His new unit had been chosen to be the first in the USAAF to receive the P-47, and he vividly recalled his initial encounter with the big fighter:

> In every respect the Thunderbolt was an airplane that lived up to her name. After the BC-1 and AT-6 trainers I had flown at Kelly Field, the Thunderbolt was a giant. I had been accustomed to 600hp – beneath the P-47B's massive cowling was 2,000hp. She was big, and on the ground she wasn't very pretty. But every inch of her structure was power, a rugged and sturdy machine with all the mass of a tank.

At the conclusion of Transition training, pilots reported to unit training groups, where they were welded into fighting teams. Between December 1942 and August 1945, 35,000 day-fighter crews were trained. All fighter units were supplied by the operational training unit program. Simultaneously, a replacement unit training program (90-day course) within the four domestic air forces provided replacements for overseas aircrew who had been lost in combat or rotated home for reassignment.

Six months were initially required after the formation of a cadre to complete the organization and training of a new group. By 1943, preparations to move an air unit overseas had been cut to just over four months. It normally took almost 120 days and 17 separate actions by HQ officers to move the unit to its port of embarkation.

GERMAN PILOT TRAINING

In 1940, the realities of war had led the Luftwaffe to modify the final stages of its training syllabus through the creation of *Erganzungsgruppen* (Operational Training Schools) for the teaching of tactics and further familiarization with frontline types. In the *Jagdwaffe*, these units were directly linked to, and controlled by, operational *Geschwader*. Designated IV Gruppe, the intention of these units was to allow new pilots to gain precious operational experience before being hurled into combat. For Bf 109 pilots in 1943–44, advanced training was usually in Ar 68 and He 51 biplanes (albeit becoming progressively rare by then), Bf 109D/Es, captured French Dewoitine D.520s and Ar 96s.

By the summer of 1942, the loss of so many experienced pilots meant that there was insufficient manpower available to carry out the training function in operational squadrons, so the importance of the *Erganzungsgruppen* was steadily reduced. Those attached to frontline fighter units were eventually disbanded in mid-1942 and replaced by three Fighter Pools located in the three main operational areas for the Luftwaffe – in the South at Cazeaux, in France (Erganzungsjagdgruppe Süd), in the West at Mannheim, in Germany (Erganzungsjagdgruppe West), and in the East at Krakow, in Poland (Erganzungsjagdgruppe Ost).

All operational units would draw replacement crews from these pools until war's end. Although the creation of these pools reduced the number of instructors required, thus freeing up more experienced pilots for frontline service, it also effectively curtailed the operational training of new pilots in the frontline at a time when such experience was critically needed for newcomers receiving their first exposure to combat. Just as serious was the elimination of a fully crewed, but only partially trained, reserve that the *Erganzungsgruppen* offered to frontline units.

For those pilots destined to fly the Bf 109 in 1943–45, the trio of *Erganzungsjagdgruppen* were equipped with a varied fleet of fighters covering all major variants. There were also a handful of two-seat Bf 109G-12s on strength with these units from late 1943, although they were vastly outnumbered by conventional single-seaters.

Between January and April 1944, the Luftwaffe's day-fighter arm lost more than a thousand pilots in action, which included the core of its experienced fighter leader cadre. The training organization was hard-pressed to make good losses of this magnitude, and in a desperate attempt to shore up flagging homeland defense units, hours were cut and courses curtailed in order to get new students expeditiously into frontline *Gruppen*. As many as 30 trainees (the equivalent of an entire *Gruppen*) per conversion course were now being lost in fatal crashes due to inexperience and a lack of flying hours in tricky types such as the Bf 109G. And those that completed their schooling were of little immediate use, other than to make up numbers. Leutnant Heinz Knoke of 5./JG 11 recalled in his book *I Flew for the Führer* how his unit dealt with fresh-faced aviators that seemed to be arriving on a near-daily basis:

> April 28, 1944. A steady stream of new pilots arrived on posting to us during recent weeks. With the exception of a flight sergeant who came from the Eastern Front, they are all young NCOs without experience, posted to us directly upon completion of courses at training schools which are altogether inadequate for operational

Although senior personnel in the Luftwaffe wanted the more heavily armed Fw 190 to be the bomber killer, leaving the higher-flying Bf 109 to deal with the escorting fighters, this photograph shows that Gustav pilots also received training in how best to down a "heavy." The experienced *Jagdflieger* appears to be advocating the head-on attack as the most effective way to engage a B-24 – the wire protruding from the latter illustrates the bomber's areas of defensive fire. Judging from their expressions, his audience – especially the pilot to his immediate right – seems to be far from convinced!

MESSERSCHMITT PILOT: THEODOR WEISSENBERGER

Born on December 21, 1914 in Mühlheim-am-Main, Theodor Weissenberger had been a keen glider pilot and instructor prewar. Having been kept away from the action teaching would-be Bf 110 *Zerstörer* pilots for the first two years of the conflict, Oberfeldwebel Weissenberger eventually succeeded in securing a posting to 1.(Z)/JG 77 in northern Norway in the autumn of 1941. He soon proved his worth, claiming his first kill on October 23, 1941. Over subsequent months Weissenberger downed a further 22 aircraft flying the Bf 110, and also destroyed 15 locomotives, two flak installations, a radio station, a railroad station on the northern Russian Murmansk line and ten large barracks.

In September 1942 he was posted to II./JG 5, which was equipped with Bf 109Es and based in Petsamo, in northern Finland. Flying with 6. Staffel, he was awarded the Knight's Cross on November 13 for 38 victories. Promoted to *Staffelkapitän* of 7./JG 5 on June 15, 1943, Weissenberger had increased his score to 104 by July 4. Later that same month he received Oak Leaves for his continuing success, and he became *Staffelkapitän* of 6./JG 5 in September.

Weissenberger became *Gruppenkommandeur* of II./JG 5 on April 20, 1944, and he had boosted his tally to 175 kills by May 18. That same month he took his unit south, where it became the last complete *Gruppe* to be added to the Defense of the Reich order of battle. On June 4 Weissenberger became *Gruppenkommandeur* of I./JG 5, and he led the unit with distinction on the D-Day front. He claimed 25 kills in the Normandy region in just a matter of days, including five P-47s on June 7, two more 24 hours later and three on June 12! He also claimed a trio of Typhoons and a P-51 on July 19.

With his accumulated score standing at 200, Major Weissenberger became *Gruppenkommandeur* of Me 262-equipped I./JG 7 on December 1, 1944, and he was promoted to lead the *Geschwader* on January 15, 1945. He claimed a further eight kills (seven B-17s, including three on March 18, and a P-51) with the Messerschmitt jet fighter. By war's end, Theodor Weissenberger had flown more than 500 combat sorties and scored 208 victories. Having survived so much aerial combat, Weissenberger was killed on June 11, 1950 whilst competing in the XV Eifelrennen motor race at the Nürburgring when his BMW-engined single-seater crashed on the first lap.

requirements. I myself take them up for about 120 training flights. Two veteran combat pilots in the unit also give them instruction in blind flying. In addition, they receive advanced instruction in bombing and gunnery.

One of the replacements sent to a Defense of the Reich unit at this time was 22-year-old Ernst Schröder, who recounted his impression of the Bf 109G in Marco Fernández-Sommerau's *Messerschmitt Bf 109 Recognition Manual*:

Although the Bf 109 could fly at higher altitudes than its great rival, the Fw 190, it was a crime to have allowed its development to last so long. To train a pilot on this aircraft took longer than in the Fw 190, and time is what we did not have in 1944. The Bf 109 had a large blind spot to the rear, but in combat a fighter pilot has to observe the rear quarter five times more than the front. In the Fw 190, I could easily see my rudder, and therefore spot the danger coming from the rear. I couldn't see my rudder in the Bf 109, and the all-round visibility was equally as poor due the heavy framework that dominated the fighter's canopy. The rear-view mirror fitted to the Bf 109 was also near useless due to excessive vibration in flight.

The Messerschmitt's handling was also outmoded by 1944, and it lacked electrical equipment to activate the flaps and to effect trim adjustments – this was all done with electrics in the Fw 190. The position of the parachute beneath the pilot also caused problems, and the cockpit canopy was difficult to jettison. The pilot had to pull a lever and then lift the 50kg canopy by hand to eject it.

The best modification that could have been made to the Bf 109G from a junior pilot's perspective would have been to have moved the undercarriage outward, and to strengthen it overall. This would have cured all the problems associated with the fighter during takeoffs and landings. The Bf 109 tended to swing on take-off or landing along the movement of the wing's axis. Although experienced pilots soon grew accustomed to this, and could use the propeller torque to their advantage, novices often found themselves being brutally pulled to the left, which caused countless accidents – particularly in the final 18 months of the war.

Although I never personally damaged any Messerschmitts while learning to become a fighter pilot with 3./JG 101 at Pau, in France, in early 1944, I still thought that the Bf 109G was a "*Scheissbock*" (shitbucket), and it was a crime that it was manufactured until 1945.

INTO COMBAT

P-47 THUNDERBOLT TACTICS

There was no official edict on how formations should be flown when the Eighth Air Force commenced fighter operations in the ETO, so P-47 groups experimented to find the most desirable for control and deployment against an increasingly elusive enemy. On April 17, 1943, 56th FG CO Col "Hub" Zemke tried out a new formation, staggering the squadrons and flights so that the group was like a giant V when viewed in plan. Twelve days later, 112 P-47s of the 4th,

56th and 78th FGs flew a high-altitude Rodeo over the enemy coastline, sweeping overland from Ostend to Woensdrecht. The 56th FG, led by Maj Dave Schilling, lost two Thunderbolts to enemy Fw 190s flying in pairs and firing short, well-aimed bursts, before diving away. A change in US tactics followed.

Hitherto, individual flights had gone out in close finger-fours, each shifting into string trail behind its leader at the enemy coast. This flight battle formation, advised by the RAF in Stateside training days, placed the rearmost pilot in a very vulnerable position. Squadronmates were usually unable to warn him of a surprise attack from the rear, and in such an event the enemy was ideally placed to pick off the remaining airplanes ahead in the line. To improve matters, Zemke staggered the two-airplane elements in a flight, and spread flights out in very loose formation to give better positioning for spotting attackers coming in from the rear. Pilots now had more flexibility for evasion too.

On May 18, when the three P-47 groups sortied along the Dutch coast once again, a dozen Bf 109Gs approached the 4th FG at 30,000ft after the Thunderbolts had turned for England. The German fighters came in astern and the P-47s broke around and dived on them. The Bf 109Gs dived away in accordance with *Jagdwaffe* standard procedure, but this was a suicidal move. The Thunderbolts turned into them with a vengeance, 1Lt Duane W. Beeson (the top ace in the 4th FG during the P-47 era) chasing Oberfeldwebel Heinz Wefes of 4./JG 54 until he baled out at 100ft for the first of his 17 victories. This was also the first Bf 109 to fall to a P-47.

The engagement on May 18 revealed the strong points of the Thunderbolt, which were exploited over and over again by USAAF pilots through to VE-Day. It had quickly become obvious to VIII Fighter Command that the P-47 was inferior to the Bf 109G and Fw 190A at altitudes up to 15,000ft, and that the German aircraft had notably better rates of climb. Indeed, according to Luftwaffe Flight Test Center pilot Hans-Werner Lerche, who extensively flew a captured P-47D-2 in late 1943, "the Thunderbolt was rather lame and sluggish near ground level, with a maximum speed of barely 310mph."

Above 15,000ft, the Thunderbolt's performance steadily improved to the point where, between 25,000ft and 30,000ft, it surpassed the Bf 109G and Fw 190A in all areas bar rate of climb and acceleration – the heavy P-47 was, after all, double the weight of either German fighter. Lerche concurred, stating "I was astonished to note how lively the Thunderbolt became at higher altitudes. Thanks to its excellent exhaust-driven turbosupercharger, this American fighter climbed to 36,000ft with ease." Under full power, the P-47 was faster than both enemy types above 15,000ft, and as much as 30mph quicker at 30,000ft. The Thunderbolt's performance at altitude, and ability to build up tremendous speeds when diving, ultimately proved to be its biggest assets in combat. USAAF bombers usually operated at heights in excess of 24,000ft, which was in the P-47's optimum performance zone.

Enemy fighters would attempt to get above the "heavies" and dive through their ranks in slashing attacks, and this suited the P-47 pilots, who would in turn try and get above the Fw 190s and Bf 109s and hunt them down as they dived on their targets.

Thanks to its weight advantage, the P-47 could soon close on a diving German fighter, even if the latter initially accelerated away from the pursuing American interceptor. Hans-Werner Lerche found that the performance of the Republic fighter when heading earthward was a revelation. "The strength of the Thunderbolt in a dive was particularly impressive. This was just as well, as it was no great dogfighter, particularly at heights below 15,000ft. It was excellent at higher altitudes, in diving attacks and when flying with maximum boost. No wonder then that the P-47s were always the decisive factor as escort fighters for bomber attacks conducted at higher altitudes."

Although acknowledging its limitations, "Hub" Zemke was also fulsome in his praise of the P-47:

> A rugged beast with a sound radial engine to pull you along, it was heavy in firepower – enough to chew up an opponent at close range. It accelerated poorly and climbed not much better. But once high cruising speed was attained, the P-47 could stand up to the opposition. Strangely, the rate of roll and maneuverability were good at high speeds. At altitude, above 20,000ft, the P-47 was superior to the German fighters. In my book, you use your aircraft as advantageously as you can. In the dive, my God, the P-47 could overtake anything. Therefore, I made it policy in my group that we used the tactic of "dive and zoom." We stayed at high altitude, dived on the enemy, then zoomed back to high altitude before the next attack. To try to engage Bf 109s and Fw 190s in dogfights below 15,000ft could be suicidal – that was not playing the game our way.

The P-47's problems at lower altitudes were subsequently cured with the introduction of paddle-blade propellers and water injection, but until these improvements arrived in early 1944, Thunderbolt pilots were advised to avoid combats at low altitudes and slow speeds – the P-47 could turn with its more nimble German opponents provided its pilot kept his speed above 200mph. They were also told never to try to climb away from an enemy fighter unless having

Maj Kenneth Gallup, commanding officer of the 353rd FG's 350th FS, plunges headlong into a formation of 30-plus Bf 109Gs from III./JG 53 on August 4, 1944. His squadron was defending some 320 B-17s sent to bomb the Hamburg oil refinery when it was bounced by the Gustavs of III./JG 53, the latter attacking the Thunderbolts at a height of 30,000ft. Gallup had "made ace" four weeks earlier, and finished his combat tour with nine victories (including seven Bf 109s) to his credit, all of them claimed whilst flying the P-47D. (Artwork by Gareth Hector, © Osprey Publishing)

gained good speed in a dive. Just how poor the early P-47s were at climbing is illustrated by the fact that a Bf 109G averaged 11 minutes to climb from near ground level to 30,000ft, an Fw 190A took 14 minutes and the Thunderbolt required a full 20 minutes!

With P-47 pilots still finding their feet in combat in 1943, and hamstrung by flying less capable versions of the Thunderbolt, they found their opponents more than ready to exploit their numerous weaknesses in these early clashes over occupied Europe. 1Lt Robert S. Johnson recalled "There was no questioning the battle experience or the skill of the German pilots, nor could we find solace in the outstanding performance of the Fw 190 or Bf 109 fighters." After one of the first clashes between the 56th FG and the *Jagdwaffe*, Johnson noted "The Germans hit the lower squadrons hard, Me 109s and Fw 190s attacking in pairs. The Luftwaffe boys were hot. They screamed in from dead ahead, working perfectly as teams, throwing their bullets and cannon shells expertly into the evading Thunderbolts."

As losses mounted due to *Jagdwaffe* units seemingly always entering the battle with a height advantage, USAAF P-47 units began flying at ever-increasing altitudes. Fighter groups would approach the enemy coastline at 30,000ft, which was well above the optimum altitude of the Fw 190A and Bf 109G. And although their presence was noted by the *Gruppen* scrambled to engage USAAF bombers at 20,000–25,000ft, they could often be ignored by the German pilots as they were rarely released to dive on them by over-cautious commanders. Numerous seasoned Luftwaffe aces developed an open contempt for the P-47s during this period, dubbing them the "non-intervenors." Such an attitude would come back to haunt the *Jagdflieger* as the year progressed and VIII Fighter Command grew more confident in its use of the Thunderbolt.

As the P-47 units accrued more experience during the bomber escort missions that they were flying over France and the Low Countries, so their toll of enemy aircraft destroyed began to steadily grow. The 56th FG's 1Lt Robert S. Johnson was among a growing band of pilots proving that the P-47 was indeed a fighter to be reckoned with when flown to its strengths. He proved this when he claimed his first Bf 109 kill (almost certainly Leutnant Werner Grupe of 12./JG 26, who was flying a Bf 109G-4) on August 19, 1943. Johnson was wingman for Capt Jerry Johnson, who had claimed two Bf 109s destroyed 48 hours earlier, and who would ultimately down eight Gustavs (he was also the 56th FG's first ace):

Using typical fighter-pilot hand gestures, the 56th FG's Robert S. Johnson describes an air-to-air engagement to two USAAF brigadier-generals. (Imperial War Museum)

> I hit the throttle, giving the P-47 her head. The moment the second Me 109 spotted me coming in, he snapped over in a sharp turn and fled to the north. Jerry was only 90 degrees to him as I swung onto his tail. I closed in rapidly to 150 yards and prepared to fire. Suddenly Jerry kicked rudder and sent a burst into the Me 109. A good boy in that Messerschmitt – he pulled into a terrific turn and kicked his plane into a spin. I rolled and dove, waiting for the Me 109 to make his first full turn. I knew just where he'd be for his second turn, and I opened fire at this spot.
>
> Sure enough! The Messerschmitt spun right into my stream of bullets. Immediately he kicked out of the spin and dove vertically.

> Oh no you don't! I rolled the Jug, and from 27,000ft raced after the fleeing Me 109. The Messerschmitt seemed to crawl as the Thunderbolt fell out of the sky. I lined up directly behind the sleek fighter and squeezed the trigger. Eight heavy guns converged their fire. My second kill vanished in a blinding explosion that tore the fighter into shreds.

As the summer turned to autumn, VIII Fighter Command began to prevail in the war-torn skies over Europe, although the restricted range of the P-47 still meant that heavy bombers were suffering terrible losses as the hands of the *Jagdwaffe*. Thunderbolt losses, however, had been drastically reduced, and the tally of German fighters being shot down was steadily growing. Eventually, the fitting of bomb shackles to the fuselage centerline and under the wings of the P-47D allowed 75gal and 108gal tanks to be carried, thus boosting the fighter's endurance beyond three hours.

In early 1944, the Eighth Air Force was still very much up against it, with its bombers incurring significant losses at the hands of a stubborn enemy as the "heavies" broadened their campaign against targets across Germany. The way in which VIII Fighter Command was to be used to combat the *Jagdwaffe* significantly changed, as "Hub" Zemke recalled:

> Gen Ira Eaker (commander of the Eighth Air Force) had always told us that our first objective was to bring back the bombers and our second was to shoot down enemy aircraft. Now LtGen James Doolittle (who took over control of the Eighth from Eaker in January 1944) told us to pursue the enemy when and wherever we could – we were now permitted to follow him down, and no longer had to break off attacks. At lower altitudes the P-47 would have to be wary of getting into dogfights, but apparently our generals believed that there were now sufficient P-47s to warrant the risk of it keeping the pressure on the now hard-pressed Luftwaffe fighter arm. It also meant official recognition of what I had long advocated – getting way out ahead to bounce the enemy fighters before they had a chance to make their attacks on the bombers.

Overleaf: The battle for the bombers

On March 8, 1944, 623 bombers from ten combat wings were sent to attack Berlin for the third time in a week. The 352nd FG was one of the fighter groups that provided withdrawal support that afternoon for the "heavies" returning from "Big B." Ten minutes after meeting the bombers, the group's 487th FS spotted three Bf 109G-6s, led by Major Klaus Mietusch of III./JG 26, performing a beam attack out of the sun on the bombers in the rear combat wing. Mietusch claimed a B-17 shot out of formation south of Zwolle-Braunschweig at 1325hrs, but he was in turn engaged by Capt Virgil K. Meroney in P-47D-5 42-8473 *Sweet Louise* and eventually shot down, giving the American his eighth victory. (Artwork by Gareth Hector, © Osprey Publishing)

A
F
LG

This change in tactics built on the successful foundations laid by the P-47 groups since spring 1943. The 56th FG led the way, claiming its 200th kill on January 30, and boasting 12 aces. But as the score grew, so the *Jagdwaffe* became more inclined to avoid combat and unnecessary attrition at the hands of VIII Fighter Command. "As we sharpened our own ability to slash and to fight, the German aggressiveness so predominant in the early days of battle began noticeably to wane" recalled 1Lt Robert S. Johnson. "By no means do I imply that the German pilot was less dangerous an opponent – once battle was committed, however, the enemy fliers no longer were so eager to slug it out with us in a free-for-all. Steadily, we shot down and killed many of their experienced men. At the same time, we gained constantly in experience, and in our ability to master battle situations as they erupted."

Echoing these sentiments was MajGen Bill Kepner, commander of VIII Fighter Command, who wrote in May 1944, "If it can be said that the P-38s struck the Luftwaffe in its vitals and the P-51s are giving it the coup de grace, it was the Thunderbolt that broke its back." Some of the heaviest blows to the *Jagdwaffe* were struck by the P-47, with a number of high-scoring *experten* falling to the guns of the Republic fighter. One such pilot who was lucky to escape with his life after an encounter with Thunderbolts from the 56th FG on May 12, 1944 was Maj Günther Rall. Hospitalized for many months with wounds suffered in this clash, he would subsequently fail to add any more victories to his 275-kill tally.

Rall's Messerschmitt was one of 18 aircraft credited to the group as destroyed on this date (including five Bf 109Gs to 1Lt Bob Rankin, making him the first ETO P-47 "ace in a day"), the haul validating the introduction of the "Zemke Fan." This tactic had been devised by the CO of the 56th in response to the enemy's increasing reluctance to engage US fighters. His plan called for a P-47 formation to fly to a good visual reference point in enemy territory such as a lake, and then the four-airplane flights that made up the formation would fan out in different directions, with a close concentration in the center to be called in should contact be made with enemy fighters.

Eighth and Ninth Air Force P-47 groups turned their attention to supporting the D-Day landings following the Normandy invasion on June 6, 1944. Initially, however, there was little sign of Luftwaffe activity in the face of such overwhelming Allied air power, although enemy aircraft did start to appear in larger numbers in the aftermath of the invasion. On June 10, for example, the 78th FG had no fewer than ten P-47s shot down (five falling to Bf 109Gs), but the American pilots in turn claimed seven and four damaged in a 30-minute dogfight that ended north of Argentan. Other Thunderbolt groups enjoyed mixed fortunes on this date too, as pilots were forced to dogfight with German aircraft at less than favorable altitudes close to the ground.

During this period, P-47 pilots formed the opinion that *Jagdwaffe* units flying Bf 109Gs had better aircraft and better aviators. However, thanks to its paddle-blade propellers and water injection, the Thunderbolt was faster in level flight and could outturn both the Bf 109G and the Fw 190A in a high-speed climbing turn. The "bubbletop" P-47D-25, with its two-inch rudder extension, could also turn tighter than both German fighters at lower speeds too, as well as effectively "turn around its tail" while in a vertical climb without stalling out.

It was the 353rd FG's turn to suffer at the hands of a Bf 109G *Gruppe* on June 12, the group losing eight P-47s while making ground attacks near Dreux. Col Glenn E. Duncan's formation of 48 P-47s were bounced by Gustavs who attacked from out of the clouds. Targeting the rear of the Thunderbolt formation, the German pilots forced their opponents to drop their bombs and belly tanks and immediately split up into flights and elements. Those that climbed through the clouds found a high cover of Bf 109s waiting to pounce on them. The Thunderbolt pilots stayed in the area, dodging in and out of the clouds, until low fuel forced them to break for base. The 353rd FG in turn claimed six Bf 109s destroyed, with ranking ace Col Duncan being credited with three of them – at one point in this ferocious clash he called for help over the radio, stating that he had six Bf 109s "surrounded"!

Large scale encounters between Bf 109 *Gruppen* and both Eighth and Ninth Air Force P-47 units at medium to low altitudes would continue well into the early autumn, although as the Allies rolled back the German forces on the ground, so *Jagdwaffe* losses continued to mount in the air. By mid-September most fighter

P-47D-30-RE 44-20571 of the Ninth Air Force's 386th FS/365th FG has its engine run up by its pilot in front of a mobile flak battery at the group's base in Metz, France, in late 1944. The 365th FG began combat operations with the Ninth Air Force in February 1944, moving to France in late June. On January 30, 1945, the group moved to Florennes/Juzaine, in Belgium, remaining there until March 16, when its P-47s were transferred to Aachen, in Germany.

units had suffered such severe losses that they were ordered to return to Germany to reequip and then commence homeland defense missions.

The "Battle of the Bulge" in the Ardennes in December 1944 briefly saw German fighters, including numerous Bf 109G/Ks, back in the skies over Allied frontlines in larger numbers. However, their effect on the war in the west was negligible, and Thunderbolt pilots again enjoyed a brief spike in the number of victories achieved. By then the 56th FG was the only P-47 unit in the Eighth Air Force, and the group continued to escort heavy bombers as they ranged at will all over Germany. Aerial targets became harder and harder to find following the all-out effort of *Bodenplatte* on January 1, 1945, and the 56th FG claimed just 23 Bf 109s destroyed in the last four months of the war.

Ninth Air Force Thunderbolt units also encountered fewer and fewer enemy aircraft, with the last official Bf 109 aerial victories to fall to P-47s being credited to aircraft from XIX TAC on April 16, 1945. Conversely, the last Thunderbolts claimed shot down by Bf 109s – credited to pilots of III./JG 53 – were also Ninth Air Force aircraft, which were downed three days later.

By VE-Day, the 56th FG had scored more aerial victories than any other group in the ETO. And it had also produced the two top-scoring American fighter aces in the theater in LtCol "Gabby" Gabreski and Capt Robert S. Johnson with 28 and 27 kills, respectively. Perhaps the most outstanding tribute to this aircraft's ability to absorb punishment as well as to hand it out is the fact that all ten of the leading Thunderbolt aces (six of whom were shot down) in the ETO survived the war.

Bf 109 TACTICS

Despite being among the most skilled, and most successful, fighter pilots to take to the skies in the history of aerial warfare, the Bf 109G/K *Jagdflieger* defending Germany from daylight bombing raids in 1943–45 faced an impossible task. Despite using tried and tested tactics that had served them well since the Spanish Civil War, and flying an aircraft bred in combat, they were steadily outnumbered and outgunned as the war progressed.

Within weeks of the first USAAF cross-Channel raids in the early autumn of 1942, the Luftwaffe high command realized the incipient threat posed by the Eighth Air Force's high-flying heavy bombers and their even higher (but as yet still short-ranged) fighter escorts. The rugged and hard-hitting Fw 190 was an ideal anti-bomber gun platform, but its performance degraded sharply at altitude. What was needed to supplement the Fw 190 was a machine designed expressly for the fighter role. And in late 1942 just such an aircraft was about to enter service

– the Bf 109G-4. It was therefore decided that the two *Jagdgeschwader* in the west (JGs 2 and 26) would henceforth operate a mix of Fw 190As and Bf 109Gs.

The tactics used by the Bf 109G *Gruppen* from 1943 until war's end were based on the philosophy for success espoused by the "Father" of the *Jagdwaffe*, Werner Mölders. His mantra for aerial combat saw the emphasis placed more on fighting then flying. His combat experiences in Spain prewar had taught Mölders that the best way to achieve success against enemy aircraft was to base all tactics around the two-aircraft *Rotte*, which in turn formed the basic fighting unit for all *Jagdwaffe* formations. Within the pair, the *Rottenführer* was responsible for making the kills and his wingman (the *Katschmarek*) protected the leader's tail. The wingman did not worry about where he was flying, or what to do next – he simply had to follow his leader. He usually held position some 200 yards away from the *Rottenführer*, flying almost in line abreast formation. Each pilot concentrated their search of the sky inwards, so as to cover his partner's blind spot.

Two *Rotten* made up a *Schwarm*, flying some 300 yards apart – roughly the turning radius of a Bf 109G at combat speed. The leading *Rotte* typically flew to one side and slightly ahead of the other, and a *Staffel* formation comprised three *Schwarme*, either stepped up in line astern or in line abreast. The *Jagdwaffe* also devised the "cross-over turn" to avoid aircraft on the outside of a *Schwarm*

In the final months of the war, most aerial clashes between P-47s and Bf 109s saw Thunderbolts being engaged while attacking ground targets. One such clash took place on February 19, 1945, when 13 Bf 109K-4s and eight Fw 190As bounced 16 P-47D-30s of the 362nd FG, shortly after the latter had strafed a railroad marshalling yard. *Staffelkäpitan* Leutnant Günther Landt dived through the Thunderbolt formation from a height of 16,000ft, and upon his return to base at Kirrlach claimed two P-47s destroyed, thus taking his tally to 18. (Artwork by Gareth Hector, © Osprey Publishing)

becoming stragglers when the formation turned at high cruising speed in an area where contact with the enemy was likely. Each pilot held his speed going into the turn and the *Rotte* simply changed position in the formation during the maneuver.

The Bf 109 had always enjoyed a superior altitude performance to the fighters it had come up against since the start of World War II, so the favored tactic of *Jagdflieger* throughout the conflict was to get above their opponents and attempt to bounce them, if possible using the sun to mask their approach. After a single firing pass, the pilot would use the speed gained in his diving attack to climb back up into a position from which to perform any repeat attacks. With enemy fighters usually being slower and more maneuverable, German pilots tried to avoid turning dogfights wherever possible.

If bounced, the *Rotte* or *Schwarm* would typically turn individually to meet the attack, and if there was no time for this, they would take advantage of the direct injection system fitted to their Bf 109Gs by bunting over into a dive. The *Abschwung* (split-ess) was also used as an alternative escape route, the pilot performing a half roll pulled through into a steep dive at full throttle – this maneuver could only be done with plenty of altitude in hand, as up to 15,000ft in height would be lost.

These formations and tactics had served the *Jagdwaffe* well in previous conflicts, with *Rottenführer* having just one job to do – find and destroy the enemy. When they were found, the formation leader was the one who went in for the kill, leaving his wingmen to cover his tail. And for much of 1943, Gustav pilots were able to exploit these battletested tactics when engaging P-47s. However, as the number of Thunderbolts escorting the "heavies" grew, and their pilots became more experienced, the Germans found that their opponents were using these very same tactics against them. The improved P-47D, which now also boasted a long range thanks to the addition of drop tanks, was able to climb higher and dive faster than the Bf 109G. These improvements meant that Gustav pilots could not long pick and choose their fights at will, waiting until the escorting fighters were low on fuel before bouncing them as the Fw 190s set about the bombers. Posted in to command II./JG 11 from the Eastern Front, Maj Günther Rall outlined the changing fortunes facing the *Jagdwaffe* in the west in 1943–44 in his autobiography *My Logbook*:

> Over the last months the Americans have been able to steadily increase the range of their P-47s. This machine is used both to provide cover for the bomber streams, as well as to range far ahead of them, sweeping German airspace clean from tree-top height up to an altitude of 11,000 meters. Thus certain *Gruppen* are employed specifically against the American forward fighter screen.

Able to take a lot of punishment, the robust Fw 190s are ideally suited to attack the carefully staggered, heavily armed bomber boxes. However, the fighter's BMW radial engine dramatically loses performance at altitudes above 5,000 meters. Fighter combats over the Reich are now often being fought at altitudes between 8,000 and 11,000 meters, where the air is too thin for the BMW powerplant to deliver sufficient power output. II./JG 11 is therefore deployed as a high-altitude *Gruppe* equipped with Me 109s whose engines are fitted with special superchargers, so that they can concentrate quite specifically in keeping the high-flying P-47s and P-51s occupied while the Fw 190s go after the bombers.

All of which sounds perfectly plausible in theory, but in reality – with the German fighter arm outnumbered by anything between seven-to-one and ten-to-one – it is not so easy to put into practice.

It does not take me long to realize that over Germany almost everything is different from the Eastern Front – with one exception, that here too we are faced by a sheer weight of numbers. But these numbers are now made up of pilots who have years of meticulous training in the American homeland behind them, and who have only been declared operational after 400 hours of flying. They are fresh, aggressive, well schooled in tactics and are flying superior equipment. Combats take place on the edge of the stratosphere, whereas, in complete contrast, I have scored the majority of my victories in Russia at much lower heights. Also here over the Reich every effort is being made to match the enemy strength for strength – to send up a single *Rotte* or *Schwarm*, as we did daily on the Eastern Front, would be unthinkable here. When the Americans come, the three *Staffeln* of the *Gruppe* are led into battle together – until, that is, everything explodes apart into individual dogfights.

The scenes in Germany's skies are indescribable. Nobody who has sat in a fighter aircraft and seen the thousands of condensation trails stretching from east to west like a huge great ruler being drawn across the heavens will ever be able to forget the sight. We regularly take off with belly tanks, but have to jettison these when contact is made with the enemy in order to be fully maneuverable for dogfighting. At combat rating, we have perhaps 40 minutes in which to fight, break off the engagement and then try to find a suitable place to land.

Although always outnumbered by their opponents, the *Jagdwaffe* had managed to hold its own for much of 1943 thanks to the experience of the pilots defending Germany, the superior equipment that they flew into battle and the aggressive tactics that they employed. However, the arrival of improved, longer-legged Thunderbolts and Mustangs in early 1944 quickly eroded any qualitative advantage previously enjoyed by the *Jagdflieger*. The issuing of new orders from Berlin only

Los
Fest
ata
km
km/h
Reststand
warnlampe
Notzug
für Fahrwerk
EIN

made the situation worse, as pilots were told to focus all their efforts on the bombers – indeed, they were expressly forbidden to engage the escort fighters. With Allied fighters now becoming more numerous, and USAAF pilots having gained more experience in combat, the gaps in the escort coverage for the "heavies" disappeared. There was now no way for the *Jagdwaffe* to attack bombers only.

Despite being progressively more outclassed by later versions of the Thunderbolt, the Bf 109G remained very much in the thick of the action through to war's end. While still an effective dogfighter, the Gustav lacked the speed necessary to initiate combat or escape from Allied fighters. Despite these serious shortcomings, an experienced pilot could use its ability to climb and turn to regain the advantage if caught by surprise. However, the majority of Bf 109G pilots by this stage of the war were far from experienced, and they proved to be easy targets.

Among the *experten* to stick with the Bf 109G through to VE-Day was Oberleutnant Kurt Bühligen, who claimed 112 kills (including nine P-47s), all in the west with JG 2. Having flown the Bf 109 and the Fw 190, he was familiar with the foibles and strengths of both. The latter's propensity to flick sharply over onto one wing during certain maneuvers was well known, and this trait was routinely employed by experienced Fw 190 pilots to extricate themselves from a tight corner. The Bf 109 possessed no such inbuilt, but propitious, flaw, so many pilots, including Bühligen, fell back on a tactic of their own devising for use in an emergency.

They would fly with their machine trimmed slightly tail heavy, keeping the nose down by applying constant forward pressure on the control column. In moments of crisis, the control column could be pulled back and the nose would

MESSERSCHMITT: THROUGH THE GUNSIGHT

All Bf 109s were fitted with reflector gunsights, universally known as the Revi – an abbreviation of *Reflexvisier*. The Bf 109B and some early versions of the C, D and E variants were fitted with the bulky Revi 3. Obsolete by 1939, this sight was replaced by the Revi C 12/C (as illustrated), and later the C 12/D. The former was optimized for fixed armament only, while the C 12/D was calibrated for both fixed gunnery and bombing. The C 12s were simple sights with no computing aids of any kind. They did, however, boast a built-in dimmer to regulate reticule intensity, and this was assisted by the fitment of "sun dark" glass to reduce glare. A small auxiliary optical sight was also fitted in case the C 12 failed.

From late 1943 until war's end, a number of Bf 109G/Ks were fitted with the new Revi 16B gunsight. Much more compact in size, pilots appreciated its smaller dimensions when sat in the cramped cockpit of the Messerschmitt fighter.

Some pilots (particularly aces) in frontline units also had telescopic sights fitted to their Bf 109s in the field, and attempted to have them harmonized with standard Revi reflector gunsights. The sights did not collimate (adjust into line-of-sight, thus allowing the Revi to be brought into play), however, and only served to identify objects that were usually beyond the pilot's clear visual range.

Finally, the Bf 109G/K was fitted with a KG 13A firing grip for operating three combinations of armament – cowling machine guns, engine-mounted cannon and underwing gondola cannon. The grip also boasted a radio actuation button and/or a rearm button for use with the MK 108 cannon if fitted. The gun-firing and radio activation function could be safely performed by the pilot using just two fingers on his right hand. (Artwork by Jim Laurier, © Osprey Publishing) immediately point upwards without the momentary "mushing" which could easily prove fatal.

Leutnant Heinze Knoke, who, like Bühligen, also enjoyed success against the P-47 (five kills), was another *experte* who relied on his years of combat experience to stay alive when dueling with seemingly countless numbers of Thunderbolts:

> The Yanks do not leave us alone. Today they attack Münster in strength. Just when I am ready to pounce with my flight on a formation of Fortresses over the burning city, we are intercepted by dozens of P-47s diving on us from above. A wild dogfight begins. The Thunderbolt has a clumsy appearance which is belied by its high speed and maneuverability. It can still be outfought, however, by a Messerschmitt in the hands of a good pilot.
>
> At my first burst of fire a Thunderbolt ahead of me blows up, and my wingman downs a second one. That brings the entire pack of Thunderbolts down on our necks. It is all we can do to shake them off. I try every trick I know, and put on quite a display of aerobatics. Finally I get away by spiraling up in a corkscrew climb. I know that the Thunderbolt cannot duplicate this maneuver.

Following the carnage of Normandy, the constant hemorrhaging of pilots in ill-fated homeland defense missions and the massive losses of *Bodenplatte*, the *Jagdwaffe* was a spent force by early 1945. Nevertheless, Bf 109G/K units continued to fly missions through to VE-Day, occasionally inflicting losses – but always at some cost to themselves – on Ninth Air Force P-47 units conducting ground support sorties.

ANALYSIS

Between December 1942 and January 1943, 200 P-47s had been sent to Britain. Range was not something that had influenced the equipment of fighter units destined for the ETO because it was thought that operations would be similar to those undertaken by RAF fighters, where high-altitude performance seemed to be the important factor. Early USAAF fighters such as the P-39, P-40 and Allison-engined P-51A had proven unable to match the performance of RAF and German fighters in the ETO, where most combats took place at higher altitudes.

However, the P-47 was built to operate at higher altitudes thanks to the turbosupercharging of its R-2800 engine, and although it was initially slower in the climb than its contemporaries, improvements such as water injection and

EIGHTH/NINTH AIR FORCE FIGHTER LOSSES IN THE ETO 1942–45				
Aircraft	Sorties	Victories air	Victories ground	Losses
P-47	423,435	3,082	3,202	3,077
P-38	129,849	1,771	749	1,758
P-51	213,873	4,950	4,131	2,520

LEADING USAAF P-47 ACES WITH Bf 109 VICTORIES IN THE ETO			
	Bf 109 kills	Overall score	Unit
LtCol Francis S. Gabreski (P-47D)	11	28 (+6.5 in F-86A/Es)	56th FG
Capt Joe H. Powers (P-47C/D)	10.5	14.5	56th FG
1Lt Robert J. Rankin (P-47D)	10	10	56th FG
Capt Robert S. Johnson (P-47C/D)	9	27	56th FG
Maj Gerald W. Johnson (P-47D)	8	16.5	56th/356th FG
Maj Leroy A. Schreiber (P-47D)	8	12	56th FG
Col Glenn E. Duncan (P-47D)	7.5	19.5	353rd FG
Col David C. Schilling (P-47C/D)	7	22.5	56th FG
Capt Duane W. Beeson (P-47C/D)	7	17.333 (5.333 in P-51Bs)	4th FG
Capt Felix D. Williamson (P-47D)	7	13	56th FG
Maj Quince L. Brown (P-47D)	7	12.333	78th FG
LtCol Kenneth W. Gallup (P-47D)	7	9	353rd FG
Maj George E. Bostwick (P-47D/M)	7	8	56th FG
Maj Walter C. Beckham (P-47D)	6	18	353rd FG
Maj Boleslaw M. Gladych (P-47D)	6	18 (8 in RAF Spitfires)	56th FG
Capt Virgil K. Meroney (P-47D)	6	9	352nd FG
Capt Frederick J. Christensen (P-47D)	5	21.5	56th FG
Capt Alwin M. Juchheim (P-47D)	5	9	78th FG

LEADING Bf 109 ACES WITH P-47 VICTORIES IN THE ETO			
	P-47 kills	Overall score	Unit(s)
Oberleutnant Theodor Weissenberger	13	208	JG 5
Major Julius Meimberg	12	53	JG 53
Oberstleutnant Kurt Bühligen	9	112	JG 2
Oberfeldwebel Heinrich Bartels	9	99	JG 27
Leutnant Günther Landt	9	23	JG 53
Leutnant Alfred Hammer	8	26	JG 53
Hauptmann Walter Krupinski	7	197	JG 5/11
Oberleutnant Herbert Rollwage	6	85	JG 53
Major Klaus Mietusch	6	75	JG 26
Hauptmann Ludwig-Wilhelm Burkhardt	6	69	JG 1
Major Hermann Staiger	5	63	JG 26
Hauptmann Heinz Knoke	5	33	JG 1/11
Hauptmann Otto Meyer	5	21	JG 27

EIGHTH AIR FORCE P-47 THUNDERBOLT GROUPS			
4th FG	P-47C/D	3/10/43 to 2/44	To P-51B 2/44
56th FG	P-47C/D/M	2/43 to 9/45	
78th FG	P-47C/D	1/43 to 1/45	To P-51D 1/45
352nd FG	P-47D	7/13/43 to 4/20/44	To P-51B 4/44
353rd FG	P-47D	7/43 to 11/10/44	To P-51D 11/44
355th FG	P-47D	7/43 to 3/13/44	To P-51B 3/44
356th FG	P-47D	9/43 to 11/44	To P-51D 11/44
358th FG	P-47D	12/43 to 1/44	To Ninth AF 1/2/44
359th FG	P-47D	11/43 to 5/44	To P-51B
361st FG	P-47D	12/43 to 5/44	To P-51B
495th FTG	P-47C/D	12/25/43 to 6/45	

NINTH AIR FORCE P-47 THUNDERBOLT GROUPS ON JUNE 9, 1944	
IX TACTICAL AIR COMMAND	
70th FW	
48th FG	P-47D
371st FG	P-47D
71st FW	
366th FG	P-47D
368th FG	P-47D
84th FW	
50th FG	P-47D
365th FG	P-47D
404th FG	P-47D
405th FG	P-47D
XIX TACTICAL AIR COMMAND	
100th FW	
358th FG	P-47D
362nd FG	P-47D
303rd FW	
36th FG	P-47D
373rd FG	P-47D
406th FG	P-47D

paddle-bladed propellers soon gave it a performance that matched the Bf 109G and Fw 190A.

In the spring of 1943, the growing strength of VIII Bomber Command increased pressure on the *Jagdgeschwaderen* in the west. At this time the Luftwaffe, unhappy with the relatively small numbers of bombers being shot down, revised its tactics. On December 20, German pilots began attacking bomber formations from dead ahead, or "12 o'clock level." Closing speeds of around 600mph made it difficult to keep targets in effective firing range for more than a split-second, and German pilots were always fearful of colliding with their targets. Larger attacking formations, and simultaneous attacks by fighters, rather than in trail, were now also used. While they would still use the head-on approach, the angle of attack would be from ten degrees above the horizontal – otherwise known as "12 o'clock high" – which, in experiments, was found to be more effective. As before, the best chance of knocking a bomber out of formation was to kill the pilots in the cockpit.

All told, the Thunderbolt was flown by 18 of the top 30 American aces in Europe during the war. Official figures credit the P-47 with the destruction of 4.6 enemy aircraft for each Thunderbolt lost in aerial combat during 1,934,000 flying hours, using 204,504,000 gallons of fuel.

During the first five months of 1945, Thunderbolts flew an average of 1,677 hours and dropped 541 tons of bombs per day. From D-Day to VE-Day, Thunderbolt ground-attack operations were claimed to have accounted for 86,000 railroad cars, 9,000 locomotives, 68,000 motor vehicles and 6,000 armored vehicles in Germany alone. Thunderbolt groups dropped 132,000 tons of bombs, expended more than 135 million rounds of ammunition, 60,000 rockets and several thousand gallons of napalm. An impressive two-thirds of all Thunderbolts produced were exported to overseas combat commands, and 54 percent of these were lost to enemy action and other causes.

Late in the war, the *Tagjagd* or day fighter pilots were badly trained and hastily thrown into the battle against all odds, and only a handful survived in the lethal skies over the Third Reich. Young replacement fighter pilots who joined the *Reichsverteidigung* (Defense of the Reich) as 1944 progressed had only limited chances to survive in air combat, as they were primarily misused as "cannon fodder." In early 1944, 50 percent of all German fighter pilots were combat experienced veterans, with the remainder being replacement pilots. The majority of the latter category had only a minimum of flying experience in first-line fighters, and no combat experience at all to compensate for the heavy losses from which the Luftwaffe then severely suffered.

It was not uncommon for replacement pilots not to have flown a fully armed Bf 109G/K prior to reaching the front line. Take-offs and landings in formation were also rarely undertaken in training units, and pilots never fired the MK 108 and MG 151 cannon prior to entering combat. The tactics employed in the frontline were entirely new tasks to be learned as well. All of this occurred during a period of about two months, with severe restrictions on flying time because gasoline supplies were becoming increasingly limited.

A graphic example of what could happen to the unwary when taking off or landing in the Bf 109G. Oberfeldwebel Alfred Müller of 4./JG 27 poses somewhat sheepishly beside the spectacular remains of his Gustav following a training accident at Fels am Wagram in June 1944. And Müller was no novice, having claimed eight victories over Allied aircraft prior to the crash. He would double his tally (which included five "heavies") prior to being killed in action on August 16, 1944.

AFTERMATH

THUNDERBOLTS OUTSIDE THE ETO

The P-47D was the first version of the Thunderbolt to serve with the USAAF in the Pacific, the 348th FG commencing escort missions from Brisbane, Australia in the spring of 1943. During 1944 the Thunderbolt became operational in all active theaters of war except for Alaska. P-47s served with the Mexican, Free French and Soviet forces, and in Burma, RAF and Tenth Air Force P-47Ds operated in the Arakan campaign. Some 830 P-47 Thunderbolts were supplied to the RAF, and they were operated by 16 squadrons almost entirely in the Far East. In Burma, No. 5 Sqn's P-47 fighter-bombers flew "cab-rank" patrols directed by ground visual control posts. Carrying three 500lb bombs and equipped with heavy machine guns, they created havoc among the Japanese troops and supply lines. Thunderbolts disappeared from the RAF inventory soon after VJ-Day.

Early in 1945, the introduction of the P-47N, with its increased internal fuel capacity, enabled the Thunderbolt to begin escorting B-29s to targets in the Japanese home islands. The 318th FG on Saipan was the first combat unit in the Pacific to receive N-models, the group commencing combat operations over Japan in spring 1945. On May 25 the 318th FG shot down 34 Japanese aircraft without suffering a single loss.

From 1947 to 1952 F-47Ns saw active service with the US Air Force and Air National Guard (ANG) units. The last active USAF Thunderbolt group was the 14th FG at Dow Field, Maine, which reequipped with F-84B Thunderjets in 1947. At least two squadrons of F-47Ns were active in Air Defense Command until 1952, and the ANG finally phased out the last of its P-47Ns for jet aircraft in 1953.

Bf 109S OUTSIDE THE ETO

During 1941 I./JG 27 was transferred to North Africa to supplement the small Luftwaffe force then operating in that area, which was still equipped with the Bf 109E-4/Trop at Ain-el-Gazala. On September 24, Leutnant Hans-Joachim Marseille claimed the destruction of five enemy aircraft, and he soon became the most celebrated German pilot in the Middle East with a total score of 158 victories, 151 of them achieved in North Africa. Marseille was killed in a flying accident in a Bf 109G on September 30, 1942.

Early in 1942, opposed only by Hawker Hurricane IIs and Curtiss Tomahawks, JG 27 destroyed large numbers of Allied aircraft. JG 53 was also based variously in Greece, Crete and Sicily, and mainly took part in operations against Malta. Nine *Gruppen* equipped with the Bf 109G were operational in July 1943, and they were heavily engaged during the Allied invasion of Sicily.

On July 5, 1943, eight fighter *Gruppen*, including II. and III./JG 3 and III./JG 52, equipped with the Bf 109G took part in Operation *Zitadelle*, a major attempt to regain the initiative in Russia. They claimed the destruction of 432 Soviet aircraft, of which II./JG 3 destroyed 77, including 62 bombers.

In 1943 around 600 Bf 109s were built in Hungary. In addition to production for the Luftwaffe, Messerschmitt exported Bf 109s to Bulgaria, Finland, Hungary, Japan, Rumania, Slovakia, Spain, Switzerland and Yugoslavia. Postwar, in Spain Hispano built Merlin-engined Bf 109s for the Spanish air force under a license negotiated in 1942. Finland, which had received Bf 109Gs in 1943, operated "Gustavs" until 1954. The Czechoslovakian air force was equipped with DB 605-engined Avia S-99s and a far larger number of S-199 aircraft powered by Junkers Jumo 211F engines. The fledgling Israeli Air Force purchased 25 early-production aircraft from Czechoslovakia, and on May 29, 1948, an S-199 flew its first combat mission for the *Chel ha'Avir*. Czechoslovakian Bf 109s remained in service until 1957.

161
Iain Wyllie

Part III

TOOTH AND CLAW: DUELS OVER CHINA, 1944

P-40 WARHAWK vs Ki-43 "OSCAR"

In the annals of aerial warfare, no aircraft type has come to symbolize a campaign as much as the Curtiss P-40 Warhawk's battles in China in 1941–45. Known the world over for the distinctive sharksmouth warpaint on their noses, P-40 fighters first saw combat in China with the legendary American Volunteer Group (AVG), and continued to fight while equipping squadrons of the USAAF throughout World War II.

Just as ubiquitous as the P-40 in the skies over China was its chief adversary in the Imperial Japanese Army Air Force (IJAAF). Codenamed "Oscar" by the Allies, the Nakajima Ki-43 or Type 1 *Hayabusa* (peregrine falcon) was the Warhawk's most common foe in the aerial battles of southeast Asia. Though never achieving the iconic status of the P-40, the Ki-43 nevertheless proved a worthy opponent whenever the aircraft met in combat.

These two aircraft types were the products of vastly different, yet contemporary, philosophies of fighter design. The P-40 reflected the thinking of American war planners in the late 1930s. It was heavily armed, sturdy and reasonably fast at medium and low altitudes, with armor plate protection for the pilot and self-sealing fuel tanks. Its inline Allison engine was powerful and reliable. The price paid by the P-40 for these attributes was weight, which contributed to its slow rate of climb and sluggish performance at high altitude.

The Ki-43 was a stiletto to the battle-ax P-40. A logical extension of World War I fighter thinking and the samurai tradition combined in one airframe, the Ki-43 design favored maneuverability over all other characteristics. Light weight and a large wing area gave it a small turning radius and a high rate of climb – just what a pilot needed for close-in dogfighting. But to achieve the Ki-43's low wing loading, its designers had to sacrifice firepower (the airplane only carried two machine guns) and survivability.

Although the P-40 and Ki-43 met in combat throughout the Pacific War from New Guinea and the Solomon Islands to the steaming jungles of Burma, their

At 1444hrs on April 24, 1943, the Japanese 1st Air Brigade launched 44 Ki-43 "Oscars" of the 25th and 33rd Sentais on a raid against the USAAF base at Ling Ling. The 23rd FG/75th FS launched 14 P-40K Warhawks in defense of its base, and intercepted the attackers some ten miles southeast of their airfield. The subsequent fight lasted an extraordinarily long 55 minutes, and ranking 75th FS ace Capt John Hampshire succeeded in claiming one "Oscar" destroyed, as did three other pilots from the squadron. No P-40s were lost in return, despite the Japanese claiming three destroyed. (Artwork by Iain Wyllie, © Osprey Publishing) duel peaked during the air campaign that accompanied the Japanese *Ichi-Go* land offensive in China during 1944. The classic engagements that took place over the Hsiang River Valley during the siege of Hengyang are our focus in this book, when day after day during the summer of 1944, P-40s and Ki-43s clashed in the skies over China. Although the Chinese and American pilots under the command of MajGen Claire L. Chennault maintained air superiority, the Japanese ground offensive ultimately achieved its goals of capturing Allied air bases in East China and completing a land link from French Indo-China to the great port city of Shanghai.

There was a very human story to the aerial clashes in *Ichi-Go*, with fighter pilots on both sides displaying courage, imagination and flying skill in great measure. Sadly, the personal accounts of this campaign that survive are largely limited to those of the P-40 pilots. Much to the author's frustration, few if any personal stories by or about Ki-43 pilots who flew in China have come to light – and certainly none in the English language. There are several reasons for this.

Firstly, it is important to understand how few Japanese fighter pilots were involved in the China campaign. The IJAAF had just two Ki-43 *sentais*, with an authorized strength of 57 pilots each, and considerably fewer pilots and aircraft actually available for operations at any given time. Combat inevitably took its toll on both men and machines, and the IJAAF was not able to provide replacements in sufficient numbers to maintain the units at full strength.

The fact that Japan ultimately lost the war also helps to explain the dearth of personal accounts. The nation's *bushido* code of warrior values, which stressed death before dishonor, caused many pilots who survived the conflict to suffer deep feelings of personal shame. They were neither inclined nor encouraged to record their stories postwar, and many records of the units in which they served were destroyed as the conflict drew to a close. So, as the succeeding years have passed, these pilots died in silence, and their stories of air combat in China went with them to their graves.

It may strike the readers of this book as ironic that we know more about the technical aspects of the Ki-43 as a weapon of war than we know about the men who risked their lives to fly it in combat. That is a fair assessment, and a sad one at that.

THE MACHINES

CURTISS P-40 WARHAWK

The Curtiss P-40 series had such a long and involved development history that it is difficult to say when the process actually began. Do the roots of the P-40 spring from the various Curtiss Hawk biplane fighters produced in the 1920s and early 1930s? Or does the story start with the XP-934 Swift of 1932, which was the unsuccessful first attempt by Curtiss to build a monoplane fighter? Perhaps the former, perhaps the latter, or perhaps a little of both. But the fact remains that by the early 1930s, those designs, and others, had helped to establish the Curtiss Aeroplane Division of the Curtiss-Wright Corporation as one of the leading manufacturers of military aircraft in the United States, if not the world.

In 1934, Curtiss initiated the design of a new monoplane fighter, the Hawk 75. The design team, led by former Northrop engineer Donovan H. Berlin, was instructed to come up with a fighter that could win a USAAC contract competition the following year. Berlin's team created a low-wing monoplane that featured a fully enclosed cockpit and retractable landing gear, and was powered by a 900hp Wright twin-row radial engine.

The airplane first flew in April 1935, but failed to win the Army contract, which went to the Seversky P-35. Instead, the Army ordered three Curtiss service test aircraft and designated them Y1P-36s. USAAC officials were greatly impressed by the improvements the company had made with this machine when compared with the original H-75, and in June 1937 they issued Curtiss with a contract to build 210 P-36s. France quickly followed with an additional order for 200 fighters.

By all accounts the P-36 was an excellent aircraft, with a robust airframe, reliable powerplant and lively flying characteristics. In fact, the Royal Air Force flew export versions of the airplane against the Japanese in Burma well into 1944. But as early as 1938, it became obvious that the 300mph top speed of the P-36 was not fast enough to allow the aircraft to remain competitive with the advanced fighter designs emerging from Europe.

Donovan Berlin went back to work on the H-75 design, replacing the radial engine with a turbosupercharged version of the new Allison V-1710 liquid-cooled inline powerplant and moving the cockpit aft to offset the additional weight in the nose. The streamlined XP-37 delivered a performance boost as expected, achieving a top speed of 340mph in initial testing. The Army ordered 13 service test models of the YP-37, but the experimental turbosupercharger proved unreliable and sightlines from the cockpit were very poor, so further development of the airplane was abandoned. The seed of an idea had been planted, however, a seed that soon would bloom in the form of the legendary Curtiss P-40.

Berlin returned to the basic P-36 design again for his next attempt to build a high-performance fighter, but this time he took a simpler path. Recognizing that the USAAC believed it needed a fighter that produced maximum performance at an altitude of just 15,000ft, Donovan did away with the complex turbosupercharging system of the P-37 and simply mated a 1,050hp Allison V-1710-19 engine, with conventional supercharging, to the airframe of the tenth production P-36A. The new fighter, already designated the XP-40 by the USAAC, had a long, pointed nose similar to the P-37's and the radiator mounted under the fuselage aft of the trailing edge of the wing.

The XP-40 made its maiden flight on October 14, 1938, with Curtiss assistant chief test pilot Ed Elliott at the controls. The airplane looked fast, but in initial testing it was unable to top 340mph at 15,000ft. Various tweaks to the design followed, including moving the radiator into a cowling under the nose and replacing the engine with a more powerful V-1710-33, but its speed remained disappointing.

The P-40 had other strengths, however. Its handling was generally good, although the airplane wasn't as maneuverable as the P-36, and it had spectacular diving speed. But, most importantly, it was available. Converting the Curtiss factory from production of the P-36 to the similar P-40 would be a relatively simple task, compared to gearing up to build an entirely new aircraft.

By January 1939, when the USAAC held its next fighter competition, tensions were already rising in Europe and southeast Asia. Although isolationist sentiment remained high in the United States, Congress had appropriated funds for a major build-up of the nation's military forces, including the acquisition of a large number of new fighter aircraft. After comparing the XP-40 to other fighter proposals that were not yet as far along in development, such as the Lockheed P-38 and the Bell P-39, the USAAC issued a record-setting contract to Curtiss on April 26, 1939 for 524 P-40s at a cost of nearly $13 million.

Although the XP-40 had yet to satisfy the desired performance specifications set out by the USAAC, the low price and quick availability of the new Curtiss fighter had carried the day. More advanced designs – especially the P-38 – promised speed and altitude performance far superior to the P-40, but their manufacturers would require at least two years before they could begin delivering them to the Army. Deliveries of the P-40 could start in half that time, allowing the USAAC to embark on its buildup while Lockheed and other manufacturers developed the next generation of American fighters.

THE P-40 THROUGH 360 DEGREES

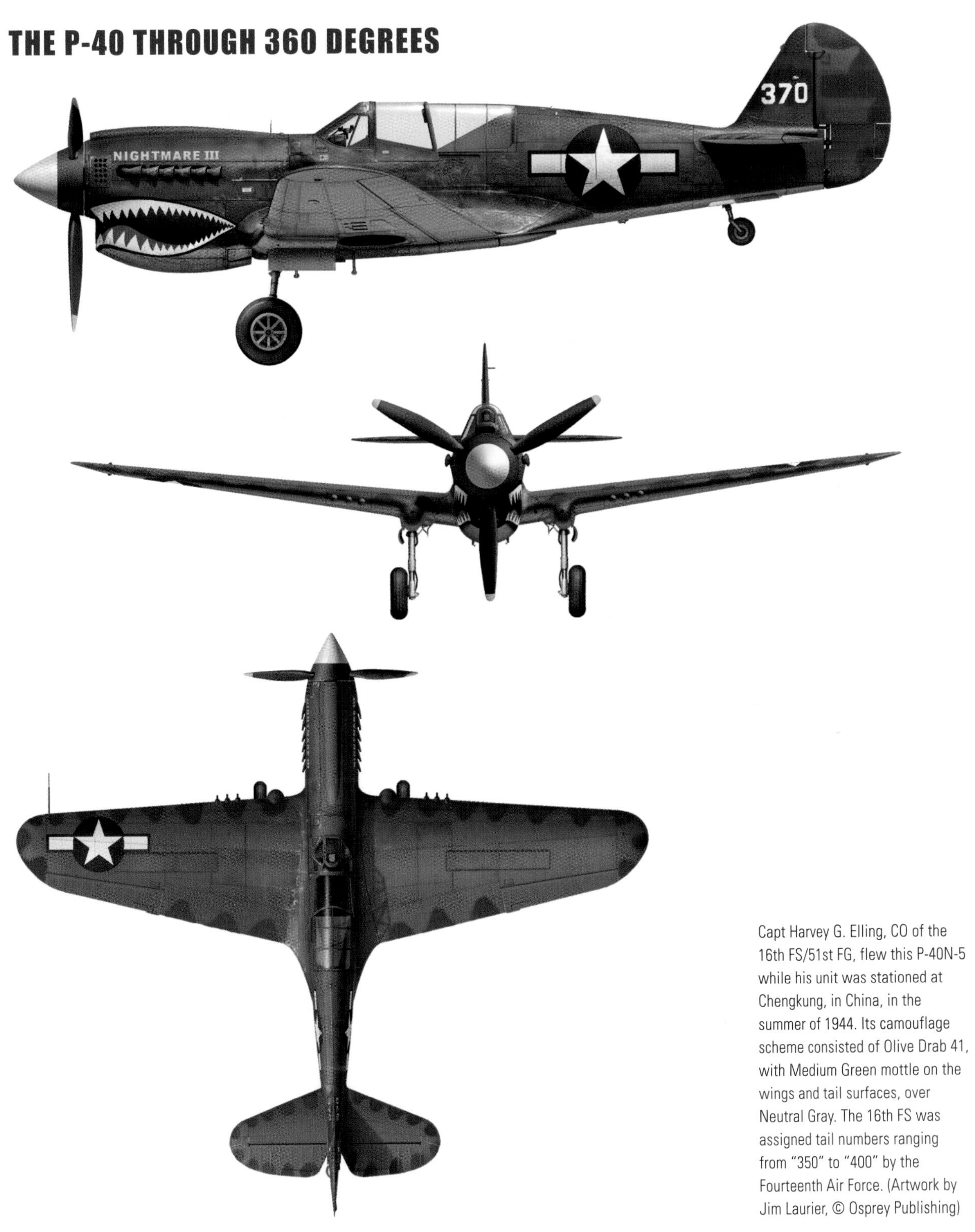

Capt Harvey G. Elling, CO of the 16th FS/51st FG, flew this P-40N-5 while his unit was stationed at Chengkung, in China, in the summer of 1944. Its camouflage scheme consisted of Olive Drab 41, with Medium Green mottle on the wings and tail surfaces, over Neutral Gray. The 16th FS was assigned tail numbers ranging from "350" to "400" by the Fourteenth Air Force. (Artwork by Jim Laurier, © Osprey Publishing)

The Army chose to skip the option of ordering Y-prefixed service test aircraft and went directly to the P-40 production model. Designated the Hawk 81 by Curtiss, the production model featured the "Dash-33" Allison engine and carried four machine guns – two .50in weapons in the upper cowling and one .30in gun in each wing. Meanwhile, the Curtiss engineers continued to massage the design in the quest for more speed. In December 1939, the modified XP-40 reached 366mph at the desired altitude, satisfying the Army that the P-40 was sufficiently developed to go into mass production.

The first production P-40 (serial number 39-156) rolled off the Curtiss production line in March 1940. The airplane, along with the next two off the line, went through a series of tests that determined its top speed was 357mph at 15,000ft, its cruising speed was 277mph and its landing speed was 80mph. The P-40's service ceiling was 32,750ft, and it could climb 3,080ft during the first minute of flight, reaching 15,000ft in 5.3 minutes. Deliveries of the first 200 P-40s to the USAAC began in June 1940. In time, the P-40 would acquire the name "Warhawk" in Army service.

Curtiss also began producing an export version of the Hawk 81, which was dubbed the Tomahawk. France had been the first country to place an order, but none of the 185 H-81-A1s it purchased in May 1939 had been delivered prior to the nation being occupied by German forces just over a year later. Great Britain was by then desperate to obtain additional fighters for the RAF so it took over the French aircraft, along with placing its own order for Tomahawks.

Sources disagree as to whether Curtiss produced a P-40A or not, but the first significant upgrade to the line was the P-40B, or H-81A-2. The changes in this model were the product of intelligence gleaned from the air battles that took place during the first year of the war in Europe. They included refinements such as self-sealing fuel tanks, armor protection for the pilot behind the seat and in the windshield and the addition of one .30in machine gun in each wing. New self-sealing tanks were introduced in the P-40C, these reducing the internal fuel capacity from 160gal down to 135gal. The provision to carry an external 52gal drop tank on the centerline was added to compensate. Each of these items added weight, and the performance of the new models – particularly their rate of climb – suffered accordingly. But these were the first models of the P-40 to be truly combat-capable.

The first P-40s to see action were actually RAF Tomahawks in North Africa in June 1941. The strengths and weaknesses of the Curtiss fighter soon made themselves apparent in combat against German and Italian adversaries. Commonwealth pilots quickly came to appreciate the Tomahawk as a stable gun platform with a reliable powerplant and a robust airframe, capable of absorbing battle damage sufficient to bring down most of its contemporaries. The British replaced the .30in wing guns with their own .303in weapons to simplify supply problems, and pilots found this armament sufficient for desert warfare. The Tomahawk's maneuverability and dive speed also made the fighter competitive with the German Bf 109E/Fs and Italian C.202s it met in combat. The Tomahawk's major shortcoming for desert combat, however, was its poor performance at higher altitudes.

Top Australian ace Clive Caldwell, who scored 20.5 victories in Curtiss fighters, noted that while the Tomahawk performed creditably in a dogfight if operating within its own altitude limitations, pilots were forced to leave the initiative with their higher flying opponents. In order to engage the enemy at the Tomahawk's best height, pilots soon learned to accept the fact that they had to endure an initial attack from above. Aviators from at least eight different nations flew P-40s and Tomahawks during the H-81's operational combat life. Perhaps the most famous of these airplanes were the 100 Tomahawks diverted from the British in 1941 to equip the AVG in Burma and China.

While the Curtiss factory worked around the clock turning out P-40s and Tomahawks, Allison engineers were busy developing a more powerful version of the V-1710 engine. The 1,150hp Allison F (V-1710-39) was initially slated for the new Curtiss XP-46 fighter, but the Army did not want to shut down the company's production plant long enough to convert to the new fighter. Curtiss, meanwhile, had redesigned the P-40 with the new engine to fill a British order in May 1940. The Army bought 22 examples of the new H-87A Kittyhawk as the P-40D in September 1940, and soon followed this initial purchase up with orders for 820 P-40Es.

Maj Bruce Holloway flies a 76th FS P-40E near Kunming in 1942. The airplane lacks the U.S. ARMY marking under its wings, indicating that it may be one of the AVG hand-me-downs. The blue 76th FS fuselage band is barely visible. (Bill Johnson)

The H-87A was a major departure from the earlier models, as it boasted a totally new fuselage. A change in gearing moved up the thrust line of the V-1710-39 engine, and thus the center of the propeller spinner, so that it was now nearly in line with the exhaust stacks. With the higher line of thrust, the fuselage was shortened by 6.75in, and the radiator/oil cooler chin scoop was deepened. The upper section of the fuselage was cut down, and a larger cockpit opening gave the pilot improved vision.

Armament also changed in the H-87A. The nose guns were removed, and two .50in weapons were installed in each wing, along with an improved system of hydraulic gun chargers. The nearly identical H-87A-3/P-40E featured six wing guns, with 281 rounds of ammunition per gun. A 500lb bomb or 52gal drop tank could be fitted on the centerline shackle, and six 20lb bombs could be mounted to attachments on the undersides of the wings.

The improvements in the P-40D/E did not translate into significantly better speed or altitude performance over prior models, however. Top speed was 355mph at 15,000ft, and the service ceiling dropped to 29,000ft. Range was a respectable 800 miles at normal speeds and 1,150 miles at 195mph.

When a supply of Rolls-Royce-designed Merlin engines became available in 1941, a P-40D was modified to accept the powerplant made famous in the RAF's Spitfire and Hurricane fighters. Designated the P-40F/Kittyhawk II, the new version had a slightly different nose that had a deeper chin inlet and lacked the air scoop on top of the cowling. Partway through its production run of 1,311, the P-40F got a 26in extension to the rear of the fuselage to improve directional stability. This feature carried over to the P-40L, which Curtiss attempted to lighten by deleting two wing guns and other equipment. The Merlin 28 engine, built in the US by Packard, featured a single-stage, two-speed supercharger that offered modestly better altitude performance than the Allison engine. Other than that, the performance of the P-40F/L was similar to earlier models. The next Allison-powered H-87, the P-40K or Kittyhawk III, featured an improved V-1710-73 and an enlarged vertical tail, the latter being yet another attempt to improve directional stability. This aircraft also got the 26in fuselage extension late in its production run, and the similar P-40M that followed it also had this feature.

The last major version of the H-87, and the most numerous, was the P-40N/Kittyhawk IV series. In the P-40N, powered by the same Allison V-1710-81 that equipped the P-40M, Curtiss engineers took the lightening efforts started in the P-40L several steps further, and in the process produced the fastest production model with a top speed of 378mph. But there was a price to pay for the slight increase in speed. The P-40N-1's armament was reduced to four guns and its front wing tank and internal starter were removed – none of these deletions were well received by frontline pilots using the N-model on combat operations.

Various improvements were introduced in the eight sub-variants of the P-40N that followed, the most visible of these being a modified cockpit canopy with a frameless sliding hood and the cut-down rear fuselage deck of the P-40N-5, which also reverted to six-gun armament.

The last Warhawk, P-40N-40 (serial number 44-47964) rolled out of the Curtiss factory on November 30, 1944, completing a production run of 13,738 aircraft.

NAKAJIMA Ki-43 "OSCAR"

Although the Nakajima Ki-43 was vastly different from the Curtiss P-40 in concept and design, the development paths of the two fighters were remarkably similar. Like Curtiss in the United States, Nakajima Hikoki KK was already an established Japanese manufacturer of military aircraft by the mid-1930s. Starting with the A1N1 naval carrier fighter – a license-built version of the Gloster Gambet – in 1925, Nakajima turned out a steady stream of successful fighters for the Imperial Japanese Naval Air Force (IJNAF) and IJAAF. Most of these in-house designs were biplanes, including the outstanding A2N carrier fighter of 1930, although Nakajima also produced the Type 91 parasol monoplane fighter for the Army.

Ki-27s of 10th Dokuritsu Hiko Chutai on May 2, 1939. This unit took part in the Hankow campaign that year, but claimed no victories then. It continued flying in China until late 1941, when the 10th returned to Japan to convert to the Ki-43-I and was redesignated the 25th Sentai in November 1942. (Yasuho Izawa)

When the IJAAF sought proposals in 1935 for a new single-seat monoplane fighter, Nakajima, and its rivals Kawasaki and Mitsubishi, responded with three designs. The Kawasaki Ki-28, Mitsubishi Ki-33 and Nakajima Ki-12 all promised a good turn of speed, but that was not to be the determining characteristic when the IJAAF flight-tested the prototypes in early 1937. Army planners were also looking for maneuverability, light weight and simplicity in their new fighter, and that is what they found in Nakajima's Ki-27.

Conceived by Nakajima engineers Yasumi Koyama and Professor Hideo Itokawa, the Ki-27 embodied the smallest practical airframe that could be designed around the best available radial engine, Nakajima's Ha-1-Ko. This nine-cylinder powerplant produced 710hp for takeoff and 650hp at 6,560ft. The airplane featured all-metal stressed-skin construction, with an oval-section semi-monocoque fuselage, a large wing employing an NN-2 airfoil section, a fixed undercarriage housed in streamlined fairings and a sliding canopy over the cockpit. The clean lines of the Ki-27 were in keeping with the old axiom that when an aircraft looks right, it usually flies well.

With a wing loading of 14.33lb per square foot, the Ki-27 was markedly more maneuverable than its rivals for the IJAAF contract, while nearly matching them in maximum speed and rate of climb. An order for ten preproduction aircraft was issued, and at the end of service trials in December 1937, the Imperial Army placed a large-quantity order for the Ki-27-Ko, featuring a more powerful Ha-1-Otsu engine, a variable-pitch propeller and two 7.7mm machine guns.

Deliveries of the new fighter began in March 1938, and within weeks the Ki-27 had scored its first combat success when Capt Tateo Kato claimed the destruction of three Chinese-flown Polikarpov I-15 fighters over northern China. Understandably, Army pilots were ecstatic about their new mount. By this time, however, Nakajima engineers were already designing the fighter that would become its successor.

Politics was to play a major role in shaping the concept and design of Nakajima's next fighter. The company had been the only manufacturer to come away from the Army fighter competition of 1937 with an order for airplanes. That meant Kawasaki and Mitsubishi had been left to bear the tremendous costs that they had invested into their prototypes. To forestall the chance of this happening again, they began lobbying the Japanese Diet (government) for a change in procurement policy to eliminate the competitive selection of military aircraft. The lawmakers agreed, and orders were passed to Army Air Headquarters that a single manufacturer would supply the next fighter.

With Nakajima being the only aircraft company that had proven its ability to produce a modern fighter to the Army's satisfaction, it was abundantly clear which manufacturer would get the contract for the Ki-27's replacement. Nakajima received the development contract for the Army's next generation fighter, the Ki-43, in December 1937.

The immediate combat success of the Ki-27 in China served to support the Army's philosophy of favoring light weight and maneuverability in its fighter aircraft. With the same generals in charge of procuring the Ki-43 and the same team of engineers designing the airplane, it is hardly a surprise that the new fighter would represent an uninspiring small step forward in aviation technology. The generals instructed Nakajima to produce a fighter that would have maneuverability at least equal to the Ki-27, but with greater speed, a faster rate of climb and longer range. And that is what Nakajima eventually gave them, but just barely.

Following the pattern set by the Ki-27, Koyama and Itokawa again set out to produce the smallest and lightest possible airplane around the best available radial engine, which was now the 14-cylinder Nakajima Ha-25. The Ki-43 was another aerodynamically clean low-wing, stressed-skin all-metal monoplane. Its three-spar, one-piece wing had metal-framed control surfaces covered in fabric and contained four fuel tanks with a total capacity of 125gal. Again, two 7.7mm machine guns were mounted in the upper decking of the forward fuselage. The only major departure from the earlier design was the inclusion of hydraulically operated folding undercarriage members.

The first Ki-43 prototype was rolled out on December 12, 1938, and it was immediately disappointing. Not only was the airplane seven percent heavier than its calculated structural weight, but initial flight tests at Tachikawa revealed it lacked the responsiveness and maneuverability of the Ki-27. To make matters worse, the Ki-43 proved barely faster than the Ki-27, and its landing gear was difficult to retract and lower. Perhaps the only successful element of the Ki-43 was its Ha-25 engine, and that was a copy of an American design.

When the disappointed IJAAF threatened to cancel further development of the Ki-43, Nakajima's designers went back to the drawing board. They refined and lightened the airframe, reducing the fuselage cross-section and redesigning the aft section and tail surfaces. An all-around-vision cockpit canopy was introduced as well.

Perhaps the most important change in the redesigned Ki-43 was the addition of the so-called "butterfly" combat flap. This Fowler-type flap could be deployed to increase lift, giving the airplane a dramatically tighter turning radius. Ten preproduction Ki-43s went into flight-testing, and this time the Army evaluators were greatly impressed with the improvements. It was found that the Ki-43 could now be looped and "Immelmanned" at speeds of 168mph or slower, stall recovery and acceleration from low airspeeds were excellent and the "butterfly" flaps produced an astounding rate of turn. What the testing did not discover was that Nakajima's efforts to lighten the wing structure had also weakened it, making the wing vulnerable to structural failure in high-g combat maneuvers.

On January 9, 1941, more than three years after Nakajima designers began working on the Ki-43 project, the Army gave approval for production of the Type 1 Fighter Model 1-Ko to begin, and formally bestowed on it the name *Hayabusa.* Nakajima's plant at Ota geared up for production, and deliveries of the Ki-43 began in June 1941. Two months later, the 59th and 64th Sentais became the first units to begin converting from the tried-and-true Ki-27 to the new Ki-43. Both units suffered accidents resulting from wing failures during dives, and their remaining fighters were hurriedly modified to rectify the problem. The modification would prove only moderately successful, however.

By November, just weeks before Japan's attack on the US installation at Pearl Harbor, Hawaii, the two Hayabusa units had completed their training and moved to bases in southeast Asia. They went into action on the first morning of the Pacific War on December 7, and within two weeks they had run up considerable scores of enemy aircraft destroyed in combat over Malaya, Burma and Singapore. Initially, the Allies assumed that all Japanese low-wing radial-engined fighters were Mitsubishi A6M Type 0s, but when it became known that the Ki-43 was indeed an entirely different aircraft, they assigned it the codename "Oscar."

From the outset of production, the IJAAF and Nakajima knew that the Ki-43-I would be an interim version of the new fighter. Design work on the definitive model of the Hayabusa began almost immediately, and in February 1942 the first of five prototype Ki-43-IIs rolled out of Nakajima's experimental workshop at Ota.

Although outwardly similar to the previous model, the Ki-43-II featured numerous important upgrades. A new optical gunsight replaced the telescopic sight, modest pilot armor protection was added, the radiator was improved and the wing tips were reengineered. The wing was strengthened internally, and provisions were added to mount bombs or drop tanks from racks under the wings. Armament was upgraded to two 12.7mm Ho-103 Type 1 machine guns, with 250 rounds of ammunition per weapon, and this would remain standard in all future models of the Hayabusa. At the front of the airplane, a redesigned air intake system was routed to the 1,150hp Ha-115 engine, which featured a two-stage supercharger and drove a fixed-pitch, three-blade propeller.

Trials of the new Hayabusa revealed it to be an improvement over the previous model, and the IJAAF ordered the fighter into production. In November 1942,

THE Ki-43 THROUGH 360 DEGREES

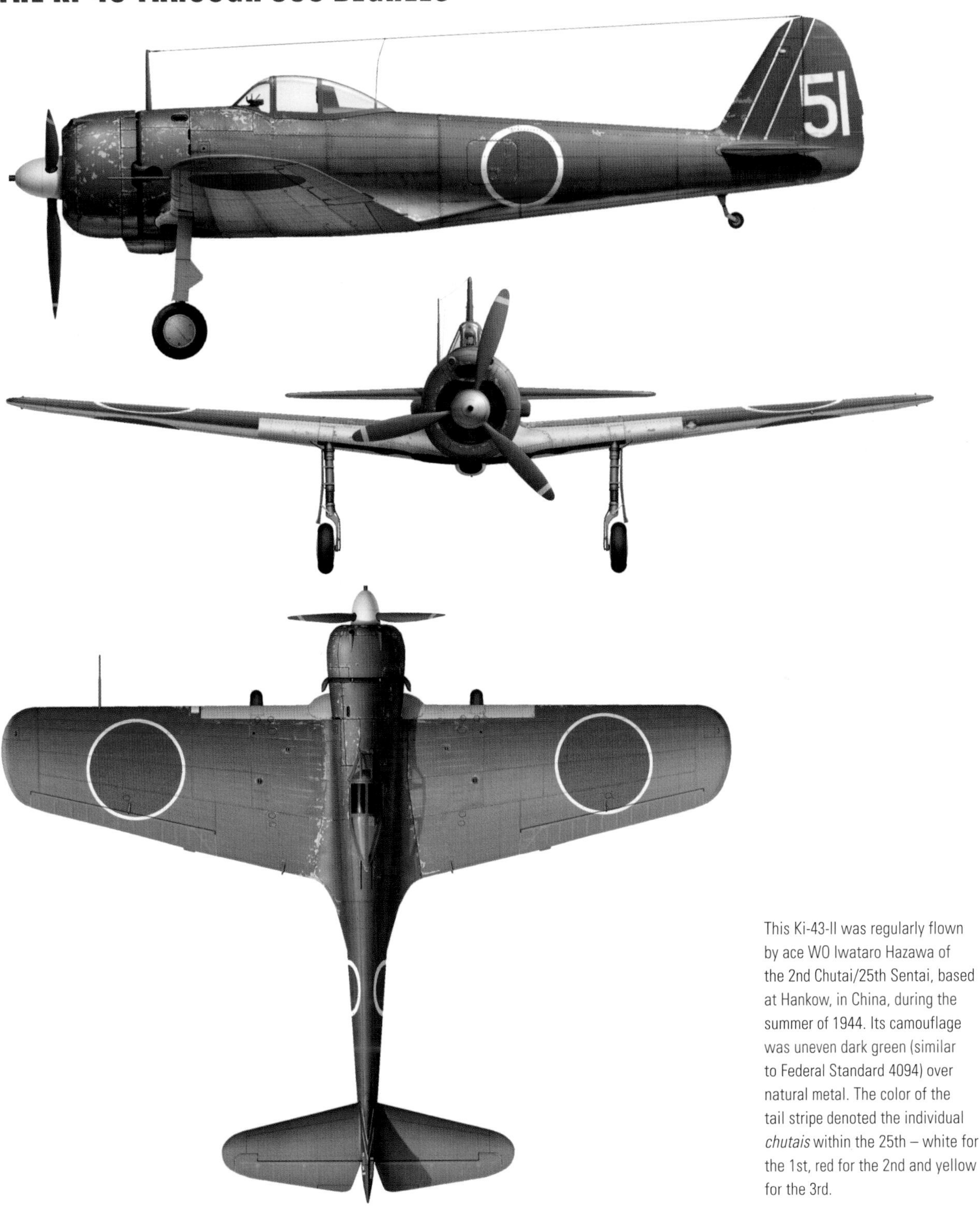

This Ki-43-II was regularly flown by ace WO Iwataro Hazawa of the 2nd Chutai/25th Sentai, based at Hankow, in China, during the summer of 1944. Its camouflage was uneven dark green (similar to Federal Standard 4094) over natural metal. The color of the tail stripe denoted the individual *chutais* within the 25th – white for the 1st, red for the 2nd and yellow for the 3rd.

Ejector-style exhaust stacks, which increased the performance of the late-build Hayabusas, were introduced on the Ki-43-II-KAI and carried over to the Ki-43-III. Here, China-based American soldiers inspect a captured Ki-43-II-KAI fitted with droppable wing tanks. (Craig Busby)

the Ki-43-II-Ko began to supplant the Ki-43-I on the assembly line at Ota, gradually claiming a greater share of the production volume until the last Ki-43-I was rolled out in February 1943. The Ki-43-II, in several versions, would go on to become the model of the Hayabusa produced in the greatest numbers. The airplane boasted a top speed of 329mph at 13,125ft, a service ceiling of 36,750ft and a normal range of 1,095 miles. It would fight on every major front of the Pacific War, and also equipped advanced training units in Japan and southeast Asia.

A final version of the Hayabusa was the Ki-43-III, which appeared in 1944. It is a testament to the decline of Japan's fortunes by this point in the war that the aircraft was produced at all, since the performance of advanced Allied fighters had long since left the nimble Hayabusa far behind. Built mainly by Tachikawa so as to allow Nakajima to concentrate on its superior Ki-84 *Hayate* fighter, the Ki-43-III mounted a more powerful Ha-115-II engine of 1,190hp, with individual exhaust stacks protruding from the rear of the cowling. The additional power allowed the Ki-43-III to reach a top speed of 358mph at 21,920ft and a service ceiling of 37,400ft, but it remained hindered by its woefully inadequate armament of two machine guns. Tachikawa manufactured close to 1,000 Ki-43-IIIs between October 1944 and June 1945.

The Ki-43 remained in frontline service with the IJAAF from the first day of the Pacific War to the last, equipping 36 fighter *sentais* and numerous independent units for at least part of that time. Although IJAAF fighters with better performance were introduced throughout the war, the Ki-43 was still in service with 18 *sentais* when the conflict finally ended.

TYPE HISTORY

CURTISS P-40

P-40/TOMAHAWK I

Aircraft in the first batch of 199 production P-40s were not truly combat-worthy, as they lacked armor-plating and self-sealing fuel tanks. Fortunately, the US had not yet entered the war when the first P-40s were delivered. Powered by an early version of the Allison V-1710 liquid-cooled V12 engine, the aircraft was fitted with two .50in machine guns in the nose and one .30in weapon in each wing. The French ordered a similar model, designated the H-81-A1, which was armed with four .30in wing guns instead of two. Most of these were taken over by the British as Tomahawk Is in mid-1940 after France fell to the Germans. They were employed by the RAF primarily as trainers, or stored for future shipment overseas.

P-40B/C/TOMAHAWK II

The first upgrade of the P-40 line addressed many of the shortcomings of the previous model. Improvements included armor protection for the pilot, upgraded radio equipment and the addition of a second .30in machine gun in each wing. The P-40C added self-sealing fuel tanks and the provision to carry a drop tank or bomb on a centerline station below the cockpit. Many P-40B/Cs found their way to USAAC squadrons in the Philippine Islands and Hawaii, thus becoming the first Warhawks to see action in American markings. The British version of these aircraft, fitted with .303in wing guns but otherwise similar, was used for low-level fighter-reconnaissance sorties over occupied Europe and in fighter-bomber operations in North Africa. Some 100 aircraft were diverted in 1941 from the British order to the CAF, where they would equip the legendary AVG, soon to be known worldwide as the "Flying Tigers."

P-40D/E/KITTYHAWK I

When Allison redesigned its V-1710 to produce the upgraded "F-series" engine, Curtiss needed to redesign the P-40's fuselage to accommodate the higher thrust line and additional horsepower produced by the new motor. With the guns having been removed from the redesigned nose of the P-40D, Curtiss replaced the four small-caliber weapons in the wings with .50in machine guns in the P-40D. The armament was increased to six .50in guns in the P-40E, as it was in late-build Kittyhawk Is and all Kittyhawk IAs. The new fuselage also introduced an improved cockpit enclosure, with a bigger windshield and deeper sliding canopy. The USAAF's P-40E-1 could carry six small bombs under the wings, and late in its production run a small dorsal fillet was added at the base of the vertical stabilizer to improve longitudinal stability. P-40Es and Kittyhawk Is saw extensive combat in the Pacific and CBI theaters, and in North Africa from 1941.

P-40F/KITTYHAWK II

In an attempt to improve the performance of the P-40 at higher altitudes, Curtiss fitted an E-model airframe with a Rolls-Royce Merlin engine – the same powerplant as in the Spitfire and Hurricane. The engine, license-built by the Packard Motor Co and equipped with the two-stage mechanical supercharger, gave the P-40F a top speed of 364mph at 20,000ft. The nose was redesigned to remove the air scoop atop the cowling because the Merlin engine had an updraft carburetor. Instead, the engine drew its air through an enlarged radiator scoop below the engine. In a further effort to improve the stability of the Warhawk, Curtiss extended the rear of the fuselage by 26in, starting with the 700th P-40F.

Because they were considered better able to cope with high-flying German and Italian fighters, most P-40Fs and Kittyhawk IIs were sent to American and Commonwealth squadrons fighting in the Mediterranean Theater of Operations (MTO).

P-40K/KITTYHAWK III

Outwardly, the P-40K-1 and K-5 Warhawks were identical to the late-production P-40E-1, with the small dorsal fillet at the base of the vertical stabilizer and flared exhaust pipes fitted to the engine. But there was a big difference under the cowling; Curtiss gave the P-40K a considerable boost in power over previous Allison-engined models with the 1,325hp V-1710-73. The armament remained six .50in guns in the wings. The added power made the P-40K the fastest Warhawk yet, even slightly outpacing the P-40F at 20,000ft. The additional speed was not wasted on its pilots. No less a proponent of the airplane than Col Bruce K. Holloway – a 13-victory ace over China with the 23rd FG – considered the P-40K his favorite Warhawk because it delivered improved performance without compromising flight characteristics or combat equipment.

With the P-40K-10/15, Curtiss went to the 26in fuselage extension introduced with the late-model P-40F. These were the first P-40s fitted with a radio antenna mast on the fuselage spine. The RAF received 192 Kittyhawk IIIs through Lend-Lease, with most of them being assigned to Commonwealth air forces.

P-40L/KITTYHAWK II

Seeing no further prospects for a significant boost in engine power any time soon, Curtiss began to strip weight from the Warhawk in the P-40L. This model was basically a Merlin-powered P-40F with several items removed or modified. Armament was reduced to four .50in wing guns, less armor plate was fitted and internal fuel capacity dropped from 157gal to 120gal. These changes lopped about 140lb from the empty weight, compared to the P-40F. A very slight improvement in performance over the F-model resulted, but the loss of combat effectiveness more than offset the gain in speed. The P-40L-1 retained the short fuselage of the early P-40F, but the 650 P-40Ls with serial numbers starting at 42-10480 had the 26in fuselage extension. The P-40Ls supplied to the RAF were designated Kittyhawk IIs, as were the P-40Fs.

As the end of the P-40F/L production run drew near in spring 1943, the USAAF decided that the new North American P-51B fighter should have the top priority for Merlin engines. This decision left 300 P-40F/L airframes lacking engines, and these were converted to Allison power and redesignated P-40Rs.

P-40M/KITTYHAWK III

Throughout the P-40's life, Curtiss was trying to develop a new fighter to replace the Warhawk in production. The Curtiss P-46 and P-60 designs failed to pan out, however, and the USAAF still needed fighters. An order for 600 new P-40M Warhawks resulted, with deliveries starting in November 1942. Outwardly, the P-40M was little changed from the long-tailed P-40K, but it was powered by the new 1,200hp Allison V-1710-81. This engine could draw bypass air for the carburetor through metal filters fed by a perforated grill on each side of the nose

P-40Ns of the 5th FG CACW on the line at Chihkiang in 1944. The aircraft in the foreground ("765" of the 17th FS) carries a drop tank under the centerline and clusters of fragmentation bombs on its wing racks. Note the chalked-in sharksmouth on the second Warhawk in the line. (Bill Mustill)

P-40E/N: IN THE COCKPIT

1. N-3A reflector gunsight
2. Ring gunsight
3. Flap and wheel indicator
4. Compass
5. Flight indicator
6. Coolant temperature gauge
7. Fuselage fuel gauge
8. Turn and bank indicator
9. Turn indicator
10. Airspeed indicator
11. Tachometer
12. Manifold pressure gauge
13. Oil temperature gauge
14. Engine gauge unit
15. Rate of climb indicator
16. Altimeter
17. Oxygen indicator
18. Oxygen pressure gauge
19. Oil pressure gauge
20. Fuel pressure gauge
21. Parking brake
22. Gun arming switch
23. Warning lights
24. Carburetor heat control
25. Canopy control crank
26. Throttle
27. Mixture control
28. Propeller control
29. Ignition switch
30. Compass control
31. Ammeter
32. Cockpit heat control
33. Rudder trim tab control
34. Elevator trim tab control
35. Fuel selector
36. Rudder pedals
37. Control column
38. Gun firing button
39. Forward wing tank fuel gauge
40. Hydraulics hand pump
41. Radio receiver
42. Radio transmitter
43. Map case
44. Fluorescent spotlight
45. Wing bomb release
46. Pilot's seat
47. Cowl flaps control
48. Radio crash switch
49. Filter switch box
50. Fluorescent spotlight
51. Oxygen regulator
52. Oxygen hose
53. Flap selector
54. Undercarriage selector handle

Ki-43: IN THE COCKPIT

1. Gunsight
2. Airspeed indicator
3. Turn and bank indicator
4. Rate of climb indicator
5. Manifold pressure gauge
6. Compass
7. Altimeter
8. Tachometer
9. Fuel pressure gauge
10. Oil pressure gauge
11. Oil temperature gauge
12. Undercarriage warning lights
13. 12.7mm gun
14. Guarded switch cover
15. Engine primer fuel pump
16. Cocking handle
17. Cabin lamp
18. Elevator trimming
19. Chronometer
20. Radio tuner
21. Radio dial
22. Cylinder temperature
23. Exhaust temperature
24. Control column
25. Canopy winding mechanism
26. Combat flap control buttons
27. Main switches
28. Oxygen control
29. Oxygen flow meter
30. Fuel gauge (main tanks)
31. Fuel gauge (auxiliary tanks)
32. Right and left auxiliary tank selector
33. Right and left main tank selector
34. Pilot's seat
35. Hydrostatic plunger for main tanks
36. Hydrostatic plunger for auxiliary tanks
37. Hydraulic brake pedals
38. Rudder pedals
39. P.4 compass
40. Emergency hydraulics hand pump
41. Magneto switch
42. Throttle lever
43. Mixture control
44. Propeller pitch control
45. Friction adjuster
46. Control handle valve (use unknown)
47. Internal tanks cock
48. Main fuel cock
49. Undercarriage emergency operation
50. Cam manipulation
51. Undercarriage selector
52. Flap selector
53. Compressed air bottle

(Artwork by Jim Laurier, © Osprey Publishing)

ahead of the exhausts. A further visual clue was the addition of a vent window in the port side of the windscreen. Another new feature was reinforced, although still fabric-covered, ailerons. The P-40M-5 introduced a permanent carburetor air filter for the engine, and a new feature on the P-40M-10 was a mechanically-operated landing gear indicator on each wing. Because the P-40M was so similar to the P-40K, the RAF designated both aircraft Kittyhawk IIIs.

P-40N/KITTYHAWK IV

The last production version of the Warhawk, the P-40N was a further attempt to cut weight from the veteran fighter. In all, 5,210 P-40Ns were built in nine sub-versions, making it the most numerous of all Warhawks, and also the most varied. The first version, the P-40N-1, was outwardly similar to the P-40M except that its armament was reduced to four wing guns. It also featured the smaller internal fuel capacity of 120gal. Another weight saving resulted from the elimination of the battery, but this meant that the airplane had to be started by an external power source, which caused headaches for combat units operating the fighter in forward areas. Most P-40Ns were retrofitted with batteries as a result.

Powered by a 1,200hp Allison V-1710-81 engine, the P-40N-1 was the fastest Warhawk, with a top speed of 378mph at 20,000ft. An improved cockpit enclosure, with a clear sliding canopy and cut-down rear deck, debuted on the P-40N-5 to give the pilot a better view out of the airplane. The main landing gear got smaller wheels made of lightweight magnesium and lacking hubcaps. In China, where supplies and spare parts were severely limited, the switch to the new wheels caused problems for the Fourteenth Air Force because the gravel runways there wore out tires in a hurry, and the stockpiled replacement tires for older P-40s would not fit the smaller-diameter wheels.

On the plus side, the P-40N-5 reverted to six wing guns, and improvements were made to the pilot's seat and the radio equipment. The 100 P-40N-10s were winterized versions of the N-5, and were the first to include a rate of climb indicator among the instruments. Internal fuel capacity grew to 161gal in the P-40N-15, and the P-40N-20 got a new engine in the form of the 1,360hp V-1710-99, along with pylons under each wing that could carry a bomb of up to 500lb or a drop tank. Minor changes continued in the P-40N-25, -30 and -35, and the last production Warhawk, the P-40N-40, was the first with metal-skinned ailerons.

Most of the 458 Lend-Lease Kittyhawk IVs went to New Zealand and Australia for service in the Pacific, although some saw action with RAF squadrons in the MTO.

NAKAJIMA Ki-43 "OSCAR"

Ki-43-I

The initial production version of the Hayabusa, the Ki-43-Ia, featured a 980hp Ha-25 Type 99 14-cylinder radial engine with a single-speed supercharger. A fixed-pitch, two-blade wooden propeller soon gave way to a variable-pitch metal propeller, also with two blades. The wingspan was 37ft 6.3in, with wing area of 237 sq ft. Armament consisted of two 7.7mm Type 89 machine guns in the upper cowling, aimed by a telescope-type gunsight protruding through the windscreen. As supplies of the new 12.7mm Ho-103 machine gun started to become available, one of the 7.7mm guns was replaced by the heavier weapon in the Ki-43-Ib.

When the Pacific War broke out in December 1941, only 40 of these machines had been delivered to combat units. Weakness in the wing spars of the early Hayabusas was only partly remedied by a modification program, and a number of them crashed when the wings collapsed as pilots were pulling out of high-speed dives. A further upgrade to the Hayabusa, the Ki-43-Ic, standardized the armament at two Ho-103 machine guns with 250 rounds per gun, and added attachment points for small bombs or drop tanks under each wing. Of the 716 Ki-43-Is manufactured, all but the first 80 were built to the -Ic specification. The slight addition in weight produced by the heavier guns had little, if any, appreciable effect on the performance of the aircraft.

Ki-43-II

Five prototypes of this first major improvement to the Hayabusa were delivered to the IJAAF beginning in February 1942, and by October the new model was in full production as the Ki-43-IIa. Further modifications to the wing cured it of its tendency to collapse under high loading, shortening the span by 23.6in and increasing the load-carrying capacity of the wing racks. The fighter was fitted with the more powerful 1,130hp Nakajima Ha-115 radial engine (which also used a two-speed supercharger) driving a three-bladed metal propeller. The engine was housed in a new cowling that was longer in chord and bigger in diameter, and also featured an air intake for the supercharger in the upper lip. Other improvements included a slightly taller windscreen and canopy, a more effective reflector gunsight, armor plating to protect the pilot and a rubber coating to protect the fuel tanks.

An oil cooler was fitted under the fuselage at the rear of the cowling. The armament, and the Type 96 Hi-3 radio, were unchanged from the previous model. Various minor modifications incorporated during the production run of the

Ki-43-II "15" of the 2nd Chutai/25th Sentai taxis at Nanking. Its pilot is SgtMaj Kyushiro Ohtake, a ten-victory ace who flew operationally from March 1941 through to the end of the war. Seriously wounded in combat over Seoul on August 13, 1945, he eventually succumbed to his injuries in 1951. (Yasuho Izawa)

Ki-43-IIa were standardized in the Ki-43-IIb, and deliveries began during the summer of 1943. Other changes included a deeper "honeycomb" oil cooler under the cowling, a revised air intake for the carburetor and an auxiliary cooler intake beneath the fuselage. Later, the hard points under the wing were moved outboard of the landing gear to prevent bombs from striking the propeller during diving attacks. A further development, designated the Ki-43-IIc (also called Ki-43-II KAI), introduced ejector exhaust stubs that gave the engine a slight boost in horsepower.

Ki-43-III

Though the Hayabusa was clearly suffering at the hands of more advanced Allied fighters by the middle of 1944, a new version was nevertheless introduced in the form of the Ki-43-IIIa. Outwardly, it was very similar to the Ki-43-IIc, but its engine was the new Ha-115-II rated at 1,190hp. Tachikawa built 1,098 examples of the Ki-43-IIIa and two prototypes of the Ki-43-IIIb. Fitted with two 20mm cannon and a more powerful Mitsubishi Ha-112-32/42 engine, the Ki-43-IIIc was intended to serve in the home islands as a B-29 interceptor, but the war ended before it could enter production.

A VIEW FROM THE COCKPIT

As the products of two vastly different design specifications, the Ki-43 and P-40 gave their pilots predictably different flight characteristics. With its light weight and relatively large wing, the Ki-43 was a delight to fly. It could "climb like an

Ki-43 "OSCAR" GUNS

The Ki-43-II was fitted with two Ho-103 Type 1 12.7mm machine guns mounted in the forward fuselage and synchronized to fire through the propeller arc. The butts of the guns extended back into the cockpit on either side of the instrument panel, and the individual magazines for each weapon carried 250 rounds apiece. The Ho-103 was very similar in design to the Browning M2.

P-40 WARHAWK GUNS

The Warhawk, from the P-40E through to the P-40N, was fitted with Browning M2 .50in machine guns, two or three in each wing. The guns were aimed slightly inward so that their streams of fire would converge at a point about 300 yards ahead of the airplane.

angel and turn like the devil." The heavy P-40 struck many pilots as truck-like, with a slow rate of climb and a marked drop-off in performance at higher altitudes. But the weight also gave it spectacular speed in a dive.

The tactics devised by Fourteenth Air Force commander Claire Chennault for his P-40 pilots in China took advantage of the fighter's strong points – speed, strength and firepower – while attempting to negate its weaknesses. Chennault's P-40 "drivers" learned to attack in a slashing dive through the enemy formation, then zoom up to make another attack. Under no circumstance were they to follow a Ki-43 in a turn or climb. The P-40's heavy armament of six .50in machine guns constituted a key advantage, as although the 12.7mm Ho-103s carried by the Ki-43 packed virtually the same punch as the Browning guns in the Curtiss fighter, the "Oscar" only had two of them. So an accurate two-second burst from a P-40 would hit the Ki-43 with 16.2lb of "slugs," which was triple the throw weight that a Ki-43 pilot could bring to bear on a Warhawk.

Outgunned as he was, the Hayabusa pilot needed superior marksmanship to score a kill, and he definitely wanted to avoid a head-on confrontation with a P-40. Finally, the superior firepower of the P-40 also made it much more effective than the Ki-43 at bringing down enemy bombers.

As in any match-up of two fighter aircraft, the advantage could go either way depending on the skill of the pilots and the situation in which combat was joined.

A pilot – Japanese or American – looking down from 15,000ft and seeing a formation of enemy fighters in front of him was in a great position to attack. But the success of that attack depended on getting close enough to open fire before the adversary had a chance to take evasive action. An alert Ki-43 pilot attacked from the rear by a P-40 could use his superior maneuverability to turn or loop out of the line of fire, while a P-40 pilot in the same situation could push over into a dive and quickly outdistance the Ki-43. In this situation, the advantage went to the Ki-43, because it could maneuver at any altitude. The P-40 needed sufficient altitude in order to dive away, and if caught "low and slow," it was likely to take a pounding.

On the other hand, the Ki-43 mounted a high-pressure oxygen cylinder behind the pilot's seat that had a nasty habit of exploding if struck by enemy fire, tearing the Hayabusa to pieces. The P-40's tough frame could absorb a lot of punishment, and its cooling system was mounted under the engine in the nose – a difficult spot to hit from behind. With their opposite strengths and weaknesses, the Ki-43 and P-40 fit together like two pieces of a puzzle. But the bottom line was this. No Ki-43 pilot wanted to trade his Hayabusa for a P-40, and even if he did, he would not have found a Warhawk pilot willing to make the swap.

P-40 vs Ki-43 COMPARISON SPECIFICATIONS		
	P-40N-15	Ki-43-II
Powerplant	1,200hp V-1710-81	1,105hp Ha-115
Dimensions		
Span	37ft 3.5in	35ft 6.75in
Length	33ft 5.75in	29ft 3.25in
Height	12ft 4.5in	10ft 8.75in
Wing area	236 sq ft	230.37 sq ft
Weights		
Empty	6,200lb	3,812lb
Loaded	8,350lb	4,891lb
Wing loading	35.38lb/sq ft	21.23lb/sq ft
Performance		
Max speed	343 mph at 15,000ft	329 mph at 13,125ft
Range	750 miles	1,006 miles
Climb	to 14,000ft in 7.3 min	to 19,685ft in 6.35 min
Service ceiling	31,000ft	36,794ft
Armament	6x .50in Brownings	2x 12.7mm Ho-103s

THE STRATEGIC SITUATION

Starting in early 1942, the P-40 and Ki-43 met in combat at various locations throughout the Pacific theater, primarily in the savage skies above New Guinea, Burma and China. These clashes reached maximum intensity during the Japanese *Ichi-Go* land offensive in China during 1944.

Although conventional history tells us the Pacific War started with Japan's attack on Pearl Harbor on December 7, 1941, the roots of the conflict go back a full decade further to September 1931, when the Japanese Kwantung Army invaded the Manchuria region of northeast China. Seeking to expand its industrial capacity, Japan occupied Manchurian cities, took over the railroads and installed a puppet government. The Chinese retaliated by boycotting Japanese goods, sparking a six-week clash between Chinese and Japanese troops in early 1932 that became known as the "Shanghai Incident." Five years of relative calm followed, during which time both nations built up their military forces – including their air arms – in expectation of future conflict.

On July 7, 1937, fighting again erupted between Japan and China, this time at the Marco Polo Bridge on the outskirts of Peking, and soon spread throughout northern China. By this time, nearly all of China's warlords had submitted to the central authority of Generalissimo Chiang Kai-shek's Kuomintang government, and a flourishing Communist movement had been bottled up in a remote area of northern China. For the next eight years China would be gripped in a state of full-scale war.

IJAAF fighter units, flying Kawasaki Ki-10 biplanes, quickly gained air superiority over Chinese pilots equipped with foreign-built aircraft such as the Curtiss Hawk II fighter and Northrop 2E light bomber. Poorly trained and haphazardly employed, the CAF suffered devastating losses. Even the hiring of retired US Army Capt Claire L. Chennault, a noted pilot and expert on fighter tactics, as an advisor to the CAF failed to change the situation.

Chennault's efforts to buy modern aircraft and train Chinese pilots to fly them were frustrated by China's rigid class system and the rampant corruption in Chiang's government. Occasionally, the CAF was able to launch effective interceptions against Japanese raiders, but these ultimately failed to slow the constantly advancing enemy. First Peking was captured, then Shanghai and Nanking. When Chiang's government moved inland to Hankow, Japanese bombers followed. In late 1938, when Hankow fell to the Japanese, the Kuomintang government retreated farther into central China, settling in the city of Chungking, on the Yangtze River.

The Chinese were finally able to stop the advancing Japanese in May 1939 at Tsaoyang, in mountainous Hupeh Province. As a stalemate ensued, the Japanese turned to a strategy of attrition. They blockaded China's coastal ports to prevent much-needed supplies from reaching the interior, and supplied their own ground forces with indigenous Chinese resources. At the same time, Japanese bombers continued to attack the cities of free China, including the new capital. Millions of civilians died.

The outbreak of war in Europe in September 1939 only worsened China's situation. When France surrendered to Germany, an ally of Japan, on June 22, 1940, the port of Hanoi, in French Indo-China (now Vietnam), was closed to supplies bound for China. The only port of entry left for China-bound goods was Rangoon, in the British colony of Burma. From there, supplies could be shipped north by rail to the new "Burma Road," and on into China. Chennault feared that China could lose this route as well if Japan and Great Britain went to war, which was looking increasingly likely, unless the Burma Road could be defended from air attack. Further, he had concluded by this time that the current CAF would not be up to the task.

Chennault and Chiang were able to convince US President Franklin D. Roosevelt to provide China with 100 American military pilots and frontline fighters for them to fly in defense of the Burma Road. The AVG formed in the summer of 1941 on a jungle airfield at Toungoo, in Burma, and immediately began training on Curtiss 81-A2 Tomahawks that had been hastily diverted from a British order for the export version of the P-40.

By coincidence, it was also during this time that the 59th and 64th sentais of the IJAAF became the first units to reequip with the new Ki-43-I. As tensions between Japan and the US grew in the weeks preceding the Pearl Harbor attack, the 59th and 64th sentais were deployed to the Malay Peninsula, while the Third Pursuit Squadron of the AVG went to Rangoon, thus setting up the first aerial duel between the P-40 and the Ki-43.

After a successful interception over Rangoon by AVG and RAF fighters on December 23, 1941, the 64th Sentai was ordered north from Malaya to bolster the escort force for a second bombing raid against Rangoon on Christmas Day. Led by Sentai Commander Maj Tateo Kato, 25 Ki-43s of the 64th met 63 Ki-21 heavy bombers over Thailand and proceeded with them west toward Rangoon. The formation eventually came apart en route, however, and Kato's Ki-43s were split into two forces.

As the Japanese aircraft crossed into Burma, two flights (totaling 13 AVG P-40s) took off from Mingladon airfield, along with a similar number of

RAF Brewster Buffalo fighters. The opposing forces duly fought a huge aerial battle that raged for about 30 minutes while the Japanese formation was withdrawing across the Gulf of Martaban. One of the AVG pilots, flight leader William N. Reed of Marion, Iowa, made several firing runs at the bombers before being forced to dive away from the fight to clear his guns after they had jammed. Reed duly described what happened next in his diary:

> I saw another P-40 who was also leaving the scrap. By now we were 140–150 miles across the gulf from Rangoon. I joined the other ship and saw that it was (Parker) Dupouy. We started back across the gulf at 17,000ft, and had only gone about 30 miles out off the shore of Moulmein when we spotted three Model Os (actually Ki-43s, which were unknown to the AVG at this time) in a V-formation below us, apparently heading home. We dropped down on their tails and surprised them. Dupouy was following me as I picked out the right-hand wingman. I fired from about 50 yards, and Dupouy fired behind me. The Jap exploded right in front of my face. I pulled sharply up to the right to avoid hitting him, and Dupouy pulled up to the left. In doing so, his right wing clipped the other Jap wingman's ship right in the wing root, and the Jap spun into the gulf, too.

Gen H. H. "Hap" Arnold (left), chief of the USAAF, inspects 23rd FG P-40s with BrigGen Chennault at Kunming in February 1943. A month later, Arnold would approve orders creating the Fourteenth Air Force to replace the CATF in China, with Chennault as its commanding officer. (Bruce Holloway)

As far as can be determined, Reed and Dupouy had scored the first two P-40 victories over the Ki-43, although they did not know it at the time. Many of the AVG P-40s were hit in the fight, and two pilots made wheels-up landings at an auxiliary airstrip, but it is not known whether they were victims of Ki-43s or other Japanese aircraft involved in the battle. In any case, it was a spectacular start to the long and bitter rivalry between the two fighter types.

When Burma fell to the Japanese five months later, the AVG withdrew to China. Now the only lifeline left for China was a slender stream of goods that could be flown into the country from India over the mountainous route that became known as the "Hump." The AVG provided air defense for Chinese cities and the "Hump" route, while also supporting Chinese forces attempting to prevent the Japanese from advancing across the Salween River into China's Yunnan Province. When the AVG was disbanded in July 1942, USAAF pilots of the new CATF took over its mission, and what remained of its tired P-40s.

Although the CATF was a small force consisting of just five P-40 squadrons and one B-25 medium-bomber unit, Chennault (now a USAAF brigadier-general) had prepared well to carry on the fight. Not only had he convinced the Chinese to build an extensive network of airfields from which the CATF could operate, he had also engineered a vast "warning net" of civilian spotters who could quickly alert Warhawk units to the presence of incoming Japanese air attacks from virtually anywhere in unoccupied China.

Chennault's headquarters for the CATF was located at Kunming, in Yunnan Province, as it had been for the AVG. Kunming was also the air terminal for cargo flying over the "Hump," as it was located about as far into China as a heavily loaded transport airplane could fly from India and still maintain a safe reserve of fuel. From Kunming, a string of airfields stretched northeastward some 600 miles to Hengyang, with others along the way at Kweilin and Lingling. To the north, airfields in the vicinity of Chungking hosted units of the CAF whose primary duty was to provide air defense for the capital.

For their part, the Japanese surrounded the CATF on three sides. The IJAAF maintained air bases in the Hankow area to the northeast, at Canton and Hong Kong, on the China coast, and to the south in French Indo-China and northern Burma. The IJAAF did not, however, have aircraft in sufficient strength to maintain offensive operations from all of these places at the same time.

A sort of cat-and-mouse war ensued therefore, with commanders on both sides moving their air units regularly to take advantage of weather conditions, supplies and/or tactical considerations. Keeping sufficient supplies of ammunition and fuel on hand to maintain operations was a constant struggle for the Americans, as all of their material had to be flown into China over the "Hump." Bad weather, enemy action and even political decisions could cut the "Hump" flow to a trickle – and often did.

Aerial clashes between the CATF's 23rd FG and the IJAAF over China began immediately after the AVG dissolved on July 4, 1942. Operating primarily from the eastern bases, the P-40s initially maintained a defensive posture as the IJAAF, flying from Hankow and Canton, attempted to wipe out the novice American

Repair facilities, such as the No. 10 Factory in Kunming, helped to keep the 23rd FG supplied with aircraft by rebuilding damaged airplanes and stripping parts from others that were beyond repair. Seen here in 1942, the factory is working on four P-40s plus a Republic P-43A at bottom left. Note the Chinese insignia on the P-40 wing in the foreground. (Don Hyatt)

pilots. A small cadre of former AVG aviators had remained in China, however, and these men provided the leadership and combat savvy needed to hold the line while the newly arrived USAAF pilots gained experience.

By late October, Chennault had built up sufficient strength to undertake substantial offensive operations. His first targets were the dock areas on the Kowloon peninsula, which B-25s, escorted by P-40s of the 23rd FG, struck on October 25, 1942. An even bigger raid hit the port facilities at Canton in November. The Japanese struck back on December 26 and again in mid-January 1943, both times sending bombers from Burma to attack the "Hump" airfield at Yunnanyi, in southwest China.

When the Fourteenth Air Force succeeded the CATF in spring 1943, it signaled the beginning of a buildup of American air power in China. By early 1944, Chennault would have at his disposal four fighter groups equipped with P-40s (the USAAF 23rd and 51st FGs and the 3rd and 5th FGs of the Chinese-American Composite Wing), a P-38 fighter squadron, two medium bomb groups with B-25s and a heavy bomb group flying B-24 Liberators.

With these aircraft, Chennault was able not only to maintain pressure on the Japanese land forces in China through steady attacks on their lines of communication, but also to harass Japanese shipping carrying vital war materials from southeast Asia to Japan through the South China Sea. In late 1943, Chennault reorganized his forces into the 68th Composite Wing (CW) on the eastern front and the 69th CW, covering the "Hump" route from bases in southwest China. In addition, squadrons of the newly formed Chinese-American Composite Wing (CACW) were arriving in China sporadically as they completed combat training in India.

To keep pace, the IJAAF upgraded its 3rd Air Division, concentrated in the Hankow area, to the 5th Air Army in January 1944. This enlarged force now included two Ki-43 *sentais* (the 25th and 48th), two interceptor *sentais* with short-range Ki-44s and various bombing and army cooperation units.

The run of defeats for Japanese forces in the South Pacific during 1943, coupled with the growing Allied strength on the Asian mainland, prompted its high command to respond with plans for a major land offensive in China. The express aim of this attack, codenamed *Ichi-Go* ('Number One'), was to drive the Fourteenth Air Force out of its eastern air bases and, if possible, force China out of the war. This would prevent long-range B-29 bombers from using Chinese bases in future raids on targets in the Japanese home islands. An added benefit would be the establishment of a rail link all the way from Hanoi to Shanghai, the great port city on China's east coast. This would allow vital war materials from southeast Asia to bypass the increasingly dangerous sea routes on their way to Japan.

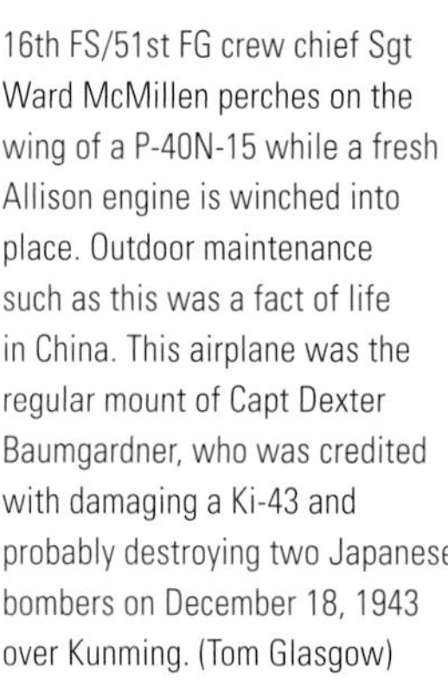

16th FS/51st FG crew chief Sgt Ward McMillen perches on the wing of a P-40N-15 while a fresh Allison engine is winched into place. Outdoor maintenance such as this was a fact of life in China. This airplane was the regular mount of Capt Dexter Baumgardner, who was credited with damaging a Ki-43 and probably destroying two Japanese bombers on December 18, 1943 over Kunming. (Tom Glasgow)

As early as January 1944, Chinese intelligence noted a buildup of Japanese land forces in the Hankow area and north of the Yellow River. Then, on April 17, 1944, Japanese troops under the command of Gen Shunroku Hada began pouring across the Yellow River at Kaifeng and heading south through Honan Province along the rail corridor to Hankow, some 250 miles away. At the same time, other Japanese forces pushed north from Hankow on the same route in this first phase of *Ichi-Go*. Their aim was to close this last gap in the railroad line between Peking and Hankow, thus opening a new route for the flow of men and supplies south for the second phase of *Ichi-Go*, which was soon to follow.

Chennault responded by moving the four P-40 squadrons of the 3rd FG CACW, plus a CACW B-25 squadron, north to air bases in eastern Szechwan Province. From there they could launch attacks on the advancing Japanese in an effort called "Mission A." Bad weather hampered the transfer, and it was not until April 30 that the CACW was able to launch its first sorties of the campaign. By that time, the two Japanese forces were well on their way toward linking up, which they soon did. From that point on, the "Mission A" forces would pound the Peking–Hankow rail corridor constantly, seeking to deny the Japanese use of it. Skirmishes between CACW P-40s and Ki-43s of the 5th Air Army became routine.

Meanwhile, the bigger picture of the Japanese battle plan became apparent to Chennault and his Fourteenth Air Force staff. The 68th CW received orders to launch attacks on the Hankow area with the aim of destroying Japanese supplies before they could be used in the second phase of *Ichi-Go*. The first mission went off as planned on May 6, with a strong force of 54 bombers and fighters led by 23rd FG CO Col David L. "Tex" Hill attacking a supply depot near the main Hankow airfield with moderate success.

The Japanese responded in kind, with the Fifth Air Army launching a series of attacks against USAAF air bases in eastern China with the goal of gaining air superiority over the area so the Americans would be unable to disrupt the offensive.

Neither the American effort to cripple the buildup nor the Japanese bid for air superiority succeeded, however. On May 26, 1944, when 60,000 assault troops of the Japanese Eleventh Army marched south out of Hankow toward the Chinese-held city of Changsha, their first objective, the 68th CW, immediately started pounding them from the skies. The *Ichi-Go* offensive, which would provide the backdrop for the last major confrontation involving the P-40 and the Ki-43, was now under way.

THE MEN

Just as the P-40 and Ki-43 differed according to the attitudes and philosophies of the nations that produced them, so did the pilots who flew these legendary fighters. The United States and Japan were two vastly different places in the 1940s, each with cultures and traditions that seemed incomprehensible to the other. The United States was a young democracy, not yet 200 years old, founded on the principles of "life, liberty and the pursuit of happiness." Japan, in contrast, was an ancient land bound in a strict class structure and ruled by its military.

It was only natural that the young men of these two countries would approach military service with different mindsets, although they certainly shared patriotic dedication to their respective homelands.

PILOT TRAINING

Aviation held a great attraction for young men of both nations during the years leading up to the Pearl Harbor attack, thanks in no small part to the heroic portrayals of World War I aces and the subsequent aerial adventures of pilots such as Charles Lindbergh and Jimmy Doolittle. Because of that, the Japanese and American air forces were able to set high standards for intelligence and physical condition in their pilot recruits.

As might be expected, the training programs of the IJAAF and USAAF were similar in structure. After completing preparatory military training, which could last for several months, student pilots began flying lessons in primary school on docile training aircraft – mostly biplanes such as the Stearman PT-17 (US) and Tachikawa Ki-17 (Japan). One of the main purposes of Primary training was to weed out those who showed no talent for flying, but the students who graduated went on to the next level, called "Basic" training in the US and "Advanced" in Japan. Here, the standard training aircraft for American Army pilots was the Vultee BT-13/15, a low-wing monoplane with fixed landing gear, while Japanese cadets flew Tachikawa Ki-9 biplanes.

American Army trainees flew the much-admired North American AT-6, a monoplane with retractable landing gear, in their final training phases, called "Advanced." The final phase for IJAAF pilots was known as "Operational" training, in which pilots flew the Tachikawa Ki-55, a low-wing monoplane with fixed landing gear that doubled as an Army cooperation aircraft.

Despite these similarities, there were three important differences in the two nations' pilot training programs. The first was flight time. An American pilot would receive his wings and officer's commission after about nine months of instruction and 200 hours of flight time. In prewar years, he would then be assigned to an active squadron, where his piloting skills would continue to develop while flying first-line combat aircraft. In December 1942, the USAAF instituted Fighter Replacement Training Units (FRTUs) to give newly minted fighter pilots experience in the types of aircraft they would be flying in combat. The FRTU courses (normally some two months in duration) included instrument training and night flying, air-to-air and air-to-ground gunnery instruction and practice in formation flying and combat maneuvering.

IJAAF fighter pilots who finished Primary training were assigned to a *Kyoiku Hiko-tai* (flying training unit) for six months. Then they were posted to a fighter *sentai*, where an additional three months of training were undertaken prior to entering combat. The Japanese fighter pilot could therefore enter combat with more flight time – some 300 hours over two years – than his American counterpart. The IJAAF did not see a need for all of its pilots to be officers, however, and as a result all but the few trainees chosen for officer status began their flying careers as enlisted men.

Pilots of the 1st Chutai/25th Sentai pose for a group photograph. They are, in the front row from left to right, Tominaga, Osawa and Kimura, and the second row, from left to right, Murakami, Lt Masao Okumura, Capt Takashi Tsuchiya (1st Chutai leader), unknown, Saito and WO Eiji Seino (an ace with an estimated ten victories). (Yasuho Izawa)

The balance in flight training would tip dramatically once the US and Japan went to war against each other, however. The Americans held tight to their 200-hour syllabus throughout the war, considering this the minimum amount of training needed for a military pilot to achieve his wings. But the IJAAF did not have this luxury. After the Allies began to gain the upper hand in the Pacific in mid-1942, shortages of fuel and equipment, plus the demand for replacement pilots on the war fronts, made it increasingly difficult for the IJAAF to maintain the quality of its flight instruction. By 1944, fledgling IJAAF pilots were being sent into combat with a pitiful 60 to 70 hours of flight experience, and the results were predictable. A striking difference between USAAF and IJAAF training was the intensity and methods of imposing discipline on their respective student pilots. Both air forces recognized the need to establish military order and teach respect for the chain of command among their pilots, but they diverged on the methods for doing so.

The Americans took a somewhat casual approach to training, with classroom instruction in military conduct supplemented by relatively gentle "hazing" from training instructors and senior student pilots. Punishments for infractions – forgetting to salute a superior or failing an inspection, for instance – were likely to be assignments to some of the unsavory tasks connected with military service, such as guard duty and kitchen cleanup. Since the goal of most student pilots was to graduate from flight school and become a military pilot, the threat of expulsion was all the motivation most cadets needed to learn the rules, and observe them.

Japanese military training was altogether different in this regard, seeking to instill total dedication to the Emperor and to Japan in its fighting men, along with complete disregard for one's self-interest. As had been the case for centuries, the Japanese were taught that they would gain greatest honor by dying for their country, with a complete disdain for suffering, surrender or death. A key element in teaching this to young men, mostly in their teens, was corporal punishment. IJAAF pilot Yasuo Kuwahara described his thoughts on this topic in his book *Kamikaze*:

> Military men, regardless of nationality, follow the same basic rules. The great difference lay in how these rules were enforced. An American, for example, who failed to be clean shaven or to have his shoes properly shined for an inspection might have his pass revoked for a day or two, or he might be given extra duty. For us, however, as for all of Nippon's basic trainees, the slightest infraction, the most infinitesimal mistake, brought excruciating punishment.
>
> What I can only describe as a siege of ruthless discipline and relentless castigation began in the first hours of our arrival, and thereafter never ceased during all the days of our training – a siege so terrible that some did not survive it.

"OSCAR" PILOT: TOSHIO SAKAGAWA

Toshio Sakagawa was born in 1910 in Awaji Shima, Hyogo Prefecture, and graduated from the Army Military Academy with the 43rd Intake in October 1931. Promoted to flying second lieutenant, he was sent to Tokorozawa for pilot training and then received instruction on fighters at Akeno. Following a posting to the 1st Rentai, Sakagawa enrolled in the commander's course and graduated in July 1936. His next posting was to the Type 91 parasol fighter-equipped 11th Rentai in Harbin, China, as commander of the 2nd Chutai.

Sakagawa's first combat experience came shortly after the outbreak of war with China in 1937, when his unit was forced to fly ground support missions in the northern regions of the country due to there being no aerial opposition of note in this area. Sent back to Japan in March 1939 to briefly serve as an instructor at Akeno, in Japan, he duly returned to China in September 1939 as commander of the Ki-27-equipped 3rd Chutai, 24th Sentai. His unit took part in the final attack on Tamsagbalu on the 15th of that month at the end of the Nomonhan Incident.

After his promotion to major in August 1941, Sakagawa assumed command of the 47th Independent Fighter Chutai, which was formed at Tachikawa from personnel previously assigned to the Flight Test Center and equipped with nine preproduction Ki-44s. Dubbed the "Shinsegumi" or "Kawasemi" unit, the 47th moved to Saigon on December 8, 1941 and operated over Malaya and Singapore until April 1942, when the unit was transferred back to Japan. Frustrated by the Ki-44's short range and poor serviceability, Sakagawa and his pilots had enjoyed little success in combat.

In October 1942 Sakagawa was posted to command the Ki-43-equipped 25th Sentai, which had just formed following the expansion of the Canton-based 10th Independent Fighter Chutai. He and his unit would enjoy considerable success through to July 1944, with the highlights for Sakagawa including the destruction of a B-24 Liberator over Hankow on August 21, 1943 – the first time a IJAAF fighter had downed a four-engined USAAF heavy bomber in China. Sakagawa's biggest day in combat came on May 6, 1944, when he claimed the destruction of three P-51 Mustangs in a single engagement over Hongchung. As CO of the 25th Sentai, he led the unit with great distinction during the opening stages of the *Ichi-Go* offensive.

In July 1944, Sakagawa transferred back to the Akeno school, and three months later he was named deputy commander of the oversized 200th Sentai. Equipped with Ki-84s, this unit boasted six *chutais* staffed with former instructors drawn from the Akeno school. Sakagawa fought with this unit in the Philippines in October and November, and was then sent to the Ki-84-equipped 22nd Sentai on December 1, 1944 as its new CO. After three more weeks in combat in the Philippines, and having lost more than 20 pilots, the 22nd was ordered back to Japan to recuperate. In a cruel twist of fate, on December 19, 1944, a transport airplane carrying surviving 22nd Sentai pilots home crashed during a night takeoff from Fabrica airstrip, on the Philippine island of Negros. Sakagawa was among those passengers killed. Postwar historians believe he claimed about 15 victories in aerial combat.

> No matter how perfectly we performed our tasks, the "hancho" (training instructor) found excuses to make us suffer. Punishment was an integral part of our training, and served two main purposes – to create unwavering discipline and to develop an invincible fighting spirit.
>
> For all of us it was a question not merely of learning skills but of survival. Anyone who could withstand the "hancho" would never run from the enemy, and would prefer death to surrender. Whether this policy really produced a superior fighting man, I am not prepared to say. Courage may have more than one connotation. Nonetheless, it did create men who were either so fearless or so dedicated that they would almost invariably fight to the death.

Sadly, a large proportion of IJAAF pilots did in fact fight to the death during World War II, although Kuwahara, by a quirk of fate, was not one of them.

The differences in training techniques of the two air forces came into play when their fighter pilots encountered each other in combat, to be sure. But ultimately it was the sheer scope of the two nations' efforts to train pilots for combat that would set them apart. From the beginning, Japanese war planners failed to understand this issue. When the Japanese Army established its Army Youth Pilot Program in 1938 to begin building up strength for the coming war, its initial intake was just 120 student pilots in two schools. By contrast, a year later when the United States started the Civilian Pilot Training Program, its first-year goal was to produce 20,000 new pilots. The numbers continued to be skewed as time passed.

By the end of the war, Japan had produced some 46,000 pilots, while no fewer than 193,440 Americans had earned their wings between 1941 and 1945. From December 1942 through to August 1945, the USAAF graduated 35,000 fighter pilots from its FRTUs alone. Even when considering that the United States was fighting on two fronts while Japan was not, the sheer weight of numbers of American pilots made the outcome of the Pacific air war a foregone conclusion.

ORGANIZATION AND TACTICS

The operational units of the USAAF and IJAAF were organized similarly. The numbered air forces of the USAAF corresponded to the IJAAF's air armies, and both were assigned to specific geographical areas. In China, the USAAF's Fourteenth Air Force was headquartered in Kunming, while the IJAAF's 5th Air Army headquarters was in Hankow.

The basic operational unit was the group in the USAAF and the *hikosentai*, usually shortened to "sentai," in the IJAAF. A USAAF group normally consisted

Air combat in China was a serious business, as can be seen on the face of Lt Tadahiko Toki of the 1st Chutai/25th Sentai as he sits in the cockpit of his Ki-43-I. Toki was killed in action during an air battle with P-40s of the 75th FS/23rd FG on April 1, 1943 over Lingling. (Yasuho Izawa)

of three or four squadrons further broken down into several flights. On paper, a USAAF squadron would have about 25 aircraft and pilots, with the basic formation being four flights of four aircraft each. This was rarely the case in the Fourteenth Air Force, however, where a full squadron formation was extremely rare due to the paucity in aircraft and pilots. More likely, twelve, eight or even as few as four fighters would be involved in a mission.

In the IJAAF, the equivalent of the squadron was the "chutai," of which there were usually three in a *sentai*. Each *chutai* normally comprised 16 aircraft and pilots, and it was further broken down into flights of three called "shotai," the smallest flying section. Later in the war, the three-airplane *shotai* gave way to the more effective four-airplane formation used by the Allies.

It was in the utilization of their fighter units that the American and Japanese commanders diverged. Gen Chennault, commander of the Fourteenth Air Force, had gained fame as the architect of the dive-and-zoom attacks on the agile Japanese fighters that his AVG pilots used so successfully during 1941–42. But an overlooked, and perhaps just as important, aspect of his tactics was the employment of P-40s in the fighter-bomber role.

Although the first P-40s in China were used primarily in pure fighter roles such as interception and bomber escort, by 1944 the majority of their missions involved attacking ground targets, including airfields, road and river traffic, railroads, troop concentrations and army compounds in Japanese-held territory. The numbers of P-40s involved in these missions varied depending on the availability of aircraft, pilots, fuel and ammunition, but the standard configuration involved 12 aircraft in three flights of four.

The assault flight would make the first attack, with the remaining two flights providing top cover. Then the assault flight would climb up and replace one of the other flights in the top cover as the second flight of four aircraft went down to attack. Finally, the third flight would follow. If enemy aircraft approached to challenge the mission, the top cover would be ready to take them on while the low flights got out of harm's way.

The IJAAF used its Ki-43s far more as pure fighters. This made sense, given the fact that the airplane, with its light armament, was designed specifically for air-to-air combat and not the bombing and strafing of ground targets. In China, Ki-43 units used two tactics to attempt to lure P-40 pilots into combat at a disadvantage. One was to send a single fighter down below a high-flying formation of Ki-43s to act as bait. If P-40s attempted to attack the lone Ki-43, the others would dive on the American adversaries from above.

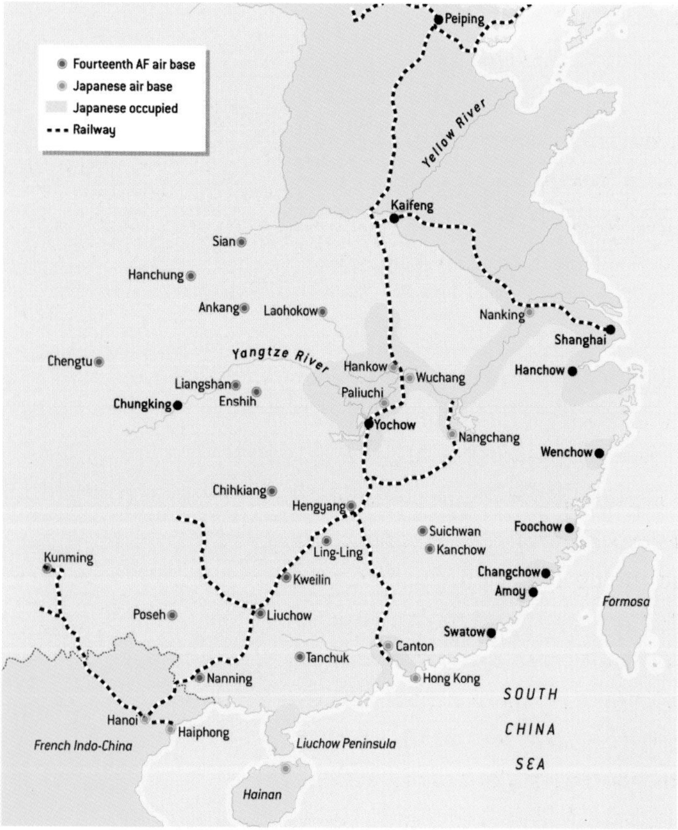

From its air bases in China, the USAAF's Fourteenth Air Force could strike targets in the Japanese-held areas of Hankow, Canton/Hong Kong, French Indo-China and Burma, as well as harassing Japanese shipping lanes in the South China Sea.

A second tactic was one the American pilots soon dubbed the "squirrel cage." In this, a formation of Ki-43s would break into two Lufbery defensive circles, one above the other, traveling in opposite directions. Every so often, Ki-43 pilots would loop, roll and perform other maneuvers in their highly agile "Oscars" as they flew in their circle. From a distance, the "squirrel cage" looked like a big dogfight, but if a Warhawk pilot approached with the idea of joining the fight, he would quickly find himself surrounded by unfriendly Ki-43s. In practice, American pilots quickly became wary of these two ploys, and rarely took the bait.

INTO COMBAT

On March 8, 1944, Col Winslow B. Morse, commander of the Fourteenth Air Force's CACW, was at his headquarters in Kweilin, China, when he received urgent orders to proceed at once with his staff to Kunming for a meeting with his commander, MajGen Chennault. Something big was in the wind. For two months, Chinese intelligence had been monitoring the Japanese movement of supplies and troops south from Peking and Manchuria via rail to the Yellow River Bridge, near Chenghsien. Chennault had concluded that the Japanese were building up for a push south across the river and through Honan Province in an attempt to complete the rail link with Hankow. In response, he devised a strategy to oppose the advance by air attack, which he called "Mission A," codename *Fateful.*

Units of Morse's CACW would provide most of the air power for "Mission A," including one B-25 squadron of the 1st Bomb Group and the four squadrons of the 3rd FG, equipped with P-40Ns, as well as two P-40 squadrons of the 4th FG CAF for support. Initially, this small force (a total of 84 aircraft on the rare days when all squadrons were at full strength) would operate from airfields at Liangshan, Hanchung, Ankang and Enshih.

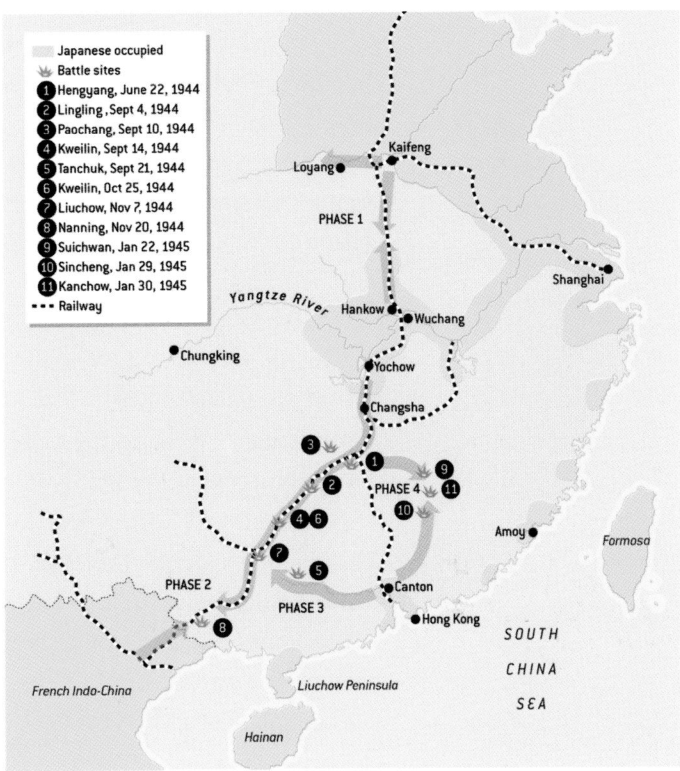

The Japanese *Ichi-Go* offensive, which would provide the impetus for the last major confrontation involving the P-40 and the Ki-43, eventually deprived the USAAF's Fourteenth Air Force of all of its major air bases in eastern China.

The CACW was perhaps the least heralded and most misunderstood of all the Fourteenth Air Force units that fought in China during World War II. In action from November 1943 to the end of the war, the CACW rolled up an impressive record against the Japanese while overcoming the challenges of culture and language posed by having Chinese and American personnel serving side-by-side in its squadrons.

The CACW was born in May 1943 at the Trident Conference in Washington, DC, when Chennault sold the conferees on a plan to build up Allied air strength in China. At that time, US-trained Chinese pilots were becoming available in substantial numbers, but the CAF was short on aircraft and leaders with combat experience. The USAAF, on the other hand, was experiencing a shortage of new combat pilots, but had plenty of new airplanes being delivered from factory assembly lines.

Under Chennault's plan, the CACW would use a mirror command structure, with Chinese and American co-commanders from wing headquarters all the way down to flight leaders and administrative positions in the wing's eight fighter squadrons and four medium bomber units. Chinese personnel would fill out the remaining slots for flight crews and technicians. The CACW would be a unit of the CAF, and its aircraft would carry Chinese markings. But unlike other CAF units, it would serve under the operational control of Chennault and the Fourteenth Air Force.

Operational training of the first three CACW squadrons commenced in August 1943 at Malir Cantonment, near Karachi, India (now Pakistan). The desert air base would be the birthplace of all CACW squadrons, which would number 12 by the time the last ones had completed training nearly a year later. The CACW itself was officially formed at Malir on October 1, 1943, under the command of Col Morse and his Chinese counterpart, Col Chiang I-Fu. Initially, the wing consisted of the 3rd FG (Provisional), with P-40Ns, and the 1st BG (Provisional), flying B-25Ds. The 5th FG (Provisional) was formed in January 1944, also flying P-40Ns. Eventually, each group consisted of four squadrons.

The 28th and 32nd FSs flew the CACW's first fighter missions on December 1, 1943, a week after they had arrived at Kweilin and set up operations. By the following spring, all four P-40 squadrons of the 3rd FG (7th, 8th, 28th and 32nd FSs) and two squadrons of the 5th FG (its last two squadrons were soon to arrive) were operating in China alongside USAAF P-40 units of the 23rd FG.

The plan behind "Mission A" was to let the Japanese concentrate their Honan forces, then smash them with air attacks before the offensive had time to begin. Air raids would continue to be flown until the Japanese withdrew. At air bases around Hankow, the 5th Air Army of the IJAAF had four fighter *sentais* (totaling roughly 100 aircraft) available to support the advance. The veteran 25th Sentai, equipped with Ki-43-IIs, had been operating in China since late 1942. Another Ki-43 unit, the 48th Sentai, was newly arrived from Manchuria, while the 9th and 85th sentais had begun receiving Ki-43s to bolster their shrinking complements of Ki-44s.

Col Morse made a flying tour of his new bases following the meeting with Chennault, then settled down to make plans for "Mission A" while awaiting the "go" order from Fourteenth Air Force headquarters. But the carefully laid plans involving notification by the Chinese four weeks prior to the peak of the buildup were quickly discarded when Japanese troops crossed the Yellow River in force on April 19, 1944 – with no warning from the Chinese! As Japanese tanks and cavalry rolled south from Chenghsien, it was obvious that the opportunity to stop the offensive before it started had been lost. To make matters worse, bad weather descended on eastern China, forcing Morse's squadrons to delay departure for their new bases for a critical week.

By May 1, three P-40 squadrons had reached Liangshan and were ready for action, but again the weather turned nasty and the airplanes went nowhere for three more days. Meanwhile, the Japanese were pushing southward in several drives, with little substantive opposition from Chinese ground forces. The 32nd FS, meanwhile, had reached its base at Hanchung and flew its first of many strikes against the Yellow River Bridge on May 3, dive-bombing the storage area on the north side of the single-track, two-mile-long span. Heavily defended and easy to repair, the bridge would be hit repeatedly in the coming months, but it was never closed for more than a few days.

On May 5, the 32nd FS registered the first claims for aerial victories of "Mission A." Led by squadron commander, Maj William L. Turner, eight P-40s were strafing a section of the Luchow–Loyang road (which would quickly be nicknamed "Slaughterhouse Alley") when Turner and Capt Keith Lindell spotted a single-engined aircraft they identified as a "Val" (probably a IJAAF Mitsubishi Ki-51 ground attack aircraft) and teamed up to shoot it down. Capt Tom Maloney and LtCol Tom Summers (3rd FG fighter control officer, assigned to fly with the 32nd FS) destroyed a twin-engined transport airplane that they encountered nearby a short while later.

The P-40s continued their strafing mission, and Summers' aircraft was struck by ground fire, forcing him to bail out. He returned to Hanchung on foot some days later. Lt Wang was wounded when an explosive shell hit his P-40 in the cockpit, and he crash-landed near Loyang. The P-40s' strafing proved effective, destroying 40 to 50 trucks, four armored cars and two pillboxes, plus killing an estimated 200 Japanese soldiers.

By this time, the full scope of the *Ichi-Go* offensive was becoming clear to the Americans. Col Clinton D. "Casey" Vincent, CO of the 68th CW at Kweilin, put together a force of 54 fighters and bombers for a strike against the Hankow area on May 6 in the hope of destroying Japanese supplies before the second phase of *Ichi-Go* could begin its drive down the Hsiang River valley toward Changsha. Led by Col David L. "Tex" Hill (legendary AVG ace now serving as commander of the 23rd FG), the fighter force consisted of P-51s of the 76th FS, P-38s of the 449th FS and P-40s of the 75th FS.

The formation pressed northeast toward Hankow through heavy haze and scattered clouds. About ten minutes out from the target – a supply area just off the edge of the main Hankow airdrome – several Ki-43s popped out of the clouds and made a head-on pass at a flight of Mustangs, and one P-51 was shot down. Soon the P-38s and P-40s joined the scrap, but only Col Hill, flying a P-51, would claim a victory. 1Lt James Folmar of the 75th FS was also credited with damaging a Ki-43. The "Oscars" were unable to engage the bombers, which successfully attacked the target.

At this point, the fight was on for aerial supremacy in the skies over the *Ichi-Go* advance. Although distracted by the CACW's aggressive attacks in Honan Province, the IJAAF 5th Air Army took on as its main assignment the securing of air superiority over the Hengyang and Suichwan areas, where the 68th CW bases were located. On May 11 and 12, the Japanese sent out strong missions against Suichwan, which was located in a pocket of Chinese-held territory midway between Hankow and Canton.

The first attack on the Suichwan area arrived in the late afternoon of the 11th when 35 Ki-43s of the 25th Sentai were reported heading toward the auxiliary air base at nearby Namyung. A small 76th FS force of three P-40Ns and two P-51Bs scrambled to meet the attack, with Capt Ed Collis leading. The P-40s attacked a "V" formation of Ki-43s from behind, and the Japanese pilots dropped their wing tanks when they saw the P-40s closing in. Collis, nevertheless, was able to get a good burst into the tail of one of the Hayabusas, which went down trailing smoke, and the Warhawk pilot later spotted a fire on the ground where he believed the airplane had crashed. Collis was credited with a confirmed victory, and the other three members of his flight each got one damaged. Lt Bill Watt described the fight:

> We in the P-40s sighted about 12 "Oscars" flying 1,000ft below us. We dove down and succeeded in each one of us killing an "Oscar." As I remember, there wasn't much to it. I just picked off one of the "Oscars" and got the hell out of there. We made it back to Suichwan without being intercepted by the Jap aeroplanes flying top cover.

The CACW was also in action on May 11, with P-40 pilots of the 7th and 32nd FSs claiming six Ki-43s shot down for no losses during a scrap near Mienchih. The results of these opening encounters of the P-40-versus-Ki-43 *Ichi-Go* duel cannot be confirmed on the Japanese side, but the advantage seems to have gone to the American fighters. The IJAAF evened the score the following day when the 5th Air Army sent more missions to the Suichwan/Namyung area.

For the first mission on May 12, the IJAAF despatched nine Ki-48 bombers of the 90th Sentai, escorted by about 50 Ki-43s of the 25th and 48th sentais. The Chinese warning net failed yet again, and the Japanese force reached Suichwan without being intercepted at about 0630hrs. Three P-40s and three P-51As of the 76th FS, along with P-40Ns of the 29th FS/5th FG CACW, scrambled late and were still climbing when the Japanese formation arrived over the base. The bombers flew past the airfield, turned around and made their bombing runs heading north in the direction of home. One flight of Ki-43s made a strafing run across the field as well.

WARHAWK PILOT: CLINTON D. VINCENT

Born in the small town of Gail, Texas, on November 29, 1914, Clinton D. Vincent was the youngest of 11 children in his family. Known throughout his life by the nickname "Casey," Vincent moved with his family to Natchez, Mississippi, while still a small boy, and grew up there. On graduating from high school in 1932, he received an appointment to the prestigious United States Military Academy at West Point.

After graduating from West Point as a second lieutenant in June 1936, Vincent undertook flight training at Randolph and Kelly Fields at San Antonio, in Texas. His first operational assignment came in November of the following year when he became the operations officer for the 19th Pursuit Squadron at Wheeler Field, in Hawaii. A move to California followed in November 1940, when Vincent transferred to the newly formed 35th Pursuit Group. He advanced rapidly in the group from squadron commander to group operations officer, executive officer and, in December 1941, group commander with the rank of major.

Vincent left for Australia in January 1942 and eventually wound up in Karachi, India, in March. There, he was assigned as Director of Pursuit Training for the Tenth Air Force. This was effectively a desk job, and he loathed it. Finally, in November 1942, Vincent obtained a transfer to BrigGen Claire Chennault's staff in China. He flew his first two combat missions on November 11 while en route to Kunming, China, from Dinjan, India. Upon arrival in China, Vincent was named operations officer of the CATF. Flying with the 23rd FG, he received credit for his first aerial victory – a fixed-gear fighter shot down over Canton – on November 27, 1942.

Vincent was promoted to full colonel in January 1943 and became chief of staff of the Fourteenth Air Force when it was activated in March. At about this time he began to be depicted in the popular Milton Caniff comic strip *Terry and the Pirates* as "Colonel Vince Casey." Then, in May 1943, he assumed command of the Forward Echelon of the Fourteenth Air Force at Kweilin, while continuing to fly missions whenever time allowed. On August 26, 1943, he scored his sixth and last confirmed victory, after which Gen Chennault grounded him from further combat flying.

After spending September and October on leave in the US, Vincent was named commander of the newly created 68th Composite Wing (an expansion of the Forward Echelon) in December 1943. His promotion to brigadier general in June 1944 at the age of 29 made him the youngest American general since the Civil War. Vincent continued to command the 68th CW throughout the *Ichi-Go* offensive, and returned to the US in December 1944.

Fellow ace BrigGen David L. "Tex" Hill, who served as Vincent's deputy in the 68th CW, recalled "'Casey' was one of the greatest officers I've ever been around. He was strong, smart – just one hell of a good man. He was never recognized for what he did. He handled it well in China. But you could tell in his diary that he felt like he'd been left hanging." Vincent served in Air Defense Command postwar and died of a heart attack in his sleep on July 5, 1955. He was just 40 years old.

Lt Steve Bonner, leading the P-40s of the 76th, dived toward the base and made a head-on pass at one of the Hayabusa strafers, seeing strikes on its engine as the two airplanes passed. Then he attacked another Ki-43 from above and behind, getting hits on the wing root and forward fuselage. The fighter went down trailing heavy smoke and fire, and ground observers confirmed its crash. This victory made Bonner an ace with five kills, all scored in P-40s.

Fellow P-40 pilot Lt Ken Elston of the 29th FS claimed a Ki-43 destroyed for the 5th FG's first confirmed victory of the war, and two P-51 pilots were also credited with victories. The Japanese lost two Ki-43s and their pilots, Sgts Katsuji Kurosaka and Souki Hoshi, from the 48th Sentai, and claimed one P-40 and one P-51 shot down. The only US loss was the P-40 of Lt Irving Saunders of the 76th FS, which belly-landed at its base, caught fire and burned – Saunders escaped injury. Another P-40 pilot, Lt Bob Kruidenier of the 29th FS, gave this account of the mission, which confirmed the stoutness of the P-40 airframe:

> I fired at plenty of Jap fighters that day, and while I was squaring away for a sure kill, a Nip let me have it with all he had. Holes appeared in the canopy, and oil and smoke filled the cockpit. In a flash I knew I had let myself become a "sitting duck" for some Jap pilot. I rolled the aeroplane over on its back and headed for Mother Earth, knowing that my would-be killer would not follow me down in a high dive, as the Jap aeroplanes were not capable of withstanding terrifically high diving speeds. I found that my wheels and flaps would still function, and I was able to make a safe landing on our own field. Not until I viewed the holes in my aeroplane did I realize what a lucky boy I had been. Except for five small needle-like steel splinters which had entered my right leg, I was still all in one piece.

The Japanese came back in the afternoon in another big formation, but this time only a few P-51s and P-40s were available to defend the base. The Japanese lost two Ki-48s, but their bombing was very effective. One string of bombs fell directly across the revetment area, destroying three P-38s and damaging three B-25s and three P-40s. After this, the 5th Air Army shifted its attention to the air bases at Hengyang, Lingling and Kweilin, also staging occasional night raids against the CACW at Liangshan.

On May 17 the 25th Sentai sent 27 Ki-43s to attack the American air base at Hengyang, hoping to cripple the 23rd FG by catching its fighters there on the ground. The plan did not work, however, as most of the P-40s were returning from a mission at the time and were diverted to Lingling for landing. Two pilots from the 75th FS, Lts Oswin "Moose" Elker and Vernon Tanner, were assigned

Pilots of the 74th FS pose with a new P-40K at Kunming in early 1943. In the front row, from left to right, are R. Turner, R. Morrison, C. Bair, W. Crooks, R. Lucia (PoW), W. Smith (behind Lucia), A. Cruikshank, J. Hinton, T. Shapou and T. Jeffreys. Sat on the nose of the fighter are F. Ladd, D. Mitchell and C. Crysler, whilst on its wing, from left to right, are L. Jones, W. Hawkins, D. Anderson, C. Bunch and W. Wanner. (Leon Klesman)

to airfield defense. They took off when the Japanese fighters were reported, and climbed to the bottom of an overcast layer at 4,000ft. Elker gave this account of what happened next:

> As the Ki-43s reached the field, they got into what we called their "squirrel cage" formation, in which some circled in one direction and some in the opposite direction. Some looped and some rolled. The purpose of this tactic was to give them good visibility in all directions against attack from any angle. More than anything else, it resembled a bee swarm.
>
> As they came below us, Tanner and I attacked those that came within our range. The attacked Japs always headed into the "squirrel cage" where, due to the diverse maneuvers of their comrades, there would always be one of them to attack the pursuer. I made short attacks and got back into the overcast to lose my pursuers, of which there were always several. After a quick turn in the overcast I'd come back down, and with so many aeroplanes in such a small patch of sky, there was a good chance I would sometimes come back down behind one within range. I would usually get in one good burst before I'd have tracers coming over my shoulder and I would have to get back into the overcast.

Elker got in a good burst at a Hayabusa on one pass and saw it spiral down trailing smoke, before breaking back into the clouds. He turned in the claim as probably destroyed, along with four damaged. Tanner also claimed a probable, but was badly hit himself and had to belly-land his P-40 at Hengyang. Several other 75th FS pilots managed to tackle the "squirrel cage" late in the fight, and total claims by the squadron were one confirmed destroyed, four probables and six damaged. The 25th Sentai claimed two P-40s shot down in exchange for two Ki-43s lost (with pilots Lt Koji Morita and Cpl Fukuji Tagami), plus three more damaged.

Elsewhere on May 17, Japanese troops in Honan Province completed their operation to link the Peking–Hankow railway line. With that, the "Mission A" units shifted their emphasis to denying the Japanese use of the line and began raining down bombs, rockets and machine-gun fire on trains and bridges from dawn until dusk. Then, on May 26, the main phase of the *Ichi-Go* campaign began when the Japanese 11th Army crossed the Yangtze River near Yochow and headed south toward the river city of Changsha. Chinese resistance was light at first, but it stiffened as the invaders crept closer to the city, where Gen Hsueh Yueh was in command of nearly 150,000 defenders.

Immediately, the pace and profile of 68th CW operations changed. Now, in addition to striking at Japanese installations and defending their own airfields, pilots would also begin attacking Japanese troop concentrations and lines of communication in the field. The flying took a toll, as the 75th FS alone lost seven P-40s (two pilots killed) between May 26 and 29, including two aircraft destroyed by Japanese bombs at Hengyang.

The IJAAF's 5th Air Army stepped up its activities as well in an effort to lend support to the ground advance. The 25th and 48th sentais began flying their Ki-43s from Paliuchi, just above Tungting Lake, which was the closest base to the Hsiang Valley fighting from which they could operate safely without the constant threat of air attack. The Hsiang Valley advance moved swiftly and was soon out of range of the short-legged Ki-44s of the 9th Sentai at Hankow, the 85th Sentai's Ki-44s having moved south to Canton in preparation for a new drive that would soon start north from there. Ki-43s were also based at Linfen to support the fighting in Honan Province, but several of these aircraft were destroyed on May 31 by rocket-firing P-40s of the 32nd FS/3rd FG.

Flying was curtailed by rain on this front during the first week of June. Then on the 9th, Chinese ground forces began a limited drive toward the city of I-ch'ang, west of Hankow. This drive was supported by CACW P-40 squadrons at Enshih and Liangshan, the 8th and 28th FSs reporting a lively scrap with Ki-43s over I-ch'ang on that date. But the Chinese soon stalled short of their objective, and the advance was called off by month-end.

June was busier for the American and Japanese pilots fighting over the Hsiang River Valley as the land offensive rolled on. Col Vincent moved 5th FG squadrons

WARHAWK: THROUGH THE GUNSIGHT

The primary gunsight in the P-40N was the USAAF's N-3A reflector sight, manufactured by Service Tool Engineering of Dayton, Ohio. The N-3A, like reflector sights used by other combatant air forces during World War II, was essentially a refined ring-and-bead, with the image of the ring-and-bead projected by a light onto a special glass in front of the pilot's eyes so that they were only visible when the pilot was looking directly down the longitudinal axis of his aircraft.

The most important improvement that the N-3A offered over the ring-and-bead sight was that the reflector's image was focused at infinity, so the pilot did not face the impossible task of trying to focus his sight on two different distances – the sight and the target – at the same time. The brightness of the image could be adjusted to suit the light conditions. The graticule could also be adjusted to the wingspan of the target aircraft, so when the latter's wingspan filled the circle, the pilot knew he was in range. The graticule was also of some help to the pilot in calculating deflection while firing at a target turning away from him, but it was basically no more helpful than a ring-and-bead sight in this regard.

P-40s were also fitted with a ring-and-bead sight as a manual backup in case the reflector sight failed. The USAAF subsequently introduced the more sophisticated K-14 gyroscopic gunsight in 1944, but few if any of these were fitted to late-production P-40N Warhawks. (Artwork by Jim Laurier, © Osprey Publishing) and the 76th FS from Suichwan to Hengyang on June 1 to bolster the defenses there. Two days later, the 76th sent its P-51s to Lingling, while the 74th FS brought its P-40s to Hengyang from Kweilin. On June 9, the 5th FG moved to a new base at Chihkiang, 175 miles northeast of Hengyang, where it would operate for the next year. A new P-40 squadron joined the 23rd FG mid-month when the 118th Tactical Reconnaissance Squadron (TRS) arrived at Kweilin under the command of future ace Maj Edward McComas.

The 23rd FG flew nine missions on June 9 alone, including five by the 74th FS. Two days later the depleted 75th FS pulled back to Kweilin. Now only the 74th FS remained at Hengyang, but this would not last for long. On June 15, Japanese ground forces bypassed Changsha, effectively accomplishing their first goal for *Ichi-Go* by bottling up the Chinese troops there, and continued heading south. This placed the air base at Hengyang, only some 80 miles away, in jeopardy. For more than two years Hengyang had been the "hot corner" in eastern China due to its close proximity to the Japanese strongholds at Hankow and Canton. Whenever Fourteenth Air Force fighter pilots got orders sending them to Hengyang, they could feel pretty confident of seeing plenty of action. Now those days were ending.

On June 16 Col Vincent ordered the 74th FS (down to eight P-40s, with just three of them fit for combat) to pull back to Kweilin. When the Japanese reached the gates of the city four days later, the last US personnel were ordered to evacuate the air base, and Vincent then had it demolished that night. By morning, nothing remained of the base that had been the scene of so many of the 23rd FG's greatest triumphs bar smoking rubble and a runway pockmarked with bomb craters.

But the Chinese 10th Army chose to make a stand at Hengyang, although the city was now surrounded. Some 10,000 troops, commanded by Gen Fong Hsien Chien, held the Japanese at bay, despite being equipped with just three old 75mm cannon and a smattering of machine guns, mortars and rifles. The siege at Hengyang would stretch on for the next six weeks, while the Japanese also continued to advance down the Hsiang Valley.

Lousy weather during the first three weeks of June – the peak of the monsoon season – did not prevent the P-40s from severely pounding the advancing Japanese forces. The majority of the missions flown were river sweeps designed to catch the Japanese hauling men and supplies by boat south to their frontline troops. In one nine-day period, the 23rd FG flew 538 sorties and lost just one aircraft when the engine failed in the P-40N flown by Lt David Rust of the 75th FS. He was forced to make a wheels-up landing ten miles north of Lingling.

For the month of June, the 23rd FG flew 1,606 offensive sorties – more than double the number flown in May, piling up 3,790 hours of combat time in the process, and claiming 17 Japanese aircraft shot down. But the price was high, with 20 P-40s and 12 P-51s lost to all causes. Few of these losses were attributed to enemy fighters, however, because the bad weather severely hampered operations of the Ki-43s from Paliuchi.

The first big engagement of the month took place on June 25, when Maj Arthur Cruikshank led a mixed formation of 74th and 75th FS P-40s out of Lingling on an offensive sweep up the river north of Hengyang. At mid-morning, the P-40s encountered eight Ki-43s of the 25th Sentai that were escorting Ki-51 ground attack aircraft sent to attack the Chinese at Hengyang. The Ki-51s turned for home as the P-40s and Ki-43s clashed. One of the American pilots on the mission was Lt Robert S. Peterson of the 75th FS, who was flying as wingman for Lt James C. Vurgaropolus. Peterson recalled fighting two enemies that day – Japanese fighters and the weather:

> I was glued to Vurgaropolus, this being my first contact with Jap fighters. We dove on a fighter (Ki-43), and when Vurgaropolus scored hits on him, he turned across my sight and I got in a good burst. As we were outnumbered, we dove away without seeing the airplane hit the ground. We claimed a probable, sharing half each.
>
> While this action was going on, the weather had moved in between us and Lingling. We had become separated from the others, so "Vurgie" told me to form up on his right wing and we would follow the Hsiang River back to Lingling. He took the left bank and I took the right. The river twisted and turned between high banks. It was typical monsoon rain. The rain was so heavy I could hardly see "Vurgie's" airplane – water was coming in around the canopy. At that moment the airplane shuddered and I saw wire draped over and around the nose and canopy. I had run through telephone lines that crossed the river. On landing, the wire was strung out 1,200ft behind me.

The P-40 pilots claimed three Japanese fighters destroyed, five probables and four damaged for the mission, while their opponents claimed one P-40 damaged. Neither side reported any losses that day. Peterson went on to complete 94 missions in China and eventually retired from the USAF Reserve as a major-general. Vurgaropolus was not so lucky. He was killed just four days after the June 25 mission when his P-40 slammed into a building during a strafing run over Changsha.

As June drew toward its close, the air base at Lingling was the next to be threatened by the Japanese advance. By this time, the crucial air raid warning net was breaking down in the Tungting Lake area, leaving the base exposed to air attack as well. The 75th FS moved to Kweilin and the 76th went farther south to Liuchow, where its Mustangs would be in position to oppose a new Japanese advance moving northwest out of Canton.

July brought further scraps between Japanese and American fighters. The IJAAF's 5th Air Army had instructed its bomber and fighter pilots to concentrate on attacking ground targets – Chinese defensive positions and supply lines – and to avoid air combat whenever possible. But considering the intense air operations over the rather narrow area of the *Ichi-Go* advance, such encounters were inevitable.

On the morning of July 5, the 75th FS sent eight P-40s, led by Maj Donald L. Quigley, from Kweilin to escort B-25s attacking a supply depot at Tungcheng, some 40 miles east of Tungting Lake. The weather cleared as they passed Lingling, and just north of Hengyang Lt Donald Lopez spotted 12 Ki-43s of the 25th Sentai coming in from above. Quigley advised the bombers to clear the area as he led the P-40s in a sharp turn to meet the Ki-43s head-on. He fired on a Ki-43 as it passed below him and saw the airplane stagger as it was hit. Quigley rolled over on his back and watched the Ki-43 dive straight down. By this time both formations had broken up, and aircraft were spread all over the sky. Quigley attacked another Ki-43 from the rear and saw it erupt in flames before he was forced to break off his attack.

Lopez, leading the second flight of four P-40s, picked up some battle damage in the opening pass and lost his wingman, Lt Al Haines, who was shot down to become a PoW. Then Lopez took a long-range shot at a Ki-43 below him. The maneuverable Hayabusa immediately stood on its wingtip and clawed into a hard turn to port – a maneuver that the P-40 pilots called a "flip" – and Lopez lost it. Next he saw a Ki-43 below him turning to the right and gave chase. Following its turn, Lopez pulled so much lead that the target dropped out of sight behind the long nose of his P-40. He opened fire with a short burst, eased off the turn enough to observe the results, then pulled hard again and fired a longer burst. This time when he eased out of his turn, he could see the Ki-43 trailing fire from its engine cowling and wing roots as it fell away.

The second element in Lopez's flight was also involved. Lt Joshua Sanford and his wingman, Lt Art Heine, shot up two Ki-43s that were attacking Lopez during the opening pass. Sanford picked out another target and was hitting it when yet another "Oscar" got on his tail and put a solid burst into the P-40's fuselage and cockpit area. Sanford was wounded in the foot and broke off into a dive. He was able to fly homeward as far as Lingling, where he belly-landed the damaged Warhawk.

This encounter between Ki-43s and P-40s occurred during the afternoon of August 8, 1944 when 16 "Oscars" of the 25th Sentai and 11 Warhawks of the 3rd FG/CACW clashed near Sinshih. Led by LtCol William N. Reed, the P-40s had been strafing river traffic on the Yangtze when the Ki-43s attacked from above and behind. The fight evolved into a swirling dogfight at low altitude, and one Ki-43 was shot down (pilot survived) and four P-40s were damaged. The CACW pilots claimed nine victories upon their return to base. (Artwork by Jim Laurier, © Osprey Publishing)

In an obvious case of misidentification, the 25th Sentai pilots claimed two P-51s shot down and two damaged against no losses. The P-40 pilots were credited with three confirmed victories for the loss of the P-40s flown by Haines and Sanford. Three more encounters took place later in the day, with the 25th Sentai losing Cpl Shoji Kanayama near Sinshih, shot down by Lt Harold Robbins of the 74th FS.

Another significant air battle that gives excellent insight into the intensity of the operations took place on July 15, when P-40s of the 74th FS ran into a formation of 48th Sentai Ki-43s – and possibly Ki-44s (referred to in the following account as "Tojos") of the 9th Sentai – during a mission to Siangtan. What follows is the post-mission narrative obtained from the flight leaders of the 74th FS:

> The 74th FS sent seven P-40s led by Capt John C. Herbst, squadron commander, from Kweilin to stage out of Namyung against the Japanese supply line from Tungchang to Tsyungyang. On July 14 they attacked several truck columns and destroyed more than 50 vehicles. Early the next morning they staged out of

Suichwan to attack barracks and flak positions near Siangtan. The dive-bombing flight, led by Capt Theodore A. Adams, carried a 250lb bomb under each wing. The trio of top cover, led by Capt Herbst, was loaded with parafrags [parachute fragmentation bombs].

The flights approached Siangtan, with the top cover at 8,000ft and the dive-bombers at 6,000ft. Capt Adams was to lead two dive-bombers in on the barracks near the airfield and Lt Virgil A. Butler and his wingman were to attack flak positions near the railway trestle north of the city.

Capt Theodore Adams supplied the following account of his experiences during the mission:

I had just located the target and peeled off on my dive-bombing run when I noticed a silver airplane below and to the right of me. It had a high, square-tipped wing and a radial engine. I kept an eye on the silver job because I figured I would come back after I bombed and get it. When I got down to about 2,000ft I saw another Jap to my left. I dropped my bombs and went after him. He was turning across my nose, so I pulled in behind him. I had built up so much speed in my dive that I closed in a hurry.

I started shooting with a 30-degree deflection and closed so fast I had to duck under to keep from hitting the Jap. He was a "Tojo" with elliptical wings and a big radial engine. I saw smoke trail out of his engine and then he fell off and hit the ground. I was at about 1,200ft when I pulled out.

Ki-43-II "55" of the 25th Sentai at Nanking. Note that the fighter's tail number does not match the number on the landing gear cover. The mottled camouflage was field-applied, thus no two Ki-43s in the 25th Sentai looked alike. (Yasuho Izawa)

> I saw a whole mass of Japs milling around the field at about 1,000ft. There were at least 20 "Tojos" and "Oscars" in a big landing circle going clockwise around the field. I did a steep 180-degree turn and came back over the field. I blacked out in the turn and headed into the Jap circle. One "Tojo" started to pull straight up away from the circle. I still had plenty of excess speed so I followed him up in a vertical climb. We were both going straight up when I opened fire. I saw two big plumes of black smoke trail from his cowling, and he stalled out. I had to duck again to avoid a collision. I saw him go down smoking like a chimney.
>
> There was a "squirrel cage" formation south of the field, with eight "Oscars" chasing their tails and edging away from the main fight. My speed was still up, so I broke into the edge of their circle. One tried to dive out so I gave him a 30-degree burst. I missed, and all of a sudden there were four other "Oscars" coming in on me from behind. They were shooting, but their deflection was off – all trailing. I dived a little and another P-40 came scooting by and scattered the Japs.
>
> I came back over the field at 500ft and saw a "Tojo" going west. I overhauled him and took a 45-degree deflection shot and then cut it down to 20 degrees. I saw pieces fly off his fuselage, but he kept on going. By this time one of my coolant lines had cracked and the fluid was boiling out. My temperature gauge was clear over on the peg, so I shoved the nose down and started for the Chinese side of the lines to the southwest. Two Japs chased me, and I could see four others on the tail of another P-40. The Japs couldn't gain on me, and the coolant saw me home. I found out later that Lt Van Sickle had shot an "Oscar" off my tail as I turned into my first "Tojo." I never even knew the Jap was there.

Lt Virgil Butler also spoke about his experiences on July 14:

> I was after some flak positions near the railway trestle north of the field. I made my bomb run and went after the silver square-winged Jap. All of a sudden I picked up three Japs on my tail. While I was diving and twisting to get away from them, a "Tojo" loomed up ahead in my sights. He had his flaps and wheels down, and was almost dead ahead below me. I lowered my nose and took a good long shot from squarely astern. He looked as though someone had struck a match along his fuselage – just a long, growing flare of flame. He rolled over and crashed, still burning. I kept on diving down to the deck and got away from the other three Japs.

Finally, Capt John Herbst gave his take on how the mission went from his point of view:

I was leading the top cover at 8,000ft when I heard Capt Adams call, "There is a Jap down here." At the same time I spotted three black fighters coming in toward us. They must have been top cover for whatever was going on below. I turned into them and they turned away. I never did see them again. We dropped our frag bombs and belly tanks and started down. We picked up a terrific speed in that dive – enough to carry us all the way through the fight with an advantage.

At 3,000ft I saw two black columns rising from two Jap airplanes that had already hit the deck. Then I spotted a lot of Japs at about 1,000ft circling clockwise, and a couple of P-40s weaving in and out of the circle. There were two dust streamers rising along the runway where two more Japs were taking off. I counted at least 16 "Oscars" and "Tojos" all strung out in the circle, apparently following their leader. They made no effort to get away – just went around and around.

I started to cut inside the circle, but I had so much speed – about 340mph – that I had to weave in and out to get shots in. It was a real slugging match. We had the speed and altitude on them, and at close range those six .50s tore them apart. I took a couple of snap shots and missed. The Japs just went round and round – none of their usual tricks, not even steep, tight turns. They seemed to be afraid to do any stunts at low altitude. Our boys had been flying on the deck for so long – strafing and dodging hills in bad weather – that nobody thought twice about racking around in vertical banks ten feet off the deck. It was just our "meat."

I spotted an "Oscar" with his wheels down at about 600ft. I slowed down and came in directly behind him and a little above. I gave him a two-second burst and he erupted in flames. I saw him crash. By then I had picked up a "Tojo" on my tail, with an "Oscar" behind him. I could also see other smoke columns rising from crashed airplanes. The "Tojo" opened fire, but all his shots were trailing. I could outturn him, but the moment I got ahead the "Oscar" would cut across the circle and cut me off. I flipped over and started turning in the opposite direction. The same thing happened. I was surprised that I could turn inside the "Tojo", but he seemed unwilling to make a tight turn at 500ft. Finally I shoved the stick down and dived under the "Oscar" as he banked across to cut me off. That cleared my tail, and I looked around.

There was a P-40 south of the field with a "Tojo" on his tail at 800ft. The P-40 was diving and the "Tojo" turning into him to get a deflection shot ahead of him. I turned into the "Tojo" from high astern. My first burst was over him, and he saw the tracers. He flipped over and tried to dive out in the opposite direction. That brought him squarely into my sights for a no-deflection shot, and I gave him another burst that nearly burned out my guns. He burned and went in. I got back up to 500ft and came back across the field. There were only three Zeros left still

P-40F Warhawk fighters on a training flight out of Moore Field, near Mission, Texas, in 1943. These pilots are conducting Advanced fighter training before joining operational squadrons. By 1943 their Warhawk was no longer a first-rate fighter in most theaters, but in China its ruggedness and firepower allowed it to more than hold its own against the IJAAF. (USAAF)

> circling the field. I went after them, along with about five other P-40s. We made a couple of passes and didn't hit anything. Leaving the field, I saw columns of smoke rising from the ground.

The Ki-43 pilots claimed one P-40 destroyed, one probable and two damaged, although in fact there were no Warhawk losses. The P-40 pilots claimed six victories, including two Ki-43s and four Ki-44s. The 48th Sentai did indeed lose two Ki-43s, with Capt Tadashi Nishikawa and SgtMaj Susumu Ito both being killed.

July also saw the 5th FG at Chihkiang fly three very effective missions against the IJAAF airfield at Paliuchi. These strikes, flown on the 14th, 24th and 28th, are probably the best-remembered missions in the history of the group. The combined score was 66 Japanese aircraft destroyed, 31 probables and 24 damaged, for the loss of one P-40 and its pilot to enemy action and one other to a flying accident.

Aggressive low-level flying and superb planning can be credited for the success of the Paliuchi missions. Each time, the P-40s approached the target by flying across Tungting Lake at wave-top height, and each time they caught the Japanese by surprise. A measure of just how unprepared the enemy was for these attacks is revealed in one simple statistic – of the 66 aircraft destroyed, only two were shot down. The rest were caught on the ground, helpless before the guns and bombs of the P-40s.

While these aerial battles were taking place, on the ground, the Chinese defenders continued to hold out in Hengyang thanks to supplies dropped to them from Fourteenth Air Force transport airplanes. Yet despite aircraft from Col Vincent's 68th CW mercilessly pounding Japanese ground troops surrounding the city, and "Mission A" units continuing to disrupt the enemy's lines of supply, Hengyang was doomed. The air action climaxed on August 8, 1944, the very day the Chinese finally capitulated after a siege lasting 44 days. That morning, P-40Ns of the 75th FS/23rd FG had an encounter with Ki-43-Iis of the 48th Sentai at low altitude near Hengshan. The 23rd FG mission recap read as follows:

> Eight P-40s of the 75th took off from Lingling at 0450hrs for an offensive sweep and patrol from Hengyang north to Siangtan, following the river. Four barges and one powered sampan damaged. Nine trucks burned and 18 damaged. After this the "Sharks" (P-40s) ran into nine "Oscars" and "Hamps" (in actuality, all Japanese fighters involved were Ki-43s). Lt (Robert) Peterson confirmed one "Hamp." Maj (Donald) Quigley got one probable "Oscar." Lt (James) Folmar probably destroyed one "Oscar." Lt (Donald) Lopez damaged one "Oscar." Lt (Joseph) Martinez damaged one "Oscar" and Lt (Paul) Moehring damaged two "Oscars." All of our aeroplanes returned safely.

The 75th FS's mission description read in part, "Maj Quigley found an 'Oscar' apparently crippled and chased it all the way to Lukow on the deck. He got in three head-on passes, and several times the airplane seemed to be out of control, but always recovered right on the deck. Maj Quigley ran out of ammunition and broke away without seeing the airplane go in." Lt Robert Peterson recalled years later "a fight down to the treetops. This was a situation we had long been warned against – dogfighting with Jap Zeroes – but I got into the fight and refused to let go until my foe went down."

The Ki-43 pilots of the 48th Sentai claimed no fewer than seven P-40s shot down, although in fact none were lost. Three Ki-43s were destroyed and their pilots killed, and *sentai* commander Maj Masao Matsuo was badly injured in a fourth machine.

Also on August 8, LtCol Bill Reed, the former AVG pilot now serving as commander of the 7th FS/3rd FG, led 11 P-40s of the 7th, 8th and 28th FSs off from Enshih at 1300hrs, heading east to sweep the Yangtze River to Hankow. The P-40s approached the target area at 3,000ft in CAVU (ceiling and visibility unlimited) weather, then descended to treetop level at Sinti and strafed several concentrations of boats spotted along the river. While at low-level, the P-40s were jumped by more than 12 Ki-43s of the 25th Sentai. The 7th FS mission report described the fight as follows:

> They proceeded toward Hankow, where they were jumped by enemy fighters. LtCol Reed got on the tail of one "Oscar" after it had pulled off a pass on a P-40 and gave it a good burst. Lt [Edward] Mulholland [Reed's wingman] saw him in an uncontrolled glide at less than 500ft. Claimed one destroyed. Lt Mulholland got a 40-degree deflection shot at an "Oscar" and gave him three good bursts. It flipped on its back with flames coming from its engine in a steady stream. Claimed one destroyed. Lt Mulholland got hits on two other "Oscars" in head-on passes. Claimed two damaged. Lt Tang became lost on the return trip and landed at Kaifeng.

The P-40 pilots claimed a total of nine Ki-43s destroyed, but the encounter was not actually that decisive. The 25th Sentai lost one Ki-43 in the fight and claimed three P-40s shot down. In fact, no P-40s were lost, although LtCol Reed came home with a big hole in the right aileron of his airplane.

The capture of Hengyang was another victory for the Japanese, but it had come at a high cost. The *Ichi-Go* ground forces, now extended like a finger into Hsiang River Valley, were fatigued, and their supply line was tenuous at best because of its continued vulnerability to air attack. Similarly, the 5th Air Army was nearing exhaustion. The 25th Sentai was down to just a handful of Ki-43s and the 48th Sentai was in even worse shape. After having lost 16 pilots and most of its Ki-43s over the previous three months, the 48th was withdrawn to reequip with

---

Overleaf: Sharknoses over China

P-40Ns of the 75th FS/23rd FG and Ki-43-IIs of the 48th Sentai clash at low altitude near Hengshan, in China, on the morning of August 8, 1944. Eight P-40s of the 75th, led by Maj Don Quigley, "ran into nine 'Oscars' near Hengshan. Maj Quigley found an 'Oscar' apparently crippled and chased it all the way to Lukow on the deck. He got in three head-on passes, and several times the airplane seemed to be out of control, but always recovered right on the deck. Maj Quigley ran out of ammunition and broke away without seeing the airplane go in." Lt Bob Peterson described the combat as "a fight down to the treetops." 75th FS pilots claimed one victory (Peterson's), two probables and four damaged. (Artwork by Jim Laurier, © Osprey Publishing)

175

new aircraft and replenish its pilot strength. Within a few weeks the 22nd Sentai would arrive from Japan, equipped with the new Nakajima Ki-84 *Hayate* – a far superior fighter to the Ki-43.

The P-40 units opposing the Japanese remained full of fight, but their ability to maintain pressure on the Japanese was compromised by shortages of fuel and ammunition. And the number of P-40s in frontline service was beginning to wane as high-performance North American P-51 Mustangs displaced them in squadron after squadron. The war in China would continue for another year, but the full-scale aerial duels between P-40s and Ki-43s were now all but over.

ANALYSIS

The air battles involving P-40s and Ki-43s over China during the summer of 1944 constituted a classic confrontation between two contemporary fighter aircraft and the pilots who flew them. The airplanes were dissimilar in design and performance, while the pilots were products of two distinctly different cultures. But in the final analysis, the difference in the war-making capabilities of the United States and Japan was the deciding factor in the outcome of the fight.

On the American side, Gen Chennault's fighter pilots achieved the immediate goal of maintaining control of the air over the various fronts in the *Ichi-Go* advance. Fourteenth Air Force interdiction missions continued unabated throughout the campaign, hindered more by bad weather than by occasional interceptions by Japanese fighters. In fact, a P-40 pilot was far more likely to be shot down by Japanese ground fire than in air-to-air combat. For example, the 23RD FG lost 20 P-40s and 12 P-51s in June 1944 to all causes, but only one loss was the result of being shot down by an enemy fighter. The group lost 24 more fighters in July and 30 in August, eight of which went down in air-to-air combat.

The ability of the Fourteenth Air Force to absorb such losses without losing control of the skies was due in part to the aggressive nature of its combat leaders, and in part to the fact that its units received sufficient replacement aircraft and pilots.

In contrast, the IJAAF's 5th Air Army sustained heavy losses in air-to-air combat and from enemy raids on its airfields. The Japanese started the *Ichi-Go* campaign with 113 Ki-43s and Ki-44s – roughly equal to the number of Fourteenth Air Force fighters opposing them – but the numbers of airplanes and pilots in the 5th Air Army quickly declined as replacements failed to cover losses.

Very early in the campaign, Japanese commanders could already see their forces being depleted, so they ordered their pilots to avoid air combat whenever possible.

But this proved impractical because the IJAAF fighter units were tasked with defending the Japanese supply lines, which were constantly under attack from American fighters and bombers. As the supply lines grew longer, so Japanese losses mounted. Pilot strength in the 25th Sentai, for example, had dropped from 44 on May 31 to just 25 by the end of August.

But the fact remains that Gen Chennault could not stop the Japanese ground advances by hitting them from the air, as he had confidently predicted he would be able to do prior to the offensive commencing. The Chinese army simply lacked the skills and equipment to hold its ground, despite all the help it got from the Fourteenth Air Force.

Perhaps the most telling statistic lies in the production numbers. The Ki-43 was the most numerous IJAAF fighter of World War II, a grand total of 5,751 being delivered in just over four years. By comparison, the P-40's production run of 13,738 aircraft ranked just third among USAAF fighters behind two superior types, the P-47 and the P-51. Even if the Ki-43 had possessed superior combat capabilities, which it definitely did not, the "Oscar" would still have fought a losing battle due to the inability of Japan, and its aircraft manufacturers, to keep pace with their counterparts in the United States.

Capt Takashi Tsuchiya (1st Chutai/25th Sentai leader) scored eight victories before he was killed in action on September 3, 1944. The label on his parachute harness read *Chutai-cho* ("Chutai leader"). His Ki-43-II was marked as aircraft "20." (Yasuho Izawa)

ACES LISTS

Several factors make it difficult, bordering on impossible, to produce a definitive statistical analysis of the P-40 vs Ki-43 duels in China. For one thing, American pilots tended to identify all Japanese radial-engine monoplane fighters as "Zeros," even after the existence of the IJAAF's Ki-43s and Ki-44s became known in 1943. The Fourteenth Air Force maintained a policy of requiring verification from a second source to confirm aerial victories, but the nature of air warfare still made confirmation an inexact art at best.

The IJAAF put far more emphasis on the overall group performance in combat, preferring to give credit for aerial victories to the unit rather than to an individual pilot. In addition, the IJAAF established no specific rules for confirming the veracity of a victory claim. Thus, the tallies listed here are based on the victory claims attributed to the pilots at the time of this publication being written.

Finally, due to the shortage of detailed Japanese records from the China campaign, it is impossible to break down all IJAAF aces' scores by enemy aircraft type. Most of the tallies attributed to the leading Japanese aces in China would almost certainly have contained at least one P-40 kill, however, as the Warhawk was the only American fighter in-theater for much of World War II.

P-40 ACES IN CHINA WITH FOUR OR MORE Ki-43 KILLS				
Name	Unit	Ki-43 kills	Total score	Notes
Maj E. W. Richardson	23rd FG	7	8-0-0	75th FS CO
Maj A. W. Cruikshank Jr	23rd FG	6	8-6-0	74th FS CO
Capt J. F. Hampshire Jr	23rd FG	6	13-3-0	KIA China, 5/2/43
Col B. K. Holloway	23rd FG	6	13-4-0	23rd FG CO
Capt J. W. Little	23rd FG	6	7-0-0	1 kill Korea
Maj R. L. Callaway	3rd FG CACW	5.5	6-1-2	32nd FS CO
Capt D. A. Clinger	23rd FG	5	5-3-0	–
Maj E. R. Goss	23rd FG	5	6-2-0	75th FS CO
LtCol R. L. Liles	23rd/51st FGs	5	5-5-2	16th FS CO
Capt J. M. Williams	23rd FG	5	6-2-1	76th FS CO
Capt H. A. Paxton Jr	3rd FG CACW	4.5	6.5-0-2	–

TOP Ki-43 ACES WHO SCORED IN CHINA 1942–45			
Name	Sentai	Total score	Notes
Capt I. Hosono	25th	26	KIA China, 10/6/43
1Lt M. Kanai	25th	26	19 victories over China
Capt N. Ozaki	25th	25	KIA China, 12/27/43
WO M. Ogura	24th	16	1st P-40 victory July 1942 China
LtCol T. Sakagawa	25th	15+	KIFA Negros, Philippines, 12/19/44
SgtMaj T. Shono	25th	14	KIA China, 10/27/44
Maj K. Namai	33rd	12	1 P-40 victory China
2Lt I. Hazawa	25th	10+	KIA China, 1/14/45
SgtMaj K. Ohtake	25th	10+	–
WO E. Seino	25th	10+	4 P-40 victories China
SgtMaj K. Kato	11th	9	3 P-40 victories early 1944 China
WO T. Tashiro	25th	8	KIA China, 1/4/45
Capt T. Tsuchiya	25th	8	KIA China, 9/3/44
SgtMaj M. Yamato	33rd	8	3 P-40 victories August 1943 China
Capt H. Shishimoto	11th	7	–

AFTERMATH

The *Ichi-Go* offensive continued after the fall of Hengyang, as did aerial clashes involving P-40s and Ki-43s. But bad weather in September and October 1944, combined with the declining number of P-40s in China, made these encounters increasingly rare.

By this time, the Fourteenth Air Force was finally getting high-performance North American P-51B/C Mustangs as replacements for its tired P-40s, as Gen Chennault had been requesting for two years. All former P-40 squadrons of the 23rd and 51st FGs had been reequipped with Mustangs by the end of 1944, and the CACW squadrons would follow suit in the spring of 1945. Meanwhile, the 5th Air Army continued to fly Hayabusas, its Ki-43-IIs slowly giving way to the new Ki-43-III model, along with Ki-44s and the vastly superior, but notoriously unreliable, Ki-84 Hayate.

On January 14, 1945, CAF Lt Yueh Kung-Cheng of the 27th FS/5th FG CACW was credited with shooting down a Ki-43 during an escort mission to Hankow, thus giving him the distinction of claiming what is likely to have been the last P-40 victory over a Hayabusa in China, if not the entire Pacific War. But the Japanese ground offensive in China wore on. Kweilin and Liuchow had fallen in November 1944, followed by Suichwan and Kanchow in January 1945. These conquests completed the *Ichi-Go* objective of establishing a rail link from Indo-China to Shanghai and Peking, but it was a hollow victory because the continuing ability of the Fourteenth Air Force to strike the railway line from its remaining bases made the link all but useless.

Seeking to put a stop to this aerial harassment, the Japanese next turned their attention to the Fourteenth Air Force's forward airfield at Chihkiang, where the 5th FG CACW and the 75th FS/23rd FG were based. An offensive by the 20th Army began in the spring of 1945, with limited aerial support from the IJAAF's diminished 5th Air Army. This time, however, the Chinese defenses held and the Japanese drive stalled short of its goal in May 1945. P-40s and Ki-43s played little or no part in this final battle of the *Ichi-Go* offensive.

The P-40 went out of frontline service in the Fourteenth Air Force when the CACW's 27th FS/5th FG converted to P-51s in June 1945. P-47 Thunderbolts had already replaced Warhawks in the fighter-bomber role in Burma and the MTO in 1944, and former P-40 squadrons in the Pacific were now flying P-38 Lightnings. Most air forces retired their remaining P-40s at the end of the war. The Netherlands East Indies Air Force flew the last known combat operations in the P-40, attacking Indonesian nationalist guerillas on occasion before leaving the country in 1949.

Although appearing at first glance to be intact, derelict Ki-43 "71" is missing its left aileron and tailwheel assembly as it sits forlornly on an airfield at Nanking in September 1945. Dumped "Oscars" littered ex-IJAAF airfields across the Pacific and China-Burma-India theater at war's end. (Yasuho Izawa)

Back in the US, the Curtiss-Wright Corporation was struggling while the rest of the nation was looking forward to the end of the war. As noted earlier, attempts to design a follow-on fighter to replace the P-40 on Curtiss production lines had proven to be unsuccessful. The final version of the Warhawk, the XP-40Q, was a big improvement over the P-40N, but was still too little, too late. Upgrades included a cut-down rear fuselage spine and a bubble canopy, radiators moved to the wing roots to allow a more streamlined nose and a more powerful Allison engine with two-stage supercharging that produced a top speed of 422mph at 20,000ft. This would have been great had North American's superior P-51D not already been in full production. The P-40Q simply was not needed, and the last Warhawk rolled out of the Curtiss factory in November 1944. Plagued by chronic mismanagement and a series of uninspired designs, the Curtiss-Wright Corporation eventually ceased all aircraft production in 1951.

The Ki-43 remained in production throughout the war. In fact, Tachikawa was testing a new model for home defense – the Ki-43-IIIb with heavier armament and a more powerful engine – when the armistice was signed. Few new Hayabusas reached China in the final year of the war, however, as virtually all fighters built in Japan were now being sent to units protecting the home islands, which were coming under attack from USAAF B-29 Superfortresses based in the Marianas Islands. By mid-November 1944, the 25th Sentai at Paliuchi had been reduced in strength to just nine Ki-43s and three Ki-84s.

In late January 1945, the 5th Air Army was ordered to prepare for an expected invasion on the east coast of China by pulling its units back to a triangular zone marked by the cities of Shanghai, Hanchow and Nanking. In its place, the smaller 13th Air Division was established at Hankow to carry on the fight in central China. After replenishment in Japan following the Hengyang siege, the 48th Sentai remained in China with its Ki-43s through to the end of the war. The 25th Sentai was ordered to Korea in June to prepare for the invasion of Japan, and it was still there when the war ended in September 1945.

The "Oscar" continued to serve in several Asian air forces until the late 1940s. As a member of the Greater East Asia Co-Prosperity Sphere, Thailand had received Ki-43-Iis from Japan in 1944, and its air force flew them in frontline service for several years after the armistice until they were replaced by more modern American and British types. The Red Army of China forces acquired Ki-43s from former Japanese bases when they occupied Manchuria, beginning in October 1945. Similarly, insurgents of the Indonesian People's Security Force built up their air force by refurbishing a number of wrecked Hayabusas that had been recovered from a large aircraft dump in Djakarta.

The French confiscated Ki-43s from the IJAAF's 64th Sentai at the end of the war and used them for a short period on counterinsurgency operations in French Indo-China until replacing them with Spitfires acquired from the British. The French pilots initially had difficulty landing their "Oscars," being unfamiliar with them, and several were wrecked. This was said to have amused the demobilized Japanese pilots still in the country, because they considered the Ki-43 very easy to handle both in the air and on the ground.

Ironically, the postwar era was kinder to Nakajima Aircraft than it was to Curtiss-Wright. At the end of the war, after producing a total of 25,935 airplanes and 46,726 aircraft engines over the previous 30 years, Nakajima was broken up into 15 smaller companies. These firms began making products utilizing aviation technologies, such as monocoque buses, scooters that rolled on bomber tail wheels and other transport-related products.

Later, five of these companies reunited into what is currently known as Fuji Heavy Industries Ltd, a manufacturer of transportation- and aerospace-related products, as well as the maker of Subaru vehicles. So, 60 years after the end of World War II, the legacy of the Nakajima Ki-43 Hayabusa is a popular car found on American highways from coast-to-coast!

MARK POSTLETHWAITE '10

Part IV

DUELING FOR THE REICH: GERMANY 1943–45

P-51 MUSTANG vs Fw 190

By early 1944, the air war in Europe was moving into its final phase. The massed heavy bombers of the USAAF and RAF had long flown raids deep into Germany, but neither Spitfires nor Thunderbolts could escort the four-engined "heavies" all the way to their targets and back. However, in late 1943 the ETO the first USAAF fighter group in to be equipped with a new, long-range escort fighter became operational. Now, and until VE-Day, the USAAF's fighters could fly head to head with the finest interceptors that the Luftwaffe could still wield, as they battled to stem the bombers' onslaught.

The legendary P-51 Mustang, the best American fighter of World War II, and the Fw 190A, one of Germany's greatest piston-engined interceptors, were thus the players in some of the most deadly combat confrontations of the war in Europe. Combining the endless power of the Packard Merlin with a beautifully designed airframe, the Mustang epitomized the might of the Eighth Air Force's VIII Fighter Command in the final 18 months of the conflict. More than 80 pilots became aces flying the classic North American fighter, a fact that bears testimony to its overall superiority in combat.

Not only was the Mustang capable of meeting the Bf 109G/K and Fw 190A on even or better terms, it could escort the four-engined bombers of VIII Bomber Command on deep penetration missions all the way to their targets and back again. Also, the Mustang's long range gave it an extra dimension by permitting fighter groups to break away and strafe enemy airfields and other targets before returning home.

The rapid improvement and success of the Mustang is even more remarkable when one considers that the Fw 190A was the result of design work begun in late 1937, and as such it had a three-year development advantage over the North American design. Furthermore, when the first Allison-engined P-51s appeared, the Mustang still had a lot of catching up to do in order to realize its potential as a multi-gunned fighter.

On the morning of January 14, 1945, II./JG 26's four *Staffeln* of Fw 190D-9 "Long-noses" took off from a foggy Nordhorn to attack American fighter-bombers reported active in the St Vith area of Belgium. However, their route south put them on a collision course with a large formation of Flying Fortresses heading for the Rhine road bridges at Cologne. Alerted to the presence of the Luftwaffe force, some two-dozen P-51 Mustangs of the 78th Fighter Group were detached from the B-17s' fighter escort and ordered to engage. They bounced the lower-flying Germans near Aachen, and one of the pilots lost in the ensuing action was the Staffelkapitän of 5./JG 26, Oberleutnant Gerhard Vogt. His "White 13" was last seen disappearing into cloud to the southeast of Cologne. (Artwork by Mark Postlethwaite, © Osprey Publishing)

In 1940, when the British were shopping for a new fighter, the Mustang was fitted with its original Allison powerplant, which was not designed to perform at high altitudes, and so the RAF operated the aircraft in great numbers in the ground attack and tactical reconnaissance roles. The Fw 190A, however, had become the scourge of Allied pilots from the moment it had appeared at German airfields in Belgium in August 1941. A nimble, fast and well-armed adversary, it was technically superior to all British and American fighters in frontline service at that time. This situation only changed with the advent of the Merlin-engined P-51B in late 1943.

In the autumn of 1942, plans had been laid to develop the Mustang as a long-range fighter, fitted with the Rolls-Royce Merlin engine. After overcoming early teething troubles, the worst of which was persistent gun jamming, the P-51B clearly demonstrated its tremendous potential. By early 1944 the aircraft had surpassed the Fw 190A in terms of performance, the latter aircraft's top speed being almost 50mph slower at all heights and 70mph slower above 28,000ft. There was little to choose between the two when it came to maximum rate of climb, while the Mustang could always outdive the Fw 190A. Again, in the turning circle both were closely matched, and if anything the Mustang was slightly better. However, not even a Mustang could approach the Fw 190A's outstanding rate of roll.

Revisions in design and armament followed, and the P-51D/K became the best of the wartime Mustang breed. Capable of outperforming German propeller-driven fighters, and able to operate far over the continent with the aid of drop tanks, the P-51D/K was the most successful of all the models to see service in World War II. It was also built in greater quantities than any other variant. In the right hands, the Mustang was superior to the Fw 190A, despite Focke-Wulf trying to keep pace with the Allied fighter through the production of a profusion of newer models that boasted technological innovations such as water/methanol fuel injection to boost engine power for short periods. But ultimately, these improvements were too little, too late.

By late 1944, an average of three German fighters and two pilots were lost for every B-17 or B-24 shot down. The *Jagdwaffe* was hampered by a lack of fuel, diminishing spares and pilot attrition, and high-scoring Fw 190 *experten* like "Pips" Priller and Heinz Bär and the handful of Focke-Wulf-equipped *Jagdgeschwader* could not overcome the overwhelming odds stacked against them in the defense of the Reich.

THE MACHINES

NORTH AMERICAN P-51 MUSTANG

In April 1940 British Purchasing Commission (BPC) officials visiting America sought a new long-range fighter to supplement the Spitfire and Hurricane. When they approached North American Aircraft with an invitation to produce the Curtiss 11-87 (P-40D) in quantity under license for the RAF, the California-based company suggested instead that it build a brand new and infinitely superior fighter using the same 1,150hp Allison V-1710-39 engine. The BPC accepted the proposal, but a 120-day limit for the construction of a prototype was imposed.

North American's only previous experience in fighter design and construction was limited to the near-identical NA-50 and NA-68, both of which were little more than reworked, single-seat trainers fitted with guns in the wings. Just 13 examples of these aircraft had been built for the Peruvian and Royal Siam air forces in 1939. Nevertheless, North American Aircraft Company president I. H. "Dutch" Kindelberger was confident that his company could produce an aircraft that answered the needs of the RAF. He and his team of engineers had studied early accounts of air combat in Europe, and these had influenced the design of a new fighter that North American already had on its drawing board prior to the BPC visit. Much useful technical data was also obtained from the Curtiss-Wright Corporation.

With the BPC contract signed, the design team, headed by Lee Atwood, Raymond Rice and German-born Austrian Edgar Schmued (the latter having previously been employed by Dutch aircraft manufacturer Fokker) hastily began work on the new fighter, which was designated the NA-73X – "73" was North American's model number and "X" denoted its experimental status.

The NA-73X prototype was assembled in 117 days, although when the aircraft was rolled out of the company's Mines Field facility its 1,100hp Allison V-1710-39 (F3R) engine was not yet installed and the prototype was fitted with wheels borrowed from an AT-6 basic trainer. The NA-73 was one of the first fighters to employ a low, square-cut laminar-flow airfoil, which had its maximum thickness well aft. The aircraft duly boasted the lowest-drag wing fitted to any fighter yet built. Drag was further reduced by streamlining a radiator scoop into the underside of the fuselage behind the pilot, whilst keeping the fuselage cross-section to the least depth possible.

On May 4, 1940, the US Army released the new design for sale to Britain, provided that two of the initial batch of fighters be transferred to the US Army Air

Corps (USAAC) for tests. After 320 NA-73s were ordered by the BPC 19 days later, the fourth and tenth aircraft were allotted the Army Air Corps designation XP-51 in a contract approved on September 20. Four days later the BPC increased its purchase to 620 examples. After several modifications, the NA-73X was flown for the first time on October 26, 1940. It crashed on November 30 following an engine failure in flight, but production was by then assured. Christened the Mustang I by the British, the first production standard aircraft was flown on April 23, 1941, and retained by the company for further testing.

The USAAC's first XP-51 arrived at Wright Field for service testing on August 24, 1941, while the second aircraft was accepted by RAF representatives in September and then sent on a long journey by ship to Liverpool, where it arrived on October 24. Tests soon showed the Mustang I to be superior to the Kittyhawk, Airacobra and Spitfire in both speed and maneuverability at low altitudes. Top speed went from 328mph at 1,000ft to 382mph at 13,000ft. Equipment included armor, leak-proof fuel tanks, two .50in machine guns – with 400rpg – placed low in the nose and two more in the wings, inboard of four .30in weapons with 500rpg.

The first production model destined for RAF service made its maiden flight on May 1, 1941, and a Lend-Lease contract approved on September 25 that same year added a further 150 Mustang IAs to the production order. These aircraft were armed with four 20mm cannon in the wings, with 125rpg. The first 20 P-51s to follow the last Mustang IAs off the line in July 1942 were taken on charge by the US Army Air Force (USAAF), fitted with two cameras for tactical reconnaissance duties and redesignated F-6As. When this contract was completed two months later, the RAF had received 93 Mustang IAs and the USAAF 55 F-6A photo-reconnaissance aircraft. Two airframes were diverted to the XP-78 project.

The Allison powerplant was not designed to perform at high altitude, so the British decided to operate the Mustang in the armed tactical reconnaissance role with a camera fitted behind the pilot. Although restricted to ceilings below 16,000ft, the Mustang I's speed of almost 353mph at 8,000ft made it ideal for ground attack and tactical reconnaissance, and it began replacing the Curtiss Tomahawk in 11 UK-based Army Cooperation squadrons in the spring of 1942. The North American machine was also issued to 12 other units. Its first operational sortie was flown on July 27 and in October Allison-powered Mustangs became the first RAF single-engined single-seat fighters to penetrate German airspace from England.

In the autumn of 1942, Maj Thomas Hitchcock (who was later killed flying a Mustang), then assistant air attaché in the US Embassy in London, suggested to

North American Aviation's factory in 1942, months after the US joined the war, bringing its vast manufacturing capacity into the struggle. Here, early P-51 Mustangs are under production in the Inglewood, California facility. (© Corbis)

senior officers in the USAAF that the Mustang could easily be developed into a long-range fighter through the fitment of the battle-tested Rolls-Royce Merlin engine. Hitchcock reported that the P-51 was one of the best (if not the best) fighter airframes developed to date, and advised that it be modified into a high-altitude fighter by "cross-breeding" it with the Merlin 61 engine, which produced a top speed of 400mph at 30,000ft.

America's ranking World War I ace, Eddie Rickenbacker, endorsed Hitchcock's proposal, as did Air Marshal Sir Trafford Leigh-Mallory (then head of the RAF's No. 11 Group, and soon to be placed in charge of Fighter Command). Five Mustang Is were subsequently delivered to Rolls-Royce for conversion into Mustang Xs through the fitment of a Merlin 65 to each airframe. At the same time the two surplus Mustang IAs retained by North American in California were modified to take license-built Packard Merlin engines in place of their Allison powerplants. Initially designated the XP-78, the aircraft had become the XP-51B by the time the first example completed its maiden flight on November 30, 1942.

A little over 12 months later, the Packard Merlin Mustang would start to provide the answer to the USAAF's prayers for a long-range fighter capable of escorting its heavy bombers to and from heavily defended targets in occupied Europe and "fortress Germany" itself. And although the marriage between the

American airframe and the British engine went remarkably smoothly, the new P-51B was still beset with other technical problems that initially nullified its abilities in combat. Its engine routinely suffered from coolant loss at high altitude during the course of long escort missions, resulting in overheating and eventually failing powerplants. Oil leaks also plagued early-build P-51Bs, and the fighter's oxygen system struggled to cope with the four- to five-hour sorties that were the norm in the ETO.

Although these problems were serious enough, it was the gun stoppages in combat that drew the most criticism from pilots flying the B-model Mustang in 1943–44. The P-51B was fitted with just four .50cal machine guns – two in each wing. Its laminar airfoil section was too thin to accommodate the weapons in the normal upright position, so they were canted over about 30 degrees. Thus, the ammunition feed trays had to curve slightly upward and then down again to enable link-belted rounds to enter the gun at the right angle. Gun jams were almost inevitable if the weapons were fired while the pilot was maneuvering at anything beyond 1.5g.

Numerous modifications were made both by the manufacturer and units in the field in an effort to solve the gun jams. An example of the latter saw an enterprising groundcrewman from the 354th FG obtain some electric ammunition feed motors that were being used in the Martin B-26 Marauder to carry shells from the ammunition boxes to the guns in the medium bomber. Once fitted to the P-51Bs, these seemed to go a long way to eradicating the jamming problem.

Capt Bill Whisner claimed 14.5 aerial victories in the Mustang in 1944–45 flying with the 352nd FG's 487th FS. His first Fw 190 victories were scored in the P-51B, and he recalled some of the technical issues that beset the early-model Mustang:

> Our first B-models did have some teething problems that needed to be worked out. The Packard Merlin engine had numerous difficulties with its coolant, oil, fuel and electrical systems. Our guns were also a continual source of frustration. Any time we pulled more than 1.5 to 2gs they would jam, usually because rounds would fail to eject from the belt. Some stopgap measures were undertaken, but the problem was not alleviated until the introduction of the D-model, which had a redesigned gun belt and ammunition feed system. Meanwhile, we had to take our chances with the guns while maneuvering in combat, or confine our firing to straight and level flight! The greenhouse canopy had the disadvantage of restricted visibility, especially to the rear, which was also a real problem in combat.

The P-51B was followed by 1,750 P-51Cs, which were virtually identical to the B-model but built in North American's new Dallas factory. A number of these aircraft were fitted with British-designed Malcolm bulged sliding frameless hoods similar to the Spitfire canopy in the UK, improving the rearward visibility for the pilot. Malcolm hoods were fitted to most RAF Mustang IIIs delivered in 1944, as well as to a number of USAAF P-51B/Cs. By late 1943, a major redesign of the Mustang's fuselage had seen a streamlined "bubble" canopy mated to a cut-down rear fuselage. The definitive P-51D would soon be rolling off the production line in California.

The D-model, powered by the Packard Merlin V-1650-7 and fitted with six .50cal machine guns (with 400rpg), was a considerably improved machine. Its wing had been thickened slightly so that the six guns could be fitted in an upright position, and this meant no more jams. Other changes less visible to the eye, but of equal or greater importance, included the K-14 100mm fixed-reticule gun sight. This replaced the P-51B/C's optical sight, with its 70mm reticule, which was too small for angle-off shooting. The new gun sight made deflection shooting and

This quartet of Bottisham-based 374th FS/361st FG Mustangs was photographed from a 91st BG B-17G when returning from a bomber escort mission to Munich on July 11, 1944. The aircraft nearest to the camera is P-51B-15 42-106839 *BALD EAGLE III*, flown by 1Lt Robert T Eckfeldt. Next in line is P-51D-5 44-13357 B7-R *TIKA IV*, which was assigned to 1Lt Vernon Richards, then P-51D-5 44-13857 and Malcolm-hooded P-51B-15 42-106942. (Courtesy of Tom Cushing)

range estimation considerably easier. The gun sight consisted principally of a piece of slanted, clear glass centered above the instrument panel directly in the pilot's line of sight. When activated, a center dot of yellow light, known as a "pipper," was projected onto the glass. The "pipper" was in turn surrounded by a circle formed of six or eight diamond-shaped dots. Using the control lever mounted on the throttle handle, the diamonds were expanded or contracted so that they continually "bracketed" the target. This automatically calculated the amount of lead needed for the range of the target, and meant the pilot had an excellent chance of scoring hits.

As previously noted, the Merlin Mustang was powered by a V-1650 engine built under license in the USA by luxury automobile company Packard. The V-1650 could be taken up to 61 inches of manifold pressure at 3,000rpm for takeoff or, if needed in combat, 67 inches for up to five minutes in Emergency Power. Normally-aspirated engines tended to run out of power as altitude increased, usually between 15,000ft and 20,000ft. The Merlin-powered P-51, however, had a two-stage blower in the induction system that was controlled automatically with a barometric switch. At around 17,000ft, when the throttle had been advanced almost all the way forward just to maintain normal cruise, the blower would kick into high, the manifold pressure would jump up and the climb could be continued to 30,000ft. The P-51 could be taken a lot higher than that, but above 30,000ft its engine power began to tail off rapidly and the pilot had to use his controls gingerly in order not to stall the fighter.

The P-51D/K was to become the most successful Mustang variant, being built in greater numbers than any other model – 6,502 were completed at Inglewood, in California, and 1,454 rolled off the Dallas production line. Early on in its production life, the P-5ID/K received a dorsal fin to compensate for the loss of keel surface due to the reduction of rear fuselage decking, and tail warning radar was also added in due course.

The P-51D first saw frontline service in Europe with the Eighth Air Force immediately prior to D-Day. It quickly excelled in high-altitude escort and combat, being superior in both speed and maneuverability to all Luftwaffe piston-engined fighters above 20,000ft. In order to make the most of the aircraft's agility, VIII Fighter Command pilots were among the first to wear anti-g suits, which inflated automatically around their calves, thighs and lower body during tight turns and when pulling out from a dive. The g-suit restricted the blood from draining from the head and trunk, and thus delayed the onset of "black-out." The only slight drawback associated with this new flying apparel was that pilots found they could then take more "g" than their P-51s, and Mustangs would regularly land following combat with deformed wings and numerous popped rivets.

THE MUSTANG THROUGH 360 DEGREES

This Mustang was the legendary Maj Leonard "Kit" Carson's P-51K-5 *Nooky Booky IV*. It was in this airplane, his fourth P-51, that Carson chalked up much of his score to become the top scorer of the 357th FG (with 18.5 victories, plus 3.5 more by strafing). From November 1944 the 357th adopted colored rudders – red for the 363rd FS, yellow for the 364th, and no color for Carson's 362nd FS. Until December 1944 most of the 357th's aircraft were camouflaged. (Artwork by Jim Laurier, © Osprey Publishing)

When production of the P-51D ended in August 1945, the total number of Mustangs completed stood at 15,484, with 5,541 of these aircraft in frontline service with the USAAF at war's end.

FOCKE-WULF Fw 190

In late 1937, a development contract was issued to Focke-Wulf Flugzeugbau GmbH for a single-seat interceptor fighter to supplement the Messerschmitt Bf 109. Under Kurt Tank's direction, a design team led by Oberingenieur Blaser created a low-wing monoplane with a fully retractable undercarriage that could be powered by either the Daimler-Benz DB 601 12-cylinder vee liquid-cooled inline engine (as fitted to the Bf 109) or the BMW 139 18-cylinder two-row radial.

A radial engine typically causes drag and is bulky, and the latter trait reduces the pilot's forward visibility during take-off and landing. However, the *Reichsluftfahrministerium* surprisingly ordered the radial-engined fighter to be developed so as not to overburden Daimler-Benz – a decision which amazed Tank and his colleagues. Detailed work on the fighter began the following summer.

Flugkapitän Hans Sander, in his capacity as Focke-Wulf's chief test pilot, flew the first prototype from the company's Bremen facility on June 1, 1939. It was powered by a fan-cooled 1,550hp BMW 139 radial which was fitted with a special ducted spinner to reduce drag. After five test flights, the aircraft was transferred to Rechlin, where a speed of 595km/h (370mph) was achieved. During October 1939 a second prototype was completed, this machine being fitted with two 13mm MG 131 and 7.92mm MG 17 machine guns.

In June 1939 the BMW 139 engine was abandoned and work began on the 14-cylinder BMW 801. In an effort to compensate for the greater weight associated with this new engine, the fighter's cockpit was moved farther aft.

Despite its bulky powerplant, the Fw 190 was small, the BMW engine being neatly faired into a slim fuselage. In stark contrast to the Bf 109, the Focke-Wulf fighter was fitted with an extensively glazed cockpit canopy which afforded the pilot an excellent all-round view. Early in 1940, Reichsmarschall Hermann Göring visited the Focke-Wulf factory and inspected the Fw 190 V2 second prototype. He was very impressed, and told Tank that he "must turn these new fighters out like so many hot rolls!"

The success of the BMW 801-engined aircraft led to the construction of 30 preproduction machines, designated Fw 190A-0, and 100 Fw 190A-1 production models were also subsequently ordered. Early trials were carried out at *Erprobungsstelle* Rechlin, and in March 1941 pilots and engineers from JG 26 prepared to introduce the new fighter into Luftwaffe service. In August the first Fw 190A-1s were delivered to 6./JG 26 at Le Bourget.

On September 18, when RAF Spitfire Vs and Fw 190s clashed for the first time, it soon became obvious that the German fighter was more maneuverable in almost every respect, and also possessed a higher maximum speed. Fw 190As fought their first major action in early February 1942, when they were among the fighters used to cover the battlecruisers *Scharnhorst* and *Gneisenau* and the heavy cruiser *Prinz Eugen* as they sailed from Brest to the safety of north German ports. *Jagdwaffe* fighters fought off British attempts to destroy the ships, and Fw 190A-1s from III./JG 26 shot down six Swordfish torpedo-bombers.

Orders soon followed for the improved Fw 190A-2, which was powered by the BMW 801C-2 engine and armed with two 7.92mm MG 17 machine guns above the engine cowling and two 20mm MG FF cannon in the wing roots – the aircraft also often carried an extra pair of MG 17 guns in the outer wings. The A-2 was followed by the Fw 190A-3, which was powered by a 1,700hp BMW 80ID-2 engine and had the MG FF cannon moved outboard and replaced by two of the much faster firing 20mm MG 151/20 cannon. The cockpit canopy could be jettisoned with the aid of explosive bolts and the pilot was protected by 8mm and 14mm armor plating. By early 1942 more than 250 Fw 190s were being produced every month. In March 1942 II./JG 26, which was often in the forefront of attacks

Two MG 131 13mm machine guns (as seen here) replaced the 7.92mm Rheinmetall-Borsig MG 17 weapons in the upper forward fuselage from the Fw 190A-7 series onward, as the latter were deemed to lack sufficient punch when it came to knocking down heavy bombers. Indeed, the MG 17 guns were disparagingly dubbed "door knockers" by frustrated *Jagdflieger*, who complained that they did not deliver an adequate weight of fire to destroy enemy aircraft – especially the USAAF's four-engined bombers. (Focke-Wulf, Bremen)

on American day bombers and their fighter escorts, was reequipped with the Fw 190A-3. In April JG 2 was also equipped with the Fw 190A-3 in the west. Four months later the Fw 190A-4, powered by the BMW 80ID-2 engine (with water-methanol injection that provided 2,100hp for short periods), entered production.

Although the Fw 190A had proven itself to be an extremely effective fighter, operational experience revealed that the power of the BMW 801 engine tended to drop off at altitudes in excess of 7,000m (22,967ft). Attempts were therefore made to improve the high-altitude performance of the aircraft during the subsequent production of Fw 190A, B and C variants.

In June 1942 Fw 190s were issued to JG 1 to combat American bomber formations appearing over the Reich, as well as to IV./JG 5 in Norway. The following month the first Spitfire IXs entered RAF service, and these aircraft met the Fw 190 on almost equal terms. However, on August 19, when the Fw 190s went into action against Allied fighters and landing craft during the ill-fated Dieppe operation, the RAF lost 106 aircraft, of which JG 2 and JG 26 claimed the lion's share. By the end of the year, with the American daylight bombing raids increasing in their intensity, several more Luftwaffe *Gruppen* were equipped with the Fw 190.

Early in 1943 the Fw 190A-5, which was essentially similar to the A-4, appeared. This version differed from its predecessor by having a revised engine mounting to allow the BMW 801D-2 to be fitted 15cm (5.9in) farther forward of the cockpit. This arrangement was designed to eliminate engine overheating problems which had consistently plagued the aircraft since its service introduction almost two years earlier.

By the start of 1943, the Eighth Air Force in East Anglia had become a potent threat, conducting raids on targets in the Reich. The situation had become so serious by July that Luftwaffe fighter units had to be transferred to airfields in the west from the Eastern Front and the Mediterranean. From late August 1943 onwards, six *Jagdgruppen* equipped with Fw 190A-4/5s were available for operations against the Allied air forces flying from Britain. On August 17, when the Eighth Air Force attacked Regensburg and Schweinfurt, more than 300 Fw 190s met the four-engined bombers. The Americans lost 60 "heavies," with almost all of them falling to German fighters. On October 14, when the Eighth Air Force attacked ball-bearing factories in Schweinfurt, Fw 190A-5/R6 fighters shot down a high proportion of the 79 bombers that were destroyed. A further 120 "heavies" were damaged.

The next major variant of the Focke-Wulf to enter service was the Fw 190A-6, which had a redesigned wing that was both lighter and could carry four 20mm MG 151/20 cannon – two MG 17 machine guns were also mounted above the

THE Fw 190 THROUGH 360 DEGREES

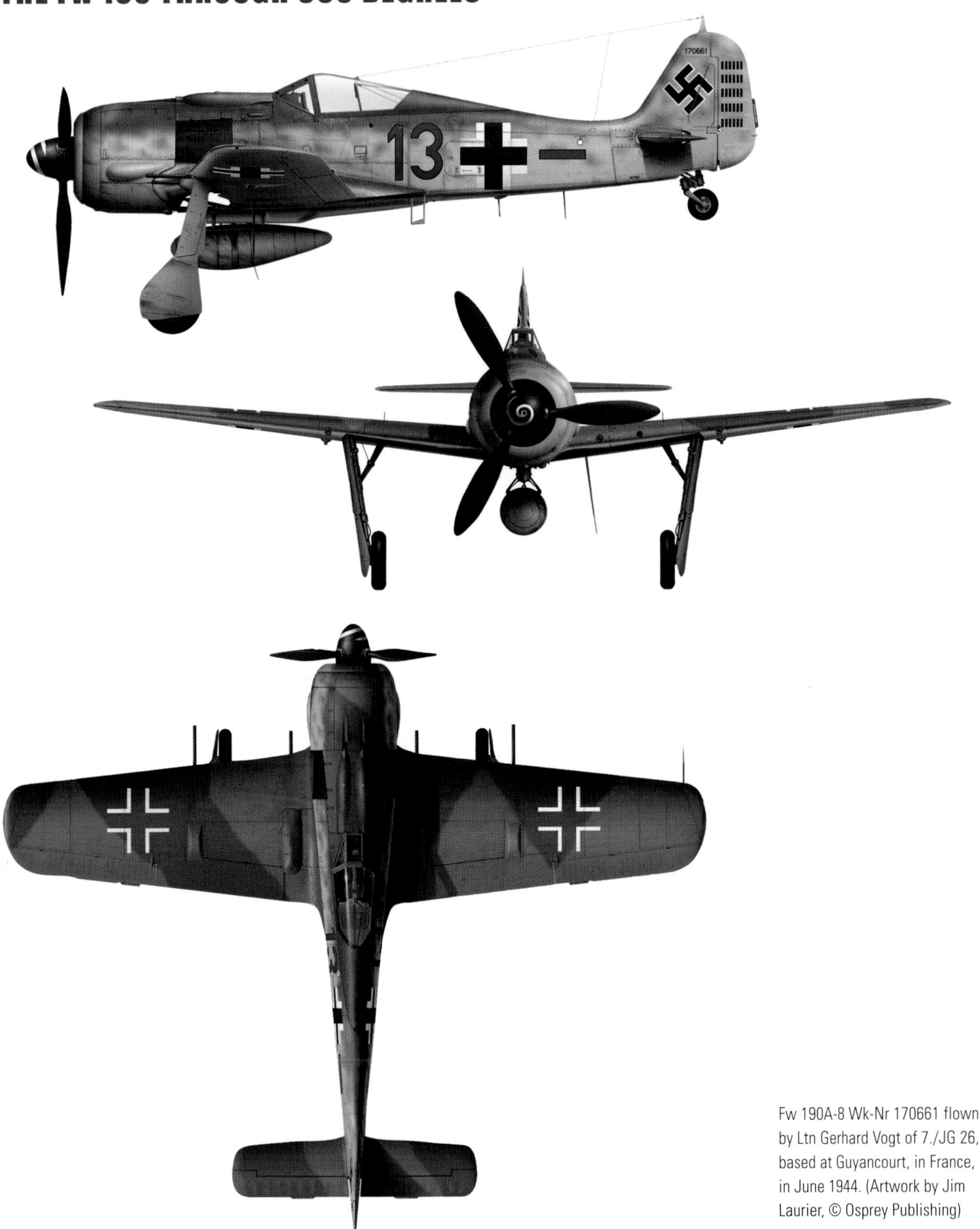

Fw 190A-8 Wk-Nr 170661 flown by Ltn Gerhard Vogt of 7./JG 26, based at Guyancourt, in France, in June 1944. (Artwork by Jim Laurier, © Osprey Publishing)

engine. The A-6/R1 carried six 20mm MG 151/20 cannon and the Fw 190A-6/R3 two 30mm MK 103 cannon in underwing gondolas. In December 1943 the Fw 190A-7 entered production.

The final large-scale production version of the A-series was the Fw 190A-8, fitted with an additional 115-litre internal fuel tank and other refinements. One of the last production variants of the A-series was the Fw 190A-9, which was similar to the A-8 but was powered by a 2,000hp BMW 801F engine. Although the radial-engined Fw 190A series was the principal variant to see service with the Luftwaffe, thousands of Fw 190F/Gs eventually replaced the Ju 87 Stuka as Germany's chief close-support aircraft. Essentially these planes were ground-attack versions of the basic Fw 190A series serving as fighter-bombers. Due to their ground-attack roles neither variant can be regarded as a direct opponent of the Merlin-engined P-51.

As good as the BMW-radial engined Fw 190A was, its performance fell away badly at high altitudes. It would struggle to be a premier air superiority fighter once the P-51D appeared in the ETO from June 1944. Following two years of development, the first of some 700 Junkers Jumo 213 inline-engined Fw 190D-9s began pouring off the Cottbus assembly line in August 1944. Although a match for the P-51D, the "Dora-9" was only ever considered "an emergency solution" by chief designer Tank, whose ultimate high-altitude fighter was the inline-engined Ta 152H. Also built at Cottbus, production examples of the Ta 152H started to leave the Focke-Wulf plant in November 1944, and by the time the factory was abandoned in early 1945, 150 examples had been delivered to the Luftwaffe. Most of these aircraft were issued to JG 301. Although the Fw 190D-9 and Ta 152H were clearly better air superiority fighters, their paucity in numbers meant that the radial-engined Fw 190A series machines remained in the vanguard of the *Jagdwaffe* through to VE-Day, opposing the thousands of Mustangs that ruled German skies in the last year of the war.

TYPE HISTORY

P-51 MUSTANG

MUSTANG I

The limitations of the Allison engine, whose power fell off dramatically above 12,000ft, resulted in the powerplant proving unsuitable for combat and interception roles in Europe, where fighter-versus-fighter engagements often took place at altitudes in excess of 20,000ft. Instead, the aircraft was used for tactical reconnaissance, armed with four .50in and four .303in machine guns, which were used to good effect in the ground attack role. RAF Mustang Is equipped with an obliquely-mounted camera served with no fewer than 23 squadrons of Army Cooperation Command. A further 300 generally similar aircraft followed, the RAF receiving 93 examples (Mustang IA). These differed from the earlier model in having self-sealing fuel tanks and four 20mm cannon – the latter fitted in the wings. Some 55 camera-equipped F-6A aircraft were used by the USAAF for tactical reconnaissance.

A-36A

RAF operation of the Mustang in the ground-attack role saw the USAAF procure 500 aircraft, which were called Apaches. These aircraft were fitted with dive brakes and underwing bomb racks. One A-36A was supplied to the RAF.

P-51A

The USAAF procured 310 examples powered by the 1,200hp V-1710-81 engine with war-emergency boost. Armament consisted of four .50in machine guns with 1,260 rounds, and two 500lb bombs or drop tanks could be carried on underwing racks. Fifty P-51As were allocated to the RAF as Mustang IIs, and 35 were converted into camera-equipped tactical reconnaissance F-6B aircraft for the USAAF.

P-51B

For evaluation purposes, two P-51As (later redesignated XP-78 and finally XP-51B) were powered by Packard-built Merlin V-1650-3 engines and two-stage superchargers rated by the USAAF at 1,295hp at 28,750ft, with 1,595hp available as a war-emergency boost setting up to 17,000ft. The XP-51Bs attained a maximum speed of 441mph at 29,800ft. The first Merlin-engined Mustang built in the US flew on November 30, 1942, with a four-bladed Hamilton propeller and the carburetor intake below, instead of above, the engine.

The first P-51B-1-NA was flown on May 5, 1943. Armament still consisted of four .50in machine guns – half the armament of the P-47 – but its 440mph top speed was the fastest among fighters then in combat. An 85gal fuel tank was fitted behind the cockpit, and together with two 108gal or 150gal drop tanks under the wings, the Mustang had the range to accompany bombers to any target in Germany. A total of 1,988 B-models were built at Inglewood, the last 550

P-51B/C GUNS

The P-51B/C was fitted with just four .50in Browning machine guns, and these were initially prone to jamming due to their angled mounting within the Mustang's thin wing.

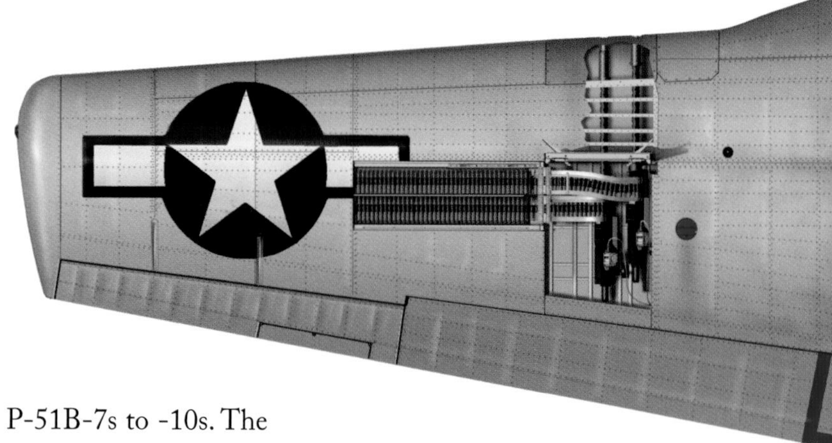

becoming P-51B-7s to -10s. The addition of an 85gal fuselage fuel tank increased the fighter's total internal fuel capacity to 269 US gallons and the normal range to 1,300 miles. This modification was also made in the field to earlier P-51B/Cs. Some 274 P-51Bs were allocated to the RAF as Mustang IIIs.

P-51C

Generally similar to the P-51B, 1,750 C-models were built at North American's new Dallas plant. Both the B- and C-models differed from earlier versions by having a strengthened fuselage and redesigned ailerons, and they were initially powered by the Packard Merlin V-1650-3, followed by the V-1650-7 Merlin 68. The latter had a war emergency rating of 1,695hp at 10,300ft, and produced a maximum speed of 439mph at 25,000ft. The sea-level climb rate was 3,900ft/min. Maximum weight with a 2,000lb bomb load was 11,200lb. Armament was four .50in machine guns in the wings, with a total of 1,260 rounds of ammunition. The RAF received 636 P-51Cs (Mustang IIIs). 71 USAAF P-51B/Cs were modified as F-6C tactical reconnaissance aircraft.

P-51D

The major production version, with a total of 7,956 built, the D-model introduced the bubble canopy to improve the pilot's field of view, a modified rear fuselage and six .50in machine guns. Fifty P-51Ds were supplied to the nationalist Chinese Air Force and 40 to the Royal Netherlands Air Force in the PTO. A modification of this series resulted in ten TP-51D trainers being built with radio equipment relocated and an additional seat, with full dual controls, behind the pilot seat. One TP-51D was further modified for use as a high-speed observation post for the Supreme Allied Commander, Gen Dwight Eisenhower, who flew in it to inspect the Normandy beachheads in June 1944.

P-51D/K GUNS

The P-51D/K was fitted with six .50in Browning machine guns, and these proved to be far more reliable than the weapons in the early-model Merlin Mustangs thanks to their upright mounting in the fighter's slightly deeper wings. (Artwork by Jim Laurier, © Osprey Publishing)

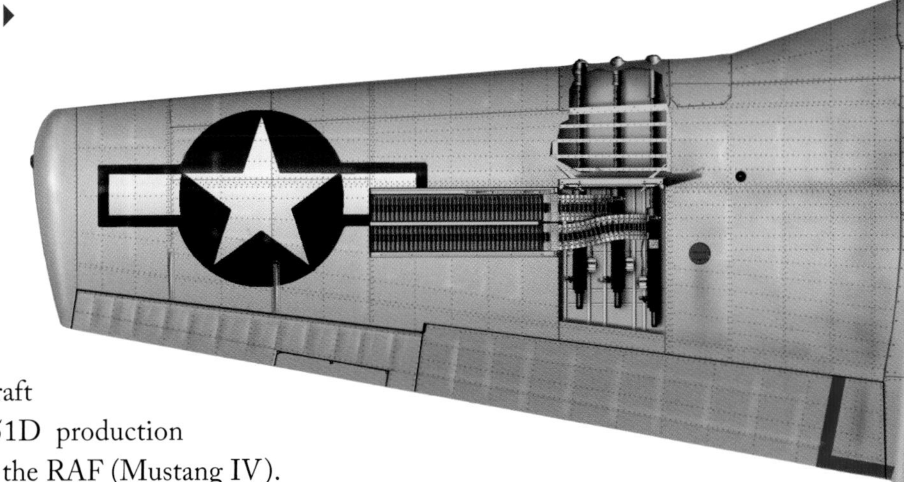

F-6D

136 tactical reconnaissance aircraft were modified from the P-51D production contract. 281 were allocated to the RAF (Mustang IV).

P-51K

1,500 generally similar examples differed only in the replacement of the Hamilton-Standard airscrew by an Aeroproduct propeller and a slightly modified canopy with a blunter rear. Weighing 11,000lb loaded, the P-51K was not fitted with rocket stubs, and it had a slightly inferior performance to the P-51D. 163 were built as F-6K tactical reconnaissance examples. 594 were allocated to the RAF (Mustang IV).

FOCKE-WULF Fw 190

Fw 190 V1 AND V2

The Fw 190 prototype (D-OPZE) was rolled out in May 1939 and flew for the first time from Bremen airfield on June 1. The aircraft was powered by a fan-cooled 1,550hp BMW 139 radial fitted with a special ducted spinner to reduce drag, but the engine overheated rapidly nevertheless, and eventually the ducted spinner was removed and replaced by a new tightly-fitting NACA cowling. Fw 190 V2 second prototype was also fitted with a large ducted spinner and powered by a BMW 139 engine. The latter was subsequently replaced by the longer and heavier BMW 801 powerplant, which necessitated structural changes to the aircraft and the relocation of the cockpit. These prototypes were armed with two 13mm MG 131 machine guns in the wings and two 7.92mm MG 17 weapons in the upper forward fuselage. The third and fourth prototypes were abandoned.

Fw 190 V5/V5G

Once powered by the new 1,660hp BMW 801C-0 engine, the V2 was modified to take a wing of increased span. To compensate for the greater engine weight, the cockpit was moved farther aft. With the introduction of the V5g ("g" standing for *gross* or large), the V5 short span version (which had a wing area of 15 sq m (161.46 sq ft) was redesignated the Fw 190 V5k ("k" standing for *klein* or small). The V5k had a wing area of 18.3 sq m (196.98 sq ft).

Fw 190A-0

The preproduction batch, nine of these aircraft were fitted with the small wing, while the remainder had the larger span version. 100 production Fw 190As were ordered, the first five of which bore the alternative designations V7 to V11.

Fw 190A-1

This initial production model was essentially similar to the V5g, being powered by a 1,660hp BMW 801C-1 radial, having the long-span wing and 7.92mm MG 17 machine guns and FuG 7a radio equipment. In August 1941 the first Fw 190A-1s were delivered to Geschwader-Stab JG 26, commanded by Obstlt Adolf Galland.

Fw 190A-2

The Fw 190 V14 first prototype had two 7.92mm MG 17 machine guns above the engine cowling and two 20mm MG FF cannon in the wing roots. The production Fw 190A-2, which was powered by the BMW 801C-2 engine, often carried an additional pair of MG 17 guns in the outboard wing panels.

Fw 190A-3

This was the first major production variant, which was powered by the 1,700hp BMW 801D-2 engine. It had the MG FF cannon moved to the outer wing panels, and their original location used instead for two of the much faster firing 20mm MG 151/20 weapons. The cockpit canopy could be jettisoned with the aid of explosive bolts and the pilot was protected by 8mm and 14mm armor plate. The first examples were introduced into service in autumn 1941.

Fw 190A-4

Delivered during the late summer of 1942 with FuG 16Z radio and a fin-mounted radio mast atop the fin. The BMW 801D-2 engine had provision for MW-50 water/methanol fuel injection to boost output to 2,100hp for short periods, and thus raise the maximum speed to 416mph at 21,000ft.

Fw 190A-4/R6

MW-50 fuel injection deleted. Capable of carrying two underwing Wurfgranaten WGr 21 210mm rocket launchers for the unguided WGr 21 Dodel missile. Fixed armament was reduced to two MG 151 cannon.

Fw 190A-4/U5

Able to carry a 66-Imperial-gallon drop tank beneath each wing and a 1,102lb bomb under the fuselage.

Fw 190A-5

Introduced in early 1943, this version was essentially similar to the A-4 but had a revised engine mounting which enabled the BMW 801D-2 to be fitted 15cm farther forward in an attempt to cure a tendency for the engine to overheat. Many sub-variants were produced, including the Fw 190A-5/U16 which was armed with 30mm MK 108 cannon in the outboard wing position as standard.

Fw 190A-6

Developed from the experimental Fw 190A-5/U10 in June 1943. A redesigned, lighter wing could take four 20mm MG 151/20 cannon whilst retaining the two MG 17 machine guns mounted above the engine. FuG 16ZE and FuG 25 radio equipment was also carried.

Fw 190A-6/R1

Developed following successful trials with the Fw 190A-5/U12, this aircraft had six 20mm MG 151/20 cannon and was used operationally by JG 11.

Fw 190 V51

Forerunner of the A-6/R2, which could carry a 30mm MK 108 in the outboard wing position.

Fw 190A-6/R3

Armed with two 30mm MK 103 cannon in underwing gondolas.

Fw 190A-6/R4

Was to be fitted with a BMW 801TS engine with a turbosupercharger. The only prototype (Fw 190 V45) was initially fitted with a BMW 801D-2 engine with GM 1 power-boosting, being re-engined with the BMW 801TS in July 1944.

Fw 190A-7 COWLING GUNS

The Fw 190A-7 boasted two 13mm MG 131 machine guns fitted in the upper forward fuselage, these weapons having replaced the 7.92mm Rheinmetall-Borsig MG 17s that had been a feature of all previous Fw 190s.

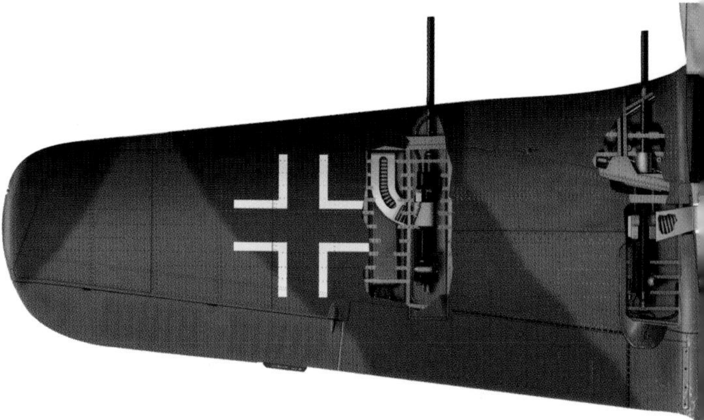

Fw 190A-7 WING GUNS

The Fw 190A-7's primary "punch" was provided by four 20mm MG 151/20 cannon fitted in the wings. (Artwork by Jim Laurier, © Osprey Publishing)

Fw 190A-6/R6

The final A-6 variant, this aircraft could carry a 210mm Wurfgranaten WGr 21 rocket tube beneath each wing.

Fw 190A-7

Introduced in December 1943, and basically similar to the Fw 190A-6, the first prototype was the Fw 190A-5/U9, which had two MG 151/20 cannon in the wings and two 13mm MG 131 machine guns above the engine cowling. The second prototype (Fw 190 V35) was similar, but had four MG 151/20s in the wings and a strengthened undercarriage. It was later re-engined with a 2,000hp BMW 801F engine, which was also tested in the V36. The *Rüstsatz* conversion packs produced for the A-7 was similar to that for the A-6, with much emphasis being placed on the A-7/R6 with Wurfgranaten WGr 210cm rocket tubes.

Fw 190A-8/R7

Fitted with an armored cockpit for use by the newly established anti-bomber *Sturmgruppen*.

Fw 190A-8/R11

All-weather fighter with heated canopy and PKS 12 radio navigation equipment.

OTHER Fw 190 VARIANTS:

The following inline-engined variants were excellent air superiority fighters, but saw very limited service.

Fw 190D-9

Powered by the inline 2,000hp Junkers Jumo 213, a "Dora-9" was a match for the P-51D. However, only 700 were ever produced, which meant that it could never hope to rival the Mustang for air superiority.

TA 152H

Featuring a wider wingspan, stretched fuselage, broad chord fin and a pressurized cockpit, the Ta 152H was powered by the Junkers Jumo 213E engine. Only 150 were ever delivered to the Luftwaffe.

A VIEW FROM THE COCKPIT

Legendary British test pilot Capt Eric Brown flew many German aircraft both during and immediately after World War II. Amongst the types to appear in his logbook was an Fw 190A-4 that had been landed by its pilot in error at the RAF fighter station at West Malling, in Kent, on April 17, 1943. Sent to Farnborough for evaluation three days later, Brown soon got to fly it:

> From any angle, in the air or on the ground, the Focke-Wulf was an aerodynamic beauty, and it oozed lethality. It sat high on the ground, and in getting into the cockpit it was immediately evident that the ground view left much to be desired, for the BMW 801D air-cooled radial engine, although beautifully cowled, could not but help be obtrusive. Nevertheless, it still offered a better view forward than was obtainable from the Bf 109, the Spitfire or the Mustang.
>
> The cockpit, while on the narrow side by Allied standards of the day, was fairly comfortable, with a semi-reclining seat for the pilot, which was ideally suited for high-g maneuvers. Contrary to expectations, the flight instruments were not quite so well arranged as those of the Bf 109, but the general layout of the cockpit was good. Perhaps its most novel feature was its ingenious *Kommandgerät* – "a brain-box" which relieved the pilot of the task of controlling mixture, airscrew pitch, boost and rpm, executing all these functions automatically.
>
> All the ancillary controls were electrically operated by a mass of pushbuttons, which were obviously intended for daintily-gloved fingers and not for the massive leather flying gauntlets issued to British aircrew – the latter converted the human hand into a bunch of bananas.
>
> The most impressive feature of the Focke-Wulf was its beautifully light ailerons and high rate of roll. The ailerons maintained their lightness from the stall up to 400mph, although they became heavier above that speed. At lower speeds the Focke-Wulf tended to tighten up in the turn, and a slight forward pressure on the

stick had to be applied. But above that figure the changeover called for some backward pressure to hold the aircraft in the turn. Rudder control was positive and effective at low speeds and satisfactory at high speeds, when it seldom had to be used for any normal maneuver.

It was when one took the three controls together rather than in isolation that one realised that the Fw 190's magic as a fighter lay in its superb harmony of control. To be a good dogfighter, and at the same time a good gun platform, required just those very characteristics that the Focke-Wulf possessed in all important matters of stability and control.

The Focke-Wulf had harsh stalling characteristics, which limited its maneuver margins. I flew several varieties of the breed many times, and each time I experienced that sense of exhilaration that came from flying an aircraft that one instinctively knew to be a top-notcher, but at the same time demanded handling skill if its high qualities were to be exploited.

Just as the Spitfire IX was probably the most outstanding British fighter aircraft to give service in World War II, its Teutonic counterpart undoubtedly deserves the same recognition for Germany. Both were supreme in their time and their class. Both were durable and technically superb, and if each had not been there to counter the other, then the balance of air power could have been dramatically altered at a crucial period in the fortunes of both combatants.

P-51 MUSTANG vs Fw 190A COMPARISON SPECIFICATIONS			
	P-51B/C	P-51D/K	Fw 190A-8
Powerplant	1,380hp V-1650-7	1,490hp V-1650-7	1,700hp BMW 801D radial
Dimensions			
Span	37ft 0in	37ft 0in	34ft 5½in
Length	32ft 3in	32ft 3in	29ft 4¼in
Height	12ft 2in	12ft 2in	13ft 0in
Wing area	235.7sq ft	235.7sq ft	196.5sq ft
Weights			
Empty	6,985lb	7,125lb	7,680lb
Loaded	11,800lb	11,600lb	9,680lb
Performance			
Max speed	440mph at 30,000ft	437mph at 25,000ft	402mph at 20,700ft
Range	400 miles	950 miles	658 miles
Climb	to 20,000ft in 7 min	to 3,475ft in 1 min	to 26,300ft in 14.4 min
Service ceiling	41,800ft	41,900ft	32,700ft
Armament	4x .50in Brownings	6x .50in Brownings	4x MG 151 20mm cannon, 2x MG 12.7mm machine guns

How did the Mustang match up against the Fw 190A? A March 1944 report by the RAF's Air Fighting Development Unit made brief comparisons between the Mustang III (P-51B-1) and the Fw 190A powered by the BMW 801D. It stated that the latter was almost 50mph slower at all heights, increasing to 70mph above 28,000ft.

There appeared to be little to choose in the maximum rate of climb. It was anticipated that the Mustang III would have a better maximum climb than the Fw 190. The Mustang was considerably faster at all heights in a zoom climb, and it could always outdive the Fw 190. When it came to the turning circle, the report stated that there was not much to choose. The Mustang was "slightly better when evading an enemy aircraft with a steep turn. The pilot will always outturn the attacking aircraft initially because of the difference in speeds. It is therefore still a worthwhile maneuver with the Mustang III when attacked."

When it came to rate of roll, not even a Mustang III could rival the Fw 190A. The report concluded that:

> In the attack, a high speed should be maintained or regained in order to regain height initiative. An Fw 190 could not evade by diving alone. In defense, a steep turn followed by a full throttle dive should increase the range before regaining height and course. Dogfighting is not altogether recommended. Do not attempt to climb away without at least 250mph showing initially.

In his "Briefing for P-51 Pilot Instructors" in August 1945, Louis S. Wait, Administrative Test Pilot for North American Aviation at Inglewood, California, said, in part:

> The new, heavier, more powerful Packard-built Rolls-Royce engine made necessary a heavier radiator for proper cooling and a heavier four-blade wide-chord propeller to utilize the increased engine power at altitude. The P-51B/C was an overloaded aeroplane since the combat weight was increased from 8,000lb to slightly over 9,000lb. As later results demonstrated, the decrease in "g" factor alone was not a serious complication. However, the increased engine power and four-blade propeller caused a marked decrease in directional stability.

Whereas the pilot previously had to use increasing rudder pressure for increasing sideslip or yaw angles, the rudder forces now tended to decrease at yaw angles greater than 100 degrees. If the pilot did not apply sufficient opposite rudder, the

P-51D/K: IN THE COCKPIT

1. Landing gear control lever
2. Elevator trim tab control wheel
3. Carburetor hot air control lever
4. Carburetor cold air control lever
5. Rudder trim tab control
6. Aileron trim tab control
7. Coolant radiator control
8. Oil radiator control
9. Landing light switch
10. Florescent light switch, left
11. Flare pistol port cover
12. Arm rest
13. Mixture control lever
14. Throttle quadrant locks
15. Throttle control
16. Propeller pitch control
17. Selector dimmer assembly
18. Instrument light
19. Rear radar warning lamp
20. K-14A gun sight
21. Laminated glass
22. Remote compass indicator
23. Clock
24. Suction gauge
25. Manifold pressure gauge
26. Air speed indicator
27. Directional gyro turn indicator
28. Artificial horizon
29. Coolant temperature
30. Tachometer
31. Altimeter
32. Turn and bank indicator
33. Rate of climb indicator
34. Carburetor temperature
35. Engine temperature gauge
36. Bomb release levers
37. Engine control panel
38. Landing gear indicator lights
39. Parking brake handle
40. Oxygen flow indicator
41. Oxygen pressure gauge
42. Ignition switch
43. Bomb and rocket switch
44. Cockpit light control
45. Rocket control panel
46. Fuel shut-off valve
47. Fuel selector valve
48. Emergency hydraulic release handle
49. Hydraulic pressure gauge
50. Oxygen hose
51. Oxygen regulator
52. Canopy release handle
53. Canopy crank
54. IFF control panel
55. IFF detonator buttons
56. VHF radio control box
57. Rear radar control panel
58. VHF volume control
59. Florescent light switch, right
60. Electrical control panel
61. Circuit breakers
62. BC-438 control box
63. Cockpit light
64. Circuit breakers
65. Rudder pedals
66. Control column
67. Flaps control lever
68. Pilot's seat
69. Flare gun storage

Fw 190A-7: IN THE COCKPIT

1–4. Controls for FuG 16ZY radio
5. Horizontal stabilizer trim control
6. Undercarriage and flaps controls
7. Horizontal stabilizer trim indicator
8. Landing gear and flaps actuation buttons
9. Throttle and propeller pitch control
10. Instrument panel lighting dimmer control
11. Fuel cock control lever
12. Engine starter brushes cut-off
13–15. IFF controls for FuG 25 equipment
16. Landing gear manual extension control
17. Cockpit ventilator
18. Fuel tank selector
19. Altimeter
20. Fuel and pressure gauge
21. Pitot tube heater light
22. Jettison lever for under-fuselage stores
23. Oil temperature gauge
24. Air speed indicator
25 & 26. MG 131 guns-armed lights
27. Artificial horizon
28. Armament switches, ammunition counter and armament control unit
29. Revi 16B gun sight
30. Engine cooling flaps control
31. Armored glass windscreen
32. Rate of climb indicator
33. AFN-2 homing indicator for FuG 16ZY
34. Compass
35. Fuel gauge
36. Propeller pitch indicator
37. Engine supercharger pressure gauge
38. Cockpit light
39. Tachometer
40. Fuel low warning light
41. Rear fuel tank switch-over light
42. Fuel tank selector switch
43. Flare gun port
44. Oxygen flow indicator
45. Oxygen pressure gauge
46. Oxygen flow valve
47. Canopy crank
48. Circuit breakers
49. Canopy jettison lever
50. Engine starter switch
51 & 52. Clock
53. Flare gun door jettison button
54. Bomb fuse activator
55. Compass deviation table
56. Fuel pump circuit breaker
57. Flare gun stowage
58. Circuit breaker panel
59. Machine guns' circuit breaker
60. Pilot's seat
61. Control column
62. Wing cannon firing button
63. Bomb release switch
64. Rudder pedals
65. Throttle lever damper control

(Artwork by Jim Laurier, © Osprey Publishing)

airplane tended to increase the skid or sideslip all by itself, eventually resulting in an unintentional snap roll or entry into a spin. Several pilots complained that they could no longer obtain their usual evasive action because of the addition of the dorsal fin and change in the rudder boost tab.

With full fuselage tanks and two 110gal external tanks, the gross weight of the P-51D was over 11,600lb, nearly 50 percent more than the design weight of the airplane. The only way to obtain increased strength or any substantial amount of increased stability would be to start from scratch and design a new airplane.

THE STRATEGIC SITUATION

After the war, the USAAF's ranking officer, Gen H. H. "Hap" Arnold, frankly admitted that it had been "the Army Air Force's own fault" that the Mustang had not been employed operationally very much earlier. Range was not something that had influenced the equipment of fighter units destined for the ETO because it was thought that operations would be similar to those undertaken by RAF fighters, where high-altitude performance seemed to be the important factor.

The Eighth Air Force had begun the bomber offensive from East Anglia in 1942 with the steadfast belief that tight bomber formations could fight their way unescorted to a target in the face of fighter opposition and still strike with acceptable losses.

The futility of the US tactics was finally rammed home during the bloody aerial battles fought in the autumn of 1943, when unescorted bombers penetrated deeper into Reich airspace than ever before and more than 60 "heavies" were lost on a single mission. Almost too late, the American chiefs of staff were immediately struck by the need to drastically overhaul the USAAF's long-range fighter cover.

At the same time, the massed raids by B-24s and B-17s on targets in Germany had sent shock waves through the Luftwaffe high command. The situation that confronted the *Jagdwaffe* in 1943 resulted in an urgent need for a fighter capable of breaking up the American combat box formations so that pilots could then pick off single bombers without fear of having to face the potentially destructive firepower that a mass formation could bring to bear. With the Fw 190 in the forefront of the defense of the Reich, the heavy bomber losses reached 18.2 percent in late 1943. A year earlier, when German targets had been defended predominantly by Bf 109Gs, the average American losses were 13.6 percent of the attacking force. In September–October 1943, almost a thousand Fw 190s were operating with units in France and Germany, and a further 270 were serving on the Eastern Front and in Italy.

After Schweinfurt, desperate attempts were made by the USAAF to improve fighter cover. The P-38 Lightning had a good escort range, but it was usually second best in combat with the Bf 109G and Fw 190A. Single-engined fighters such as the nimble Spitfire IX and P-47D Thunderbolt (an aircraft double the weight of a Bf 109 and half as much again as the Fw 190) had only enough range to escort the bombers part of the way and then meet them on their return. Eighth Air Force commander Gen Ira Eaker knew that deep penetration missions were finished unless a proven long-range escort fighter could be found. "At this point nothing was more critical than the early arrival of the P-38s and P-51s," he stated postwar. The P-51B was not only capable of meeting the Bf 109s and Fw 190s on even or better terms, it could also escort the B-24s and B-17s all the way to their targets and back home again.

The Mustang's range of 2,080 miles was far in excess of that available in other fighters of the day, and this was achieved through the combination of internal fuel tanks and external drop tanks. A total of 92gal were contained in fuel cells in each wing, and this was supplemented by two 75gal underwing drop tanks and an

Single-engined fighter plants were near the top of the target list for the bombing campaign Operation *Pointblank*. Here, 100 unescorted B-17s attack a Focke-Wulf plant in a precision daylight raid. (NARA)

85gal fuselage-mounted tank fitted as an afterthought behind the cockpit. When the latter was anything more than two-thirds full, the Mustang was afflicted by a potentially vicious handling peculiarity that meant that pilots could not perform even modest combat maneuvers. This left the fighter vulnerable, as even an average German fighter pilot could easily outmaneuver a Mustang that had a full fuselage tank. If such an attack occurred, the P-51 pilot would usually lose control due to the fighter's aft-loaded center of gravity, pitching over and entering a fatal spin.

It was not long after Mustang pilots started flying long-range missions into occupied Europe that reports began filtering back from the frontline concerning the fighter's handling when fueled up. With the full 85gal in the fuselage tank, the aft center of gravity in a maximum-rate turn caused a stick reversal – the airplane tended to wrap the turn tighter without any backpressure on the stick. Pilots were quoted as stating that the P-51 "behaved like a pregnant sow."

The *Jagdwaffe* based its highly valued anti-bomber *Sturm* units primarily at airfields to the south and west of Germany's major industrial complexes in a vain attempt to defend these key locations from daylight bombing raids undertaken by the USAAF's Eighth and Fifteenth Air Forces.

The standard procedure was to burn the fuselage tank down to about 30gal immediately after take-off, and prior to switching to external tanks. That way if the latter had to be jettisoned unexpectedly, the P-51 pilot was already in a condition from which he could fight. Theoretically, pilots would be well inside Germany before they exhausted their external fuel load, and the longer they could retain their external tanks the better.

The fuel-tank selector, which had five positions corresponding to the five tanks, controlled fuel flow. The selector was in the center of the cockpit below the instrument panel and just forward of the control column. Pilots would take off using fuel from the left-side 75gal wing tank, and once airborne and in formation, they would switch to the fuselage tank situated aft of the cockpit. If the fuel selector was on one of the External positions when the tanks were dropped, the engine would start to run roughly as it sucked air, rather than fuel. No permanent harm was done, but the momentary silence of the Merlin in the cockpit invariably rattled the nerves of an already fraught new pilot – veterans reported that it scared them too!

Although the Mustang would eventually be the straw that would break the back of the *Jagdgruppen*, from late 1943 until the early spring of 1944, the daylight bomber crews were, for the most part, still very much on their own against the Luftwaffe. Inexplicably, USAAF planners considered the P-51B better suited to tactical operations rather than strategic long-range bomber escort, and therefore in November 1943 the first deliveries of Merlin-powered Mustangs were made to three groups of the tactical Ninth Air Force in the UK, instead of the Eighth Air Force's VII Fighter Command, whose need was critical.

However, by the time the Ninth Air Force's first Mustang-equipped group (the 354th FG, aptly dubbed the "Mustang Pioneer Group") arrived in England in November 1943, Gen "Hap" Arnold had worked out a plan that would see P-51Bs escorting his clearly vulnerable heavy bombers before the year was out. Although the 354th FG was assigned to the Ninth Air Force for administration, operationally it would be controlled by the Eighth Air Force's VIII Fighter Command. Once in the UK, the "Mustang Pioneer Group" would have just two weeks to get itself ready for combat operations.

The unit flew its first operational mission over enemy territory from Boxted, on the Essex–Suffolk border, on December 1, and four days later it helped provide bomber escort for 452 B-17s and 96 B-24s sent to attack targets in the French city of Amiens – 34 P-38s and 266 P-47s also participated in this mission. On the 13th, when a record 649 bombers struck naval targets in Bremen, Hamburg and Kiel, P-51Bs reached the limit of their escort range for the first time.

Mustangs of the 78th FG escort B-17s into Germany during the final months of the war. The lead ship is Col John Landers well-known mount *Big Beautiful Doll*. (Artwork by Gareth Hector, © Gareth Hector)

On February 10, 1944, some 40 long-ranging P-51s accompanied the "heavies" to their targets and back again, but they were powerless to prevent a much larger force of German fighters destroying 29 of the 169 Flying Fortresses despatched. The very next day the first P-51Bs to be permanently assigned to VIII Fighter Command became operational with the 357th FG at Raydon, in Essex.

During "Big Week" (February 20–25), Eighth and Fifteenth Air Force bombers (the latter flying from bases in Italy) and 1,000 fighters were despatched almost daily on the deepest penetrations into Germany thus far. On March 6, 730 B-17s and B-24s and 801 P-38, P-47 and P-51 escort fighters headed for targets in the suburbs of Berlin in the first American air raid on "Big-B," as the German capital was nicknamed by USAAF crews. Eleven fighters and 69 bombers were lost, with a further 102 "heavies" seriously damaged.

"Big Week" and the early attacks on Berlin provided the heyday for the P-47 Thunderbolt in its role as a bomber escort with VIII Fighter Command. Thereafter, the Luftwaffe would be opposed primarily by Mustangs, as its fighters vainly attempted to blunt the daylight bombing campaign. By war's end only one of VIII Fighter Command's fifteen fighter groups was not equipped with the P-51D/K, the Mustang's advantage of greater endurance over the P-47 having seen the aircraft wreak havoc throughout occupied Europe whilst escorting bombers on long-penetration raids deep into Germany and beyond.

D-DAY AND ONWARD

On June 6, 1944, when the Allies stormed the beaches of Normandy, the Fw 190 fighter force, like the rest of the Luftwaffe in western France, offered little in the way of resistance when faced with overwhelming RAF and USAAF air power. More than 4,100 Allied fighters were committed in support of the D-Day landings, with some 2,300 of these being USAAF day fighters. In response, the Luftwaffe had just 425 fighters of all types in the area, of which only 250–280 were serviceable on any given day. Nevertheless, on occasion German fighters inflicted significant losses on the massed ranks of USAAF bombers and their escorts, but replacement aircrew and aircraft were rapidly drafted in and the offensive never wavered.

By early July the Allies had firmly established themselves in France, and VIII Fighter Command returned to its primary mission of heavy bomber support as the Eighth Air Force once again shifted its focus back to daylight raids on strategic targets. The Mustang pilots, dubbed "Little Friends" by the USAAF bomber crews, soon added ground strafing to their close escort and dogfighting repertoire as airfields and communications targets were battered by rockets, machine guns and bombs once the Allies gained the initiative in the skies over Germany.

The Luftwaffe, however, was still far from defeated, and production of fighter aircraft actually increased in 1944 and into 1945. It peaked in September 1944,

As this map clearly shows, the Merlin-engined Mustang possessed an awesome range for a piston-engined fighter.

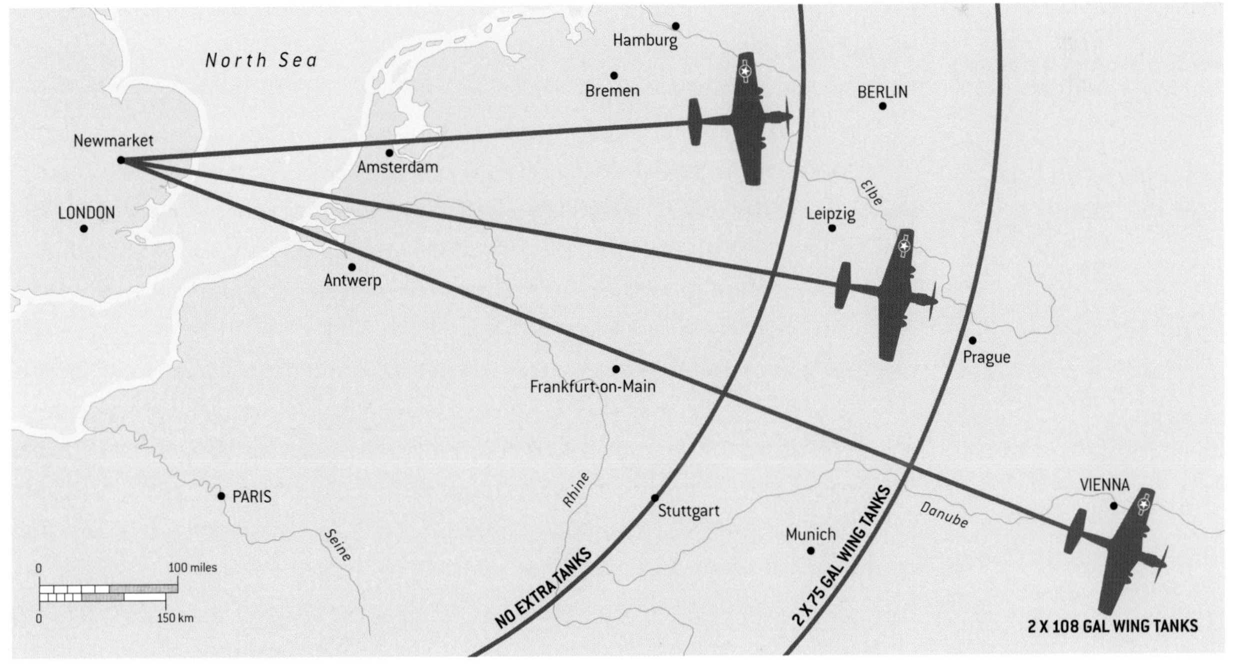

This Fw 190A-8/R2 (Wk-Nr. 681497) was flown by 5./JG 4's Gefreiter Walter Wagner during Operation *Bodenplatte* on January 1, 1945. Attacking the Allied airfield at St Trond, in Belgium, on what was only his third-ever combat mission, Wagner was forced to land near his target when the engine of his fighter cut out after being hit by groundfire. (Courtesy of Eddie Creek)

when an astonishing 1,874 Bf 109s and 1,002 Fw 190s were completed. That same month, an average of three German fighters and two pilots were killed in action for every B-17 or B-24 shot down. The US Strategic Air Forces were clearly winning the war of attrition in the conflict with the *Jagdwaffe*, which was forced on to the defensive. Irreparable harm was now being inflicted on the German fighter force through shortages of pilots, aircraft and fuel – problems that never afflicted American fighter groups.

January 1945 marked the Eighth Air Force's third year of operations, and it seemed as if the end of the war in Europe was now in sight. The Wehrmacht's December 1944 offensive in the Ardennes had ultimately petered out due to superior Allied air power, and in the east, the Red Army was in the early stages of its final push towards Germany.

Although an Allied victory was no longer in doubt, the last months of the war saw the surviving elements of the German armed forces put up a dogged defense of their homeland. And the dispersed manufacturing plants established throughout the Third Reich proved very difficult for the Eighth Air Force to neutralize, despite heavy bombers continuing to strike at these targets well into April 1945. And while the "heavies" sortied into enemy territory on a near-daily basis, so the Mustang escorts continued to offer them protection against the final remnants of the once-mighty Luftwaffe in its final death throes.

THE MEN

The Fw 190A and the Merlin-engined Mustang were two of the truly great aircraft of World War II, the exploits of those that flew them ranking both types amongst the finest fighters in the annals of military aviation. Each possessed their own intrinsic and distinctive merits and, as with all fighters, they also had their shortcomings. But in the right hands these limitations could usually be compensated for.

Almost all the top American aces in the ETO flew the Mustang, and many of the leading German *experten* claimed their victories in the Fw 190A. When pitched against each other, combat experience, or the lack of it, was often the deciding factor. It must be remembered that by 1943–44, American Mustang pilots confronted scores of German fighter pilots that had been in continuous action in Europe since 1940. Apart from a few who had flown with the RAF in Spitfire-equipped "Eagle" squadrons, USAAF pilots arriving in the ETO from 1942 onward were relatively new to their trade, and were not combat experienced. Most of their German opponents, by contrast, had already seen several years of aerial combat either on the Channel Front or in the east against the USSR.

Luftwaffe pilot training could trace its lineage back to the late 1920s, when many future military aviators were trained to fly gliders due to the outlawing of an official German air arm by the Treaty of Versailles, signed in the aftermath of World War I. Then, in 1933, Adolf Hitler came to power and World War I ace Hermann Göring was appointed Germany's first Air Minister. Rearmament gathered pace, and on March 1, 1935, Nazi Germany revealed the Luftwaffe to the world. It comprised 20,000 men, many of whom had received flying training either as co-pilots with Lufthansa or in schools secretly set up for the purpose in the USSR. An opportunity to try out Luftwaffe tactics and aircraft came in 1936 when the Spanish Civil War between General Franco's Nationalist forces and the Republicans began. Hitler supported the Nationalists, and his pilots and crews in the Condor Legion learned many invaluable lessons which determined Luftwaffe fighter tactics in World War II.

For those pilots destined to fly the Fw 190 in 1943–45, the trio of *Erganzungsjagdgruppen* were equipped with a varied fleet of Focke-Wulf fighters covering all major variants. There were also a handful of two-seat Fw 190S-5/8s (S standing for *Schule*) on strength, although these were vastly outnumbered by conventional single-seaters.

Between January and April 1944, the Luftwaffe's day-fighter arm lost more than 1,000 aviators in action (many to P-51 pilots), which included the core of its

The Luftwaffe's usual training of pilots for Defense of the Reich duties was at times rudimentary in the extreme. Here, a white-capped Oberleutnant uses models to demonstrate a frontal attack on a trio of B-17s. (Courtesy of John Weal)

experienced fighter leader cadre. One of the replacements drafted in to make good these losses was 21-year-old Helmut Peter Rix:

> As soon as I was old enough I took up gliding, and with a C Class glider pilot's license, I joined the Luftwaffe on March 1, 1943. I had been accepted as an officer candidate and reported to Oschatz, in Saxony, for six weeks' basic training. From there we were posted to Luftkriegsschule [LKS] 3 at Werder/Havel, near Potsdam. Apart from more basic training, this was the stage at which serious officer training really commenced. Those with glider experience were placed in a special group, which worked up to the advanced glider pilot license using aircraft tow. Our powered flying then began with instruction on Bü 131 and Bü 181 primary trainers, and I eventually went solo on my 32nd circuit. For the A2 license, we branched out into aerobatics and were introduced to long-distance flying. Parallel with our flying went instruction related to aircraft technical data, navigation and to becoming future officers.
>
> Flying progression was subsequently made onto B2 training aircraft, bringing us into contact with W 33s and W 34s and twin-engined Caudron C 445s. These types were bigger and heavier, and this training phase included blind flying, formation flying, target landings and long distance triangular flights, with students alternating as first and second pilots. Nightflying, "circuits and bumps" and instrument flying was also included. My time at the officers' cadet school was hard

FOCKE-WULF PILOT: WILHELM HOFMANN

Wilhelm Hofmann was born on March 24, 1921 in Reichelsheim, in the Oderwald region of Hessen. A future stalwart of JG 26, he joined the unit upon the completion of his operational training with Ergänzungsjagdgruppe West on June 11, 1942. Unteroffizier Hofmann was duly assigned to Fw 190-equipped 1./JG 26, and gained his first victory on October 11, 1942 when he shot down a No. 64 Sqn Spitfire IX near Cassel. On December 9 Hofmann's Fw 190 A-4 (Wk-Nr. 5617) suffered engine failure in flight and he was forced to crash-land near Watten. He suffered severe injuries in the accident, and was hospitalized for four months.

Hofmann eventually returned to 1./JG 26 on March 31, 1943, by which time the unit had been posted to the Eastern Front. Here, he shot down a Soviet LaGG-3 fighter on May 14, thus doubling his score – this was his sole claim in the East. Hofmann's unit returned to the West in the autumn, and in September 1943 Feldwebel Hofmann transferred to 10./JG 26. However, his stay with this *Staffel* was short, for he was serving with 8./JG 26 by the time he claimed his third victory (a No. 132 Sqn Spitfire IX) on October 18.

On February 29, 1944, recently promoted Leutnant Hofmann was appointed *Staffelkapitän* of 8./JG 26, and on March 15 he recorded his tenth victory. Included in this tally were two Mustangs – the first, an RAF Mustang I from No. 2 Sqn on January 28, 1944, and the second a P-51B from the 363rd FG on March 8. Hofmann was to enjoy considerable success over Normandy following the Allied landings, being awarded the *Deutsches Kreuz* in Gold on July 22 for 26 victories (including six Mustangs). He brought his score to 30 on August 20 by claiming two USAAF P-47s.

On October 22 Hofmann suffered an injury to his left eye in a ground accident when the bolt in a dismounted aircraft machine gun suddenly closed whilst he was examining it. Unperturbed, the ace continued to fly combat missions whilst wearing an eyepatch! Leutnant Hofmann was awarded the *Ritterkreuz* on October 24, by which point he had claimed 40 victories – remarkably, a quarter of this tally was comprised of RAF Mustangs and USAAF P-51s.

On January 1, 1945, Hofmann led 8./JG 26 on Operation *Bodenplatte*, attacking Brussels-Evere airfield. Two weeks later he assumed command of 5./JG 26, whilst also retaining control of 8./JG 26. However, on February 15, 8./JG 26 was disbanded and he became the permanent leader of 5./JG 26. Hofmann led a formation of eight Fw 190s from Drope on a *Jabojagd* mission in the Wesel-Bocholt area on March 26, 1945, and the formation soon encountered USAAF B-26s near Münster. He expertly led a bounce of the RAF Tempest V fighter escort, shooting down a No. 33 Sqn aircraft for his 44th victory. However, during the ensuing confusion Hofmann went missing, and it was later determined that he had been shot down in error by his wingman and crashed between Hasselünne and Flechum. The ace had managed to bail out, but he was too low for his parachute to deploy properly.

By the time of his death, Wilhelm Hofmann had been credited with 44 victories achieved during the course of 260 missions. Some 43 of these successes had been gained on the Western Front, and included five four-engined bombers, 13 P-47s and ten P-51s.

in both the physical and mental sense, but it proved to be very rewarding. We were given our pilot's wings and I was promoted to *fahnenjünker gefreiter*.

Having been streamed for multi-engined nightfighters rather than day fighters, in early January 1944 I was posted to the B34 Blind Flying School at Kastrup, in Copenhagen. Here, I flew Ju 88A-4/5s, Ju 86s, He 111s, Siebel 204s and Ju 52/3ms. This was a very intensive program, with technical instruction on all the foregoing types, especially the Si 204 and Ju 88. Conversion went without a hitch and I was soon flying solo.

When our course ended in July 1944, we received our advanced pilot's wings, and as I waited to become a nightfighter pilot on Bf 110s and Me 410s, we were posted to Bad Aibling, in southern Germany. At the same time I was promoted to *fahnenjünker-unteroffizier*. Out of the blue came the announcement that our nightfighter training program had been canceled, and we were given a choice of becoming single-seat all-weather fighter pilots or going to the parachute regiment! For me the choice was easy – I wanted to fly, and with all the specialized training we had had, choosing the Fw 190 was obvious. Things then happened fast.

At the beginning of September 1944 I was posted to Jagdgeschwader 110 (part of Erganzungsjagdgruppe West) at Pretzsch, on the River Elbe, for conversion training. After flying heavy twins, it was quite something to sit in an advanced trainer like the single-engined Ar 96. The handling qualities were completely different to anything I had flown before – the effect was similar to having been driving a bus then being told to switch to a racing car. I soon settled in to enjoy the freedom and excitement of flying the Arado. Besides carrying on from where I had left off with instrument flying, I also got a taste of close formation flying in *Rotte* and *Schwarm* elements, nightflying and, for the first time, target practice.

On November 2, 1944 we moved to Altenburg for conversion onto the Fw 190. After three flights in a two-seat Fw 190S-8, I went solo while carrying out circuits – we were limited to five take-offs and landings each day under normal circumstances due to fuel shortages and Allied fighter activity. We continued fighter training over the firing range and made close formation flights in twos and fours at altitudes up to 30,000ft. In mid-December we moved to Neustadt/Glewe to join 1 Staffel of the operational training unit I./JG 2 Erganzungsgeschwader for more intensive combat training, which took in high-altitude flying with the entire *Staffel* and dogfighting. We did not stay long, and on January 12, 1945 I was posted to II./JG 301's 8 Staffel at Welzow.

My introduction to frontline flying was not good. My fellow pilots and I had hardly had time to get acquainted before the "scramble" order came through – eight out of ten of my new comrades did not return! Things were beginning to get very

> bad, with shortages of everything. We newly trained fighter pilots were supposed to gain some flying experience with the squadron before being sent into action, but that never materialized. Instead, we were just thrown straight into action.

At 1015hrs on March 2, 1945, Helmut Peter Rix was scrambled in an Fw 190 from Stendal with other elements of JG 301 when Eighth Air Force heavy bombers and their escorts were detected heading for targets in Germany. He was part of a *Schwarm* led by *Staffelkapitän* Leutnant Walter Kropp, with the remaining aircraft being flown by Unteroffiziers H. Hager and W. Ehrlich. Rix recalled:

> It was a beautiful morning, with clear blue sky, but with a cloud cover of eight-tenths at about 14,000ft. I climbed on a southeastly course to 24,000ft, where we spotted our target – a formation of B-17s at 27,000ft dead ahead. We were in line abreast formation and ready for a frontal attack when Kropp broke away to the left into a dive. Following our leader down, we got into a line astern formation – I was No. 4.

At approximately 1100hrs, Rix's Fw 190 was destroyed by gunfire from P-51Ds flown by Capt Lee Kilgo and Lt Earl Mundell of the 486th FS/352nd FG, which was escorting B-17s. All four Fw 190s were shot down during this battle, with Rix being the only one to survive.

INTO COMBAT

MUSTANG TACTICS

When it came to implementing aerial tactics, the P-51's group leader was the "quarterback of the team." VIII Fighter Command units invariably employed the standard three-squadron formation when escorting bombers over occupied Europe, with each squadron composed of a quartet of four-ship flights and two aircraft as mission spares. The down-sun squadron flew 2,000–3,000ft above the lead unit, while the up-sun squadron positioned itself about 1,000ft below the lead unit. Each squadron flew about 3,000ft horizontally apart from the lead unit.

Overleaf: Dueling for the Reich

Piloting the *Jersey Jerk*, Don Strait escapes from a near miss with an oncoming Fw 190. (Artwork by Gareth Hector, © Gareth Hector)

When it came to offensive tactics, 17.5-victory ace Capt John B. England, CO of the 362nd FS/357th FG, opined that the most perfect bounce would be made from out of the sun, and from 3,000–5,000ft above the enemy:

> A pilot making a bounce should always instinctively have the advantage in speed or altitude, since one can be converted into the other. Flights should fly close formation, relying on mutual support for protection. The enemy will think twice before he jumps 18 airplanes in good formation. This has been proven many times by our experience.
>
> The best defensive maneuver for the P-51 against the common enemy fighter airplane is just a simple tight turn. I have never seen one of our fighters shot down in a tight turn, but I have seen our fighters shot down while trying to evade the enemy by diving to the deck, or pulling some fancy maneuvers. I say never be on the defensive list – if you are on the defensive, turn it into an offensive situation immediately. Always let the Hun know you're after him from the beginning.

Fellow ace Maj John A. Storch (10.5 kills), who was CO of the 357th FG's 364th FS, related at the time:

> The basic defensive maneuver is to turn into the attacking enemy. Often this will automatically turn a defensive situation into an offensive one. If the German turns with you, the P-51 should be on the tail of the average enemy airplane in short order. If, as we have found to be more often the case, the German split-esses for the deck, without top cover, you can split-ess after him. He may outdive you on the way down and outmaneuver you during this dive, but when you level out on the deck you will probably be able to catch him.
>
> When attacked by superior numbers, if no cloud cover or help is available, about the only thing you can do is to keep turning into his attacks and take such shots as you can get, hoping to even things up. You should, under such circumstances, continue to watch all the time for an opportunity to make a break for home. However, it does not pay to straighten out on a course unless you are very sure you will be out of accurate firing range. My own opinion is that the best way to make the break is a shallow dive with everything full forward. If the enemy starts to overhaul you again and gets within accurate range, about the only thing to do is to turn again and force him to take a deflection shot at you.
>
> When attacked I like to have my wingman stay close enough that he can take an airplane off my tail, and I can do the same for him. He is of no help, however, if he stays in so tight that we cannot maneuver, and are practically one target.

The preceding and following statements are completely dependent upon circumstances, and no hard and fast rules can be set down.

When attacking an enemy aircraft, the leader should go in for the first shot while his wingman drops out and back far enough that he can watch the sky and clear his own, and his leader's, tail. If the leader overshoots or has to break off his attack, his wingman will be in position to start firing with the leader covering him. If you have to break off combat but want another shot later, break up and either turn to the right or left, but not in a turn of 360 degrees, as you probably will be unable to catch the enemy aircraft after you complete it.

Fw 190 TACTICS

Maj Storch also accurately described the tactics used by Fw 190s that he encountered over Germany in 1944–45:

The main enemy evasive tactics we have noticed are split-essing for the deck, going to cloud cover, rolling, sliding, slipping and bailing out. In any case, except for the last, the only thing to do is to follow him shooting, or if you think he will be unable to get away, wait until he straightens out and gives you a decent target. If the German has superior numbers in a large gaggle formation, you can usually get on a straggler or take on one of the airplanes towards the edges of the formation and try to separate him from the others. The others may not miss him.

If the enemy aircraft are flying in a gaggle-type formation, there isn't a lot they can do about it. Of course, you must have altitude on the German so you will have

Pilots from II./JG 26 walk out to their Fw 190A-6s at Cambrai-Epinoy in February 1944. Third from left is Oberfeldwebel "Addi" Glunz, then *Staffelkapitän* of 5./JG 26. He was one of the most successful German fighter pilots in the west in early 1944, and survived the war with 71 kills (including 19 heavy bombers) to his credit. (Courtesy of Eddie Creek)

> superior speed to break away should you get into trouble. Flaps can be used to avoid overshooting, but once you put them down you will have lost your speed advantage, and perhaps become vulnerable to attack. The best shooting method for us is get in as close as you can and still avoid hitting his aeroplane, or any pieces that by chance may fall off it, and let 'er rip. Anyone will do his best shooting when he is so close that he cannot miss.

These tactics took time to refine, and their success was ably demonstrated on several occasions. On April 8, 1944, for example, Mustangs in the 4th FG were one of the fighter groups that supported the bombers attacking Brunswick, and they attacked three separate gaggles of Fw 190s and Bf 109s over a 30-mile area from 23,000ft down to the deck. Altogether, the 4th FG claimed 33 fighters destroyed and nine damaged. Three days later, when the 352nd FG provided penetration and withdrawal support for B-17s, the "Blue Nosed Bastards" (the group's P-51s were marked with blue noses as their identifying color) flew 40 minutes of escort before breaking away to strafe ground targets. They claimed three aerial victories and seven more aircraft destroyed on the ground.

Amongst those pilots to achieve success on this date was future 7.5-kill ace 1Lt Frank A. Cutler in P-51B-7 *Soldier's Vote*. Spotting a locomotive just leaving the bridge across the Elbe River at Torgau, Cutler made his pass at the engine and saw pieces of it thrown up in the cloud of steam from its erupting boiler.

He then flew over the town of Torgau at rooftop height, heading west for a mile or two. Minutes later Cutler shared in the destruction of a lone Ju 52/3m, and as he headed north, watching the unfortunate transport aircraft go down, he spotted two light blue/gray Fw 190A-7s flying wingtip to wingtip directly below him in a westerly direction at about 1,000ft. Unteroffiziers Heinz Voigt and Karl Weiss of 4./JG 26 were flying the fighters on what should have been a routine transfer flight between bases. However, they happened to be in the wrong place at the wrong time. Cutler headed for them and closed fast, firing on the Fw 190 on the right from a distance of about 100 yards. His combat report stated:

> I saw strikes on the tail section, so I skidded left and fired at the second airplane, which had not yet taken any evasive action. All my ammo was gone, but the pilot must have been hit since the Focke-Wulf whipped over to the left and exploded in the middle of the field. Then I noticed that the first Fw 190 was burning in the next field a few hundred yards away. I was separated from my flight and the Group, so I climbed to 23,000ft and came home alone.

FOCKE-WULF: THROUGH THE GUNSIGHT

The more heavily armed of the two main Luftwaffe fighters, the Fw 190 was designated the chief bomber-killer and the A-7, A-8 and A-9 variants were all fitted with the Revi 16B reflector gunsight. This sight required the pilot to estimate the angle of deflection to the target according to combat conditions, but in reality, this was only possible with any degree of accuracy when engaging at short range and/or when attacking from a central position with minimum deflection. To shoot down a large target thus required considerable pilot skill. When attacking from either the side or behind – which would attract determined fire from a bomber's tail, top and ball turrets, as well as the waist guns – the pilot of a Fw 190 would have to remain equally determined and focused on his gunnery skills.

In a gunnery instruction document dealing with rear-mounted attacks on bombers of July 1944, German fighter pilots were instructed:

"You must fire your weapons only at the ranges for which they were designed. Normally, you should not fire at ranges greater than 400m, as beyond this distance the trajectory quickly falls away. This also applies to larger weapons such as the MK 108. It is a common fallacy to believe that it must be possible to fire larger-caliber weapons at greater ranges, and that the aiming of these need not be as precise as for small-caliber weapons. The opposite is true! You have little ammunition! Use it sparingly. With the MK 108 you have only 60 rounds, so reduce range, aim carefully, fire accurately.

"Commence firing at a maximum range of 400m. Experience has shown that combat ranges are being greatly underestimated. The distances given in combat reports are almost never correct. When, for example, a combat range of 50–100m is reported, it actually varies from between 200 and 400m, as established by analysis of combat films. Frequently, range estimation errors are even greater. In attacks against bombers, many fighters open fire at 2,500–3,000m. This is a senseless waste of ammunition!

"A four-engined bomber has a wingspan of about 30m. If it appears as large as the diameter of the deflection circle, it is at 300m range. For a four-engined bomber, the estimated value corresponding to a span of 30m is multiplied by three. Therefore, a four-engined bomber with 30m span fits in the circle one time – 1 x 3 = 300m; fits in the circle 2 times – 2 x 3 = 600m; fits in the circle 3 times – 3 x 3 = 900m.

"Learn this thoroughly and practice range estimation at every opportunity, then during combat you will no longer make gross errors."

Promoted to captain on May 2, 1944, Frank Cutler would subsequently lose his own life nine days later when his Mustang (P-51B-10 42-106483) collided with a Bf 109G south of Grimmen, in Germany.

ACES HIGH

On May 19, 1944, 1Lt Ray S. Wetmore (who already had 4.25 kills to his name flying P-47Ds) of the 359th FG's 370th FS claimed the first of his 16 victories in Mustangs when he destroyed two Bf 109Gs. He downed two Fw 190s ten days later, and by war's end had increased his tally to 21.25 victories – 9.5 of these were Focke-Wulf fighters, including four destroyed and one shared destroyed on January 14, 1945.

The ranking ace of the 359th FG, Ray Wetmore's philosophy in combat was to close in to a distance where he still had a reasonable chance of being able to break off his attack without colliding with the enemy aircraft. He did not believe in head-on attacks, and would not break head-on into Fw 190s that boasted two 20mm cannon as part of their armament. He usually chose to break to one side of the Focke-Wulf and wait for his opponent's next move. Wetmore relied on the P-51's unmatched rate of turn, firmly believing that the Mustang was absolutely the best defensive weapon in the skies over Germany.

He also preferred the half roll to the split-ess. This was because during a half roll, the Mustang pilot could see the enemy much better than when performing

An Fw 190A-8/R6 of Stab JG 26 has a 21cm mortar round carefully loaded into its underwing WGr 21 "stovepipe" in the spring of 1944. This weapon was introduced in the summer of 1943 in the hope that it would help break up bomber formations. Although a direct hit could have a devastating effect on a B-17 or B-24, the drag and weight associated with the tubes in turn had a detrimental effect on the Fw 190's performance. Most units were therefore reluctant to use this weapon in areas where bombers were escorted by fighters. (Courtesy of Eddie Creek)

a split-ess, and the American fighter did not gain too much speed during the maneuver. The P-51 was at its best when making a coordinated turn on the verge of stalling, regardless of its speed – Wetmore would consider a high-speed stall at any altitude above 500ft. He also said that German fighter pilots were at their most vulnerable when trying to take evasive action.

Yet despite the Mustang's superiority, well-flown Fw 190As could still inflict losses on VIII Fighter Command. For example, on September 17, 1944, the 4th and 361st FGs were among those groups who tussled with JG 26 in the mid-afternoon. For four pilots killed in action, the *Jagdflieger* claimed three Mustangs from the latter group and two from the 4th FG.

The 335th FS/4th FG had been bounced by 15 Fw 190A-8s from 8./JG 26 near Emmerich at the beginning of the engagement, and Leutnant Wilhelm Hofmann and Oberfahnrich Gerhard "Bubi" Schulwitz had shot down two of the P-51s. Moments later, 10.333-victory ace Capt Louis H. Norley latched onto the tail of another 8th Staffel aircraft and quickly destroyed it. Fellow ten-kill ace 1Lt Ted E. Lines claimed three more Fw 190s during the clash:

> When we were bounced from behind and above by 15 Fw 190s, my wingman hollered for me to break whilst I was trying to discard my right external wing tank. When I broke, I was head-on with five Fw 190s and immediately started firing, causing one to burst into flames. I turned to starboard, still trying to drop my tank, as two Fw 190s came under me, heading in the same direction as I was. I got on the tail of the one nearest to me and started firing, and the pilot bailed out.
>
> At this point an Fw 190 closed on my tail and fired at me, hitting me in the tail and wing. My tank finally came off and I was able to maneuver onto the tail of the Fw 190 that had been firing at me. After three orbits, he broke for the deck, with me right on his tail. I fired from 500 yards down to about 100 yards, and saw strikes on his engine, canopy, fuselage, wings and tail. He burst into flames and went into the ground and exploded.

The Fw 190 force again fought back on September 27, when 315 unescorted Liberators of the 2nd Bomb Division went to the Henschel engine and vehicle assembly plants at Kassel, in central Germany. The 445th BG flew into an area a few miles from Eisenach where II./JG 4, IV./JG 3 and II./JG 300, each with a strength of around 30 specially configured Fw 190A-8/R2s boasting heavy armor plate, were maneuvering into their preferred line abreast formation for an attack. From 1003hrs, the B-24s were subjected to a ferocious mauling by approximately 40 Focke-Wulf fighters, the aircraft attacking in three waves.

In less than five minutes the *Sturmgruppen* attacks had decimated the 445th BG, with no fewer than 22 Liberators being shot down in just three minutes, followed by three more in the following three minutes. *Staffelkapitän* Oskar Romm of IV.(Sturm)/JG 3 destroyed three of the bombers in one single attack. B-24 pilots put out frantic calls for help on the Fighter Channel, and immediately two Mustang groups covering the 3rd Division some 75 miles away near Frankfurt, and the 361st FG, escorting the 1st Division 100 miles distant, came speeding to the rescue. However, six precious minutes were to elapse before the 361st FG could reach the beleaguered 445th BG, and the other two P-51 groups arrived after the enemy had departed.

One of the pilots involved in the subsequent melee between the *Sturmgruppen* Fw 190s and the yellow-nose P-51s of the 361st FG was Unteroffizier Ernst Schröder of 5.(Sturm)/JG 300. He had taken off from Finsterwalde in his Fw 190A-8/R2 "Red 19" *Kölle-alaaf!* ("Up with Cologne!") along with the rest of his *Gruppe*, hell-bent on attacking Eighth Air Force *Viermots*. The unit intercepted the 445th BG formation heading for Kassel, and Schröder downed two of the group's B-24s. There was so much debris in the sky that he closed his eyes because he believed he would run into something.

Below him, ten to fifteen columns of smoke from the explosions of the crashing aircraft rose up through the cloud layer 3,300ft above the ground. There was burning wreckage everywhere, and the fields were covered with white parachutes. Having descended to low level to make good his escape, Schröder could clearly see crewmen who had bailed out running through the fields:

> When I flew over them they stood and raised their hands high. Soldiers and policemen were running towards them to take them captive. Suddenly, a P-51B with a yellow nose (from the 376th FS/361st FG) shot towards me. In the wink of an eye we raced closely by each other on an opposite course. When we had flown by one another, the maneuver began anew, so that we flew towards one another like jousting knights of the Middle Ages. Both of us opened fire simultaneously. The American hit my tail section. My heavy MG 151/20 20mm cannon and MG 131 machine guns failed after a few shots.
>
> Since I could not fire a shot, I began evasive maneuvers the moment the American opened fire so that he could not aim correctly. It was a strange feeling each time looking into the flash of his four 12.7mm guns. After we had played this little game five or six times, I escaped by flying low over the ground. The American turned sharply, but the camouflage paint on my Fw 190 made it difficult for him to find me against the dappled ground.

Unteroffizier Ernst Schröder of 5.(Sturm)/JG 300 fights for his life in his Fw 190A-8/R2 on September 27, 1944. His opponent in this duel was 2Lt Robert Volkman of the 376th FS/361st FG, who was flying a P-51B. (Artwork by Mark Postlethwaite, © Osprey Publishing)

I landed after minutes of fearful sweating at 1130hrs at Langensala Airport after 90 minutes of flight time. An inspection of my fighter showed some hits in the tail section and a part of the covering of my rudder had been torn off, but the damage was so slight that I could take off again at noon. I landed at 1215hrs at Erfurt-Bindersleben, where my bird had to be repaired in the hangar.

This event made it very clear to me that the Americans had now achieved air superiority, as their fighter escorts were very effective. Indeed, we had only achieved such great successes on this day because the bombers we had attacked were for some reason unescorted.

It appears that Unteroffizier Ernst Schröder's opponent during this mission was 2Lt Robert Volkman of the 361st FG's 376th FS, who had followed his formation leader, 1Lt Victor Bocquin, down through the cloud cover in pursuit of the fleeing Fw 190s while the remainder of the group continued to escort the remnants of the B-24 formation to the target. During the fight that ensued, pilots from the 376th FS operated singly or in groups of two or three as they chased down the Focke-

Wulfs. Bocquin claimed three Fw 190s destroyed and 1Lt William "Bill" Rockefeller Beyer was credited with downing five. In all, the American fighters and bombers claimed 29 fighters destroyed during the course of this mission (the Luftwaffe officially acknowledged the deaths of 18 pilots).

Credited with a total of 18 German fighters destroyed in the air and another three on the ground, the 376th FS had set a temporary record among the fighter groups of the Eighth Air Force for enemy aircraft destroyed by a single squadron on a single mission.

On November 27, II.(Sturm)/JG 300's Unteroffizier Ernst Schröder again took on an overwhelming number of Eighth Air Force "heavies" which were out in significant numbers attacking various transportation targets. He and his fellow pilots, who were part of a large *Gefechtsverband* led by 128-kill ace Oberstleutnant Walther Dahl, were set upon by the now seemingly ever-present Mustangs.

In a series of wide-ranging dogfights over the Halberstadt–Quedlingburg area – the scene of so many *Sturm* assaults in the past – the *Gruppe* lost seven pilots killed and four wounded. Unteroffizier Ernst Schröder was very nearly one of

Green-nosed P-51B/Ds of the 359th FG's 369th (IV) and 370th (CS) FSs head back to East Wretham, in Norfolk, in formation on November 14, 1944, after their escort mission had been scrubbed due to bad weather. Each VIII Fighter Command group was usually assigned 48 aircraft, which were in turn split between three squadrons. (USAF)

them. With his trusty "Red 19" having been hit in the rudder, thus making it almost impossible to turn, Schröder was attempting to escape at low level when:

> Suddenly a bare metal P-51, looking brand new, appeared just above to my left. I could clearly see the pilot peering down at me from his large glass canopy. He obviously didn't want to overshoot and get ahead of me so, using his excess of speed, he pulled up and away to port.
>
> I could no longer see him but, expecting him to attack at any second, I nearly dislocated my neck trying to look behind me. When I glanced forward again, the edge of a forest of large trees was filling my windscreen. I heaved back on the stick, but there was an almighty crash as my "Bock" tore through the top branches of a huge tree at something over 500km/h [310mph]. My cockpit immediately filled with blue smoke as I carefully tried to gain enough height to bail out.

In fact, Unteroffizier Schröder managed to belly-land his machine on a nearby airfield. It was a sorry sight. The spinner and wing leading-edges looked as if they had been "attacked with an axe," there were at least 25 bullet holes in the wings and fuselage, and lumps of tree were found embedded in the radiator. It was the end of the road for Schröder's well-known "Red 19" *Kölle Alaaf!*

The Luftwaffe lost more than 50 fighters that day. Things did not improve come the New Year, and on January 14, 1945, the red and yellow-nosed P-51s of the 357th FG based at Leiston, in Suffolk, shot down 60.5 enemy aircraft – a record for any Eighth Air Force fighter group which remained unbeaten through to VE-Day. The 20th FG claimed 19.5 victories that same day and the 353rd FG downed nine enemy aircraft. In all, 161 enemy aircraft were destroyed by VIII Fighter Command units.

Since flying its first combat mission on February 11, 1944, the 357th FG, commanded by five-kill ace Col Irwin H. Dregne, had been credited with 517 victories. No fewer than 42 pilots had attained ace status whilst flying with the group, and its ranking ace, Capt Leonard "Kit" Carson of the 362nd FS, who, on November 27, 1944, had become an ace in a day by shooting down five Fw 190s, added three more kills to his score on January 14, 1945. His first victim was an Fw 190 singled out at the rear of a gaggle flying 20 miles northwest of Berlin:

Overleaf: Dueling for the Reich

On May 24, 1944, 4th FG ace Ralph "Kid" Hofer is about to score his 20th kill. Slipping his P-51B in behind an Fw 190 intent on bringing down a crippled B-17, Hofer opens up and causes massive damage to the Focke-Wulf. Moments later the German pilot bails out just before his aircraft plummets earthwards. The "Kid" would add another Fw 190 to his tally on this day, but sadly Hofer was not to survive the war. He was lost in action on July 2, 1944. His final tally of enemy aircraft would end at 30.5. (Artwork by Gareth Hector, © Gareth Hector)

2106924
QP

> I closed to about 400 yards, firing a good burst and getting strikes all over his fuselage. I believe the pilot was killed. I went back up to the bombers, looked around for a couple of minutes and saw a formation of about 40 to 50 Fw 190s coming up about 1,000 yards behind us. There were a couple of P-51s nearby, and they broke with me. We met the enemy airplanes head-on. They didn't fire but we did.
>
> I opened fire from 600 yards, closing to 200 yards, getting strikes on both wings. The Jerry split-essed for the deck and I followed him down, firing some more and getting additional strikes. At about 18,000ft the pilot bailed out, and I watched his 'chute open. Shortly thereafter, one of my wingmen, 2Lt John F. Duncan, shot down his second Fw 190. This time the pilot did not get out of the exploding fighter. I then fired a burst from 350 to 400 yards at yet another Fw 190, getting strikes. He did a couple of snaps to the right with his belly tank on, and wound up on his back. I fired again, getting more hits on the fuselage. Pieces came off the enemy ship and he began smoking. He split-essed and headed for the deck. I followed him down until he hit, bounced and crashed. The pilot did not get out.

By 1445hrs all the 357th FG Mustangs had landed back at Leiston, and pilots were soon telling their mission accounts to amazed interrogation officers. As the story went up the line to 66th Fighter Wing and higher headquarters, recounts were ordered. However, the score remained the same. Only 13 P-51s and three Thunderbolts had been lost during the great air battle of January 14. JG 300 reported 27 pilots killed and six wounded, while JG 301 had 22 pilots killed and eight wounded. The 357th FG was duly awarded a Distinguished Unit Citation for its exploits on this day.

ANALYSIS

In the spring of 1943, the growing strength of VIII Bomber Command began to exert great pressure on the *Jagdwaffe* in the west, and this would only continue as the war dragged on. By the end of the year the Luftwaffe, unhappy with the relatively small number of bombers being shot down, had drastically revised its tactics. On December 20 the fighter force made its attacks from dead ahead, or "12 o'clock level." Closing speeds of around 550mph made it difficult to keep targets in effective firing range for more than a split second, and there was always the fear of collision at the back of the German pilots' minds. Larger attacking formations, and simultaneous attacks by fighters, rather than in trail, were now also being used.

Fighter *Geschwader* perfected their head-on approaches in early 1944, increasing the angle of attack to ten degrees above the horizontal in an effort to increase the time targets were in effective firing range. This approach was soon dubbed the "twelve o'clock high" attack by USAAF bomber crews. As before, the best chance of knocking a bomber out of formation was to kill the pilots in the cockpit.

Luftwaffe fighter pilots observed a points system in combat for aerial successes, and these were in turn converted into various awards. An *Abschuss* or shoot down of a *Viermot* (a four-engined bomber such as a B-17, B-24, Lancaster, Halifax or Stirling), earned three points, while a *Herausschuss*, or separation, was worth two. A pilot who finished off an already shot-up four-engined bomber was awarded one point for *endgültige Vernichtung*, or final destruction. Damaging a bomber sufficiently to force it from its combat box was recognized as being more difficult than the final destruction of a damaged straggler. Shooting down a fighter was also worth one point while a *Herausschuss* or *endgültige Vernichtung* did not carry any points.

Decorations were awarded after points totals were reached. One point earned the recipient the Iron Cross Second Class, and three resulted in the awarding of the Iron Cross First Class. Forty points were needed for the *Ritterkreuz*, although this varied in practice. Of course this system often led to overclaiming.

Capt Don Gentile of the Debden-based 336th FS/4th FG watches his crew chief, Sgt John Ferra, update his victory tally beneath the cockpit of P-51B-7 43-6913 *Shangri-La*. Gentile claimed 21.833 aerial and six strafing kills flying Spitfire VBs, P-47C/Ds and P-51Bs in the ETO between August 1942 and April 1944. No fewer than 13 of these victories were against Fw 190s, including a trio of Focke-Wulf fighters knocked down near Ruhrburg on the afternoon of April 8, 1944. (USAAF)

One of the most effective anti-bomber tactics devised by the *Jagdwaffe* in late 1943 was the employment of specially armored Fw 190s to attack boxes of "heavies" from behind in tight and massed formations. Major Hans-Gunther von Kornatzki is acknowledged to have been the driving force behind this concept, which he put into practice in the *Reichsverteidigung* (Defense of the Reich) with Sturmstaffel 1 ("Storm Squadron 1") between October 1943 and April 1944. Flying the Fw 190A-6 (from February 1944 the A-7 and from April the A-8) *Sturmjäger* ("Storm Fighters"), Sturmstaffel 1 became operational from Dortmund in January 1944.

Although during the ensuing months the unit managed to notch up a fair number of *Viermot* victories whilst operating from Dortmund and Salzwedel airfields, losses from defensive fire and American escort fighters were also very heavy – at least 14 of the volunteer pilots had perished by April 1944. Incorporating the remains of Sturmstaffel 1 as its 11th Staffel at Salzwedel airfield in April 1944, IV./JG 3 became IV.(Sturm)/JG 3, practicing the same "Storm" tactics in the *Reichsverteidigung*.

Fw 190A-8/R1 to R6 variants that followed were similar to the A-6/R1-R6, but the A-8/R8 used by the *Sturmgruppen* had a specially armored cockpit. The *Rammjäger* notched some notable successes against American bombers, with the most successful mission being flown on July 7, 1944 when 32 "heavies" were destroyed for the loss of just two Fw 190A-8/R7 fighters. It was an isolated success, however, and after D-Day, many Fw 190 *Gruppen* were reduced to flying ground attack sorties against invading Allied forces.

Late in the war the *Tagjagd* or day fighter pilots were badly trained and hastily thrown into the battle against all odds, and only a handful survived in the lethal skies over the Third Reich. Unteroffizier Fritz Wiener, born on July 24, 1925, was one of the young replacement fighter pilots who joined the *Reichsverteidigung* at the end of 1944:

> The young pilots, who had only limited chances to survive in air combat, were misused as "cannon fodder." In 1944 half the German fighter force consisted of combat-experienced pilots about three to four years older than myself, whilst the rest were inexperienced replacements. The majority of the latter category had only minimal flying hours in first-line fighters, and no combat experience at all. It was not uncommon for replacement pilots to arrive in the frontline having never flown the Fw 190, or having practiced take-offs and landings in formation. Firing the MK 108 cannon and MG 151 machine guns prior to going into combat was also a rare feat.

MUSTANG PILOT: JOHN C. MEYER

John C. Meyer was born on April 3, 1919 in Brooklyn, New York, and he subsequently attended Dartmouth College. He joined the Army Reserves and became a flying cadet, being commissioned a pilot and second lieutenant on July 26, 1940 at Kelly Field, in Texas. His first assignment was as a flight instructor, and he remained in this posting for a year. Meyer was then transferred to the 33rd Pursuit Squadron in Iceland to fly convoy patrols, before returning to the USA to join the 352nd FG in Massachusetts. He was made commanding officer of the group's 487th FS on December 28, 1942.

Meyer became a captain on January 21, 1943 and took the P-47-equipped 487th to Britain that June. The unit commenced combat operations in September, flying a series of bomber escort missions. On November 26, the now Maj Meyer scored his first victory when he downed a Bf 109. During April 1944 the unit began converting to the Mustang, and Meyer enjoyed his first success in the North American fighter on April 10, when he shared in the destruction of an Fw 190 and downed another Bf 109. On May 8, he celebrated his promotion to the rank of lieutenant colonel with a triple-kill haul that gave him ace status.

Meyer and the Mustang were a formidable duo, and he pushed his score past the 20-kill mark – this tally included two "triples" and a "double" haul, and he downed 8.5 Fw 190s in total. It is believed that Meyer claimed as many as 11.5 aerial kills in P-51D-15 44-15041 *Petie 3rd*. He is seen here sitting in that aircraft.

Perhaps Meyer's "finest hour" as CO of the 487th FS came in the battle now known as the legend of Y-29, when the "Bluenosers" destroyed 23 German fighters sent to attack the 352nd FG's Asch base, in Belgium, at dawn on January 1, 1945 as part of Operation *Bodenplatte*. The 487th FS was responsible for the bulk of these victories, earning the squadron the Distinguished Unit Citation – an honor usually reserved for groups. Meyer, who claimed two Fw 190s destroyed, was awarded his third DSC. This action cemented his reputation as one of the best fighter leaders in the ETO, as his long-time armorer Sgt Jim Bleidner recalled:

"While it is true that he showed extraordinary heroism on New Year's Day 1945, it is also true that his planning ahead and ability to think 'like a German' played a very important role. In this case, he was convinced that the Germans would believe that the forward airfields would be vulnerable on New Year's Day because the pilots and crews would have large hangovers from the night before. Meyer called his pilots together on New Year's Eve and said no parties until the following night. As it happened, he was correct in his analysis."

On January 4,1945, Meyer's second combat tour in the ETO came to a premature end when the ammunition carrier he was traveling in as a passenger left a snow-covered road in Belgium and he suffered a serious leg injury. He was sent home to recuperate.

Staying in the air force postwar, Meyer served in Korea (with two MiG-15 kills to his name) and eventually rose to the rank of general. He retired in 1974 and died the following year. His final victory tally was 26 confirmed, one probable and three damaged, plus 13 strafing kills.

USAAF FIGHTERS IN THE ETO/MTO 1942–45					
Type	No of sorties	Lost in combat	Enemy a/c claimed destroyed in air	Enemy a/c claimed destroyed on ground	Combat missions loss rate per sortie
P-51	213,873	2,520	4,950	4,131	1.2%
P-47	423,435	3,077	3,082	3,202	0.7%
P-38	129,849	1,758	1,771	749	1.4%
P-40	67,059	553	481	40	0.8%
Spitfire	28,981	191	256	3	0.7%
A-36	23,373	177	84	17	0.8%
P-39	30,547	107	14	18	0.4%

LEADING Fw 190 ACES WITH P-51 VICTORIES IN THE ETO		
	P-51 kills	Overall score
Oberstleutnant Heinz Bär	11	221
Oberleutnant Wilhelm Hofmann	10	44
Hauptmann Emil Lang	9	173
Oberleutnant Konrad Bauer	7	68
Oberstleutnant Walther Dahl	6	128
Oberleutnant Hans Dortenmann	6	38
Hauptmann Siegfried Lemke	6	96
Oberleutnant Peter Crump	5	31
Oberleutnant Gerhard Vogt	5	48
Leutnant Wilhelm Mayer	5	27

LEADING USAAF P-51 MUSTANG ACES IN THE ETO	
	Aerial victories
Maj George F. Preddy (P-51B/D)	23.833 (+3 in P-47D)
Lt Col John C. Meyer (P-51B/D)	21 (+3 in P-47D)
Capt Leonard K. Carson (P-51B/D/K)	18.5
Maj Glenn T. Eagleston (P-51B/D)	18.5
Maj John B. England (P-51B/D)	17.5
Capt Ray S. Wetmore (P-51B/D)	17 (+4.25 in P-47D)
Capt Clarence E. Anderson (P-51B/D)	16.25
Capt Donald S. Gentile (P-51B)	15.5 (+2 in Spitfire & 4.33 in P-47D)
Capt Donald M. Beerbower (P-51B)	15.5
Capt Richard A. Peterson (P-51B/D)	15.5
Lt Col Jack T. Bradley (P-51B/D)	15
Maj Robert W. Foy (P-51B/D)	15
1Lt Bruce W. Carr (P-51B/D)	15
Capt William T. Whisner Jr (P-51B/D)	14.5 (+1 in P-47D)
Capt Henry W. Brown (P-51B/D)	14.2
Capt Wallace N. Emmer (P-51B/D)	14

Combat tactics, combat formation flying and combat maneuvering in formation were entirely new tasks to be learned. All of this was taught to replacement pilots during a period of just two months, with periodic restrictions on flying time because the Luftwaffe's fuel supply was already becoming limited to even combat units. Although there was no shortage of aircraft in which to fly, the build quality of some of these machines left much to be desired due to poor workmanship and sabotage in the production plants in Poland and Czechoslovakia.

AFTERMATH

VIII Fighter Command veteran Capt Pete Hardiman was a great fan of the P-51 Mustang, which he flew in the ETO in 1944–45:

> My only complaint was that we did not get P-51s a year sooner. Even Herman Göring knew he was licked when he saw B-17s escorted by P-51s over Berlin. My first meeting with the Mustang was in March 1944. Compared to any fighter I had seen or flown before, she was beautiful. I fell in love at first sight. Finally, I knew that North American had kept its word and given us the best fighter ever designed. The P-51B could be everything a Spitfire could (except climb), and much more. It was the most honest aeroplane I ever flew, possessing no bad flying habits. The threat of liquid-cooled engine vulnerability to combat damage with the Merlin

This impressive line-up photograph was taken at Debden on June 16, 1944. The P-51B/Cs of the 486th FS/ 352nd FG had flown south from their base at Bodney to the home of the 4th FG in preparation for the first "Shuttle Mission" to the USSR, but bad weather had caused the operation to be postponed. Codenamed Operation *Frantic*, Shuttle missions were an abortive attempt by the Americans to cooperate with the Soviet forces in the east. The shuttle-bombing program saw the Eighth Air Force's heavy bombers, escorted by Mustangs, hitting targets in eastern Germany and then continuing on to land at Russian bases. The first *Frantic* missions were flown in late June 1944, and the operation proved to be of minimal success. (USAF Museum)

> was only true if all coolant was lost immediately – some nursing was quite possible if the oil cooling remained intact, particularly in colder air. I personally nursed mine home some 600 miles from Frankfurt with a coolant leak. Going to Berlin and back was not the most comfortable way to spend one's day, but doing it in a P-51 negated the discomfort somewhat. Nevertheless, we could not stand or straighten our legs upon returning to base. Long high-altitude flying on oxygen saps one's stamina, but having the P-51 Mustang to do it in was a life saver.

Fellow ETO Mustang pilot LtCol Bill Crump was just as enthusiastic:

> The P-51D was the answer to a fighter pilot's dream. A wonderful flying machine, it possessed an excellent view of the world around, was a fantastic gun platform and was designed to combat all enemies at any distance from base. With a well trained pilot aboard, the P-51D was a match for any and all piston-engined fighters. When you shove 61 inches of manifold pressure to that Rolls-Royce Merlin, and that enormous four-bladed propeller starts chewing on the atmosphere up ahead, you receive an undeniable communiqué. You are going somewhere aloft, and fast. Then when you start maneuvering this creature and become aware of the positively sensual balance of the controls, you just might find yourself humming a love song. Every airman worth his tin wings nurses a sneaking suspicion he is a natural as a fighter pilot, and those of us who were blessed enough to fly the Mustang were certain of it.

MUSTANGS OUTSIDE THE ETO

In spring 1942, 500 of the A-36A version of the P-51A were built for dive-bombing. Fitted with wing-mounted dive brakes, these aircraft were the first USAAF Mustangs to see combat, equipping two groups in Sicily and Italy in 1943. The first P-51A group was the 54th, which remained in Florida for replacement training, while later A-models went to Asia for the 23rd and 311th FGs and the 1st Air Commando Group, flying their first missions in the China-Burma-India theater on Thanksgiving Day 1943.

In the early months of 1944 US Mustangs began operating in Burma in support of airborne troops attacking Japanese lines of communication 200 miles behind the Assam–Burma front. P-51Bs were also introduced in the Fifteenth Air Force in Italy at this time, and on May 5, 1944 RAF Mustangs operating from eastern Italy destroyed the Pescara Dam through dive-bombing.

The RAF was second only to the USAAF in the number of Mustangs it used in World War II. The Mustang III (British equivalent to the P-51B/C) entered service with the RAF in February 1944 when it began equipping No. 19 Sqn at Ford. The first 250 ordered had the older, hinged cockpit canopy. With a maximum speed of 442mph at 24,500ft, the Mustang III was more than a match for German propeller-driven fighters in 1944, and could operate far over the continent with the aid of drop tanks. Mustang IIIs continued to escort medium and heavy bombers on the Channel front into the autumn of 1944, before moving into liberated airfields in France and serving with the 2nd Tactical Air Force (TAF) as fighter-bombers.

Mustang IIIs and Vs equipped 18 RAF squadrons in the UK and western Europe and six units in the Mediterranean theater. At the end of 1944, Mustangs serving with the 2nd TAF were withdrawn and rejoined Fighter Command in the UK, and Mustangs of Nos 11 and 13 Groups continued to escort USAAF Eighth Air Force daylight raids until war's end. Some Mustangs were still serving with Fighter Command as late as November 1946. Only 280 P-51Ds were supplied to the RAF (which designated the aircraft the Mustang IV) because of the USAAF's demand for long-range fighters in the Pacific.

The Mustang's "long legs" made it a natural choice for bomber-escort and fighter sweeps across the vast Pacific theater. Following the capture of Iwo Jima in February 1945, P-51Ds began escorting B-29 Superfortresses in the USAAF's

During the final months of the war, P-51 Mustangs based on Iwo Jima escorted long-range bombers to the heart of the Japanese home islands. These Mustangs are of the 15th FG. (Tom Ivie)

brutal assault on the Japanese mainland. With external tanks giving a total of 489 US gallons of fuel, an 11,600lb P-51D had an absolute range of 2,080 miles and an endurance of 8½ hours.

On April 7, 1945, P-51Ds penetrated Tokyo airspace for the first time. That same month production of the P-51D ended with total Mustang numbers standing at 15,484. Of that total, some 5,541 were on strength with the USAAF on VJ-Day. The D-model's replacement, the lightweight P-51H, appeared too late to take part in operations in Europe, but a few of the 555 H-models built served in the Pacific towards the end of the war, although none saw combat. On November 9, 1945 the last production Mustang (a P-51H) was built, although several more development aircraft appeared beyond this date.

Postwar, Mustangs served with at least 55 air forces. Some were operated by the newly formed Strategic Air Command until 1949, and the P-51K was withdrawn from service in 1951. When the Korean War began in June 1950, many of the 1,804 Mustangs (now designated F-51s) in service with the Air National Guard (ANG) or in storage were recalled to active service. Within a year the USAF had ten F-51 wings, and three of these saw considerable combat in the first 18 months of the conflict in Korea, as did Mustang units of the South Korean, South African and Australian air forces committed to the war.

The final F-51Ds serving with the USAF's ANG were retired in March 1957, although examples remained in frontline service with Central and South American air arms well into the 1970s.

Fw 190

During World War II, some 13,367 Fw 190s, 6,634 Fw 190 fighter-bomber and close-support aircraft and 67 Ta 152 reconnaissance and high-altitude fighters were produced by Focke-Wulf and other German aircraft manufacturers. A tropicalized version for use in the Mediterranean theater saw the Fw 190A-4/Trop built with tropical filters and a rack for a 550lb bomb under the fuselage. The A-4/R6 had no MW 50 power-boost equipment but could carry a WG 21 rocket missile tube under each wing, and the A-4/U8 was a long-range fighter-bomber variant, which carried a single 1100lb bomb under the fuselage and a 300-litre drop tank under each wing. Armament was reduced to two 20mm MG 151 cannon in the wing roots.

In 1942 1,850 Fw 190A-3 and A-4 fighters and 68 Fw 190A-4/Trop and A-4/U8 fighter-bombers were delivered to the Luftwaffe. Fw 190A-5/U2 versions equipped with anti-glare shields and flame-shrouders over the exhaust outlets were used with limited success at night on *Wilde Sau* (Wild Boar) operations – a form of freelance nightfighting with the aid of searchlights.

The Fw 190A-5/U3 was a fighter-bomber variant carrying two 550lb bombs and one 1,100lb bomb.

Perhaps the last word on the Fw 190 should go not to a German aviator but to British test pilot Capt Eric Brown, whose vast flying experience on all manner of military types has allowed him to recognize the true greatness of the Focke-Wulf fighter:

> Several fighters were to display the hallmark of the thoroughbred during World War II – aircraft that were outstanding to varying degrees of excellence in their combat performance, their amenability to a variety of operational scenarios, their ease of pilot handling and their field maintenance tractability – but none more so than Kurt Tank's remarkable creation sporting the prosaic designation of Focke-Wulf Fw 190, but dubbed more emotively, if unofficially, the *Würger* (Butcher-bird) by its designer himself.

ROYAL NAVY

Part V

LAST COMBAT OVER THE PACIFIC: JAPAN 1945

SEAFIRE vs A6M ZERO

The Spitfire/Seafire and the A6M Zero-sen are two of the most recognizable and iconic fighters of World War II. While one has come to represent a symbol of freedom, the Zero-sen has been cast as the aggressor. In terms of form and function, they are arguably two of the most elegant and beautiful fighters ever built.

Designed and constructed for very different purposes, the Spitfire/Seafire and A6M Zero-sen should have never met in combat. While the Spitfire was adapted to fulfill a role for which it was never intended, the A6M Zero-sen was purpose-built from the ground up as a naval fighter, and it proved to be one of the finest aircraft of its type to see action in World War II. And when both met for the final air combats of this global conflict, their roles had ironically been reversed. Seafire IIIs were flying from carrier decks while late mark A6M Zero-sens were being used as ground-based interceptors and suicide bombers. Tasked with carrying out very different roles for which they were designed, only one would be victorious.

The Seafire emerged from an urgent requirement by the Fleet Air Arm for a fast single-engined fighter (it did not possess such an aircraft at the beginning of the war) capable of meeting land-based opponents on better or equal terms. After proving itself during the Battle of Britain, the Spitfire was soon being closely scrutinised by the Admiralty, who quickly demanded a navalized version for its carriers. A Spitfire V was duly fitted with an arrestor hook and slinging points, and during Christmas week 1941, deck suitability trials were conducted aboard HMS *Illustrious*. Further carrier trials took place during March–April 1942, and they proved completely successful.

Meanwhile, in the Pacific, A6M2 Zero-sens were flying circles around a mixed force of British, Dutch, Australian and American fighters. The Allies were waging a battle for survival, as their P-36s, P-39s, P-40s, Hurricanes and Buffalos were proving to be little more than cannon fodder for the Imperial Japanese Navy's Zero-sen units.

At 0725hrs on April 1, 1945, Sub Lt R. H. Reynolds of 894 NAS engaged his first kamikaze after pursuing the Zero-sen through the British fleet's Gun Defence Zone. The Seafire pilot opened fire on the A6M5 at long range and with extreme deflection. Nevertheless, Reynolds scored cannon strikes on the port wing root of the Japanese naval fighter. Before he could attain a better shooting angle, however, the Zero-sen rolled and dove straight into the aircraft carrier HMS *Indefatigable*. (Artwork by Wiek Luijken, © Osprey Publishing)

The psychological impact of the A6M2's initial success on Allied pilots was profound. It raised the bar, and soon all British and American fighters were being judged by the standards it set. But as the war progressed, and the Allies forced the Japanese onto the defensive, it fell upon the Zero-sen to defend the empire.

When the Seafire III entered the Pacific War, the Imperial Japanese Navy Air Force that had once wreaked havoc against the Allies was a mere shadow of its former self – it was critically short of fuel, pilots and quality aircraft. The once vaunted Zero-sen was forced to soldier on, and while new versions had been produced, it remained completely outclassed by the latest crop of Allied fighters such as the P-38, Corsair, Hellcat, P-47, P-51 and Seafire.

By mid-1944, the fate of Japan was all but sealed. In the race towards the Philippines, USAAF and carrier-based US Navy squadrons had all but wiped out whole units of the IJAAF and IJNAF. What bases they had not shattered they simply bypassed in one of the most effective tactics of the war. Whole units were left to rot and starve where they stood.

In order to support the United States' final offensive push towards the Japanese home islands, a formidable British carrier fleet was proposed. On November 22, 1944, Adm Sir Bruce Fraser hoisted his flag as commander-in-chief of the newly formed British Pacific Fleet (BPF). Aboard the carriers, No. 24 Naval Fighter Wing (joined in March 1945 by No. 38 Naval Fighter Wing) was equipped with Seafire F IIIs and L IIIs. Their assigned task was a formidable one. The 40 Seafires of 887 and 894 Naval Air Squadrons (NAS) were to provide the bulk of the fleet fighter defense – they made up just 27 percent of the total BPF fighter strength. The rest of the fighters, namely 12 Fireflies, 38 Hellcats and 73 Corsairs, would be used in the escort and fighter sweep roles.

The Seafire F III and L III would prove to be two of the best medium- and low-level fighters of the war. In 1945, they were still the fastest and steepest-climbing Allied interceptors. Even against the latest marks of the Zero-sen – the A6M5c – the Seafire had a considerable edge in level speed, rate of climb and diving speed. If it could not always force an opponent to fight, it could at least break off combat at will and return to fight another day. Developed from the Spitfire, the Seafire was a remarkable achievement, and its performance as a naval fighter was a lasting tribute to its brilliant design.

THE MACHINES

SUPERMARINE SEAFIRE

The Seafire was a fighter born out of desperation. When war broke out in September 1939, the Royal Navy's fleet structure had been designed mainly to fight Japan, not Germany. The fear that Japan would seize the riches of its Eastern empire drove Britain to develop aircraft carriers that did not require fighter aircraft. British naval aircraft procurement concentrated on the problems of a decisive fleet battle, and during the interwar period the Royal Navy assumed that if its aircraft could not sink the enemy's capital ships alone, the best they could do was to slow down the enemy fleet and leave it to the battleships to finish them off.

The Royal Navy's aircraft carrier design (which featured armored hangars), and the belief that the vessels' antiaircraft guns would offer sufficient protection, also greatly influenced aircraft procurement. Limited by the number of aircraft its carriers could hold, the Royal Navy concentrated on procuring machines that could fill multiple roles (bomber, torpedo-bomber, long-range scout, gunfire spotting etc.) like the Fairey Swordfish, Albacore and Blackburn Skua. An aircraft that performed exclusively as a fighter was last on the list.

In September 1939, the Fleet Air Arm was equipped with 232 operational aircraft. In the majority was the fabric-covered Swordfish torpedo scout bomber. The only modern aircraft on strength were 30 Skuas. The latter was designed as a fighter/dive-bomber, but was more accurately a poor dive-bomber. Along with 18 biplane Sea Gladiators (adapted from the land-based version), they made up the entire fighter force available to the Royal Navy at the start of World War II.

Operations during the German invasion of Norway and subsequent actions in the Mediterranean against the Italians showed that the Fleet Air Arm did not have a fighter capable of engaging Axis fighters, or bombers for that matter. As a result, the Royal Navy quickly accepted a number of Hawker Hurricanes and transformed them into Sea Hurricanes through the fitment of an arrestor hook. This proved to the powers-that-be that high-performance shore-based fighters could operate from a carrier deck. While the Sea Hurricane was a success, the limits of its performance were soon exposed. What was needed was a fast, agile fighter, and the Admiralty soon demanded Spitfires.

The idea of operating a Spitfire from a carrier deck was met with mixed feelings by Fleet Air Arm pilots. While many admired the Spitfire, and were more than happy to fly one, they questioned how it would realistically perform from a pitching carrier deck. Despite being a weapon of war, the Spitfire could, ironically, be described as elegant, and when asked to fly from an aircraft carrier, as fragile. Could its slender fuselage and narrow-track undercarriage stand up to the harsh deceleration of an arrested landing? What about its landing speed and view from the cockpit over its long nose? The difficulties were many, but the urgency of war pushed those worries aside, and soon the "Sea Spitfire" would take to the air.

The first Spitfire to be "hooked" was Mk VB BL676 in late 1941. An A-frame arrestor hook was attached to the bottom longerons and slinging points were introduced on the center longerons. During the Christmas week of 1941, Lt Cdr H. P. Bramwell made 12 successful deck landings, seven take-offs and four catapult launches from the fleet carrier HMS *Illustrious*. Bramwell's report was encouraging enough for the Admiralty, and soon 250 Spitfire Mk VBs and VCs were earmarked for conversion. The first to be delivered would be 48 existing, but modified, Mk VBs, with the remaining 202 being new production Mk VCs.

Adaptation for shipboard use was a very simple matter. Naval high frequency (HF) radios, IFF, and homing beacon receivers were fitted, along with a hydraulically damped A-frame arrestor hook and slinging points. The Mk VBs became Seafire IBs and the Mk VCs were designated as Seafire IICs. The only difference between the Mk IB and IIC was in the wing. The Mk VB was fitted with the "B" wing, which could accommodate one 20mm Hispano-Suiza cannon (120 rounds) and two Browning .303in machine guns (350 rounds per gun), with a firing time of between 10 and 12 seconds. The "C" wing was designed to carry two 20mm cannons or one 20mm cannon and two machine guns. The extra weight associated with two additional 20mm cannons proved to be unacceptable, and the "C" wing was therefore never used. The Seafire's built-in armament remained unchanged during the war at two cannons and four machine guns. With the modifications complete, the new Seafire's overall weight rose by only 5 percent, and maximum speed was only reduced by 5–6 mph. It was a good start.

The Seafire IB was viewed as an interim model only, and a grand total of 211 were produced. The majority was assigned to Nos 1 and 2 Naval Fighter Schools at Yeovilton and Henstridge, while others served with the School of Naval Air Warfare. The only frontline squadron to be completely equipped with the Seafire IB was 801 NAS, which served aboard the old fleet carrier HMS *Furious* from October 1942 through to September 1944.

The Seafire IIC was the first purpose-built naval fighter to enter Fleet Air Arm service. While the Seafire IBs had been conversions of Spitfire VB airframes, the 372 Seafire IIC/L IICs that followed were purpose-built on the production line for naval service. The primary difference between the Mk IB and Mk IIC was the addition of catapult spools. This required strengthening around the spools,

THE SEAFIRE THROUGH 360 DEGREES

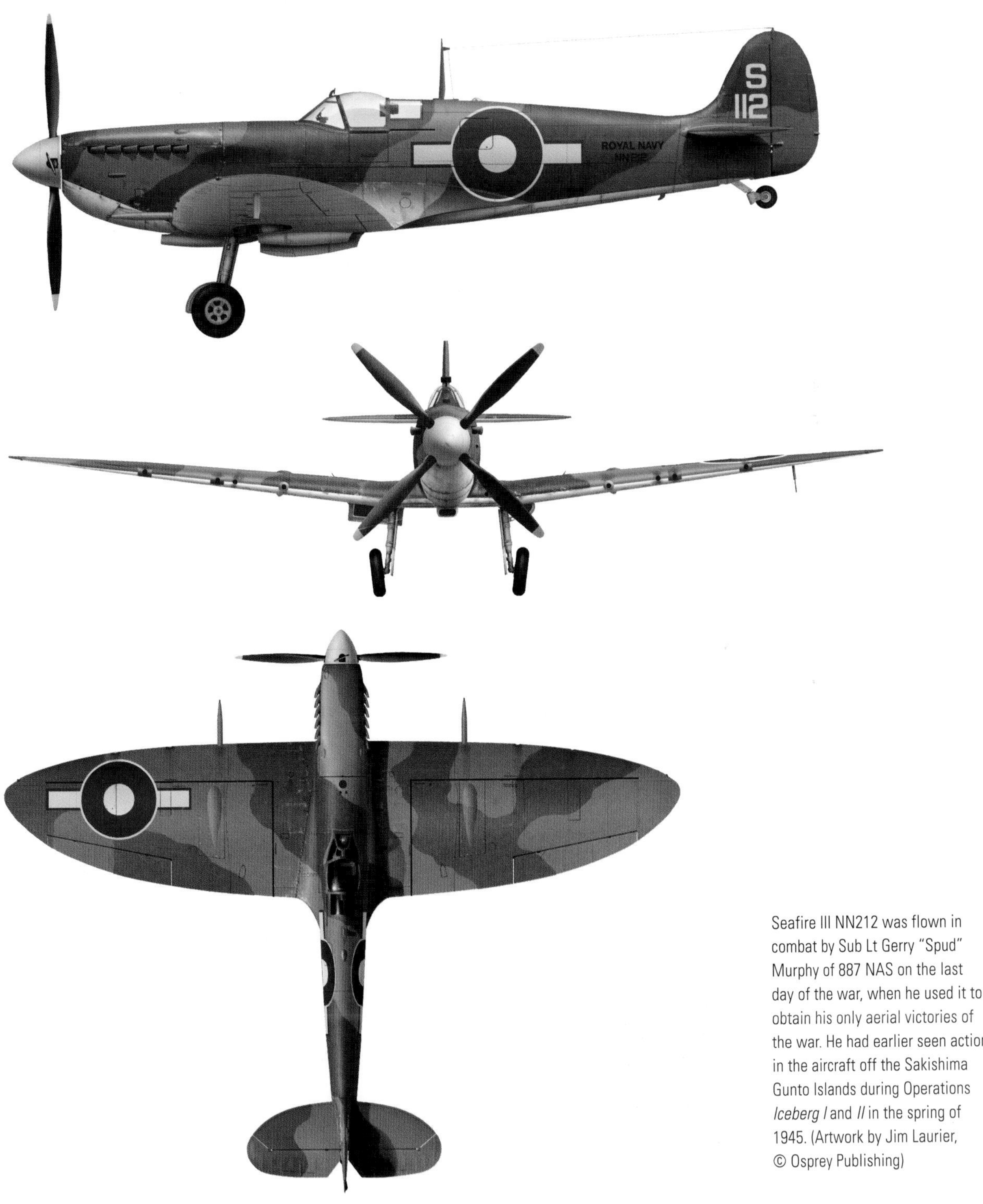

Seafire III NN212 was flown in combat by Sub Lt Gerry "Spud" Murphy of 887 NAS on the last day of the war, when he used it to obtain his only aerial victories of the war. He had earlier seen action in the aircraft off the Sakishima Gunto Islands during Operations *Iceberg I* and *II* in the spring of 1945. (Artwork by Jim Laurier, © Osprey Publishing)

but the most significant beefing up took the form of an external fishplate. This ran along the line of the mid-fuselage longeron, between the forward cockpit bulkhead and radio bay.

This additional strengthening and installation resulted in even more weight being added to the fighter. Compensating balance weights then had to be added to restore the fighter's center of gravity to acceptable limits. Add in 25lbs of armor, the heavier "C" wing and the strengthened undercarriage, and the Mk IIC's empty weight rose by an additional 6 percent over that of the Mk IB. Equipped with the same Merlin 45 or 46 as the latter, the Mk IIC proved to be 15mph slower than the Mk IB.

Operation *Torch* in North Africa in November 1942 was the first Allied amphibious assault to enjoy carrier-borne cooperation between the US and Royal Navies. It was also the first time that the Seafire was used in combat, but the results were mixed. Four squadrons were equipped with Mk IICs and one, 801 NAS, used the Mk IB. They flew 180 sorties and shot down three aircraft, damaged three others in the air and destroyed four on the ground. However, no fewer than 21 Seafires were lost, but only three as a result of enemy action. These operational losses were mainly due to the extremely poor visibility in thick haze on the first day of operations.

Despite the Seafire IIC proving to be slower than the Mk IB, its combat performance had been deemed successful, although there was concern over its shortcomings. Initial rate of climb and low-altitude speed left something to be desired, and in an effort to rectify these problems the aircraft was fitted with a Merlin 32 engine, which boasted a cropped supercharger impeller to boost the powerplant's performance closer to the ground.

A Spitfire VB transformed into a Seafire IB. BL687 has been equipped with an A-frame arrestor hook. This conversion took just over 1,000 hours to complete, and it was not until June 15, 1942 that the first Seafire IB was taken on charge by the Royal Navy. (ww2images.com)

While the Seafire IB and IIC (with their Rolls-Royce Merlin 45 and 46 engines) had been designed as medium- to high-altitude fighters, the majority of interceptions involving Fleet Air Arm aircraft in the European theater took place below 10,000ft. As if to prove this point, the first three interceptions of Ju 88s by Seafire IBs proved disappointing when the British fighters failed to catch the nimble German bombers that had attacked at low level. At the end of 1942 it was decided that the Mk IIC should be re-engined with the Merlin 32, which produced 1,640hp at 1,750ft. To take advantage of the increased horsepower, a four-bladed propeller was fitted. With a new engine and propeller, the Seafire L IIC was born.

Legendary British test pilot Capt Eric Brown was deeply involved with the testing of the Seafire. Here, he describes his experience with the new Seafire L IIC in a quote taken from the *Air International* (Volume 15, Number 3) article "Spitfires with Sea Legs":

> The Seafire L Mk IIC was the most exciting aircraft that I had flown to that time. Its initial rate of climb and acceleration were little short of magnificent, and at maximum boost it could maintain 4,600ft/min up to 6,000ft. Another result of the installation of the Merlin 32 was a quite dramatic reduction in take-off distance and, in fact, the L Mk IIC without flap could get airborne in a shorter distance than the standard Mk IIC using full flap! My enthusiasm for this new Seafire variant was such that, one afternoon, in sheer exhilaration, I looped it around both spans of the Forth Bridge in succession – court martial stuff nowadays, but during a war nobody has the time to bother with such formalities.

The result of Capt Eric Brown's flight tests led to the decision to convert all Mk IICs to L Mk IIC configuration. A sub-type of the Seafire L IIC was the LR IIC, which was a fighter-reconnaissance aircraft. Two cameras were fitted and full cannon and machine gun armament was retained. It is believed that about 30 aircraft were modified for the fighter/reconnaissance role. Although the L Mk IIC was progressively replaced by the F Mk III, its performance was, in many respects, better than the later machine, and it was not until the very end of 1944 that the Seafire L IIC was finally supplanted in frontline service.

After the quick invasion of Sicily in 1943, and with the knowledge that Italy was negotiating a separate armistice, the Allies swiftly drew up a plan for an amphibious assault in the Bay of Salerno on September 9, 1943. It was here that the Allies believed they could cut Italy in half and drive on to Naples. It was also where the Seafire earned its negative reputation.

HMS *Fledgling*, in Staffordshire, was in 1944–45 home to one of the Women's Royal Naval Service aircraft maintenance training courses. This evocative color photograph shows a rather well-worn Seafire I with its cannon armament removed. It also reveals just how many types of fighters the Royal Navy employed during World War II (the most by any navy). We can see a Corsair, two Wildcats, two Sea Hurricanes and a Fulmar, as well as two Barracudas. (DND Canadian Archives)

Carrier-based air cover for the invasion was essential. Airfields in Sicily were 220 to 240 miles from the landing beaches, and while 2,000 land-based fighters were available, they would be unable to provide more than 36 aircraft with a patrol time of between 20 to 40 minutes, depending on the type, over the invasion fleet. The Seafire, even with its short legs, could provide more than an hour of patrol time. For the invasion, the Royal Navy brought 121 Seafires to battle – 15 Mk IICs and 106 L Mk IICs. All of the latter were embarked in four small escort (HMS *Attacker*, *Battler*, *Hunter* and *Stalker*) and two fleet (HMS *Formidable* and *Illustrious*) carriers.

While the landings at Salerno were ultimately successful, the reputation afforded the Seafire was not. Statistically, the numbers were grim. Although only two Seafires were lost in action, just two enemy aircraft had been destroyed. In all, 42 Seafires were lost or written off in accidents, which amounted to one aircraft destroyed or seriously damaged for every ninth sortie flown. The reasons for the Seafire's poor performance were twofold – operating conditions and pilot inexperience. Many of the pilots had never flown off a small escort carrier before, and the lack of wind meant an increase in approach speeds of 10 to 15 knots. But when one looks closely at the sortie rate per serviceable aircraft, the Seafire did very well. It went from 2.5 to 4.1 sorties per serviceable aircraft and, in the process, protected the fleet by forcing enemy aircraft to turn back or jettison their bombs prematurely.

The next Seafire variants to see service in World War II were the F Mk III and L Mk III – the first to feature folding wings. The F Mk III was equipped with the Merlin 55 engine and a four-bladed propeller. The "C" wing was further modified through the elimination of the outboard cannon bay and blast tube stub. The Merlin 55 had an automatic boost control and barometric governing, which relieved the pilot of the need to use his judgment to get the most out of his engine. These modifications resulted in an aircraft superior to the Mk IIC. The F Mk III was 20mph faster at all heights, with an increase in rate of climb. Below 10,000ft, it was still inferior to the Mk IIC, however, but the F Mk III was built as a medium- to high-level fighter, so this was of no great concern. Only 103 F Mk IIIs were built before production switched to the L Mk III, and 887 NAS would be the only unit equipped with this variant through to war's end.

Legendary US Navy test pilot "Corky" Meyer, who attended the Joint USAAF/US Navy Fighter Conference of March 1943 at Eglin Army airfield, in Florida, had the chance to fly an early Seafire F III at this event:

> Without argument, the Spitfire/Seafire configuration was probably the most beautiful fighter ever to emerge from a drawing board. Its elliptical wing and long, slim fuselage were visually most delightful, and its flight characteristics equaled its aerodynamic beauty.
>
> The Seafire had such delightful upright flying qualities that knowing it had an inverted fuel and oil system, I decided to try inverted "figure-8s." They were as easy as pie, even when hanging by the complicated, but comfortable, British pilot restraint harness. I was surprised to hear myself laughing as if I were crazy. I have never enjoyed a flight in a fighter as much before or since, or felt so comfortable in an aeroplane at any flight attitude. It was clear to see how so few exhausted, hastily trained, Battle of Britain pilots were able to fight off Hitler's hordes for so long, and so successfully, with it.
>
> The Lend-Lease Royal Navy Wildcats, Hellcats and Corsair fighters were only workhorses. The Seafire III was a dashing stallion!

This unidentified Mk III Seafire banks towards the camera, its British Pacific Fleet markings clearly visible on the upper surface of its port wing and fuselage – note the old roundel on the starboard wing, however. These were adopted in April 1945, and were designed "to be similar to those used in the insignia of the United States Navy." The official dimensions for these BPF markings were based on two sizes – 32in- or 48in-diameter roundel. The 32in and 48in roundels proved to be either too small or too big for the Seafire's slim fuselage, so a semi-official 40in-diameter roundel was applied instead. (Phil Jarrett)

The final Merlin-engined version to see service, and the one built in the greatest numbers, was the L Mk III. First flown in the autumn of 1943, it was the logical successor to the L Mk IIC. The only difference between the F Mk III and L Mk III was the substitution of the Merlin 55 with the 55M. Like the Merlin 32, this engine was optimised for low-level performance through the fitment of a cropped supercharger impeller that helped the powerplant deliver 1,585hp at 2,750ft. Later model L Mk IIIs would receive a minor armament change when the Mk V version of the 20mm Hispano-Suiza cannon replaced the Mk II. It was a lighter weapon with a shorter barrel. The "C" wing was also modified to carry two rocket-projectile launchers under each main plane. A photo-reconnaissance version was also produced as the FR Mk III (129 built). The L Mk III and FR Mk III were the most successful Seafire variants, and were built in the greatest numbers – 808 completed by Westland Aircraft Limited and 252 by Cunliffe-Owen Aircraft Limited.

When the Royal Navy committed carriers to the Indian and Pacific theaters in 1944, close to a third of the entire fighter force available was made up of Seafire F IIIs and L IIIs. With the Fleet Air Arm also operating a mixed force of American-built Hellcats and Corsairs, the Seafire would be relegated to short-range Combat Air Patrols (CAP) and antisubmarine patrols. Only when drop tanks were made available did the Seafires participate in escort and strike operations against targets on the Japanese home islands.

It was here that the Seafire pilots of the Fleet Air Arm would meet the remnants of the once powerful IJAAF and IJNAF. In the last desperate battles of the war, the Seafire would compile a small but impressive score, and participate in the war's last dogfight between British and Japanese aircraft.

MITSUBISHI A6M ZERO-SEN

Any discussion of Japanese aircraft in World War II must be dominated by the Mitsubishi A6M *Reisen* (Zero-sen being the rough translation). It formed the backbone of Japanese naval fighter forces from the beginning of the war right up until the end.

In mid-1937 the IJNAF issued specifications for a new fighter – 12-Shi – that were far in excess of those of the A5M "Claude" that was just beginning to enter service. The IJNAF wanted a fighter capable of intercepting and destroying enemy bombers, and to serve as an escort fighter with a combat performance greater than that of enemy interceptors. It was a tall order, but the war against China accelerated the development of Japan's air arm. Japanese success with the nimble "Claude" reinforced a strong belief among IJNAF pilots in the continuing need for a highly maneuverable fighter designed for tight-turning air-to-air combat. The lessons learned in China would not serve the new fighter well. The belief that a light, nimble aircraft would dominate the skies was misplaced. The Allies had learned that maneuverability was the least important attribute when it came to fighter design.

Japanese designers were also highly influenced by their pilots, especially those of the IJNAF's Yokosuka Naval Air Corps. Requirements for the new fighter were revealed to representatives of Nakajima and Mitsubishi at Yokosuka on January 17, 1938. Nakajima quickly withdrew, convinced the job was not possible. Mitsubishi at the time was in the process of developing the IJNAF's 11-Shi bomber, and it was therefore extremely hesitant to invest resources into something that showed little hope of success. The company was persuaded to accept the project, however, and in exchange it was allowed to drop the 11-Shi bomber project. Under these strict circumstances Mitsubishi designer Hiro Horikoshi and his team created a minor miracle.

In order to produce what was in essence a "super Claude," the Zero was designed to be as light as possible. The wing was built as one piece, and it made use of a unique lightweight material called Extra-Super Duralumin. Engine power was another important factor in the new fighter's outstanding performance. At the time Japanese engine manufacturers were only producing powerplants in the 800–1,000hp range. There were a number of advanced engines in the design and experimental stages, but to move the project forward Horikoshi and his team needed a reliable one. At the time there were three available – the 875hp Mitsubishi Zuisei 13, the 950hp Nakajima Sakae 12 and the 1,070hp Mitsubishi Kinsei 46. The first two prototypes would be fitted with the Zuisei 13 engine, and the Sakae 12 was installed in the third prototype. The latter produced better performance than the Mitsubishi engine, and it would duly power the Zero-sen through its entire combat career. Saddled with an engine that developed just 950hp, Horikoshi had little choice but to dispense with anything that added unnecessary weight and drag. Items such as armor plate and self-sealing fuel tanks were out of the question.

The Zero-sen symbolised both Japan's military success and its inability to fight a protracted conflict with a major power. So it was a bad omen when, on March 23, 1939, the Zero-sen prototype had to be taken apart at the Mitsubishi plant, loaded onto two oxcarts and moved some 25 miles to the naval air base at Kagamigahara for its first flight. Powered by an 875hp Mitsubishi Zuisei 13 engine, the new A6M1 prototype took to the air for the first time on April 1, 1939. Production models of the Zero-sen would be powered by the Nakajima Sakae 12 engine, rated at 950hp at take-off. The IJNAF subsequently took delivery of the second prototype on October 25, 1939, and less than a year later, on the last day of July 1940, the Zero-sen entered frontline service. Aerodynamically, the A6M was extremely efficient. Saburo Sakai, who was Japan's highest scoring surviving ace at war's end, described the Zero-sen thus:

> The Zero excited me as nothing else had ever done. Even on the ground it had the cleanest lines I had ever seen in an aeroplane. It was a dream to fly.

Because of its low weight relative to engine power, clean design and high lift, the Zero-sen was one of the most maneuverable fighters of World War II. At low speeds it could turn inside any Allied fighter with ease. It also had a nasty bite, however. Many historians have listed the many advanced performance qualities of the A6M, but what is sometimes overlooked is the selection of armament. Boasting two license-built 20mm Oerlikon cannons and two Type 97 7.7mm machines guns, the Zero-sen packed a powerful punch. Fitting the fighter with cannon was a bold step forward, and one that would soon be followed by the Allies. The fighter's light weight had another benefit – range. The Zero-sen was extremely fuel-efficient, and as a result it had a range of more than 1,100 miles. During the battle for Guadalcanal in August 1942, the A6M was the only fighter in the world at the time that could fly the 560 miles from Rabual to Guadalcanal.

The first Zero-sens to experience combat were those assigned to the 12th Rengo Kokutai (Combined Naval Air Corps) in China. This force was made up of 15 preproduction A6M2 Model 11s. On September 13, 1940, 13 fighters escorted a small force of bombers sent to attack the city of Chungking. As the Japanese aircraft left the target area, Chinese fighters appeared. The Zero-sens quickly turned around and pounced on the mixed force of Soviet-built Polikarpov I-15 biplanes and I-16 monoplane fighters. In the one-sided battle that ensued, no fewer than 27 Chinese aircraft were shot down.

After a year of combat, the small force of Zero-sens had chalked up an impressive score – 354 sorties, 44 enemy aircraft shot down and 62 damaged for the loss of two A6M2s to antiaircraft fire. The extreme confidence generated by the Zero-sen's initial success gave IJNAF commanders an unshakable faith in the aircraft, and belief that their future military operations would be nothing but successful. When war broke out in the Pacific, the Japanese had approximately 400 A6M2 Model 21 Zero-sens on strength, of which 108 took part in the attack on Pearl Harbor on December 7, 1941. It was an incredibly small number of fighters with which to start a war, but Japanese commanders believed the Zero-sen to be the equal of two to five enemy fighters.

THE A6M ZERO THROUGH 360 DEGREES

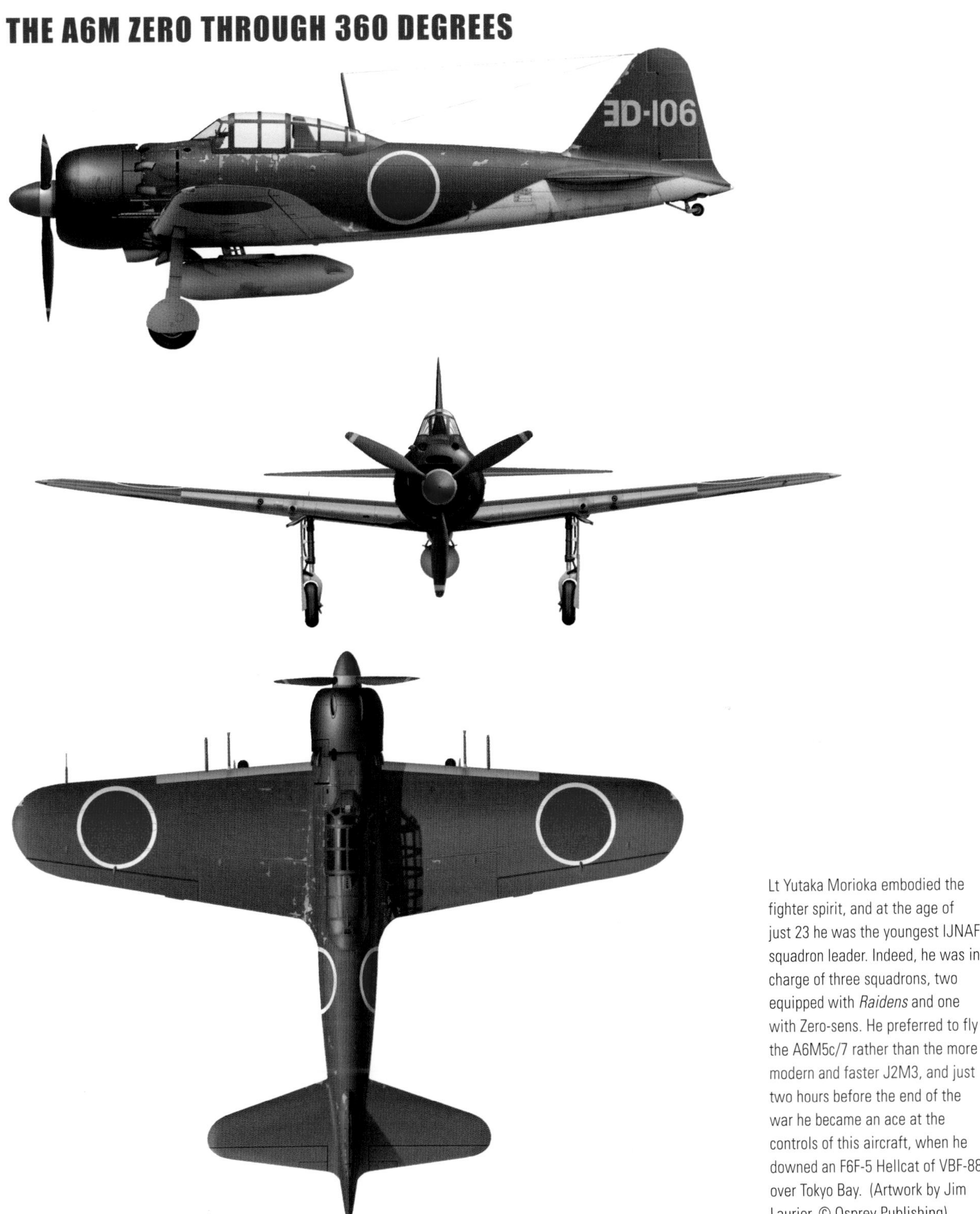

Lt Yutaka Morioka embodied the fighter spirit, and at the age of just 23 he was the youngest IJNAF squadron leader. Indeed, he was in charge of three squadrons, two equipped with *Raidens* and one with Zero-sens. He preferred to fly the A6M5c/7 rather than the more modern and faster J2M3, and just two hours before the end of the war he became an ace at the controls of this aircraft, when he downed an F6F-5 Hellcat of VBF-88 over Tokyo Bay. (Artwork by Jim Laurier, © Osprey Publishing)

The Model 21 was the same as the Model 11 except for its folding wing tips. Carrier trials had shown that the Zero-sen was a snug fit while riding the elevator between the hanger and flightdeck. Each folding wing tip was 20in long. Had the entire wing been made to fold, Japanese carriers could have carried considerably more A6Ms, but it would have increased the weight of the fighter and thus seriously degraded its overall performance.

The appearance of the Zero-sen came as a complete and utter surprise to both the Americans and the British. They were also completely unaware of its astonishing performance capabilities. Observers in China had passed their observations along, but these were ignored. Allied ignorance was complete. Their lack of knowledge, or stubborn racist belief that the Japanese could not possibly produce a fighter like the Zero-sen, led them to believe that its genius was imitative. When US fighters proved unable to cope with the A6M, embarrassed government officials were quick to claim that the Mitsubishi fighter was in fact a copy of an American design. Once that was accepted, the Zero-sen was considered to be a good fighter!

The major variants of the Zero that would see extensive combat during World War II were the A6M2 Model 21 (740 built), A6M3 Model 32 (343 built), A6M5 Model 52 (approximately 5,000 built, including all sub-variants) and A6M7 Model 63 (exact number built unknown).

During the early months of the war, the A6M2 Model 21 ruled the skies. From Pearl Harbor to the Philippines, Wake Island to Australia, the Zero-sen established a reputation like no other. Its phenomenal range caused great confusion and consternation among American commanders. The day following the attack on

A6M2s of *Shokaku's* fighter squadron run up as the carrier sails into wind for the dawn launch northeast of Hawaii on December 7, 1941. Six Zero-sens from this unit participated in the first wave attack, strafing Kaneohe and Bellows airfields. (via Aerospace Publishing)

SEAFIRE L III/F III WING GUNS

The Seafire L III/ F III was fitted with four .303in Browning machine guns and two 20mm Hispano-Suiza cannons. The cannons had a useful range of 600 yards, with a total firing time of between ten and 12 seconds. The machine guns had a further five seconds of firing.

A6M5c TYPE 52c COWLING/WING GUNS

The A6M5c Type 52c replaced the two ineffective 7.7mm machine guns housed in the cowling of previous versions of the Zero-sen with a single Type 3 13.2mm machine gun. The fighter's heavy punch was provided by two Type 99 20mm cannons in the wings, supported by two more Type 3 13.2mm machine guns. (Artwork by Jim Laurier, © Osprey Publishing)

Pearl Harbor, Clark Field, in the Philippines, was savaged by Japanese bombers escorted by Zero-sens of the Tainan Kokutai. The Americans were convinced that the fighters had been launched from a nearby aircraft carrier. In fact these A6M2s were operating from bases on Formosa – a round trip of 900 nautical miles.

For nearly six months Japanese military expansion went unchecked. It was not until the Battle of the Coral Sea on May 7–8, 1942, that the Zero-sen and the IJN first tasted defeat. The following month, on June 4–5, the Japanese suffered a catastrophic reversal that proved to be a major turning point in the war. The battle of Midway pitted four Japanese carriers against three American "flattops." When the engagement was over the Japanese had lost all four carriers, 234 aircraft and more than 10 percent of its veteran fighter pilots. It was a stunning loss.

In order to make good this pilot attrition, the IJNAF recalled many veterans from land-based units across the empire back to Japan to serve as instructors.

Flight training was shortened and entrance requirements were lowered in order to make up the numbers. These factors ultimately combined to start a process that would produce pilots that were ill-equipped for frontline combat flying come 1944.

In October 1942, the next major variant of the Zero-sen appeared. To compete with the expected increase in performance in Allied fighters, the A6M's altitude and climb performance had to be improved. Additional power was added with the fitment of the new Sakae 21 engine, which delivered 1,100hp. The new engine had a change in reduction gearing that allowed for a larger propeller, and it also incorporated a two-speed supercharger. Despite the increase in power, the Zero-sen's performance remained relatively the same, however. During flight tests, pilots recommended removing the folding wing tips. The new squared-off wing variant was designated the A6M3 Model 32 – it was codenamed "Hamp" by the Allies.

The defeats would continue unabated. As the Allies introduced better fighters with greater speed and firepower, the A6M could not keep up. New models were introduced, but by the end of the war the Zero-sen remained essentially the same aircraft. By 1945, most units were equipped with the A6M5 Model 52 and its sub-variants, the 52a, 52b and 52c. The new model, introduced in the summer of 1943, was designed to improve the rate at which Zero-sens could be produced.

All four were powered by the Sakae 21 engine, developing just 1,130hp. Capable of increased speeds in a dive, the fighter's performance was also improved through the replacement of the previous model's exhaust collector ring with straight individual stacks – the high-velocity exhaust gas was directed backward for additional thrust. In the end, the new Model 52 had a top speed of just 351mph at 19,700ft, which was only a 20mph increase over the Model 21. The Model 52 was the most widely used A6M variant of them all.

In experienced hands the fabled Zero-sen was still a deadly foe even in 1945, but in the final months of the war the once fearsome A6M was turned into something even more desperate – the kamikaze.

TYPE HISTORY

SEAFIRE

In the early autumn of 1941 the Admiralty was painfully aware of its deficiencies when it came to fielding a modern carrier-based interceptor. As fighter production made up for the losses following the Battle of Britain, the Air Ministry finally agreed to release Hurricanes for Fleet Air Arm use. While the Sea Hurricane proved capable, it was not the answer. A new naval interceptor in the form of the Blackburn Firebrand was under development, but it would not be ready for production until late 1943 at the earliest – in actuality, the first production aircraft did not fly until May 1945! The Grumman F4F Wildcat began reaching the fleet in small numbers in late 1940, but its design "stretch" was limited. It was time to add a hook to the Spitfire and turn it into the Seafire.

PROTOTYPE SEAFIRE BL676

Production Spitfire VB BL676 (fitted with a chin-mounted tropical filter) was modified through the fitment of an A-frame arrestor hook attached to the bottom longerons of its fuselage. Under-fuselage slinging points were also introduced by Vickers-Supermarine to the center longerons aft of the fighter's engine firewall and at the rear of its cockpit. The aircraft was subsequently modified to full Seafire IB specification.

SEAFIRE IB

Forty-eight existing Mk VB airframes were converted into Seafire IBs, some of which were themselves remanufactured Spitfire Is. The aircraft were fitted with A-frame arrestor hooks, released via a Bowden cable, and slinging points, with necessary local strengthening. The Seafire IB also boasted naval HF R/T, IFF and the Type 72 homing beacon. The fighter's empty weight rose by only 5 percent, however. Power was provided by either a Rolls-Royce Merlin 45 or 46 engine rated at 1,415hp. Armament consisted of four .303in Browning machine guns with 350rpg and two 20mm Hispano-Suiza Mk 2 cannons with 120rpg (armament would remain the same for all marks for the entire war). Air Service Training Limited produced 48 Mk IBs and Cunliffe-Owen Aircraft Limited was responsible for 118 examples. A further 45 Spitfires were "hooked" at RAF Maintenance Units, with associated R/T and IFF modifications also being carried out, but no slinging points or homing beacons were added.

SEAFIRE IIC

The Seafire IIC was built from the outset as a naval fighter. Mk VC airframes on the production line were converted by Vickers-Supermarine and the rest were built from the ground up by Westland Aircraft Limited. The latter was also given responsibility for the further development of the Merlin-engined Seafire series. Naval modifications were the same as for the Mk IB, but with the addition of catapult spools for the first time. Strengthening had to be provided around the spools, with the most significant visual difference being the external fishplate that

SEAFIRE L III: IN THE COCKPIT

1. GGS Mk II Gyro gunsight
2. Flaps control
3. Engine speed indicator
4. Oxygen regulator
5. Oxygen regulator
6. Airspeed indictor
7. Artificial horizon
8. Rate of climb indicator
9. Stowage for reflector gunsight lamp
10. Radio controller
11. Clock
12. Landing gear indicator
13. Altimeter
14. Gun and cannon three-position push button
15. Turning indicator
16. Oil pressure gauge
17. Fuel pressure warning lamp
18. Boost pressure gauge
19. Oil temperature gauge
20. Radiator temperature gauge
21. Fuel contents gauge
22. Slow running cut-out control
23. Signaling switchbox
24. Camera indicator supply plug
25. Instrument panel light
26. Ignition switch
27. Brake triple pressure gauge
28. Elevator tabs position indicator
29. Compass
30. Control column
31. Priming pump
32. Fuel tank pressurizing cock control
33. R.1147 Remote control wave tuner
34. Throttle, mixture, propeller control
35. Rudder pedal
36. Undercarriage control lever
37. T.R. 1196 morsing key
38. Elevator trimming tab hand wheel
39. Air intake control
40. Radiator flap control lever
41. R. 1147/RT switch
42. Door hatch
43. Jettisonable control unit lever
44. IFF controls
45. Harness release
46. R. 1147 controller
47. Pressure head heater on/off switch
48. Seat
49. Undercarriage emergency lowering control
50. Map case
51. Oil dilution pushbutton
52. Oxygen supply cock
53. Arrestor hook lamp
54. Rudder trim wheel
55. Navigation lights switch

A6M5c/7 ZERO: IN THE COCKPIT

1. Type 98 reflector gunsight
2. Artificial horizon
3. Turn and bank indicator
4. Type 3 13.2mm machine gun
5. High-altitude automatic mixture control
6. Exhaust temperature gauge
7. Clock
8. Airspeed indicator
9. Magnetic compass
10. Rate of climb indicator
11. Fuel and oil pressure gauge
12. Tachometer
13. Emergency fuel pump lever
14. Direction finder control unit
15. Emergency power boost
16. Radio direction indicator
17. Magneto switch
18. Altimeter
19. Control column
20. Manifold pressure gauge
21. Oil temperature gauge
22. Cylinder head temperature gauge
23. Cockpit light
24. Throttle quadrant/20mm cannon firing lever
25. Primer
26. Oxygen supply gauge
27. Hydraulic pressure gauge
28. 20mm cannon master switch
29. Oil cooler shutter control
30. Cowl flap control
31. Radio control unit
32. Elevator trimming tab control
33. Circuit breakers
34. Rudder pedals
35. Wing tanks cooling air intake control
36. Emergency gear down lever
37. Loop antenna handle
38. Seat up/down lever
39. Fuel tank jettison handle
40. Fuselage tank fuel gauge
41. Wing tanks fuel gauge
42. Emergency fuel jettison lever
43. Fuselage/wing tanks switching cock
44. Wings tank selector lever
45. Bomb release lever
46. Seat
47. Arresting hook winding wheel
48. Wing tank fuel switching cock

(Artwork by Jim Laurier, © Osprey Publishing)

ran along the line of the mid-fuselage longeron between the forward cockpit bulkhead and the radio bay. Empty weight rose by another 6 percent over the Mk IB without any increase in engine power – the Merlin 45/46 was retained. Increased drag from the catapult spools alone accounted for a drop of 7mph. The extra weight of the universal "C" wing and an additional 25lb of armor plate resulted in the main undercarriage being strengthened and raked forward by 2in. As a result, the Mk IIC was 15mph slower at all heights than the Mk IB. The strengthened undercarriage allowed the Mk IIC to carry a 45-Imperial-gallon jettisonable "slipper" tank or a 500lb bomb. The first Seafire IIC flew on May 28, 1943, and was delivered on June 15.

SEAFIRE L IIC

While the Seafire was designed as a medium- to high-level fighter, the majority of naval interceptions in the European theater took place below 10,000ft. While the Rolls-Royce Merlin 45 gave its maximum power at 13,000ft, and the Merlin 46 at 20,000ft, it was clear a new engine was required. At the end of 1942 it was decided that all aircraft with the Merlin 46 would be re-engined with the Merlin 32. The latter possessed a smaller, cropped supercharger impeller that added more power to the propeller instead of being used to provide more airflow for operations at high altitudes. Full throttle output at 3,000ft rose by 430hp to 1,640hp. To take advantage of the increase in power, a four-bladed Rotol propeller was fitted, replacing the three-blade unit that had been standard to the Mk IIC and IB. The Seafire L IIC had outstanding low-level performance, and its rate of climb and initial acceleration were far better than any other naval fighter produced during the war. The L Mk IIC, at maximum emergency boost, could climb at 4,600ft per minute up to 6,000ft, and could reach 20,000ft a full two minutes ahead of the Mk IIC. This was some 1,500ft per minute better than the Corsair or Hellcat. Maximum speed was 316mph at sea level and 335mph at 6,000ft. Later, some LIICs had their wingtips clipped to increase their rate of roll. This slightly increased maximum speed, but landing and take-off runs were longer. In many respects the L Mk IIC variant was the best Seafire of the war. Some 262 Mk IICs and L Mk IICs were built by Vickers-Supermarine and 110 by Westland Aircraft Limited.

SEAFIRE LR IIC

In 1943 a number of Seafire L IICs were modified along the lines of the photo-reconnaissance Spitfire PR XIII (itself based on the Spitfire VII). While the latter was equipped with three cameras, the LR Mk IIC had only two F24 type cameras due to the position of the arrestor hook. The Seafire LR IIC entered frontline service with No. 4 Naval Fighter Wing in late 1943, each of its three squadrons being equipped with between two and five aircraft. Unlike the PR XIII, the LR Mk IIC retained the full cannon and machine gun armament. There are no records of how many conversions were made, but about 30 aircraft are believed to have been produced.

SEAFIRE F III

From the very beginning, the Royal Navy was keen for a folding-wing version of the Seafire to be built. The Corsair and Hellcat were due to enter service during the second half of 1943, but competition from the US Navy and Marine Corps created a degree of uncertainty regarding a secure supply of aircraft. In order to permit unrestricted frontline service on all of Her Majesty's carriers, the Seafire needed a folding wing. The first production Mk IIC was duly pulled from the production line and used for the development of the folding wing Mk III. The folding system was simple enough, and consisted of one break just inboard of the inner cannon bay and a second at the wing tip. No power-assist folding was ever considered due to weight restrictions, and in the end the new wing added just 125lb per aircraft. It was also at this point that the Seafire would consolidate its armament. This allowed the "C" wing to be modified internally, with both the outboard cannon

The folding wings of the Seafire III were not hydraulically powered (unlike their American counterparts), and this photo reveals just how labor-intensive this work really was. This Seafire of No. 38 Naval Fighter Wing is being made ready for another sortie in June 1945. The weight penalty that came with the folding wing was 125lb. (Australian War Memorial Negative No. 019032)

bays and the blast-tube stubs being deleted. The Martin-Baker Patent Belt-Fed Mechanism was also adapted. This unit had a lower profile than that of the original, and as a consequence, the large wing blisters over the feed mechanisms were replaced by small teardrop fairings. These two modifications added close to 10mph to the fighter's top speed. The F Mk III was also given a different engine in the shape of the Merlin 55. It had the same output as the Merlin 45, but was more efficient due to the automatic boost control and barometric governing of the "full throttle height." The Merlin 55, along with a cleaner wing and four-bladed propeller, increased the F Mk III's speed by 20mph at all heights over the Mk IIC. Between 3,000ft and 14,000ft, the Seafire F III was faster than the F6F-3 Hellcat, and was evenly matched with the F4U-1A from 6,000ft to 10,000ft. The F Mk III was designed to fight at heights between 8,000ft and 15,000ft, thus making it a true medium-level fighter. Westland built a total of 103 F Mk IIIs.

SEAFIRE L III

First flown in the autumn of 1943, the L Mk III version of the Seafire would be produced in the greatest numbers. The logical successor to the L Mk IIC, the new version was identical to the F Mk III except that it was powered by the Rolls-Royce Merlin 55M engine. While the latter had slightly less power than the Merlin 32 (1,585hp for the 55M at 2,750ft versus 1,640hp at 1,750ft for the 32), the new L Mk III was actually faster in level flight. The fastest of all the Merlin-engined Seafires, the L Mk III was capable of 358mph at 6,000ft, and in 1945 it was still the fastest and steepest-climbing Allied carrier interceptor. Later production L Mk IIIs received the Hispano-Suiza Mk V cannon. This was a lighter weapon with a shorter barrel. The final version of the L Mk III was the FR Mk III. It was basically the same as the LR Mk IIC, but with a slight difference in the camera installation. Some 129 aircraft of this type were built by Cunliffe-Owen. In total, 1,060 L Mk IIIs and FR Mk IIIs were constructed by Westland Aircraft Limited and Cunliffe-Owen Aircraft Limited.

A6M ZERO-SEN

The Mitsubishi A6M Zero-sen was undoubtedly the best carrier fighter until the advent of the F6F Hellcat in late 1943. Its introduction and early aerial victories were impressive. During the first year of the war, A6M2s and A6M3s were as fast or faster than most Allied fighters in the Pacific (mainly P-36 Hawks, P-39 Airacobras, P-40 Warhawks, F2A Buffaloes, F4F Wildcats and Hurricanes). The Zero-sen's early success was due in large part to the well-trained pilots who flew it. Typically, most IJNAF aviators by the time of Pearl Harbor averaged some

800 flying hours apiece, and many had extensive combat experience from China. As the war progressed the A6M's fighting qualities began to deteriorate, and so did the quality of its pilots.

MITSUBISHI 12-SHI (A6M1)

This designation applied to the first two prototypes powered by the 875hp Mitsubishi Zuisei engine. Armament consisted of two 7.7mm machine guns and two 20mm cannon. Top speed was 304mph at 12,470ft.

A6M2 MODEL 11

The third prototype was powered by the more powerful 950hp Nakajima Sakae engine. Production started in December 1939, and it was the first model to see combat in China. A total of 64 were built.

A6M2 MODEL 21

The Model 11 proved itself in combat in China and performed well during carrier trials, but its snug fit while riding on carrier elevators proved a problem. The possible damage to the wingtips resulted in these sections being made to fold

This Nakajima Sakae 12 radial engine was taken from the first Zero-sen to be captured intact and flight-tested by US forces – the A6M2 was discovered in the Aleutian Islands in July 1942. The 14-cylinder twin-row radial produced just 950hp, which did not compare well with the engines that powered Allied fighters at the time. The Merlin 45 fitted to the first Seafires in December 1941 developed 1,415hp at 11,000ft. (Naval Historical Center)

manually. This reduced the span by 20in, and warranted a new designation. The Nakajima Aircraft Company began manufacturing the Zero-sen in November 1941, and along with Mitsubishi produced 740 A6M2s. This particular variant was given the Allied codename "Zeke 21."

A6M3 MODEL 32

To improve the Zero-sen's altitude and climb performance, the fighter was fitted with the Nakajima NK1F Sakae 21 engine, which boasted a two-speed supercharger – the powerplant was rated at 1,100hp. The engine alone added an extra 280lb in weight over the Model 21, and fuel capacity was also reduced by 21gal due to the increase in the dimensional size of the NK1F Sakae 21. Tactical combat radius suffered considerably because of the difference in fuel capacity combined with the new engine's consumption at full power. Even with the improved powerplant, the performance gains were negligible. Test pilots flying the new model suggested removing the folding wing tips, and the squared-wing model did indeed have an improved maximum speed, but little else. When the A6M3 was first encountered in combat in October 1942, it was given the codename "Hamp," which was subsequently changed to "Zeke 32." Ammunition for the 20mm cannon was increased from 60 to 100rpg. Some 343 were delivered to the IJNAF.

A6M3 MODEL 22

This aircraft actually preceded the Model 32, but in order to meet the demand for a squared wing version its production was delayed. The Model 22 was built simply because the IJNAF needed to claw back the lost range due to the reduced wing area of the Model 32. Although the Sakae 21 engine was retained, the fighter's fuel

A6M3a Model 22s of the 251st Kokutai head out on patrol from Rabaul in 1943. This particular fighter was routinely flown by veteran 86-kill ace WO Hiroyoshi Nishizawa, and it is seen here carrying a 330-liter drop tank. (via Aerospace Publishing)

capacity was increased by 24 US gallons. This gave the Model 22 the greatest range of all the Zero-sen variants, and it arrived in the frontline just in time to fly the 560 nautical miles from Rabaul to the combat zone over Guadalcanal in August 1942.

A6M5 MODEL 52

By late 1943 the Zero-sen's poor performance against newer Allied fighters like the F4U Corsair, P-38 Lightning and Spitfire was clear to both the Allies and the Japanese. Promises of a new interceptor did not materialize, and the Japanese were forced to modify the existing A6M3. The Model 52 was designed to simplify and speed up production, as well as to increase its diving speed. Wingspan remained the same as the square-tip Model 32, but modifications included the elimination of the wingtip folding mechanism. To increase diving speed, heavy-gauge wing skinning was added and the exhaust collector ring was replaced with straight individual stacks. This directed high-velocity exhaust gas backward for additional thrust. Maximum speed reached 351mph in level flight at 19,000ft. The A6M5 Model 52 was the most widely used model, with 1,701 manufactured.

A6M5a MODEL 52a

Heavier-gauge wing skin was added to increase diving speed to 460mph – just 20mph slower than the F4U Corsair. This was to be the highest diving speed attained by any Zero-sen variant. Firepower was improved with the addition of new Type 99 Model 2 Mk 4 20mm cannons. Mitsubishi produced 391 examples. The total built by Nakajima is unknown.

A6M5b MODEL 52b

CO_2 fire extinguishers were built into the fuel tank areas of the fuselage and around the firewall. Pilot protection was increased with the addition of a 5mm bullet-resistant windshield and firepower was also improved for the first time when one of the two Type 97 7.7mm fuselage machine guns was replaced by a larger Type 3 13mm machine gun. Mitsubishi produced 470 examples.

A6M5c MODEL 52c

Increased firepower, more fuel and pilot protection. The Model 52c's armament was increased to three Type 3 13mm machines guns (one fuselage-mounted and two in the wings) and two 20mm cannon – the 7.7mm machine gun was deleted to save weight. Armor plate was installed for the first time behind the pilot's seat, along with a 37gal self-sealing fuel tank. Mitsubishi produced 93 examples of the 52c.

This detailed close up shows the wing-mounted armament of the late model A6M5c. This variant was the most heavily armed and best-protected of the Zero-sen family, having an armored glass windshield, self-sealing fuel tanks and pilot head armor. Within each wing was a 20mm cannon, and outboard of the cannon was a 13mm machine gun. A further heavy machine gun was installed above the engine on the starboard side. The A6M5c was equipped with the Nakajima Sakae Model 31A engine, which boasted water-methanol injection. (*Aeroplane Monthly*)

A6M6c MODEL 53c

The Sakae Model 31 A engine with water-methanol injection was fitted, but it proved unreliable and performance suffered as a result. Mitsubishi produced only one 53c.

A6M7 MODEL 63

This was the fighter/dive-bomber variant of the Zero-sen. Armament was the same as for the 52c, and in place of the normal centerline drop tank Mitsubishi developed a bomb rack that was capable of carrying a 500lb bomb. Two wing-mounted 33-Imperial-gallon (150-liter) drop tanks were provided in place of the centerline 72-Imperial-gallon (330-liter) drop tank.

A6M8c MODEL 54c

For only the second time in the war, the Zero-sen was fitted with a more powerful engine in the form of Mitsubishi's Kinsei 62, developing 1,340hp. The larger-diameter Kinsei required a redesign of the forward fuselage that resulted in the fuselage-mounted machine gun being eliminated. The centerline bomb rack and wing-mounted drop tanks were retained. Maximum speed was 356mph at 19,685ft. Test pilots agreed it was the best model of the Zero-sen yet produced, and the fastest of them all. Only two were built.

SEAFIRE L III vs A6M5c MODEL 52c COMPARISON SPECIFICATIONS		
	Seafire L III	A6M5c Model 52
Powerplant	1,585hp Merlin 55M	1,100hp Sakae Model 21
Dimensions		
Span	36ft 10in	36ft 1in
Length	30ft 2.5in	29ft 11in
Height	8ft (over cowling)	11ft 6in
Wing area	242 sq ft	229.27 sq ft
Weights		
Empty	6,204lb	4,136lb
Loaded	7,104lb	6,025lb
Performance	358mph at 6,000ft	348mph at 19,685ft
Range	400 miles (with drop tank)	657 miles
Climb	to 15,000ft in 5 min 30 sec	to 16,405ft in 5 min 50sec
Useful Ceiling	24,000ft	36,255ft
Armament	2x 20mm Hispano cannon, 4x .303in Brownings	2x 20mm Type 99s, 3x 13.2mm Type 3s

A VIEW FROM THE COCKPIT

Very little was known about the Zero-sen in the early stages of the war, and it was not until July 1942 that the US managed to obtain a complete airframe (an A6M2 that had force-landed in the Aleutians the previous month) that could be test-flown. On September 4, 1942, the Headquarters, US Army Air Forces Director of Intelligence Service issued *Informational Intelligence Summary No. 59*:

> **The Japanese Zero Fighter**
>
> For sometime past, incomplete, confusing and occasionally conflicting information has prevailed regarding the Japanese Zero Fighter. During recent weeks, examinations and investigations of crashed Zeros in various parts of the world have clarified the situation. For this reason, it is believed that the following detailed summary will prove of interest.
>
> **Cockpit**
>
> Although perhaps somewhat smaller than average, the cockpit provides ample room for a pilot of normal size. Instruments are conveniently arranged and visibility is good. No automatic flight control apparatus is installed, but the instrument panel contains practically all other flight and navigational instruments found in modern fighters, including artificial horizon, radio compass dial and bank-and-turn indicator. A rudder bar is provided rather than individual rudder pedals. Metal stirrup loops in hinged toe plates mounted at each end of the bar provide individual brake control, which is obtained through built-in Bowden wire connections to two hydraulic cylinders mounted on the cockpit floor just in front of the rudder bar. The entire rudder bar and fittings are manually adjustable fore and aft by means of a screw to accommodate pilots of different leg length.
>
> The control stick is of normal design, but contains neither trigger nor gun selector switches. These are found upon the throttle handle on the left side of the cockpit. A small rocking-thumb lever in the top of the throttle selects in the forward position the 7.7mm nose guns and in the rearward position both the 7.7s and the 20mm wing guns. A long, curved trigger is fitted to the forward side of the throttle handle.
>
> On the next inner quadrant, slightly below the throttle, a supercharger control lever is mounted. Inboard and slightly below the supercharger handle is the handle for the propeller pitch control. The mixture control handle is mounted on a separate quadrant, slightly higher and forward of the other group.
>
> The air speed indicator is calibrated in knots and reads through a double scale from 40 to 160 and from 160 to 300 knots, equivalent to a range of 46 to 345 statute miles per hour.

This fine study of a captured A6M5 in flight shows its clean and compact lines. The Zero-sen was one of the most maneuverable fighters of World War II thanks to its large wing area and generously proportioned ailerons – both clearly visible in this photograph. But this maneuverability came at a price, for at high altitude the aerodynamic lift of a large wing area, combined with light weight, made the Zero-sen a poor performer. Above 15,000ft the Zero-sen lost its exceptional maneuverability, which was its greatest asset. The fighter was unmatched at lower altitudes and slower speeds, however. (National Archives)

The altimeter is of somewhat unusual calibration and reads from 0 to 8 through a double circular scale with a single hand indicator. The unit of measurement, although not as yet definitely determined, is presumably kilometres.

How did the Seafire match up against the A6M5 Zero-sen? In October 1944, flight trials between a Seafire L IIC and a captured A6M5 Model 52 took place at the US Naval Air Station at Patuxent River, in Maryland. A subsequent report detailing the results of the trials read as follows:

Maximum Speed

The Seafire L IIC was faster below about 17,000ft, and the Zeke 52 was faster above that altitude.

At sea level the Seafire L IIC was 24mph faster than the Zeke 52.

At 5,000ft the Seafire L IIC was 24mph faster than the Zeke 52.

At 10,000ft the Seafire L IIC was 18mph faster than the Zeke 52.

At 15,000ft the Seafire L IIC was 8mph faster than the Zeke 52.

At 20,000ft the Seafire L IIC was 5mph slower than the Zeke 52.

At 25,000ft the Seafire L IIC was 10mph slower than the Zeke 52.

Top speeds attained were 338mph at 5,500ft for the Seafire and 335mph at 18,000ft for the Zeke 52.

Climb

The Zeke 52 climbs at a very steep angle, and gives an impression of a very high rate of climb. The Seafire L IIC, however, has a much better initial climb, and remains slightly superior up to 25,000ft. The climb of the Seafire is at a faster speed, but at a more shallow angle. The best climbing speeds for the Seafire and Zeke 52 were 160mph and 123mph respectively.

Dive

The Seafire is superior in the dive, although initial acceleration is similar. The "Zeke" is a most unpleasant aircraft in a dive due to heavy stick forces and excessive vibration.

Turning Circle

The "Zeke" can turn inside the Seafire L IIC at all heights.

Rate of Roll

The rate of roll of the two aircraft is similar at speeds below 180mph indicated, but above that the aileron stick forces of the "Zeke" increase tremendously, and the Seafire becomes progressively superior.

Conclusions

Never dogfight with a "Zeke 52" – it is too manoeuvrable. At low altitudes where the Seafire is at its best, it should make use of its superior rate of climb and speed to obtain a height advantage before attacking. If jumped, the Seafire should evade by using its superior rate of roll. The "Zeke" cannot follow high-speed rolls and aileron turns. The Seafire L III, with the Merlin 55M, performed better than the L Mk IIC at all heights. At 6,000ft the L Mk III was capable of 358mph, making it the fastest of all the Merlin-engined Seafires.

All Allied fighter pilots were severely warned against dogfighting the Zero-sen. While the A6M could roll, turn and climb inside faster than any Allied fighter, that was not the whole story. The A6M5 was a slow-speed fighter. Its preferred speed was just 180mph or less, causing many Allied pilots to fight on its terms. The only Allied fighter that could outclimb the A6M5 was the Seafire, this fact alone depriving the Zero-sen pilot of one of his major advantages. By climbing and diving, the Seafire would use its strengths to its advantage, and if the Zero-sen tried to emulate the Seafire, it could only do so by increasing its speed, which reduced its maneuverability to that of the Seafire. The latter's considerable edge in level speed and rate of climb at low and medium levels gave it the ability to disengage combat at will.

Amongst the pilots to use these attributes in combat in the final months of the war was Lt Gerry Murphy of 887 NAS, who claimed two victories in the Seafire's final aerial action of World War II:

> When I first flew the Seafire it was pure exhilaration. Having flown the standard training aircraft, which didn't have anything approaching the speed and response, it was great in a climb and when turning, and you felt really in control. It was extremely responsive. I also flew the Hellcat, which was a very robust aircraft, but it was like flying a steamroller compared to the Seafire. It was big and heavy, but a great warhorse, and it could take an awful lot of punishment. Compared to the Hellcat, the Seafire was rather delicate. The Hellcat didn't have the response of the Seafire. It was the difference between a racehorse and a carthorse. The Seafire III was about 16 knots faster than the Hellcat and Corsair at low and medium altitudes.

THE STRATEGIC SITUATION

The British Pacific Fleet, formed in November 1944, was designed to fight alongside the Americans in the Central Pacific. It was a formidable force centered on three fleet carriers – HMS *Illustrious*, *Victorious* and *Indomitable*, which were subsequently joined by *Formidable*, *Indefatigable* and *Implacable*. This would be the largest deployment of Royal Navy fleet carriers and aircraft during the war.

The units embarked in these vessels formed the 1st Aircraft Carrier Squadron (ACS), which consisted of 215 aircraft (later 255). The fighter component numbered 40 Seafires of No. 24 Naval Fighter Wing (887 and 894 NASs), along with 12 Fireflies, 38 Hellcats and 73 Corsairs – the Seafires represented 27 percent of the total Fleet Air Arm fighter strength in the Pacific. The bulk of the fleet fighter defense was to be performed by the Seafire, leaving escort missions and fighter sweeps to be undertaken by "longer-legged" Hellcats and Corsairs.

Typically, the carriers would conduct two days of strikes followed by two days of replenishment. From first light to dusk, the Seafires of No. 24 Naval Fighter Wing would be required to fly 50 to 60 Combat Air Patrol sorties. The F Mk IIIs would fly medium-level CAPs below a Corsair or Hellcat HiCAP and the L Mk IIIs would provide the low-level component close to the fleet.

Performing these missions was an incredible responsibility for the pilots involved when one considers the new threat posed to the fleet by the kamikaze, and their

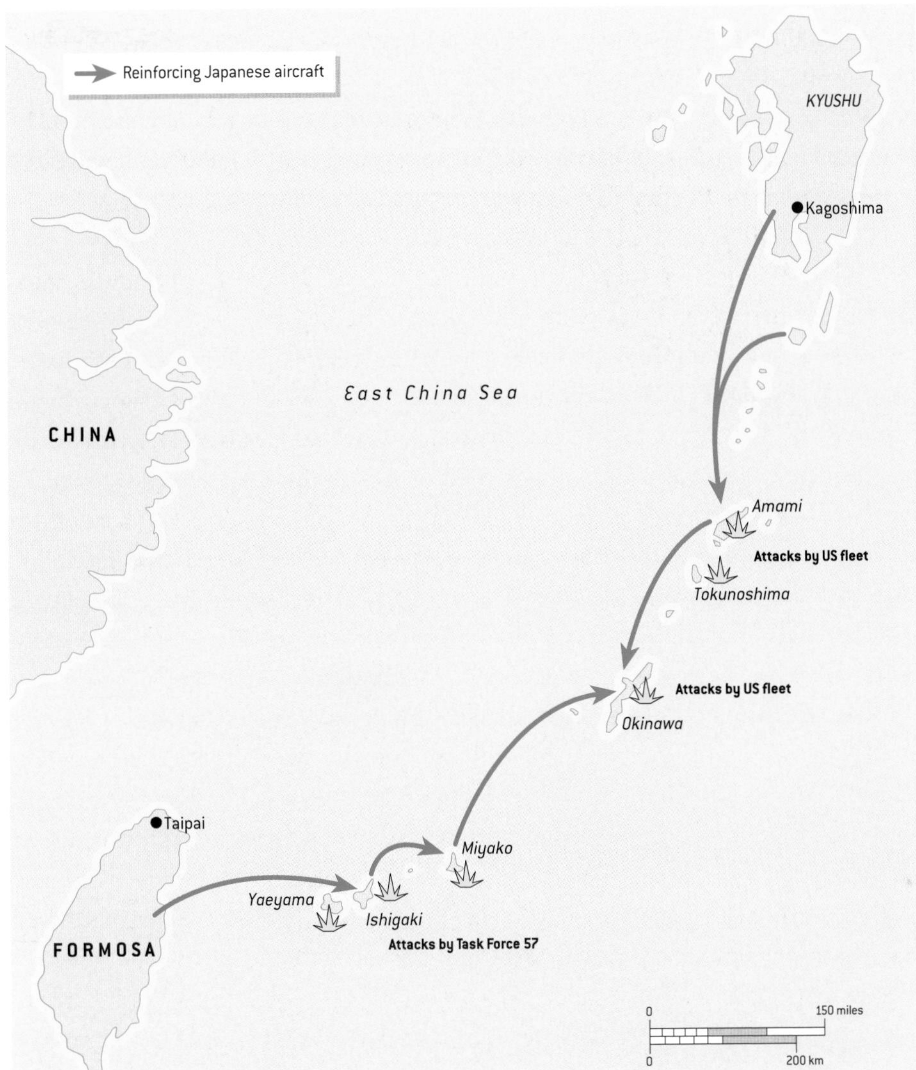

In late March 1945, the British Pacific Fleet, operating as Task Force 57, was given the job of neutralizing Japanese airfields in the Sakishima Gunto archipelago, thus preventing kamikaze aircraft movements between Formosa and Okinawa.

fanatical ability to hit, sink or damage surface vessels. In many ways the kamikaze threat was tailor-made for the Seafire III, as its low-level performance and acceleration made it the premier interceptor against sea-skimming Japanese attacks.

While the Royal Navy and Fleet Air Arm had made great strides in providing the men and materiel for the war in the Pacific, No. 24 Naval Fighter Wing was in a precarious position. Basic spare parts like propellers, undercarriage oleos and gunsights were in short supply in the Far East, and replacement Seafire IIIs were few and far between. There was also a serious shortage of experienced pilots. While the wing's leadership was of high quality, the majority of its pilots had little deck-landing experience and even less combat time.

When the fleet left Sydney harbor on March 10, 1945, for combat operations, there were only 37 Seafire pilots aboard HMS *Indefatigable* – 13 under the established complement. To deal with the low-level kamikaze threat, the number of Seafire L IIIs had been increased from 16 to 22 aircraft in 894 NAS, while the number of F Mk IIIs in 887 NAS was dropped from 24 to 18.

The British Pacific Fleet was now given the designation of Task Force 57, and on March 25, 1945, it would join with American Task Force 58 and 52.1 for Operation *Iceberg*, the invasion of Okinawa. *Iceberg* enjoyed the heaviest support for any open-sea amphibious operation of the war. Task Force 58 comprised 16 attack and light carriers, embarking more than 1,200 aircraft between them. The units to which the latter aircraft were assigned had the job of securing the northern approaches to Okinawa, as well as providing offensive and defensive support. Task Force 52.1, with its 15 CVEs (light carriers), undertook the close air support for the ground troops and provided local air defense. Task Force 57, with four carriers, two battleships, four cruisers, 11 destroyers and 231 aircraft, was the smallest of the task forces. To help support the invasion of Okinawa, the Royal Navy had been given the necessary, if thankless, task of flank protection.

The Sakishima Gunto archipelago was strategically placed between Formosa and Okinawa. The Imperial Japanese Navy still had many experienced units on Formosa, along with reinforcements on mainland China. The Royal Navy was tasked with neutralizing the airfields in the Sakishima Gunto archipelago, thus

Boasting a mix of blue and sky propeller spinners, Seafire IIIs from 801 and 880 NAS run their engines up on the deck of HMS *Implacable* as the vessel turns into wind prior to launching its air wing in early August 1945. Note that all of the Seafires are fitted with ex-P-40 drop tanks. 828 NAS's Avengers are "chocked and chained" on the stern of the carrier. (Author's collection)

preventing the movement of aircraft between Formosa and Okinawa. On March 26, all 40 Seafires of No. 24 Naval Fighter Wing were ready for action. The first day of the operation went well for the Seafire units involved, with 72 sorties launched – 32 on medium-level CAPs and 40 on new "Jack Patrols." The latter was an American innovation designed as a last-ditch counter to the kamikazes that approached at sea level. The Seafire L III was the best fighter for this particular job. Held at less than 3,000ft, the patrols were controlled by visual fighter directors using a common local air defense R/T frequency.

An A6M5 being refueled. This crude and somewhat ineffective refueling system was symptomatic of the Japanese inability to appreciate the basic needs required to field and equip an effective fighter force. Gasoline trucks were almost non-existent, and most units refueled their aircraft using 200gal drums and a hand pump. (National Archives)

After 12 days of strikes and numerous kamikaze attacks – *Indefatigable* was hit once – Task Force 57 had contributed 2,886 sorties, of which 450 were flown by aircraft from No. 24 Naval Fighter Wing for an average of 36 sorties per strike day. The victory tallies for the Seafire pilots were slim, but they did shoot down three A6M Zero-sens and possibly damaged a Ki-61 "Tony." The Seafire was now proven against the Zero-sen. With the experience gained, the pilots of No. 24 Naval Fighter Wing would see even more action during *Iceberg II.*

By the time the invasion of Okinawa took place, the IJNAF and IJAAF had virtually ceased to exist. The battles of attrition that had taken place in 1942–43 in the southwest Pacific and New Guinea had gutted both air arms of pilots and aircraft. Most of the war's early veterans were now gone, and as their replacements had little experience their combat effectiveness was negligible. In the battle for the Marianas Islands in June 1944, for example, the IJNAF would suffer one of its greatest defeats of the war.

In what has been recorded as the "Great Marianas Turkey Shoot," the Japanese were able to field a force of nine aircraft carriers and 440 aircraft. The US Navy countered with 18 carriers and 475 Hellcats. When the smoke finally cleared, the Japanese had lost three carriers, with two others seriously damaged, and more than 300 aircraft (mostly Zero-sens) and pilots.

By the time of the Okinawa invasion the remnants of the IJN's heavy surface fleet were stranded in port due to a lack of fuel, aircraft and personnel. All remaining air groups were now ground-based, with the vast majority equipped with late mark versions of the Zero-sen. For the Japanese, the war situation was hopeless, and this is when they turned to the kamikaze. Whole fighter units were converted to the new role, and the aircraft most widely used was the battle-tested A6M.

After a short spell to rest and replenish, Task Force 57 was soon back in action as part of Operation *Iceberg II*. From May 4 to 25, Task Force 57 once again flew strikes against the airfields in the Sakishima Gunto archipelago. The return to operations allowed No. 24 Naval Fighter Wing to improve its score, and of the 11 Japanese fighters destroyed by Fleet Air Arm fighters during this period, five were credited to Seafires. Although this was a minuscule number when compared to US Navy claims during *Iceberg II*, one has to remember that the British carriers had only seen 16 days of operations in 1945 up to May 4. It must also be remembered that the Seafire was tied to a defensive role – they had to wait for the enemy to come to them. No. 24 Naval Fighter Wing also improved its deck-landing record, as only nine aircraft were written off during the course of 578 sorties.

A Seafire of No. 38 Naval Fighter Wing is warmed up on board *Implacable* in mid-1945. The P-40 drop tank installation can be clearly seen. The latter adaptation was very successful, and proved more reliable than the standard 90gal slipper tank used by No. 24 Naval Fighter Wing. No. 38 Naval Fighter Wing obtained its drop tanks through a trade with the USAAF – the going rate was two crates of Johnnie Walker whisky for 60 tanks. The Seafire's short range limited its usefulness for more than two years in the frontline. Why it took so long to hang a suitable drop tank on to the Spitfire/Seafire family is one of the war's great mysteries. If they had been available when the Seafire first entered service in late 1942, its contribution would have been greater, and its reputation may not have suffered as much. (Australian War Memorial Negative No. 019029)

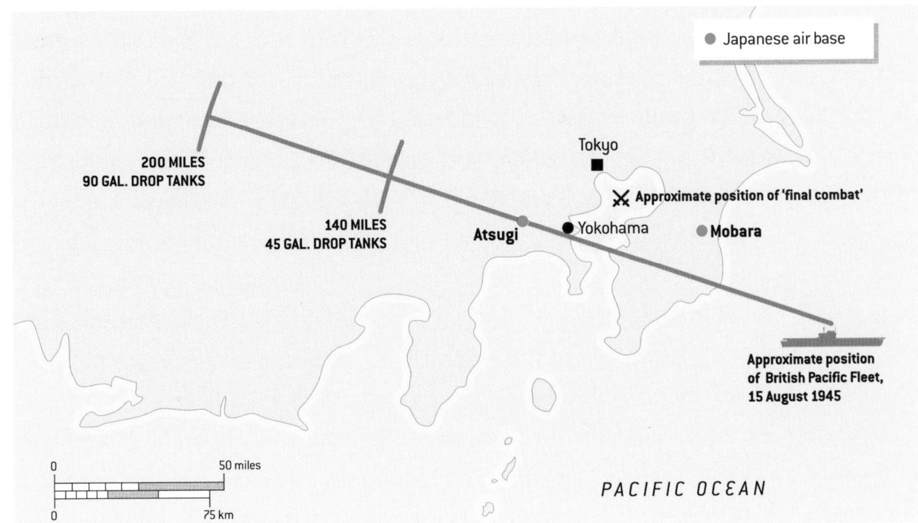

The Seafire was hamstrung for much of World War II by its poor range on internal fuel. However, by the time the British Pacific Fleet was committed to the final attacks on the Japanese home islands, its Seafire units had equipped their aircraft with either purpose-built 90gal Spitfire slipper tanks or surplus P-40 89gal drop tanks. As this map shows, these allowed the fighters to range deep inland.

On May 25, Task Force 57 withdrew from the operational area and headed for Sydney, Australia. There, it was joined by HMS *Implacable* and the Seafires of 801 and 880 NAS, assigned to No. 38 Naval Fighter Wing. Their addition brought the fleet's overall strength to 88 Seafire IIIs.

While ashore, attention was turned to the Seafire's endurance problem. No. 24 Naval Fighter Wing opted for the standard Spitfire pattern 90-Imperial-gallon slipper tank, examples of which were obtained from the Royal Australian Air Force (RAAF). No. 38 Naval Fighter Wing took a different approach to solving the range issue, however. After some experimentation, the P-40's 89-Imperial-gallon drop tank was selected. Sufficient stocks were made available (paid for with two crates of Johnnie Walker scotch) from a USAAF Warhawk unit in New Guinea, and using a modified bomb rack, all 48 of the wing's aircraft were modified. Following just three weeks of refit and repair, all preparations were made for the next round of strikes that would see the British Pacific Fleet directly targeting the Japanese home islands.

THE MEN

In January 1945 the Fleet Air Arm and the IJNAF were two vastly different forces. One was reaching the peak of its efficiency and combat strength, whilst the other was desperately short of fuel, aircraft and well-trained aircrew. In many ways, the years of conflict during World War II had seen a reversal of roles for the British and Japanese naval air arms.

At the beginning of the war, the Fleet Air Arm was comprised of a motley collection of obsolete biplanes and monoplanes, while the IJN had the world's foremost carrier striking force. Early victories in December 1941 shocked the world, and proved that the Japanese were masters in the art of carrier warfare. However, by January 1945 the Fleet Air Arm was a transformed force. Equipped with modern carriers and American Hellcats, Corsairs, Avengers and British-built Seafires and Fireflies, the Fleet Air Arm began striking at Japanese targets in Sumatra and the Bay of Bengal. In November 1944 the British Pacific Fleet was formed around the carriers HMS *Illustrious*, *Victorious* and *Indomitable*.

For the Japanese, the war had become a savage battle for survival by the autumn of 1944. Mostly equipped with the now obsolete A6M Zero-sen, the IJNAF had introduced a new weapon, the kamikaze. For all intents and purposes a force of little consequence, the IJNAF consisted of units that were manned in the main by pilots with only moderate levels of training. Incapable of taking on the vast Allied fleet sent to invade Okinawa through conventional means, novice naval aviators were turned into suicide bombers, while the more experienced pilots (who were few in number and exhausted from years of constant combat) navigated them to their targets, providing the kamikazes with a modicum of fighter protection along the way.

By 1945 the British Commonwealth Air Training Plan and the American output of pilots and aircrew had reached such a high level that they actually had a surplus of men ready to fly combat aircraft in the frontline. But even with this amazing output, Seafire pilot strength for both Nos 24 and 38 Naval Fighter Wings remained just at or below strength. In the early summer of 1945, the RAAF found itself with a large number of fighter pilots surplus to requirements. Many of these men had extensive operational experience in the Spitfire. Aware of the Fleet Air Arm's difficulties, the RAAF offered the services of 24 pilots, but the end of hostilities prevented them from seeing any combat.

FLEET AIR ARM TRAINING

By the final year of the war, a Fleet Air Arm trainee pilot could be found in one of two training systems. One was based in Great Britain and the other was in the United States, run by the US Navy under what was known as the "Towers Scheme." The latter was initially designed to train 30 pilots per month for the Fleet Air Arm and 100, mainly flying-boat crews, for the RAF.

In wartime Britain, everyone had to register for National Service, and for those who were keen on flying, most did not leave it to chance to express their interest in serving with the RAF. However, many who tried to enrol in the latter service, particularly after its widely publicized success in the Battle of Britain, were turned away because it had more volunteer pilots than it knew what to do with at the time. This was exactly what happened to future ace (and CO of 880 NAS in 1945) Lt Cdr Mike Crosley, who signed up to join the RAF in 1940, only to be told that it was effectively "full"! Eager to get into the fight, he (and hundreds like him) was immediately accepted into the Fleet Air Arm to begin his training.

The first step in the long journey to becoming a Fleet Air Arm fighter pilot began at HMS *St Vincent*, at Gosport. Here, the new recruits were given a medical, followed by an interview, during which the new recruit was asked if he wanted to be a pilot or observer. Once he had passed through this process, the new recruit would be sent home to await orders.

For naval aviators in Britain, wartime training started with a return to HMS *St Vincent*, where recruits joined in batches of 50 to 60 every four weeks. Each naval airman was kitted out with standard naval rating's uniform, and they were classified as Naval Airmen 2nd Class. Recruits spent up to seven weeks at *St Vincent* marching, saluting, looking after their kit and learning how to handle a machine gun, as well as being taught basic navigation, Morse, semaphore and meteorology. At the end of "basic" an examination had to be passed before elementary flying training could begin.

Initially, elementary flight training was handled by the RAF at Elmdon, now Birmingham International Airport, or Luton, now London Luton Airport. As training ramped up, additional facilities came on stream, with bases constructed throughout the Commonwealth that were made available through the British Commonwealth Air Training Plan. Training also took place at Naval Air Station (NAS) Pensacola, Florida.

After graduating from *St Vincent* as a leading naval airman, the new recruit could go one of two ways – to Elmdon or Luton, or on a troopship to Canada or Pensacola. For those sent to an RAF station in the UK, basic training or Elementary Flight Training (EFTS) would begin on the Miles Magister or de Havilland Tiger Moth.

It was during EFTS that the young student pilot came face to face with the mysteries of heavier-than-air flight. On the ground, the theory of flight made sense, but once in the air this frequently vanished, and the young pilot soon found himself battling a new force – panic. Squeezed into a tiny cockpit in a small and fragile aircraft, the young pilot had to master his fear and take control of his machine. Many did not, and on average one in four washed out during elementary training.

After three months of flying, the new pilot could have expected to have logged approximately 78 hours in the air. The next step was to the RAF's No. 1 Service

Flying Training School (SFTS) at Netheravon, where student pilots were streamed to fly either fighters or bombers. SFTS also meant bigger, more powerful aircraft such as the North American Harvard (SNJ-3 in US Navy service). Early on in the war, new students would have cut their teeth on old Hawker Hart biplanes and Fairey Battle monoplanes, as well as Harvards. The latter aircraft, compared to the Miles Magister or Tiger Moth, was a major step up. With a fully enclosed cockpit, it presented the student with a sea of instruments all powered by a big Pratt & Whitney engine. If the young pilot could handle the Harvard, he could then progress to a high-performance fighter.

SFTS was where pilots learned formation flying, as well as aerobatics, navigation, instrument flying and fighter tactics. After three-and-half months of classes and flying, the new student would have approximately 120 hours of flying time, including 20 hours at night. It was at this stage in their training that the new pilots were given their wings and commissioned into the Royal Navy Volunteer Reserve.

After a week of leave, newly minted pilots would return to the Royal Navy for their operational training. While the RAF had operational training units, the Fleet Air Arm had naval squadrons with numbers in the 700 series. Units like 761 NAS were designated as the advanced training squadrons of the Fleet Fighter School. By June 1944, 68 Seafires were being used for deck-landing training – a number of Miles Master IIs were also on strength.

Based at Yeovilton from its formation on August 1, 1941, and then Henstridge from April 10, 1943, 761 NAS was where new pilots learned to fly fighters. Early in the war they would have flown Sea Gladiators, Fulmars and Sea Hurricanes, but by 1944 the aircraft in the frontline were more advanced – Hellcats, Corsairs, Fireflies and Seafires.

It was also during this period of advanced training that the young students would make their first launches and landings from a carrier deck. Before a student was allowed near a carrier, he had to perform a number of Aerodrome Dummy Deck Landings on the airfield. The runway had white lines painted across it to represent make-believe arrestor hook wires. Directed by a "batsman" or landing signal officer, the young pilot would be guided down to the runway, and hopefully to a successful landing. Once this was achieved the next step was to test his skills on a moving carrier. After six or more successful launches and landings, the new fighter pilot was ready for a squadron posting.

If assigned to train in the United States, the new recruit would be bound for NAS Pensacola. Here, the student would follow a similar training syllabus, with pre-flight, primary, intermediate and advanced pilot training, as well as advanced carrier training. He would fly different aircraft from his contemporaries in the

SEAFIRE PILOT: RICHARD HENRY REYNOLDS

Sub Lt Richard Reynolds of 894 NAS was the highest-scoring Seafire pilot of the war, and he had the honor of shooting down more kamikaze aircraft than any other naval aviator in the entire Fleet Air Arm. Richard Henry Reynolds was born October 12, 1923, and went to school in Cambridge. He then joined the Royal Navy as a naval airman at HMS *St Vincent*, in Gosport. During the autumn of 1943 he underwent deck-landing training aboard the carrier HMS *Ravager* in the Firth of Clyde, and in March 1944 he was commissioned as a sub-lieutenant in the Royal Navy Volunteer Reserve. Shortly after Reynolds joined 894 NAS aboard *Indefatigable*.

On August 29, 1944, he would score his first aerial victories. During Operation *Goodwood* (a series of four Fleet Air Arm strikes against the German battleship *Tirpitz*, holed up in a Norwegian fjord), Sub Lt Reynolds and Lt H. T. Palmer sighted a German Bv 138C flying-boat shadowing the fleet. With a cloud base of just 700ft and visibility a mere half-mile, the Seafire pilots caught the German aircraft before could disappear. They made quick work of their prey, and within minutes another Bv 138C had also been downed. Reynolds was mentioned in despatches. Later that year *Indefatigable* went out to the Far East to join the British Pacific Fleet. In January 1945, 894 NAS flew CAPs while the fleet carried out strikes against Sumatran oil refineries. Starting in April, *Indefatigable* and three other British carriers took part in Operation *Iceberg*.

At 0725 hrs on April 1, a lone kamikaze pilot in a Zero-sen broke through the cloud and strafed the battleship HMS *King George V*. As it pulled out of its dive, Sub Lt Reynolds entered the Gun Defence Zone and gave chase. At long range, and with extreme deflection, Reynolds managed to score cannon hits along the enemy fighter's port wing-root, but it was not enough. Before he could reach a better firing position, the IJNAF pilot rolled the A6M onto its back and plunged into *Indefatigable*. Four officers and ten ratings were killed and 16 wounded. The armored deck saved the carrier from further damage, and flying operations resumed less than an hour later.

Twenty minutes later, a second Zero-sen appeared and dropped a bomb, narrowly missing the destroyer HMS *Ulster*. Reynolds gave chase, and in two short firing passes despatched the intruder. Moments later, he sighted another A6M, and this one chose to stay and fight. The Japanese pilot tried to force Reynolds into a turning fight, but he kept up his speed and used the Seafire's superior climbing and diving performance to reach a favorable firing position. With his fifth, and final, burst he sent the A6M crashing into the Pacific. Sub Lt Reynolds would share in the destruction of another Zero-sen during Operation *Iceberg II* on May 4. He was awarded a Distinguished Service Cross for his performance in both operations.

Sub Lt Reynold's exceptional flying abilities saw him offered a regular Royal Navy commission in 1946. In 1948 he joined 806 NAS, flying the Hawker Sea Fury. He passed the Empire Test Pilots' Course and went to Boscombe Down as a test pilot. In 1952 Reynolds went back to sea aboard the carrier HMS *Eagle*, and flew Supermarine Attackers with 803 NAS. From March 1955 to May 1956 he commanded 811 NAS, flying the Hawker Sea Hawk. In 1957 he returned to HMS *Eagle* as ship's company, and after promotion to commander in December of that year, Reynolds had his first, and only, sea command, the destroyer HMS *Contest*. Commander (Air) aboard HMS *Ark Royal* from 1959 to 1961, Richard Reynolds retired from service in 1971 and passed away in 1999.

UK, however, including the Naval Aircraft Factory N3N, Stearman N2S, North American NJ-1, SNJ Texan and Vultee SNV Valiant.

The training offered in the US came with many advantages. Firstly, there was no fear of enemy attack, and secondly, excellent flying weather and higher performance aircraft, plus the accommodation and access to American amenities, made Pensacola a very pleasant place to be.

JAPANESE PILOT TRAINING

At the time of Pearl Harbor the IJNAF was an extremely well-trained force with a core of superbly trained carrier pilots. Many averaged 800 hours' flying time, and some had totals of up to 2,500 hours. At the beginning of the war, the IJNAF had between 3,000 and 4,000 pilots, of which around 1,500 were trained for carrier operations. The Eleventh Air Fleet that attacked Pearl Harbor boasted 600 pilots, each of which had an average of more than 600 hours' flying time.

By mid-1944, the inability of the Japanese to replace lost aviators resulted in a force that had just 50 percent of the average flying time of pilots flying in January 1942. In 1945 that average was down to less than 400 hours, with a minimum of 150. The Seafire pilots of the Fleet Air Arm would, therefore, find themselves fighting against three types of Japanese pilots – the kamikaze, the poorly trained new pilot and a handful of aces and experts.

Japan was an authoritarian regime with a rigid social structure and hierarchy. The methods employed to enlist and train aircrew were in many ways harsh and lengthy. The pool of healthy well-educated men eligible for flight training was far smaller than in the West. The cult of the big gun remained dominant in the IJN during the early part of the war, with naval officers expected to be seamen first. Carrier and air group commanders were not expected to be aviators. At the time of Pearl Harbor, only 10 percent of all IJNAF pilots were officers and academy graduates of the Naval Academy at Eta Jima. Naval Academy graduates were not encouraged to enter aviation, and instead of integrating naval aviators like the US Navy did, the IJN segregated them.

In order to bolster the number of aviators, the Japanese set up the Flight Reserve Enlisted Training Program in 1928. Physically and academically gifted teenagers between the ages of 15 and 17 were chosen, and all had to be primary school graduates – in 1937 the standard was raised to middle school. These young men would spend up to three years at sea prior to being sent to aviation training.

Like their brother aviators who had been recruited from the fleet, the reserve youths were enlisted men. Amazingly, 90 percent of Japanese naval pilots were either enlisted men or "non-coms." As the war progressed, the huge divide that separated the enlisted men from officers did nothing for morale in the field.

1941 saw a major expansion of the reserve pilot program, but the results were not felt on the frontlines until 1943. Like the training methods in the West, the Japanese followed a similar program, but their methods were harsh and very selective. Japanese ace Saburo Sakai recalled that only 75 men from a pool of 1,500 were accepted for flight training. The harsh training regime that followed was designed to create a warrior mentality.

In addition to ground and flight instruction, the new recruits were also subjected to a grueling physical program which included swimming, holding one's breath, standing on heads, wrestling, diving off a platform onto the ground, hanging with one hand from an iron bar and walking on one's hands! If one performed poorly, the shame of expulsion was the result. How much of this physical training helped in the creation of a fighter pilot is open to debate, and as the war progressed the IJNAF dispensed with it.

After the war the US Navy studied the Japanese air training system and produced a detailed report, a portion of which follows:

Training

1. The Bureau of Training, Kyoiku Kyoku, at Naval Air Headquarters lays down the lines for the training of all Naval Air Personnel. A single Combined Air Training Command, Rengo Koku Sotai, based at Gifu, is responsible for carrying out the policy thus laid down.
2. There are six Combined Air Groups (Rengo Kokutai), Nos 11–14 and 18 and 19, subordinate to this command in which all IJNAF personnel are trained. These combined Air Groups are Headquarter Staffs, the training itself being given in Training Air Groups (Kokutai), under the overall supervision of the Combined Air Group Headquarters.
3. Each Combined Air Group is responsible for training in a particular area. At the same time the training given by one Combined Air Group is not the same as that given by another. The following table show the location of each group, and the nature of the training it conducts:

COMMAND	LOCATION	FUNCTION
Combined Air Group 11	Central Honshu	mainly elementary flying training
Combined Air Group 12	Kyushu	mainly advanced flying training
Combined Air Group 13	Japan/China	navigation, W/T air gunnery
Combined Air Group 14	Formosa	advanced flying training
Combined Air Group 18	Japan	unknown
Combined Air Group 19	Japan	unknown

Pilots of the 203rd Kokutai's 303rd Hikotai study their day's assignment at Kagoshima Naval Air Station in May 1945. On the left is CPO Takeo Tanimizu (32 victories), whilst the pilot on the right has an 8mm Nambu pistol in his hand. (Takeo Tanimizu)

4. Training Air Groups carrying out the training of flying and ground personnel number about 100 in total. Apart from six in Formosa, and isolated ones in the Philippines, Indo-China, China and Korea, all these Air Groups are in Japan (unlike the JAAF, most of whose training units are overseas).

5. There are five types of Training Air Groups:

A) Preparatory

Pre-flight training air groups for potential aircrews. Recruits are drawn from the IJN, from civil life or from the Youth Air Training Corps (an organization similar to the Air Training Corps in the RAF). At the end of this training, which varies in length according to the age of the recruit, trainees are classified into pilots, navigators, bomb-aimers, air-gunners and wireless operators.

B) Disciplinary

"Boot-training" groups for potential ground personnel.

C) Specialist Training

Specialist training groups exist for providing courses of instruction for other than pilot aircrews graduating from (A) and (B).

D) Elementary Flying Training

The elementary flying training groups are fed by recruits from the groups under (A) who have graduated as potential pilots. These groups specialise in fighter, bomber or reconnaissance training for pilots graduating from the elementary flying training groups.

E) Operational Training

Operational flying training is carried out in operational units, to which pilots are posted after completing their advanced flying training. Often, these units are ones being newly formed in Japan. Operational training is supervised by the command to which the operational unit is subordinated. This, in most cases, is an Air Flotilla, which for training purposes is normally given the use of two or three airfields, one or two "target" ships and, when required, a training aircraft carrier.

ZERO PILOT: YUTAKA MORIOKA

By August 1945, there were three kinds of Japanese fighter pilot – the surviving experts, most of whom had joined Capt Minoru Genda's elite squadron (343rd Kokutai), armed with the very effective N1K2-J *Shiden Kai* ("George") fighter, the novices straight out of flight school and those assigned to the kamikaze units. But in August 1945, Lt Yutaka Morioka did not fit into any of these groups. He was one of the few who actually gained in experience in the last few months of the war and survived. Hours before the final surrender announcement on August 15, 1945, Lt Morioka would achieve ace status with his fifth, and final, victory. He was probably the last pilot to do so in World War II.

Born on March 8, 1922, to parents who worked in firearms and explosives distribution, Yutaka Morioka was a fearless leader and late starter in the fighter game. Entering the Naval Academy at Etajima in the 70th Class, he graduated on November 11, 1941 and began his training as a D3A "Val" dive-bomber pilot. Morioka did not see any combat in the dive-bomber role, however, and instead became an instructor with the Usa Air Group in northern Kyushu. With the war situation turning critical, Morioka, like hundreds of other pilots, was retrained to fly fighters.

In April 1944 he joined the Atsugi-based 302nd Kokutai, whose job it was to shoot down B-29s heading for Tokyo and surrounding areas. The conversion for many pilots was not easy, but with the help of 27-kill Ens Sadaaki Akamatsu (the unit's ranking fighter ace), Morioka would be taught the finer points of aerial combat. In their first mock dogfighting session, Akamastu "shot down" Morioka four times in just ten minutes. After two months of intensive training, Morioka was presented with a diploma.

Critical manpower shortages led Lt Morioka to become the youngest IJNAF squadron leader at the age of 23. Incredibly, he was given command of three squadrons, two equipped with Raidens and one with Zero-sens – Morioka preferred to fly the latter. On January 23, 1945, Morioka would lose his left hand when attacking a B-29 near Nagoya. The tail gunner managed to damage his Zero-sen and one of the .50in bullets severed Morioka's left hand. After a short stay in hospital, Morioka returned to his unit with an iron claw fitted in place of his missing hand.

His fourth victory occurred on August 3, when Morioka led four Zero-sens in an attempt to thwart the rescue of P-51 pilot Capt Edward Mikes Jr of the 458th FS, who had baled out over Tokyo Bay. Four Mustangs, two PB4Y-2 Privateers, a B-17, a B-29 and a submarine were all involved in the operation, and Morioka managed to shoot down a P-51 from the 457th FS. He and his comrades also strafed Capt Mikes in his lifeboat (which had been dropped by a B-17G from the 4th Emergency Rescue Squadron). Mikes survived with only a few scratches, and was later rescued.

Lt Morioka led another attack on a rescue mission ten days later when he and his pilots spotted a PBY that was trying to pick up a Hellcat pilot. Morioka and his formation of eight Zero-sens chased after the Catalina, which had managed to take off and was heading for open water across Tokyo Bay at wave-top height. The PBY was eventually brought down by the IJNAF fighters at the very mouth of Tokyo Bay. Becoming a certified practicing accountant postwar, Morioka eventually passed away in July 1993.

Expansion of JNAF Training System

As a result of the increasing demands of the war, considerable expansion in the training system took place in late 1943 and the spring of 1944. This expansion was of two kinds:

A. an increase in the number of training groups of all kinds.

B. an increase in the numbers of aircraft used at many of the elementary and advanced Flying Training Groups.

The supply of personnel for the enlarged system was drawn mostly from university and higher school graduate classes, conscripted in 1943.

Individual Training of IJNAF Personnel

Pre-flight Training

The length of the pre-flight course for potential aircrew varies according to the age and educational background of the entrant. For volunteers straight from school, there is a course lasting for 1½–2½ years that is primarily educational and cultural in nature, but including instruction of an elementary kind in various aspects of IJNAF work. Recruits of military age take a six- or eight-week pre-flight course designed to improve their physique and introduce them generally to the IJNAF routine. An "aptitude for flying" test is given at the end of both of these courses, after which recruits are divided into three classes, pilots, navigators and W/T operators, and posted to other Air Groups for further training. Pilots go onto elementary flying training Air Groups.

This poor-quality, but extremely rare, air-to-air shot shows four A6M2-K trainers in flight. Many of the fighting air forces of World War II developed two-seat trainer versions of their frontline fighter aircraft, but very few made widespread use of them. The IJNAF championed the two-seat trainer, however, utilizing both the A6M2-K and A6M5-K. These aircraft filled the gap between the Navy Type 93 Intermediate Trainer and operational single-seat fighter aircraft. Most of the standard A6M2 fighter airframe was retained, but the wing guns were removed to save weight and a new two-seat cockpit with dual controls was fitted. Small horizontal fins were also added to the rear fuselage sides just above the main tailplane (they can be seen in this photograph) to improve spin recovery. (National Museum of the USAF)

Elementary Flying Training

No distinction is made at this stage between fighter, bomber or reconnaissance pilots, all of whom train together on an elementary biplane trainer (most likely the Yokosuka K2Y2 Navy Type 3 basic trainer). The course lasts four months, instruction being given in take-offs, landings and circuits. Flying time is about 100 hours, most of which are flown on aircraft with dual control. Classes are held in the principles of flying, with some instruction also in aircraft maintenance and meteorology. At the end of this course trainees are designated as fighter, bomber or reconnaissance pilots and posted to Air Groups specializing in these types.

Advanced Flying Training

Four months are spent at the Advanced Flying Training Air Groups. Advanced trainers and obsolescent operational aircraft are used, flying time being in the region of 100 hours for fighter pilots, including about ten on "conversion" [aircraft used would include the Yokosuka K5Y1 biplane Navy Type 93 Intermediate Trainer, Mitsubishi A5M4 "Claude" Navy Type 96 monoplane fighter and, later in the war, Mitsubishi A6M2-K and A6M5-K two-seat advanced trainer versions of the Zero-sen]. Combat tactics, air-firing, navigation, etc., are taught, with more importance being attached to the pilot's actual performance in the air than to his theoretical knowledge. In the case of fighters, for example, no theoretical test at all is given.

Operational Training

Having completed the advanced flying course, pilots are posted to an operational unit for operational training. Operational training is intensive, considerable time being spent teaching formation flying, as well as combat tactics, carrier landings and night flying. The time spent on operational training varies from two to six months according to operational requirements, and, therefore, no definite figure can be given for flying hours. The minimum target is believed to be 60 hours.

Pilot training for both the IJAAF and IJNAF was slow in providing well-trained pilots to replace combat losses. By 1945 the threat of invasion of the Japanese homeland was the primary concern of the IJAAF and IJNAF. By the end of the war nearly 10,700 aircraft had been assigned the kamikaze role, and the 18,000 pilots available for combat had, on average, just 100 flying hours apiece. By March 1945 all flying training had been terminated.

INTO COMBAT

SEAFIRE TACTICS

The evolution of the aircraft carrier during World War II was extraordinary. For the Royal Navy, it was a complete transformation. British carrier doctrine prewar was based on the Fleet Air Arm using its aircraft to shadow an enemy fleet and slowing it down with its torpedo-bombers. Once that was accomplished, battleships would provide the final blow. However, by 1945 the aircraft carrier, and its aircraft, could accomplish all that and more.

The aircraft carrier and the new "carrier task forces" now gave naval commanders the ability to strike at the enemy directly. The British Pacific Fleet, equipped with American-built Hellcats, Corsairs and Avengers and British-built Fireflies and Seafires, had proven itself to be an effective offensive force. Now it would turn its attention to the Japanese home islands and the last Fleet Air Arm offensive of the war.

By the time the Seafire reached the Pacific theater of war, Spitfire Mk VIIIs, Mk IXs and Griffon-engined Mk XIVs were dominating the skies over Europe. These variants were the most advanced versions of the legendary Vickers-Supermarine fighter to see combat in World War II, yet the Fleet Air Arm's Seafire III was, for all intents and purposes, a 1941 Spitfire V! The roles it was asked to perform were many and varied – interceptor, fighter escort, dive-bomber and reconnaissance – all from the deck of an aircraft carrier.

While the faults of the Seafire as a carrier aircraft were many, its performance as a combat aircraft was superb. In the Pacific, the Seafire would also battle a new and unyielding foe – the kamikaze. For this role the Seafire was well equipped. Because of its exceptional performance at medium and low altitudes, the Seafire was assigned as a last-ditch interceptor. If the kamikazes made it through the higher-level Corsairs and Hellcats, it would be up to the Seafires to engage them at altitudes of less than 3,000ft within ten miles of the destroyer screen. Each CAP would consist of eight Seafires, equipped with 90gal slipper tanks. The latter would allow the fighters to remain airborne for three hours and ten minutes.

The first kamikaze Zero-sen confirmed shot down fell to the guns of Sub Lt Richard H. Reynolds. On April 1, 1945, four A6Ms, led by a radar-equipped search and attack aircraft, were intercepted by high-level Hellcats. One Zero-sen was shot down and three escaped into cloud, later to reappear over the British carriers. At 0725hrs the battleship HMS *King George V* was strafed by one of the A6Ms. As it pulled out of its dive, the fighter was intercepted by Sub Lt Reynolds of 890 NAS. Although well within the Gun Defense Zone, the Seafire pilot pressed home his attack nevertheless. Scoring cannon strikes on the enemy fighter's port wing, Reynolds watched as the Zero-sen rolled over and dived into *Indefatigable*.

Twenty minutes later, Reynolds was able to despatch two more kamikaze Zero-sens to become the Fleet Air Arm's sole Seafire ace – he had shared in the destruction of two German Bv 138 flying-boats in the Arctic in August 1944.

Fellow ace Lt Cdr "Mike" Crosley of 880 NAS, embarked in *Implacable*, had these thoughts regarding the kamikaze threat:

> The kamikaze was a weird form of terrorism which seemed to us to deserve nothing but a painful death and eternal damnation. With their clever, decoy-led, low-level approach below the radar of the carrier air defense, it was worrying to think that 100 percent kills would be necessary before a sure defense could be provided. Each one of these part-trained, one-way aviators could park a 500lb bomb within a few feet of his aiming point if he was allowed to get within a few miles of the fleet. However, we felt that the Seafire, of all aircraft, would be the best possible defense in such circumstances, and we were not too frightened provided we could see the kamikazes coming.

This blurred, but revealing, photograph graphically reveals what the young Seafire pilots were up against. The kamikaze was a new and frightening foe, and one that required a defence with a 100 percent kill ratio for any hope of success. This Zero-sen, carrying a 550lb bomb, was photographed diving on USS *Enterprise* in May 1945. (National Archives)

In the ground attack dive-bombing role the Seafire was also effective. Here, Lt Cdr Crosley developed a method of attack that would greatly reduce losses due to flak. Instead of running into the target from line astern, one aircraft following the other, Crosley devised a method in which up to 16 Seafires would dive on it simultaneously from three different directions. Using this method, an attack could be completed within about 20 seconds, thus giving the enemy gunners a confusing array of targets, and little time to find their mark. This method also significantly reduced the time taken for the unit to re-form, thus saving valuable fuel.

On June 14, 1945, Seafires from No. 38 Naval Fighter Wing, embarked in *Implacable*, dive-bombed the oil storage tanks on Dublon Island, at Truk Lagoon. No direct hits were recorded, but the near misses fissured the tanks.

The British carriers *Victorious*, *Formidable* and *Implacable* (designated Task Force 37) rendezvoused with American Task Force 38 2,500 miles north of Manus on July 16, 1945. *Indefatigable* would join them four days later. On July 17 Task Force 37 launched its first missions against Japan – the first by any British or Commonwealth aircraft of the war. The Seafires of No. 38 Naval Fighter Wing flew "Ramrod" missions – a fighter sweep against targets of opportunity within briefed areas – as part of this strike. The wing attacked Kionoke, Naruto and Miyakawa airfields.

July 24 was the high-water mark for Task Force 37, with a total of 416 sorties being flown. Some 261 were against Japanese land and inshore targets, with the remaining 155 being defensive patrols, CAP and antisubmarine patrols. The Seafires from Nos 24 and 38 Naval Fighter Wings provided 76 of the offensive sorties – a very high number when one considers that they were also responsible for the fighter defense of the fleet.

Incredibly, August 9 (the date of the second atomic bomb attack on Japan) would mark the supreme moment for the Fleet Air Arm's strike aircraft. Some 258 Avengers, Corsairs, Hellcats, Fireflies and Seafires found and attacked targets, delivering the greatest weight of ordnance dropped or fired on "any enemy on any one day" by aircraft operating from British carriers during the whole war. More than 120 tons of bombs and cannon shells were expended. The attacks on the Japanese mainland ended on August 10 with 372 sorties flown. Task Force 37 withdrew the following day.

A6M ZERO-SEN TACTICS

Japanese "fighter tactics" at this point in the war can best be described as desperate. Putting aside the kamikaze attacks, the tactics used by the IJNAF pilots were of little consequence, as good pilots and aircraft were too few in number to make any difference. Squadrons were forced to soldier on with the now completely obsolete A6M Zero-sen, and while it was still an effective opponent in skilled hands, these were being killed off rapidly.

Early in the war the Japanese adopted the three-airplane section known as the *shotai* as its standard tactical formation. It was similar to the British V-formation, but was much more flexible. In the Japanese version, the flight leader flew well ahead of his two wingmen. While the leader held a steady course, his wingmen would weave from left to right and up and down. This protected the formation from surprise attack by covering many of the blind spots. Once a target was found, instead of attacking as a single formation, the wingmen trailed the leader and attacked the target in succession. When several *shotai* were involved, the impact was devastating.

While effective in the attack mode, the *shotai* was a liability when attacked. Once broken up, the Japanese pilots would have to fight individually, hoping to use their superior maneuverability to deadly effect. The Zero-sen performed well below 20,000ft, and was at its best in a slow-turning combat of 200 knots or less.

On the morning of August 15, 1945, Sub Lt Hockley was leading five Seafire IIIs as close and middle cover for six Avengers over Odaki Bay, near Tokyo. Twelve A6M Zero-sens approached the formation from above and astern and began their attack. Sufficient time was available for the Seafires to counter the bounce, but owing to R/T failure, Hockley failed to see the danger and was shot down. It is not clear as to which Japanese unit was responsible. Two groups were active that morning – Zero-sens and J2M Raidens from the 302nd Kokutai and Zero-sens from the 252nd Kokutai. (Artwork by Gareth Hector, © Osprey Publishing)

This system worked well for several years, but by 1944 the IJNAF had converted to the Allied four-airplane formation.

By 1945 the Japanese war effort was a lost cause. Defeats in the Philippines and on Iwo Jima had placed Allied forces right on the doorstep of Japan, and starting in February American carrier aircraft from Task Force 58 began to attack airfields in the Tokyo area. The air defense of Japan was now the top priority. Units like the 203rd Kokutai, having suffered heavy losses over the Philippines and Okinawa, were re-formed. Although the 203rd Kokutai was led by an experienced veteran (Capt Ryutaro Yamanaka), the unit was comprised mostly of fresh flight school graduates flying the venerable Zero-sen. Added to the fact that most IJNAF fighter units were ordered to conserve fuel and fighters for one big kamikaze attack, few if any of the new graduates were able to obtain any combat experience.

KAMIKAZE TACTICS

The invasion of the Philippines by American forces and the humiliating defeat of Vice-Adm Jisaburo Osawa's fleet at the Battle of the Philippine Sea forced the IJNAF to adopt tactics of the most desperate nature. Vice-Adm Takijiro Onishi, CO of the 1st Air Fleet, devised the radical idea of strapping a 250kg bomb to the Zero-sen and asking for volunteers to crash themselves on to American aircraft carriers. Newer versions of the A6M would provide escort, navigation and confirmation of the results.

With few airplanes and no fuel to train new pilots, most, if not all, of the IJNAF's naval aviators knew their situation was hopeless. This in turn led them to volunteer in droves. Success would soon follow on October 25, 1944, when bomb-carrying Zero-sens from the 201st Kokutai managed to sink the escort carrier USS *St Lo* and damage six other vessels. A6Ms were used in the vast majority of kamikaze attacks simply because they were available in the greatest numbers, and their performance gave the pilots their best chance of surviving the screen of fighters and antiaircraft fire.

The Japanese quickly realized that the radar coverage of a ship was not very good past 20 miles, so they adapted a "zero feet" approach with a twist. Most of the suicide pilots were inexperienced naval aviators, and they needed an escort to guide them to their targets. At approximately 20 miles from the Allied fleet, the experienced naval aviators would pull up and expose themselves to radar, thus hopefully drawing away the high-flying Hellcat and Corsair CAPs and leaving the low-flying kamikazes to approach their targets unseen.

After March 1945, more than half of the Japanese pilots available sacrificed themselves in suicide attacks. These last-ditch tactics cost the IJNAF dearly, and

On May 4, 1945, a kamikaze Zero-sen carrying a 250kg bomb struck HMS *Formidable*. The impact produced a 2ft-square hole and a 24x40ft depression in the armored deck. Speed was reduced to 18 knots and the vessel was out of action for five hours. Eleven aircraft were destroyed, eight sailors killed and 51 wounded. (Fleet Air Arm Museum)

as it did in the beginning of the war, the Zero-sen played a leading role in the campaign. Of the 2,363 IJNAF airplanes that took off on kamikaze flights, 1,189 were A6M fighters. Approximately 2,530 IJNAF pilots and aircrew lost their lives. In sharp contrast to those astounding numbers, Seafire pilots succeeded in downing just eight kamikaze Zero-sens.

During operations off Okinawa, the British carriers were hit seven times, but they were never put out of action. The survivability of the British "flattops" when compared to their American cousins is legendary. All Royal Navy carriers were built with an armored deck and hangers, this prewar design trait being born out of necessity. Hobbled for funding by the RAF, the Fleet Air Arm was allocated few resources, in particular advanced fighters. Worried, therefore, about the potential lack of fighter cover, the Royal Navy wisely built their carriers to take damage, specifically from 6in shells and 500lb bombs. The US Navy based its

Overleaf: Last combat over the Pacific

On May 4, 1945, during Operation *Iceberg II*, three Seafire L IIIs of 894 NAS intercepted a group of kamikazes attempting to attack the British Pacific Fleet. The latter aircraft were part of a force of 15 fighters that had taken off from Giran, on Formosa. Four of the A6Ms, flying at just 500ft, were sighted at 1730hrs and Lt Lieutenant A. S. Macleod RNZNVR (Senior Pilot of 894 NAS) led his CAP in a head-on attack and began firing at the leading enemy aircraft. The closing speed between the two fighters was very high, and, incredibly, Lt Macleod expended only 20 rounds per cannon and 15 rounds per machine gun to down the enemy aircraft that he had been targeting. The Zero-sen burst into flames and plunged into the sea. (Artwork by Wiek Luijken, © Osprey Publishing)

S
145
ROYAL NAVY
02-06

construction philosophy on the fact that its carriers would be well defended by embarked fighters.

Throughout World War II, British carriers proved themselves capable of taking direct hits either from bombs or, latterly, kamikazes. However, this protection came at a price. Because of their armor, the vessels carried fewer aircraft – the four British carriers between them had only 151 fighters, whereas one American *Essex*-class carrier of comparable size was capable of operating 74. The Royal Navy carriers were also slower.

LAST COMBAT

While the Allies waited for any signs of surrender from the Japanese, American Task Force 38 would remain off the coast of Japan. It was joined by a token Royal Navy group built around the carrier *Indefatigable* and the battleship *King George V*, designated Task Force 38.5.

Between August 13 and 15, *Indefatigable* continued to attack targets around the Tokyo area. With no signs of immediate surrender, strikes were ordered to commence again at dawn on the 15th. At 0400hrs a Firefly "Ramrod" was launched, followed by six Avengers with an escort of eight Seafires from 887 and 894 NASs. Five L Mk IIIs, led by Lt F. Hockley, would provide close and middle cover, while Sub Lt Vic Lowden led the top cover with the remaining three Seafire F IIIs. As the Avengers approached their designated target, Kisarazu airfield, they found it shrouded in cloud, forcing them to attack their alternate target – a chemical factory near Odaki Bay.

Despite the war being all but over, the IJNAF was still mounting air defense sorties and kamikaze attacks. One of the units involved was the 302nd Kokutai, based at Atsugi air base on the Kanto Plain southwest of Tokyo. Formed on March 1, 1944 and given the task of protecting the nation's capital against USAAF B-29 bombers, the 302nd had been credited with 300 victories by August 1945. The group initially boasted a mixed interceptor force comprising 48 fighters (A6M5c/7 Zero-sens and J2M3 Raidens) and 24 nightfighters (J1N2 Model 21 Gekkos).

There were very few veterans left in its ranks by the final weeks of the conflict, however, and most of its pilots had been transferred in from other branches such as seaplanes, flying-boats and carrier bombers. By May 1945, the 302nd Kokutai was down to just ten operational aircraft, most of which had been dispersed in anticipation of the final battle. The 252nd Kokutai, based at Mobara airfield, east of Tokyo Bay, was also assigned the task of air defense. Like the 302nd, it too was equipped with a limited number of late model Zero-sens.

On the morning of August 15, Allied carrier aircraft were detected heading for the Tokyo area. The 302nd commander, Capt Yasuna Kozono, ordered all serviceable fighters airborne. Led by Lt Yutaka Morioka (who was destined to become an ace that day), four J2M3 Raidens and eight A6M5c/A6M7 Zero-sens took to the air. The 252nd Kokutai also launched fighters, with Lt Cdr Moriyasu Hidaka leading a group of eight or nine Zero-sens towards a large formation of enemy aircraft.

The airspace over Tokyo Bay and surrounding areas proved to be a crowded place on the 15th. Along with the aircraft from *Indefatigable*, there were six F6F-5 Hellcats from VF-88 and an unknown number of FG-1 Corsairs from VBF-88 (both from Carrier Air Group 88, embarked in USS *Yorktown* (CV-10)) heading for the IJNAF airfields at Atsugi and Hokoda.

It has recently been claimed that the Japanese fighters encountered by the Fleet Air Arm that morning were almost certainly from the 302nd Kokutai, led by Lt Morioka. This does not mesh with Lt Morioka's claim for a single Hellcat shot down that day, however. His original orders were to head to Kisarazu airfield, and once overhead the base, he found a hangar on fire, smoking violently. Could the earlier Firefly "Ramrod" launched ahead of the Avengers and Seafires have reached Kisarazu airfield and attacked it before the weather closed in? According to Lt Morioka, his flight was then ordered back to Atsugi, which was "now under attack by Grummans." There, he spotted six F6F-5s from VF-88 and shot one down.

The six inexperienced Hellcat pilots – Lt Howard Harrison, Lt(jg)s Maury Proctor, T. W. Hansen, Joseph Shaloff and Ens Wright Hobbs and Eugene Mandeberg – claimed that they were bounced by "Franks" and "Jacks" (the former being the IJAAF's Nakajima Ki-84 and the "Jack" being the IJNAF Raiden). They claimed eight Japanese aircraft shot down for the loss of four of their own (Harrison, Shaloff, Hobbs and Mandeberg).

As the 14 Fleet Air Arm aircraft climbed through low cloud, they finally reached better weather at 6,000–8,000ft. The Seafire pilots were greeted by the new day's summer sun, and all was quiet except for the steady throb of their trusty Merlin engines. As the tiny strike force was crossing Tokyo Bay, a pair of A6M5 Zero-sens was sighted well below the Avengers. This was a common decoy tactic used by the Japanese, but the Seafire pilots did not bite. However, things became a little more interesting a few minutes later when a gaggle of a dozen A6M5s was seen coming down from the "three o'clock-high" position. The R/Ts quickly crackled into life with the calls of "Bogies – three o'clock-high."

The diving Zero-sens passed the top cover and headed for the Avengers, as well as the close-escort Seafires below them. Sufficient warning was given for the pilots to counter the bounce, but not all were able to jettison their drop tanks.

R/T failure doomed Sub Lt Freddie Hockley, and he was shot down in the first pass. He was the last Royal Navy casualty of the war.

In his memoirs, Lt Saburo Abe of the 252nd AG claims to have shot down a Seafire on August 15, but his description does not match what happened to Seafire pilot Sub Lt Hockley:

> Immediately, it turned into a chaotic battle. Both the enemy fighters and ours were coming and going from all directions. I did not know how to determine my target. Suddenly, an enemy aeroplane appeared from my right and flew down to the left. At that moment, I remembered what Tetsuzo Iwamoto, a pilot officer, had taught me. Quickly, I banked to the left with full-throttle and chased the enemy fighter.
>
> On the ground, I was pretty good at shooting. However, it was not the same when I had to shoot while flying a fighter aeroplane. I always missed my targets. So, I had decided that I would not pull the trigger lever until I was close enough to see an expression on my opponent's face. On that day, I did the same.
>
> The enemy pilot probably felt my presence, and he looked back. Our eyes met for a moment. I saw his despairing look, and I opened fire at the same time. I did not need to use a gunsight. If I remember well, the distance between us was less than 20 metres. I pulled the trigger lever, and the next moment I saw that half of the pilot's head had been blown off. The windscreen of his aeroplane went red, being covered with blood. His fighter was tossed upward into the air as if it was bending its back. I flew under him and just managed to avoid a crash.

Lt Saburo Abe also claims to have been shot at by Seafires a few minutes later, causing him to force-land his fighter:

> I heard a loud noise and felt pain in my right leg as if someone had hit it with an iron bar. I felt like I was awakened from my trance or something. Still, I was thinking "Idiot! Who are those stupid ones that cannot tell their friends from the enemy? I'm going to punch them when they get out of their airplanes," still thinking that I was being shot at by Japanese fighters. I looked up, and the two fighters that had shot at me passed above my Zero-sen and flew off to the left. "There was no 'rising sun' painted on them," I said to myself. They were not the American fighters. Their marking was different. "Who is that? They're British. What are they doing here?"

Despite Lt Abe claiming to have inflicted a grievous head wound on Sub Lt Hockley, the later managed to bale out of his stricken Seafire prior to it hitting the water. He was later captured and executed by his captors.

SEAFIRE: THROUGH THE GUNSIGHT

One of the hardest shots to make in aerial combat was the deflection shot. The majority of fighter pilots found it extremely difficult, and only the best mastered the art. In order to shoot at a target with high deflection, the pilot first had to position his fighter in the right part of the sky. Next, he had to aim at a point in space somewhere in front of his intended victim. This required the pilot to quickly calculate distance, angle, approach speed, convergences, line of target flight and deflection, and then fly and shoot at the same time. If everything went as planned, his bullets and the intended victim would meet at the same time.

The new GGS Mk 2 gyro gunsight fitted to most Seafires in 1945 was created in an attempt to solve the problems associated with deflection shooting. However, in a twisting, turning, dogfight the sight was seldom on target for more than a few seconds, and the tracking was not very smooth. The GGS Mk 2 proved to be far more adept when used against a target that was steadily approached from astern. It did have a "fixed cross" aiming point for dogfighting maneuveres, although this gave the pilot less aiming information than the old GM 2 gunsight that the GGS Mk 2 had replaced! (Artwork by Jim Laurier, © Osprey Publishing)

The remaining Seafires turned into the Japanese fighters. With the first element of Zero-sens now out of range, Sub Lt Lowden moved his flight into line abreast and engaged the second group of aircraft. The first Zero-sen was shot down at long range by Sub Lt Lowden. Opening fire at 800 yards and ceasing at 450, he hit the Zero-sen hard, causing its undercarriage oleos to drop. Lowden's No. 3, Sub Lt "Taffy" Williams, also scored some hits, and was credited with a shared victory. With his port cannon now jammed, Sub Lt Lowden continued to strike a second Zero-sen from a distance of 250 yards – after three short bursts it blew up.

The opening moves had proved decisive for the Seafire pilots, with Lowden having shot down two Zero-sens, shared in the destruction of a third and damaged two more. Williams shot down an A6M on his own and also shared one with Lowden. Now it was Sub Lt Gerry "Spud" Murphy's turn:

> The enemy approached our Avengers in fairly close starboard echelon, but with flights in line astern. They peeled off smartly in fours from down sun and headed for the Avengers. One section of four appeared to be coming head-on for us, but I didn't observe their guns firing. Their original attack was well coordinated, but they seemed to lose each other after that, and could not have kept a good lookout astern.
>
> I opened fire with my flight leader from the enemy's port quarter and saw strikes on the fuselage of the enemy, which was finished off by my flight leader or No. 3. I disengaged from above to attack another "Zeke" to port and 500ft below. Closed from above and astern, obtaining hits on its belly and engine, but I was closing too fast and overshot. I pulled up my nose to re-attack the No. 2 and saw a lone "Zeke" at my level doing a shallow turn to starboard. He evidently didn't see me, and I held my fire till 100 yards away. I observed immediate strikes on the cockpit and engine, which burst into flames. The enemy fighter rolled onto its back and plummeted in flames into cloud.

The close escort, tied as they were to the Avengers, still managed an impressive score. Sub Lt Don Duncan RNVR chose to retain his slipper tank, and keeping his speed up (as recommended in *Naval Air Tactic Notes*), he engaged three of the Zero-sens and came away with two probables to his name. The last Seafire to leave the combat area was flown by Duncan's section leader, Sub Lt Randy Kay. As an A6M closed on the Avengers, he made a quarter attack that set the enemy fighter's port wing root area on fire. Switching targets, he then concentrated on another Zero-sen, and with a high deflection shot blew its tail off with his first burst. Searching for a third target Kay found, and damaged, another A6M5c.

All six of the Avengers delivered their bombs on target. Only one had been badly damaged by the surprise Zero-sen attack, and its pilot nursed the crippled aircraft back to the fleet and ditched alongside one of the radar picket destroyers. Returning to *Indefatigable* on his own, Sub Lt Lowden encountered a dozen Corsairs (probably from VBF-88). They had seen the combat from a distance and were eager to make a contribution. By lowering his wheels and flaps and turning tightly to show his markings, Lowden was able to convince his potentially trigger-happy allies that he was a "friendly."

302nd Kokutai records for August 15 indicate that a mixed formation of 12-plus interceptors engaged enemy carrier aircraft in the Tokyo area and claimed a single kill and two probables for the loss of four fighters. These statistics closely match British records, as Seafires from the 24th Naval Fighter Wing claimed to have engaged 12 Zero-sens and shot seven of them down. Three more were claimed as probables and four damaged. The 252nd Kokutai was credited with downing nine enemy aircraft and damaging four more that day. Finally, VF-88 claimed eight enemy aircraft destroyed for the loss of four of its own.

The stress and confusion of aerial combat routinely caused inflated and overoptimistic claims to be made on both sides, and the events of that day were most certainly clouded by the "fog of war." Which Japanese unit actually found and attacked the Fleet Air Arm Avengers and Seafires remains a mystery. It is quite possible that elements from both the 302nd and 252nd Kokutais were involved. What is for certain is the fact that these engagements over Tokyo Bay were the very last dogfights to be fought in World War II. Which group of fighters actually participated in the final air combat of the conflict remains unknown to this day.

ANALYSIS

In terms of numbers of aircraft shot down, the Seafire's contribution during World War II was negligible at best. The Fleet Air Arm was credited with 455.5 aerial victories in six years of war, and American-built fighters contributed more than a third of these –52 for the F6F Hellcat, 52.5 for the F4U Corsair and 67 for the F4F Wildcat. Seafire pilots claimed 37 kills, 15 of which were Zero-sens. The remaining 247 aircraft were credited to the Sea Hurricanes, Fireflies, Fulmars, Sea Gladiators and Skuas.

As detailed in the previous chapter, the Seafire's last aerial combat of the war proved to be a resounding success. Starved of action since May 9, 1945, the young pilots of No. 24 Naval Fighter Wing had shown the aircraft to be an excellent fighter. The efforts of wing leaders, squadron COs, pilots and maintenance personnel in the Pacific had effectively extinguished the Seafire's poor reputation. When operated by motivated and well-trained personnel, the fighter was able to achieve some remarkable results.

In eight days of action between July 17 and August 15, 1945, 2,331 combat sorties were flown off the four British carriers in-theater. Some 1,186 of those were by the 88 Seafires of Nos 24 and 38 Naval Fighter Wings. That is 51 percent of the sorties flown by 35 percent of the aircraft embarked!

When fitted with 89gal and 90gal drop tanks, the Seafires were able to achieve some outstanding offensive numbers. With a radius of action in the 200-mile range, they contributed 324 sorties against airfields and flew 157 antishipping strikes. These sorties saw 43,600 rounds of 20mm cannon and 169,270 rounds of .303in machine gun ammunition expended. The damage dished out was extensive – 87 aircraft destroyed on the ground, 3,700 tons of shipping sunk and 24,700 tons damaged.

In return, Seafire losses were slight. Just eight aircraft were lost to flak and one to enemy fighters, with six pilots killed in action – a loss rate of 1.9 percent, which was lower than the 2.4 percent figure for Fleet Air Arm squadrons within Task Force 37. Twenty Seafires were also written off aboard the two carriers, seven of which were damaged beyond local repair and seven lost operationally.

What the Seafire achieved in the last few months of the Pacific War had more to do with the personnel who flew and maintained it rather than the aircraft itself. While it was a poor carrier fighter in terms of its poor range and ruggedness for deck operations (arguably, there were only two ideal carrier fighters built during World War II, the Hellcat and Zero-sen), the Seafire's combat ability as a fighter at the end of the war was still second to none.

The Spitfire's contribution to Allied victory was immense. The "stretch" in the Spitfire's design allowed it to add more horsepower and armament without degrading its performance. The Griffon-powered Mk XIV (the last version to see widespread service during the war) was considered by many to be the best piston-engined fighter of the conflict. The IJNAF's reluctance to add more horsepower to the Zero-sen doomed the fighter well before the appearance of the Seafire. Indeed, it was not until November 1944 that Mitsubishi was finally given the go-ahead to install its Kinsei 62 engine, rated at 1,350hp (still 235hp less than the Merlin 55M). Only two prototypes were ever built.

The inability of the Japanese to produce better versions of the Zero-sen, or to introduce a replacement, meant its fighter pilots were forced to fly the A6M until the very end of the war. Japanese industry also underperformed throughout the war. Between January and July 1945, Mitsubishi and Nakajima were able to produce only 1,578 Zero-sens.

In the end, the Zero-sen was both an example of Japanese genius and hard-headedness. Ironically, the last three months of air combat in the Pacific actually saved the lives of hundreds of young IJNAF airmen. The hoarding of aircraft and fuel for one last kamikaze effort had the opposite effect. The final battle never came, and the thousands of pilots trained for Imperial service were spared.

The Seafire's shortcomings were many and varied, but it was more than fitting that on the last day of the war Reginald Mitchell's elegant elliptical-winged fighter took part in what might have been the last dogfight of World War II.

SEAFIRE vs A6M ZERO-SEN CONFIRMED KILLS					
Pilot	Unit	Date	Aircraft serial	Kill(s)	Aircraft carrier
Sub Lt R H. Reynolds	894 NAS	4/1/45	Seafire L III PR256/S 146	2x A6Ms	*Indefatigable*
Sub Lt J.H. Kernahan	887 NAS	4/12/45	Seafire L III ?????/S 137	A6M	*Indefatigable*
CPO I.B. Bird	887 NAS	5/4/45	Seafire L III NN363/S ???	1x A6M	*Indefatigable*
Sub Lt D.T. Challick	887 NAS	5/4/45	Seafire L III ?????/S 131	1x A6M	*Indefatigable*
Sub Lt C.S. Randal	894 NAS	5/4/45	Seafire L III NF521/S 130	0.5x A6M	*Indefatigable*
Lt A.S. Macleod	894 NAS	5/4/45	Seafire L III PR254/S 145	1x A6M	*Indefatigable*
Sub Lt R.H. Reynolds	894 NAS	5/4/45	Seafire L III ?????/S 141	0.5x A6M	*Indefatigable*
Sub Lt A.W. Bradley	894 NAS	5/8/45	Seafire L III NN284/S 153	0.25x A6M	*Indefatigable*
Sub Lt K.D. Gall	894 NAS	5/8/45	Seafire L III ?????/S 136	0.25x A6M	*Indefatigable*
Sub Lt F.S. Hockley	894 NAS	5/8/45	Seafire L III ?????/S 143	0.25x A6M	*Indefatigable*
Sub Lt J.C. Taylor	894 NAS	5/8/45	Seafire L III ?????/S 137	0.25x A6M	*Indefatigable*
Sub Lt V.S. Lowden	887 NAS	8/15/45	Seafire L III LR866/S 121	2x A6Ms	*Indefatigable*
Sub Lt V.S. Lowden	887 NAS	8/15/45	Seafire L III LR866/S 121	0.5x A6M	*Indefatigable*
Sub Lt C.S. Randal	894 NAS	8/15/45	Seafire L III NN584/S ???	1x A6M	*Indefatigable*
Sub Lt G.J. Murphy	887 NAS	8/15/45	Seafire L III NN212/S 112	2x A6Ms	*Indefatigable*
Sub Lt W.J. Williams	887 NAS	8/15/45	Seafire L III ?????/S ???	1x A6M	*Indefatigable*
Sub Lt W.J. Williams	887 NAS	8/15/45	Seafire L III ?????/S ???	0.5x A6M	*Indefatigable*

AFTERMATH

The war in the Pacific was now over, and Royal Navy strength in the Far East was quickly reduced. By mid-September 1945, the only operational carriers in-theater were *Indefatigable*, *Implacable* and three new light fleet carriers. No. 24 Naval Fighter Wing was finally disbanded on March 15, 1946, while No. 38 Naval Fighter Wing was redesignated as 801 NAS after absorbing 880 NAS on September 13, 1945. It would later be equipped with 18 Seafire IIIs and, eventually, 18 new Seafire XVs.

Because the latter were not cleared for deck landing, 801 NAS continued to operate Mk IIIs, and it was the last frontline unit in Royal Navy service to be equipped with the type. The squadron disbanded on June 3, 1946. Many L Mk IIIs were used by fighter training squadrons, and they served for two more years until replaced by later marks. A total of 1,163 Seafire IIIs were built.

Four other air forces were issued with surplus Seafires postwar. Canada was the only Commonwealth country to choose the aircraft for its navy, and it formed two squadrons with Seafire L IIIs – these were later replaced by Mk XVs between June and September 1945. The French Navy's Aeronavale was also equipped with no fewer than 113 L IIIs between March 1946 and June 1948 – a further 15 Griffon-powered Seafire XVs were acquired in June 1949. The French used their Seafires in operations against communist Viet Minh insurgents in Indochina in November 1949. Burma obtained 20 Seafire XVs in 1951 for operations against several groups, including Chinese Nationalists, Burmese separatists and communists. Finally, the Irish Air Corps received a dozen de-navalized L Mk IIIs in 1947.

For all of its faults, the Seafire continued to be produced, and used, by the Royal Navy. The last version to see service, and the last to see combat, was the FR Mk 47. This was the ultimate stage in the development of the Griffon-engined Seafire line (comprised of the Mks XV, 17, 45, 46 and 47). The FR Mk 47 did not look like the aircraft conceived by R. J Mitchell 14 years earlier. It was a streamlined but musclebound fighter, with a massive fin and rudder. The armament was increased to four 20mm cannon. The Griffon 88 engine gave combat outputs of 2,350hp at 1,250ft and 2,145hp at 15,500ft. A six-bladed contra-rotating propeller was required to absorb all of this raw power, and the landing gear was strengthened and widened in track by a foot.

The Mk 47 version of the Seafire would experience combat operations following the invasion of South Korea by the North Korean People's Army on June 25, 1950. The carrier HMS *Triumph* was ordered to provide support for the

With the war now over, the British Pacific Fleet was quickly reduced in strength. Even with its poor deck handling and landing performance, the Seafire continued to soldier on with No. 24 Naval Fighter Wing, seen here aboard HMS *Indefatigable* in September 1945. The wing then went ashore at RNAS Schofields in Australia from September 18 to November 22, 1945. (Fleet Air Arm Museum)

retreating army of the Republic of Korea. Between July 1 and September 20, 1950, the 12 Seafires of 800 NAS flew 245 CAP and search sorties and 115 strike sorties for the loss of just two aircraft – one suffered an arrestor gear malfunction and subsequently ditched and the other Seafire was shot down in error by a nervous gunner in a USAF B-29. The Seafire finally passed from frontline service in November 1950, although Royal Navy Volunteer Reserve unit 1833 NAS did not retire its last Seafire 47 until 1954. After a decade of fleet service, and nearly 10,000 combat sorties, the Seafire had done its part.

At the time of the Japanese surrender, A6M5s of various sub-types served with only six frontline units (the 203rd, 252nd, 302nd, 352nd, 721st and Yokosuka Kokutais) on the home islands. With a few exceptions (several airframes were shipped to the United States for evaluation), all remaining Zero-sens were burned or destroyed where they stood. Others located on island bases and areas the Allies had bypassed were simply left to rot. A grand total of 10,094 Zero-sens had been built, along with a further 327 floatplane fighters and 517 two-seat trainers. Mitsubishi was responsible for 3,879 airframes and Nakajima produced 6,215 A6M1 to A6M8 fighters.

The IJNAF did not plan for a long war, nor did it see the Zero-sen having a prolonged service life. As a consequence, there were no new fighters being planned or developed to replace the venerable A6M. Not until March 20, 1942, did the new Mitsubishi J2M1 Raiden, codenamed "Jack" by the Allies, take flight. This aircraft was designed as an interceptor to destroy enemy bombers and outperform enemy fighters. Armed with four 20mm cannon, the J2M3 Model 21 had a top speed of 371mph at 17,860ft. Poor production management limited the number of Raidens built to just 470, however.

The other IJNAF fighter to see mass production towards the end of the war was the Kawanishi N1K2 Shiden-Kai, codenamed "George." It was hoped that this aircraft would finally replace the Zero-sen, but only 1,400 examples of this outstanding fighter were ever built.

Today, there are a handful of Zero-sens flying, mostly in the United States, with approximately 13 others that can be found in museums around the world. There are presently no airworthy Merlin-engined Seafires.

GLOSSARY

Abschuss	Confirmed victory in air combat
Abshüsse	Confirmed victories in air combat
Abschussteiligung	Contribution to a confirmed air-combat victory
Alarmstart	Scramble
BG	Bomb Group
CBI	China-Burma-India theater
chutai	Japanese equivalent of a squadron
Deutsche Kreuz im Gold	German Cross in gold
Einsatz	Operational flight
Erganzungsgruppe	Replacement or complement wing
ETO	European Theater of Operations
Feindberuhrung	Contact with an enemy aircraft
FG	Fighter Group
Flak	Antiaircraft artillery
FS	Fighter Squadron
Führer	Leader
Geschwader	Roughly equivalent to three RAF wings, comprising three or four *Gruppen*
Gruppe	Group containing three or four *Staffeln*, designated by Roman figures, e.g. IV./JG 26
Gruppenkommandeur	Commander or Captain, a *Gruppe* command position rather than a rank
Herausschuss	Claim for a bomber shot out of formation
Horrido!	Tally ho!
IJNAF	Imperial Japanese Navy Air Force
IJAAF	Imperial Japanese Army Air Force
Jagdbomber (Jabo)	Fighter-bomber
Jagdgeschwader (JG)	Fighter wing, includes three or four *Gruppen*
Jagdwaffe	Fighter Arm or Fighter Force
Jäger	Fighter
Kachmarek	Wingman
Kommandeur	Commanding officer of a *Gruppe*
Kommodore	Commodore or Captain, a *Geschwader* command position rather than a rank

Luftwaffe	Air Force
Maschinen Gewehr (MG)	Machine gun
Maschinen Kanone (MK)	Machine cannon
PTO	Pacific Theater of Operations
Reflex Visier (Revi)	Gunsight
Reichsluftfahrtministerium	German Air Ministry
Reichsverteidigung	Air Defense of Germany
Ritterkreuz (träger)	Knight's Cross (holder)
Rotte	Tactical element of two aircraft
Rottenflieger	Wingman, the second man in the *Rotte*
R/T	Radio telephony
Schlachtgeschwader (SG)	Ground attack wing
Schwarm	Flight of four aircraft
Schwarmführer	Flight leader
Schwarzemänner	Groundcrews or "black men," so-called because of the color of their tunics
Sentai	IJAAF equivalent of a group
Shotai	the smallest flying section in the IJAAF, comprising three aircraft
Stab	Staff flight
Staffel	Roughly equivalent to a squadron, designated sequentially within the *Geschwader* by Arabic figures, e.g. 4./JG 1
Staffelkapitän	Captain, a *Staffel* command position rather than a rank
USSTAF	United States Strategic Air Forces (Eighth and Fifteenth Air Forces)
Viermot	Four-engined bomber
Wilde Sau	"Wild Boar," freelance nightfighting tactic over bomber command's targets
Zerstörer	"Destroyer," Bf 110 fighter aircraft
Zerstörergeschwader (ZG)	Heavy fighter wing (Bf 110 or Me 410 twin-engined fighter)
Zweimot	Twin-engined bomber

SELECT BIBLIOGRAPHY

PART I

Bungay, S., *The Most Dangerous Enemy* (Aurum, 2000)

Caldwell, D.J., *The JG 26 War Diary Vol 1.* (Grub Street, 1998)

Cossey, B., *A Tiger's Tale* (J&KH, 2002)

Cull, B., Lander, B. with Weiss, H. *Twelve Days in May* (Grub Street, 1995)

Deere, A., *Nine Lives* (Wingham Press, 1991)

Deighton, L., *Fighter* (Book Club Associates, 1978)

Doe, B., *Fighter Pilot* (CCB, 2004)

Ekkehard-Bob, H., *Betrayed Ideals* (Cerberus, 2004)

Franks, N., *Sky Tiger* (Crécy, 1994)

Galland, A., *The First and the Last* (Fontana, 1971)

Goss, C., *The Luftwaffe Fighters" Battle of Britain* (Crécy, 2000)

Green, W., *Warplanes of the Third Reich* (Doubleday, 1972)

van Ishoven, A., *Messerschmitt Bf 109 at War* (Ian Allan, 1977)

Jefford, C. G., *RAF Squadrons* (Airlife, 2001)

Ketley, B. and Rolfe, M., *Luftwaffe Fledglings 1935–1945* (Hikoki Publications, 1996)

Lake, J., *The Battle of Britain* (Silverdale Books, 2000)

Morgan, E., and Shacklady, E., *Spitfire – The History* (Key Publishing, 1993)

Price, Dr A., *Spitfire – A Complete Fighting History* (Promotional Reprint Company, 1991)

Price, Dr A., *Aircraft of the Aces 1:2 Spitfire Mark I/II Aces 1939–41* (Osprey, 1996)

Ramsey, W., (ed.), *The Battle of Britain Then and Now Mk IV* (After The Battle, 1987)

Shores, C., and Williams, C., *Aces High* (Grub Street, 1994)

Steinhilper, U., and Osborne, P., *Spitfire On My Tail* (Independent Books, 1989)

Townsend, P., *Duel of Eagles* (Weidenfeld, 1990)

Wilson, S., *Spitfire* (Aerospace Publications, 1999)

PART II

Boiten, Theo and Martin W. Bowman, *Raiders of the Reich. Air Battle Western Europe: 1942–1945* (Airlife, 1996)

Boiten, Theo and Martin W. Bowman, *Battles With the Luftwaffe* (Janes, 2001)

Bowman, Martin W., *Great American Air Battles of World War 2* (Airlife, 1994)

Caldwell, Donald J., *JG 26 – Top Guns of the Luftwaffe* (New York, 1991)

Caldwell, Donald J., *The JG 26 War Diary Vol 2* (Grub Street, 1998)

Cora, Paul B., *Yellowjackets! The 361st FG in World War II* (Schiffer, 2002)

Davis, Larry, *P-47 Thunderbolt In Action* (Squadron Signal No. 67, 1984)

Drendel, Lou, *Walk Around No 11 P-47 Thunderbolt* (Squadron Signal, 1997)

Drendel, Lou, *Duxford Diary 1942–45* (W. Heffer & Sons, 1945)

Freeman, Roger A., *Osprey Aviation Elite Units 2: 56th Fighter Group* (Osprey, 2000)

Held, Werner, *Fighter! Luftwaffe Fighter Planes and Pilots* (New York, 1979)

Johnson, Air Vice Marshal J. E. "Johnnie," *Full Circle: The Story of Air Fighting* (Pan, 1964)

Johnson, Robert S., *THUNDERBOLT!* (Honoribus Press, 1973)

Knoke, Heinz, *I Flew for the Führer* (Time Life Books, 1990)

Lerche, Hans-Werner, *Luftwaffe Test Pilot* (Jane's, 1980)

McLachlan, Ian, *USAAF Fighter Stories* (Haynes Publishing, 1997)

McLachlan, Ian, USAAF *Fighter Stories – A New Selection* (Sutton Publishing, 2005)

Miller, Kent D., *Fighter Units & Pilots of the 8th Air Force* (Schiffer Military History, 2001)

Mombeek, Eric, *Defending The Reich – The History of JG 1 "Oesau"* (JAC Publications, 1992)

Morris, Danny, *Aces and Wingmen* (Neville Spearman, 1972)

O'Leary, Michael, *USAAF Fighters of World War 2* (Blandford Press, 1986)

O'Leary, Michael, *Osprey Aircraft of the Aces 31: VIII Fighter Command at War "Long Reach"* (Osprey, 2000)

Olynyk, Frank, Stars & Bars: *A Tribute to the American Fighter Ace 1920–1973* (Grub Street, 1995)

Price, Dr Alfred, *Luftwaffe Handbook 1939–1945* (Ian Allan, 1986)

Rall, Günther, *My Logbook* (Editions TwentynineSix, 2006)

Rust, Kenn C., *The 9th Air Force in World War II* (Aero Publishers, 1967)

Scutts, Jerry, *Osprey Aircraft of the Aces 24: P-47 Thunderbolt Aces of the Eighth Air Force* (Osprey, 1998)

Speer, Frank E., *The Debden Warbirds: The 4th FG in World War II* (Schiffer Military History, 1999)

Weal, John, *Osprey Aircraft of the Aces 29: Bf 109F/G/K Aces of the Western Front* (Osprey, 1999)

Weal, John, *Osprey Aircraft of the Aces 68: Bf 109 Defense of the Reich Aces* (Osprey, 2006)

Weal, John, *Osprey Aviation Elite Units 12: Jagdgeschwader 27 "Afrika"* (Osprey, 2003)

Weal, John, *Osprey Aviation Elite Units 25: Jagdgeschwader 53 "Pik As"* (Osprey, 2007)

Zemke, "Hub", as told to Roger A. Freeman, *Zemke's Wolfpack* (Orion, 1998)

PART III

Band, William F. X., *Warriors Who Ride The Wind* (Castle Books, 1993)

Bueschel, Richard M., *Nakajima Ki-27A-B* (Arco Publishing, 1970)

Bueschel, Richard M., *Nakajima Ki-43 Hayabusa I-III* (Arco Publishing, 1970)

Byrd, Martha, *Chennault giving Wings to the Tiger* (University of Alabama Press, 1987)

Christy, Joe and Jeff Ethell, *P-40 Warhawks At War* (Charles Scribner's Sons, 1980)

Hata, Ikuhiko, Izawa, Yasuho and Christopher Shores, *Japanese Army Air Force Fighter Units and their Aces 1931–1945* (Grub Street, 2002)

Heiferman, Ron, *Flying Tigers – Chennault in China* (Ballantine Books Inc, 1971)

Johnsen, Frederick A., *P-40 Warhawk* (MBI Publishing, 1998)

Kawahara, Yasuo and Gordon T. Allred, *Kamikaze* (Ballantine Books, 1957)

Kissick, Luther C., *Guerrilla One* (Sunflower University Press, 1983)

Lopez, Donald S., *Into the Teeth of the Tiger* (Bantam Books Inc, 1986)

McClure, Glenn E., *Fire and Fall Back* (Barnes Press, 1975)

McDowell, Ernest R., *Curtiss P-40 in Action (*Squadron/Signal Publications, 1976)

Molesworth, Carl and H. Stephens Moseley, *Wing To Wing* (Orion Books, 1990)

Molesworth, Carl, *Sharks Over China* (Brassey's, 1994)

Molesworth, Carl, *Osprey Aircraft of the Aces 35: P-40 Warhawk Aces of the CBI* (Osprey Publishing, 2000)

Rosholt, Malcolm, *Days of the Ching Pao* (Rosholt House, 1978)

Rosholt, Malcolm, *Flight in the China Air Space, 1910–1950* (Rosholt House, 1984)

Sakaida, Henry, *Osprey Aircraft of the Aces 13: Japanese Army Air Force Aces 1937–45* (Osprey Publishing, 1997)

Windrow, Martin C. and René J. Francillon, *The Nakajima Ki 43 Hayabusa* (Profile Publications, 1969)

PART IV

Boiten, Theo and Martin W. Bowman, *Raiders of the Reich – Air Battle Western Europe: 1942–1945* (Airlife, 1996)

Boiten, Theo and Martin W. Bowman, *Battles With the Luftwaffe* (Janes, 2001)

Bowman, Martin W., *Great American Air Battles of World War II* (Airlife, 1994)

Bowman, Martin W., *Four Miles High* (PSL, 1992)

Brown, Capt Eric, *Four of the Finest* (RAF Yearbook, 1975)

Brown, Capt Eric, *Wings of the Luftwaffe* (Airlife, 1987)

Cora, Paul B., *Yellowjackets! The 361st Fighter Group in World War II* (Schiffer, 2002)

Caldwell, Donald J., JG 26 – *Top Guns of the Luftwaffe* (New York, 1991)

Campbell, J., *Focke-Wulf Fw 190 In Action* (Squadron Signal, 1975)

Davis, Larry, *P-51 Mustang In Action* (Squadron Signal, 1981)

Davis, Larry, *Duxford Diary 1942–45 (*W Heffer & Sons, 1945)

Gruenhagen, Robert W., *Mustang – The story of the P-51 fighter* (Arco, 1976)

Hall, Grover C., *One Thousand Destroyed* (Morgan Aviation Books, 1946)

Held, Werner, *Fighter! Luftwaffe Fighter Planes and Pilots* (Arms & Armor Press, 1979)

Hess, William, *Osprey Aviation Elite Units 7: 354th Fighter Group* (Osprey, 2002)

Ivie, Thomas G., *Osprey Aviation Elite Units 8: 352nd Fighter Group* (Osprey, 2002)

Jarrett, Philip, *Aircraft of the Second World War* (Putnam, 1997)

Johnson, Air Vice Marshal J. E. "Johnnie", *Full Circle – The Story of Air Fighting* (Pan, 1964)

Miller, Kent D., *The 363rd Fighter Group in WWII – In Action over Europe with the P-51 Mustang* (Schiffer, 2002)

Mombeek, Eric, *Defending The Reich – The History of JG 1 "Oesau"* (JAC Publications, 1992)

Morris, Danny, *Aces and Wingmen* (Neville Spearman, 1972)

Nowarra, Heinz J., *The Focke Wulf 190 – A Famous German Fighter* (Harleyford, 1965)

Olynyk, Frank, Stars & Bars: *A Tribute to the American Fighter Ace 1920–1973* (Grub Street, 1995)

Scutts, Jerry, *Aircraft of the Aces 1: Mustang Aces of the Eighth Air Force* (Osprey, 1994)

Smith, Jack H., *Aviation Elite Units 10 – 359th Fighter Group* (Osprey, 2002)

Smith, J. R. and Antony, Kay, *German Aircraft of the Second World War* (Putnam, 1972)

Speer, Frank E., *The Debden Warbirds – The 4th Fighter Group in WW II (*Schiffer, 1999)

Spick, Mike, *Luftwaffe Fighter Aces* (Ivy Books, 1996)

Weal, John, *Aircraft of the Aces 9: Focke-Wulf Fw 190 Aces of the Western Front* (Osprey, 1996)

Weal, John, *Aviation Elite Units 1: Jagdgeschwader 2 "Richthofen"* (Osprey, 2000)

Weal, John, *Aviation Elite Units 20: Luftwaffe Sturmgruppen* (Osprey, 2005)

Wood, Tony and Gunston, Bill, *Hitler's Luftwaffe* (Chartwell, 1979)

PART V

Bergerud, E. M., *Fire In the Sky* (Westview Press, 2001)

Bodie, W. M. and Ethell, J., *World War II Pacific War Eagles in Original Color* (Widewing Publications, 1997)

Brown, D., *The British Pacific and East Indies Fleets – "The Forgotten Fleets' 50th Anniversary"* (Brodie Publishing Ltd, 1995)

Brown, D., *The Seafire* (Ian Allen, 1973)

Caidin, M., *Zero Fighter* (Ballantine Books Inc, 1971)

Crosley, Cdr R. M., *They Gave Me a Seafire* (Airlife, 2001)

Ethell, J. L. et al., *Great Book of World War II Airplanes* (Bonanza Books, 1984)

Francillon, R. J., *Japanese Aircraft of the Pacific War* (Naval Institute Press, 1994)

Hata, I. and Yasuho, I., *Japanese Naval Aces and Fighter Units in World War II (*Naval Institute Press, 1989)

Hata, K., August 15th Sky (Bungeishunju-sha Publishing)

Jarrett, P., *Aircraft of the Second World War* (Putnam 1997)

Mikesh, R. C., *Broken Wing of the Samurai: The Destruction of the Japanese Air Force* (Airlife, 1993)

Nijboer, D., Cockpit: An Illustrated History (Boston Mills Press, 1998)

Nijboer, D., *Graphic War – The Secret Aviation Drawings and Illustrations of World War II* (Boston Mills Press, 2005)

Nohara, S., *A6M Zero in Action* (Squadron/Signal Publications, 1983)

Okumiya, M. Horikoshi, and Caidin, M., *Zero* (Ballantine Books, 1973)

Price, A., *Spitfire at War* (Ian Allan Ltd, 1974)

Sakai, S., *Samurai* (Ballantine Books, 1963)

Sakaida, H., *Aircraft of the Aces 22: Imperial Japanese Navy Aces 1937–45* (Osprey Publishing, 1998)

Smith, P. C., *Task Force 57: The British Pacific Fleet 1944–45* (William Kimber & Company Ltd, 1969)

Sturtivant, R., and Balance, T., *The Squadrons of the Fleet Air Arm* (Air Britain, 1994)

Thomas, A., *Aircraft of the Aces 75: Royal Navy Aces of World War 2* (Osprey Publishing, 2007)

Wragg, D., *Fleet Air Arm Handbook* (Sutton Publishing Ltd, 2003)

INDEX

References to illustrations are shown in **bold**.